D1474077

A Cultural History of Tarot

Helen Farley is Lecturer in Studies in Religion and Esotericism at the University of Queensland. She is editor of the international journal *Khthónios: A Journal for the Study of Religion* and has written widely on a variety of topics and subjects, including ritual, divination, esotericism and magic.

A Cultural History of Tarot

From Entertainment to Esotericism

HELEN FARLEY

BLOOMSBURY ACADEMIC

LONDON • NEW YORK • OXFORD • NEW DELHI • SYDNEY

BLOOMSBURY ACADEMIC
Bloomsbury Publishing Plc
50 Bedford Square, London, WC1B 3DP, UK
1385 Broadway, New York, NY 10018, USA

BLOOMSBURY, BLOOMSBURY ACADEMIC and the Diana logo
are trademarks of Bloomsbury Publishing Plc

First published 2009 by I.B. Tauris & Co. Ltd.
Paperback edition first published 2019 by Bloomsbury Academic

Copyright © Helen Farley, 2009

Helen Farley has asserted her right under the Copyright,
Designs and Patents Act, 1988, to be identified as Author of this work.

For legal purposes the Acknowledgements on p. xi constitute
an extension of this copyright page.

All rights reserved. No part of this publication may be reproduced or
transmitted in any form or by any means, electronic or mechanical,
including photocopying, recording, or any information storage or retrieval
system, without prior permission in writing from the publishers.

Bloomsbury Publishing Plc does not have any control over, or responsibility for,
any third-party websites referred to or in this book. All internet addresses given
in this book were correct at the time of going to press. The author and publisher
regret any inconvenience caused if addresses have changed or sites have
ceased to exist, but can accept no responsibility for any such changes.

A catalogue record for this book is available from the British Library.

A catalog record for this book is available from the Library of Congress.

ISBN: HB: 978-1-8488-5053-8
PB: 978-1-7883-1491-6
ePDF: 978-0-8577-1182-3
ePub: 978-0-7556-9769-4

To find out more about our authors and books visit
www.bloomsbury.com and sign up for our newsletters.

Contents

Illustrations

Tables

Acknowledgements

A book is a substantial undertaking and it cannot be completed without considerable support from colleagues, friends and family. I am fortunate in that I am well-endowed with all those people such that I hardly know how to whittle down my list. I would like first to thank Professor Emeritus Philip Almond who has uncomplainingly read drafts and made many helpful suggestions.

Research travel is very expensive and I could not have undertaken it without the generous financial support of the University of Queensland Graduate School through the Graduate School Research Travel Award scheme. I would also like to acknowledge the generous support of the School of History, Philosophy, Religion and Classics and also to the Australian Association for the Study of Religion (AASR) for providing me with the funds to attend conferences and spread the seeds of my academic exploration.

My research in Milan and London was greatly facilitated by many people who had not previously met me yet bent over backwards to meet my needs. I would particularly like to mention Patrizia Foglia at la Raccolta Bertarelli at the Castello Sforzesco in Milan. In London, I would like to extend my gratitude to John Fisher of the Guildhall Library; Jo Norman of the Department of Prints and Drawings at the British Museum; Frances Rankine of the Prints and the Book, Word & Image Department of the Victoria and Albert Museum and the staff of the National Art Library.

From I.B.Tauris I would like to express my gratitude to Alex Wright who believes that a book about tarot is viable! Thanks must also go to Jayne Hill who has tirelessly pored over my copy; every comma and fullstop.

I reserve my thanks til last to my partner, James Boland, for his encouragement, support and good humour; for listening to the complicated exposition of my arguments when he would rather have been playing his guitar and for celebrating every word, every chapter and every milestone along the way.

Introduction

When we think of tarot, images of fortune-tellers, crystals and incense flash past our mind's eye. Those with more romantic dispositions may imagine dark-eyed gypsies in colourful caravans, wending their way through the countryside, telling fortunes with cards for the curious few brazen enough to peek at their destiny before its blossoming. Outsized cards are shuffled, laid out and 'read'; the order in which they are drawn, their symbolism and their position relative to each other are all significant for folk with eyes to see. Those who wish to possess a pack for themselves are confronted by a bewildering variety of decks: pagan tarots, astrological tarots, gypsy tarots, any number of Egyptian tarots, even a Metrosexual Tarot.[1]

In contemporary society where empirical scientific enquiry and strict rationalism are paramount, tarot has been associated with shoddy soothsayers and confidence tricksters, and it is in part for this reason that academics have deemed the area unsuitable for detailed examination. Though there is a paucity of scholarly works, there are numbers almost without limit of popular tarot monographs, which line the shelves of New Age bookstores and 'Self-Help' corners of department stores. In embarking on an academic study, it is difficult to separate historical fact from esoteric fiction, where elegant myths are recycled *ad infinitum*. Many authors would have us believe that the tarot contains the lost Hermetic knowledge of a proud and noble Egyptian race who encoded their secrets when faced with untimely extinction. Such myths, never verified by their perpetrators, have their origin in the desire for pseudo-legitimacy through an ancient, though false, lineage and the dogged persistence of a pre-Rosetta infatuation with all things Egyptian.

In order to correct this deficiency, this book forms the first comprehensive cultural history of the tarot deck and its imagery. The symbolism, changes in patterns of use and theories of tarot origin become entirely comprehensible when viewed in conjunction with the cultural contexts in which they occurred. Four significant periods in tarot's history are considered, beginning with an investagation of the popular theories of the deck's provenance in order to accurately determine the circumstances of its invention. The reclusive Duke Filippo Maria Visconti of Milan is the most likely candidate for inventor of that first deck, sometime early in the fifteenth century. A close investigation of the spiritual and mundane concerns of the Italian

Renaissance brings to light the meaning in the mysterious symbolism of these early decks; at this time used solely for game playing. Could it have been that that this innocuous game of some skill and much chance was an allegory for the life of the Viscontis as rulers of Milan, similarly characterised by a dizzying mix of rat-cunning and luck?

In late-eighteenth-century France, tarot was so far removed from its original cultural context that the ready decryption of its symbolism became impossible. Instead it was reinterpreted according to a new set of intellectual currents which included an infatuation with exotic cultures, esoteric doctrines and an ardent yearning for a lost Golden Age. In particular, France was gripped by Egyptomania, fuelled by Napoleon's conquest of that exotic land. The failure of the Church to adapt to the changing political, social and spiritual circumstances enabled the emergence of the alternative and esoteric doctrines which would constitute the French Occult Revival. It was in this milieu that tarot was transformed from a Renaissance game to an esoteric device, legendarily created in an Egypt still perceived to be the repository of arcane knowledge. It was linked to all manner of abstruse schemes including Hermeticism, astrology and kabbalah by esotericists, most notably Éliphas Lévi and Gérard Encausse, otherwise known as Papus.

The next significant development in tarot occurred in England, also in the grip of the Occult Revival. Under the influence of the Hermetic Order of the Golden Dawn, tarot would become central. Though never possessing more than 300 members, the Golden Dawn was enormously influential on the practice of magic and tarot interpretation. These nineteenth-century magicians altered the trump sequence and linked each card to one of the twenty-two pathways between the *sephiroth* on the kabbalistic Tree of Life. These pathways lent a divinatory interpretation to each card which forms the basis of contemporary divinatory meanings.

Two Golden Dawn members who would play a significant role in the evolution of tarot were Aleister Crowley and Arthur Edward Waite. Crowley extended the lists of correspondences between the tarot trumps and other esoteric systems. But it was Waite who was to be the major innovator by designing a pack in which the minor arcana or pip cards were illustrated to facilitate divination. The deck he designed, commonly known as the Rider-Waite deck, was to become the most popular in the history of tarot.

With the advent of the New Age, the tarot underwent yet another transformation. Though retaining its primary purpose of divination, the nature of that divination shifted; where once the deck was used for fortune-telling, the object became healing and self-development, both central to the New Age movement. In addition, New Age seekers were intrigued with Eastern and indigenous religions, searching for commonalities that would expose an underlying truth in all the world's spiritual systems. The New Age adoption of Jungian psychology justified many of its practices including the liberal use of the theory of archetypes to validate ad hoc borrowings and substitutions from other cultures in the symbolism of tarot. So too, the structure of the deck became fluid, subservient to its ultimate purpose.

In glaring contrast to religious trends in the West which were moving towards greater secularisation, tarot has shifted from the mundane towards the sacred. It began its life as a game with no purpose beyond providing mental stimulation. It contained no esoteric wisdom, could provide no spiritual advice and gave no clue as to how to conduct one's life. True enough, these matters were implied in the symbolism of the trump sequence, but it was not the purpose of the deck to provide answers, merely to acknowledge the existence of such factors. In contrast, the esotericists of the Occult Revival imbued tarot symbolism with esoteric meaning. Still, tarot was used only by a select few who were initiated into its mysteries; being seen as too powerful a tool to be left in the hands of anyone without the appropriate knowledge and skill; madness and ruin lay along that path. In contrast, New Age tarot is nothing if not accessible. Though there are large numbers of professional readers, a tarot deck and instructional guide are available to anyone with some money and a little time.[2] Obviously, it is the social and cultural context in which tarot is operating that imbues the deck with meaning and given the variety of contexts, it becomes more realistic to discuss the 'cultural histories' of tarot, rather than 'cultural history' in the singular.

Most tarot historians examine an aspect of the deck in isolation. Scholars of western esotericism busy themselves with the possible occult significance of the cards and forge tenuous links to other arcane traditions while turning a blind eye to alternative explanations of the symbolism. Historians of games are entirely focused on that aspect of the deck's multifaceted history. Art historians focus only on the artistic significance of a card within the wider context of that period's art. I will draw on all of these disciplines to posit the significance of tarot symbolism and trace the development of the tarot deck.

This book will form part of the lively discourse surrounding the academic study of the history of esotericism. Because of the changing function of the deck and the ambiguity surrounding its origins, it has been difficult to locate tarot within this discourse. Further, in an area where scholars are clambering to gain recognition for the discipline, they are inclined to distance themselves from tarot which is still regarded as suspect in contemporary society.

In recent times there has been some recognition that occultism has played a significant role in the development of Western thought. Warburg scholar Dame Frances Yates has been very influential in this arena. Her works including *The Rosicrucian Enlightenment*,[3] *Giordano Bruno and the Hermetic Tradition*[4] and *The Occult Philosophy in the Elizabethan Age*[5] have done much to legitimise the study of esotericism in the academic world. In more recent times Antoine Faivre and Wouter J. Hanegraaff have taken up the baton, working to establish the study of esotericism as a legitimate discipline.[6] Their focus, however, tends to be narrow and larger social, economic and cultural currents are downplayed or disregarded in their desire to elevate the investigation of the development of esoteric doctrine and practice. This approach, when applied to tarot, becomes especially problematic as tarot's origins were firmly grounded in the secular, only achieving esoteric significance towards the end of the eighteenth century. The study of esotericism finds little of interest in the early genesis of the game of *tarocchi* in the courts of northern Italy.

Similarly, the focus of art historical studies is stiflingly narrow. Authors in this area are primarily concerned with how tarot fits into the larger schema of Renaissance art. They are concerned with the 'who' and 'when' of tarot, rather than the 'why'. These studies help to determine when a work was likely to have been created, the original geographical location and under whose patronage the work was undertaken, certain courts or church administrators favouring particular artists at specific times. Art historians, however, show little interest in the subject of the artistry, the symbolism portrayed therein, the subsequent development of the deck or the cultural milieu in which it resided.

Playing card collectors and enthusiasts have done much to augment the available information about tarot. Alas, most collectors are at best enthusiastic amateurs, frequently ignorant of academic rigour, regurgitating popular myths without corroboration. However, there is much to be gleaned from them and their collections. In later years there have been a few names that are synonymous with reliable and careful research including Detlef Hoffmann,[7] Sylvia Mann and philosopher cum tarot enthusiast Michael Dummett.[8] Dummett in particular has contributed some works which have become the starting point for anyone interested in the field, including *The Game of Tarot* (written with Sylvia Mann), *A Wicked Pack of Cards* (authored with Ronald Decker and Thierry Depaulis) and *A History of the Occult Tarot: 1870–1970* (authored with Ronald Decker). Though Dummett exhibits careful scholarship, he is barely able to contain his contempt for the esotericists who have 'appropriated' the game of tarot for their own ends. Admittedly, he tends to moderate his opinion in his later works.[9]

Prejudices aside, card collectors have made a careful study of the evolution of both ordinary playing cards and tarot cards. They have traced the origins of playing cards in Europe from those imported from Egypt; recognising a similarity in suit signs without obvious precursors. Card collectors are interested not only in standardised packs but also non-standard packs, though they do tend to play down the significance of the latter, preferring to trace a linear development. In doing so they are neglecting a valuable clue. By looking at the larger corpus, similarities between superficially divergent decks and trends in symbolic representation may be observed. A close scrutiny of contemporaneous decks may provide a unique snapshot of the interplay of competing currents in Renaissance thought and life.

The study of tarot requires a multidisciplinary approach. First, the paucity of material precludes any claim that one discipline is able to provide sufficient information to achieve the objectives of this study. Second, the history of tarot sees the usage of the deck undergo a radical change from that of card-playing in the Italian Renaissance to its use as an esoteric document towards the end of the eighteenth century. Art historical studies and the data amassed by card collectors can help determine the early history of tarot but it is the study of esotericism that charts its subsequent course.

Though cultural historians have made no particular study of tarot, their work is invaluable in helping to determine prevailing attitudes during the periods under consideration. Looking beyond the significant names and dates which are the fodder of conventional historical studies, cultural historians seek to reconstruct the culture and ideas of a particular group or groups of people.[10] It becomes possible to speculate about a population's attitude to religion and to the supernatural, popular pastimes and familial relationships. What once may have seemed irrational and illogical to us as twenty-first century observers, becomes rational when presented within the framework of a fifteenth-century worldview for example, one burdened with a distinct cosmogony and the firsthand experience of plague, war and a growing individualism. If we can look at tarot in this context, it ceases to become the mysterious and slightly dangerous entity it first appears. Instead, it becomes the wholly comprehensible reflection of the people that created and used it. Cultural historical studies can provide the context in which tarot resides; providing clues as to why tarot was used so differently at different times. An awareness of the modes of culture and prevailing attitudes both during the Renaissance and during the Occult Revival will help us to make sense of the symbolism of each period's tarot decks.

1

Origins and Antecedents

To a contemporary user of tarot, the original meanings of the mysterious images displayed on the cards are hidden. In our world, the skeletal figure of death does not ride a horse and people are rarely hanged (and never by their feet). In order to discern the original significance of tarot symbolism, it becomes necessary to establish the true provenance of the deck. Images that held an implicit meaning in a certain context may have an altered connotation in another. The theories regarding the origins of tarot are diverse, ranging from its creation in ancient Egypt by a mysterious priesthood or an evolution from any of a number of extant games. Careful consideration must be given to each because the implications for the interpretation of tarot symbolism are considerable. Does tarot contain a carefully coded esoteric doctrine or was it designed merely as an innocent distraction? The question cannot be answered without a clear picture of the origins of the tarot deck and the use for which it was designed.

It is counterintuitive to suppose that any new invention would first appear in its final form. It is far more likely that there would be a series of false starts, refinements and revisions and so it was with tarot. Evidence suggests that the tarot deck evolved from the card-playing deck familiar in most western countries. There are certain similarities in structure and symbolism which are suggestive of this close relationship. The playing-card deck consisted of fifty-two cards distributed through four suits. Each suit contained numbered cards 1 (Ace) to 10, with three court cards. Henceforth, this pack will be referred to as the 'ordinary playing card deck' or 'regular deck'.

Though tarot exists in many variations, the standard tarot deck consists of seventy-eight cards. Of these, twenty-one are ordered trumps, which are often counted with an unnumbered 'wild' or *Fou* (Fool) card.[1] It is the symbolism resplendent on these that forms the main focus of this enquiry. Possessing a similar structure to the ordinary playing card deck, the complement of the tarot deck contains four suits of sixteen pip cards, indicative of tarot's original role in game-playing.[2] Each suit boasts numbered cards from 1 (Ace) to 10, with the addition of the four court cards of Knave,

Knight, Queen and King. Originally, tarot adopted the Italian suit signs of the regular playing card deck which predated it; these are Cups (*Coppe*), Batons (*Bastoni*), Coins (*Denari*) and Swords (*Spade*). These marks correspond to the modern English and French suit signs of Hearts (*Coeur*), Clubs (*Trèfle*), Diamonds (*Carreau*) and Spades (*Pique*) respectively. As card games played with both the regular deck and tarot deck spread from Italy across Europe, suit signs developed into distinctive, region-specific patterns as evidenced in the table below.

	CUPS	BATONS	COINS	SWORDS
ITALIAN	Coppe	Bastoni	Denari	Spade
ENGLISH	Hearts	Clubs	Diamonds	Spades
FRENCH	Coeur	Trèfle	Carreau	Picque
SPANISH	Copas (Cups)	Bastos (Batons)	Oros (Gold)	Espados
GERMAN	Herzen (Hearts)	Eicheln (Acorns)	Schellen (Bells)	Laube or Grüne (Leaves)
SWITZERLAND	Rosen (Roses)	Eicheln	Schellen	Schilten (Shields)

Table 1: Region-specific suit signs of tarot and ordinary playing cards.[3]

Certainly, the most intriguing feature of the tarot deck was the novel addition of the twenty-one trump cards and Fool to the cards of the four suits. In this way, the structure of the tarot deck diverged markedly from that of its progenitor. Originally unlabelled, the trumps bear the names of the Magician, the Popess, the Empress, the Emperor, the Pope, the Lovers, the Chariot, Strength, the Hermit, the Wheel of Fortune, Justice, the Hanged Man, Death, Temperance, the Devil, the Tower, the Star, the Moon, the Sun, Judgment and the World. The names of the trumps, the elaboration of the symbolism on them and their rank order, varied between individual decks, depending on their geographical origin, purpose and the intent of the artist who created them. These factors will be examined in more detail later.

In addition, tarot distinguishes itself from the regular playing card deck by possessing four court cards instead of three. Because of our familiarity with English decks, it is tempting to assume that the additional card in the court of tarot was the Knight, but in reality the Queen was the interloper.[4] It is only in the regular French and English decks that we find a female presence. Outside of these dominions, the court is an all-male affair. For instance, the

courts of decks from Germany and Switzerland are populated by the *König,
Obermann* and *Untermann,* all of which are male.[5]

As games played with tarot evolved, so did the deck to reflect these
changes. *Tarocchino* (or 'little tarot'), was a reduced deck of just sixty-two
cards; the pip cards from 2 to 5 being omitted.[6] Count Leopoldo Cicognara
erroneously attributed the invention of this modified deck to Francesco
Antelminelli Castracani Fibbia, the prince of Pisa who was exiled in Bologna
in the fifteenth century.[7] The *Minchiate* of Florence was yet another variation
on the theme of tarot. The controversial Popess card was removed but the
number of trumps was augmented by the addition of the Cardinal Virtue of
Prudence, the three Theological Virtues, the four elements and the twelve
signs of the zodiac, to create a deck of ninety-seven cards.[8]

The Emergence of the Playing Card Deck

Many commentators on the history of tarot have reported that the ordinary
playing card deck evolved from the tarot deck by a process of simplification.[9]
As evidence, they frequently presented the Joker of contemporary playing
cards as the last remnant of the tarot trumps, representing the Fool.[10] But in
reality, the Joker did not supplement the deck until the mid-nineteenth
century, when it was added to decks in America in order to play certain card
games.[11] Further, the Joker and the Fool had different roles in the games in
which they were utilised. Given this slim evidence, it is exceedingly unlikely
that the invention of the tarot deck predated the creation of regular playing
cards.

Ample circumstantial evidence supports the hypothesis that the regular
deck appeared in Europe before the creation of tarot. The first references to
the ordinary playing card deck appeared in prohibitions against gambling and
in sermons at least fifty years before the first documented appearance of
tarot.[12] In the prodigious catalogue of books describing the history of playing
cards, historians report the existence of manuscripts which place the first
appearance of cards sometime towards the end of the thirteenth century.[13]
Alas, these references are impossible to verify and a more reliable date can
be set at 1371 when Peter IV, King of Aragorn, commissioned a deck of
cards from the Catalan Jaume March.[14] A scant half dozen years later in
1377, the German monk Johannes of Rheinfelden in Switzerland, described
a deck as 'the common form and that in which it first reached us,' consisting
of thirteen cards in four suits, each made up of ten numeral cards and three
court cards consisting of a King, an upper Marshal and a lower Marshal.[15]
The *ludus cartarum* ('game of cards') had been introduced into Switzerland
in the same year and was quickly prohibited.[16] Almost simultaneously, cards
were mentioned in a range of bureaucratic documents including inventories

of possessions, edicts, city chronicles and account books in the cities of Siena, Florence, Paris and Basle.[17]

From the mid-fourteenth century, cards were frequently mentioned, usually incidentally, across Europe. In 1480, Juzzo da Coveluzzo wrote in his *Istoria della citta di Viterbo* (*History of the City of Viterbo*): 'There were encamped about Viterbo paid troops of the opposing factions of Clement VII and Urban VI, who did commit depredations of all kinds, and robberies in the Roman states. In this year of such great tribulations the game of cards was introduced into Viterbo, which came from the Saracens and was called "Naib".' This narrative passage described events that took place in 1379,[18] and was also reported by Nicolo delle Tuccia in 1476.[19] In many areas, card games went by the name of 'naib' or 'naipes'.

In 1380, the first references to cards in Spain appeared in an inventory of the goods owned by Nicholas Sarmona. The wording referred to 'a game of cards comprising forty-four pieces'.[20] Unfortunately, from this scant information, it is impossible to deduce the exact composition of the pack. A prohibition against card games in Ulm, Germany, dates from 1397.[21] Certainly, there was no mention of the trump cards that distinguish tarot from the regular deck in any of the references so far cited, and it is logical to deduce that tarot was not yet evident in Europe.

From the proliferation of references to cards from the 1370s and the prior absence of such mentions before this, it is safe to assume that playing cards entered Europe in the last quarter of the fourteenth century.[22] The deck's entry point was almost certainly through the prosperous seaport of Venice which conducted a brisk trade with the countries of the East and the Near East.[23] By this time, the deck already had a stable structure of fifty-two cards distributed through four suits. It seems highly unlikely that cards were a local invention, there being no evidence of progenitor or transitional decks.[24] If the concept of the regular playing card deck was imported into Europe, there were several popular theories as to its origin and likely route to the Continent. Frequently, playing-card historians have looked to contemporary or near contemporary card-game or even board-games in other parts of the world on which to base their hypotheses.

There are many theses regarding the provenance of the fifty-two-card deck. One of the most popular suggests that the Indian game of Ganjifa was the progenitor of the regular deck.[25] The cards were round and made of layers of lacquered wood or cloth, usually hand-painted and the customary suit signs represented the various incarnations of the Hindu god Viṣṇu.[26] There were twelve cards to each suit, numbered from 1 to 10 with two court cards. One of the court cards represented one of the ten incarnations of Viṣṇu, and the other showed some incident associated with this incarnation.[27] The suit signs were:

1. The Suit of Fish that signified Matsya the Fish, who towed the ship containing Manu (the first man) and saved him from the great Deluge.[28]
2. The Suit of Tortoises that signified Kurma the Tortoise, on which rested the mountain that, when turned by the serpent Vasuki, disturbed the sea of milk and produced the Fourteen Gems which had been lost in the Deluge.[29]
3. The Suit of Boars that signified Varaha the Boar, who destroyed the giant Hiranyaksha and raised the earth up out of the ocean.[30]
4. The Suit of Lions which represented Narasimha the Lion, who destroyed the giant Hiranyakashipu.[31]
5. The Suit of Dwarves or Water Jars which symbolised Vamana the Dwarf Brahmin, who saved men from the giant king Bali, who was to have dominion over the lower world.[32]
6. The Suit of Axes that represented Paraśurāma of the Axe, who punished the military caste (Kshatriya) and obliterated their power twenty-one times.[33]
7. The Suit of Arrows which signified Rāmachandra. Rāma avenged men and the gods for the crimes perpetuated by Ravana, the demon king of Ceylon. He won his wife Sītā in a contest with arrows.
8. The Suit of Quoits representative of Kṛṣṇa, believed to be the perfect manifestation of Viṣṇu. His emblem was the Chakra or quoit of lightning which he hurled at his enemies. This suit was sometimes called the Suit of Cows, because Kṛṣṇa, as a youth, lived among the cowherds.
9. The Suit of Shells was symbolic of Buddha the Enlightened, who sat upon his shell-shaped throne in meditation.
10. The Suit of Swords or occasionally called Horses represented Kalki, the White Horse. This incarnation is yet to come and Viṣṇu, with sword in hand, will sweep triumphant through the world, eliminating the powers of darkness and ushering in a better age.[34]

There is an intriguing connection between Indian and European card games: in both cases, numeral cards were reversed for some suits during play. But this is insufficient to confirm a relationship between the two. Games utilising this strategy were common in Europe long before sea trade between the two regions was enabled by Vasco da Gama of Portugal in 1498.[35] Further substantiation is required to demonstrate an Indian provenance and a deck intermediate between the European pack and Indian Ganjifa could expose such a direct evolutionary relationship. A particular eighteenth-century Ganjifa pack housed in the British Museum was a possible candidate. Even though this deck shared two suit signs with the original Latin playing card decks and each suit boasted court cards in a manner suggestive of European decks, it seems probable given its late date of manufacture, that this Ganjifa pack was influenced by the European deck rather than the other way around.[36] Further, the theory that advanced Ganjifa cards as the immediate progenitors of the standard deck was confounded by the late appearance of the Indian cards which were unknown on the subcontinent before the sixteenth century.[37]

An alternate theory advocating an Indian ancestry for European cards utilised images of the four-armed, androgynous Hindu god Ardhanari. Traditionally, Ardhanari was represented as being the composite of Śiva and his consort Devi, and was often depicted holding a cup, a sceptre, a sword and a ring. Sometimes it was the monkey-god Hanuman who was pictured holding these emblems. This theory contended that the Italian suit signs of cups, batons, coins and swords were derived from these emblems, though the possible motivations for transferring this symbolism to European playing cards was unclear; as was the special relevance that this deity had over all those represented in Indian culture.[38] The absence of Indian decks utilising this symbolism and the lack of documentation relating to transitional decks, made this hypothesis untenable.

Another long-cherished theory of an Eastern derivation for the regular deck put the creation of the cards firmly in China. After all, the northern Italian cities such as Venice had established a trade relationship with China and it is readily conceivable that returning sailors or travellers could have brought decks or the idea of a deck home with them.[39] Another theory yet more exotic had the cards travelling along the Peking-to-Samarkand silk route in caravans of camels carrying spices and rhinoceros horns. Once at Samarkand, the cards (together with the other precious cargoes), would be transported through Persia and the Holy Land, being brought to Europe with Arab traders or Christian Crusaders.[40] Some theories have the cards directly transported by that great adventurer of the medieval world, Marco Polo.[41] The Far East also seemed a likely choice because the production of cards required both the technology of printing and paper, both of which were invented in China long before their appearance in Europe.[42] American scholar Thomas Francis Carter thought that it was probable that Chinese playing cards evolved from certain forms of divination, the drawing of lots and paper money. These 'sheet-dice' almost certainly constituted the earliest form of block printing and according to Ou-yang Hsiu (1007–1072CE), began to appear before the end of the T'ang dynasty (618–907CE). Interestingly, Carter hypothesised that these 'sheet-dice' were also the remote ancestors of dominoes.[43]

The earliest source that specifically referred to playing cards was the *Liao shih* of T'o-t'o, a history of the Liao dynasty dating back to 969CE, stating that the Emperor Mu-tsung played cards (*yeh ke hsi)* on the night of New

Year's Eve.[44] The oldest extant Chinese playing card dates from the eleventh century, around 300 years later. Found by Dr A. von Le Coq in 1905, it is known as the Turfan card, named for where it was found in Chinese Turkistan. It appears to be a direct ancestor of the cards used for *chiup'ai*, a game still evident in the eighteenth and nineteenth centuries.[45]

The Chinese deck most like the regular European deck was that consisting of 'money' cards. The deck consisted either of three or four suits representing monetary values, with cards numbered from 1 to 9 in each suit. The suits typically consisted of Cash, Strings (of cash), Myriads (of strings) and Tens (of myriads).[46] The deck did differ from European decks in that there was no division of suits into numeral and court cards. Further, some cards did not possess genuine suit signs, instead bearing their number and the name of the suit.[47]

Though the Chinese were certainly using playing cards for at least 200 years before the deck's arrival in Europe, this fact alone is insufficient to nominate the Chinese pack as the immediate forerunner of the European deck. The Chinese cards lacked court cards and there would have to have been considerable development before the pack's appearance in Europe.[48] In addition, the idea that the Chinese suit signs were misrepresented in European packs, erroneously manifesting as Cups, Batons, Coins and Swords seems highly improbable.[49] Documentary evidence also fails to back up the theory of Chinese origin. The only record of such a theory before recent times comes from the Italian author Valère Zani writing in 1696. He stated that: 'The Abbe Tressan [a French missionary to Palestine, 1618–1684] showed me when I was at Paris a pack of Chinese cards and told me that a Venetian was the first who brought cards from China to Venice, and that that city was the first place in Europe where they were known.'[50] Though it is possible that the Venetian sailor did bring back a pack of Chinese cards, for the reasons outlined above, it is unlikely that these significantly influenced the design of the first European playing cards. This does not rule out Chinese cards as the *remote* ancestors of European playing cards.[51]

Almost by a process of elimination, it becomes likely that the immediate progenitor of the regular European deck was from the Islamic world, as Europe had little direct contact with countries not mediated by Islam. The cards could have entered Europe via Muslim Spain or via Italy.[52] In fact, the commercial privileges of Venetian traders were protected by a treaty negotiated with the Mamlūk Empire of Egypt and Syria in 1302 and again in 1345.[53] Sometimes, the Papacy and Crusading powers would impose trade embargoes against the Mamlūks, but these were readily circumvented, using Cyprus as an intermediary.[54]

Not only was there a direct trade with the Muslim countries providing the opportunity, but documentary evidence also favours an Arabic derivation for the progenitor of the European playing card deck. An inventory of the possessions of the Duke of Orléans written in 1408, expressly detailed 'a Saracen card deck'.[55] Dummett also cited an inventory of 1460 contained in the archive of the Barcelona notary Don Jaume Those, which included the entry: 'Packs of ordinary playing cards and other Moorish games.'[56] The most famous reference was the one revealed earlier in this chapter, that of Juzzo da Coveluzzo in his *Istoria della citta di Viterbo* (*History of the City of Viterbo*), where he described the deck as a 'Saracen invention'.[57] There is also mention of Saracen decks in Arabic sources. Playing cards were remarked upon in the classic tale of Arab adventure *Thousand and One Nights*.[58] Also, the sixteenth-century writer Ibn Hajar al-Haytamī wrote in the *Annals of Ibn Tagrī-Birdī*, that the future Sultan al-Malik al-Mu'ayyad won a large sum of money in a game of cards around the year 1400.[59]

More particularly, in 1939, archaeologist L. A. Mayer stumbled across an almost complete pack of cards from the Egyptian Mamlūk Empire in the Topkapi Sarayi Museum in Istanbul.[60] The deck was dated as being from the fifteenth century by comparison with Egyptian illuminated manuscripts of this period.[61] Of fifty-two cards, forty-eight had survived consisting of four suits: Swords, Polo-Sticks, Cups and Coins, each composed of ten numeral cards and three court cards headed by the King.[62] Five of the cards were obviously from another deck, not being consistent in style and probably were obtained to replace missing cards.[63] Though there were court cards present in the Mamlūk deck, they differed from those in the European decks; the figures of the court cards were not illustrated: Instead, they bore the appropriate suit-sign and an inscription giving the rank and suit of King (*malik*), Viceroy (*nā'ib malik*) and Second Viceroy (*thānī nā'ib*).[64] A fragment of an Egyptian card has since been located that indicated that some Islamic card decks carried representations of court subjects. A seated king or governor can be discerned on an Egyptian card fragment that has been dated to the thirteenth century.[65]

There are a number of striking similarities between the Mamlūk deck and those early Italian decks. Unfortunately, as there are no surviving early Italian regular card decks, early tarot decks must be used for comparison.[66] By way of example, the Swords suit of the Italian Brambilla and Visconti di Modrone decks resembles that of the Muslim pack very closely. In both these European and Muslim decks, the swords curve in opposition to each other, only to intersect at the top and the bottom.[67] Further, in all extant Italian decks the batons were straight and intersected once in the middle of the cards, as do the polo sticks in the Istanbul deck.[68] Because the Mamlūk deck did not itself predate the European decks, some scholars have suggested that the European cards may have been representative of the original decks.[69] This is unlikely as several Egyptian cards older than the

Mamlūk deck have since been unearthed, one of which has been dated to the late twelfth century, demonstrating a long tradition of card-making in Egypt.[70] Further, the playing-card deck appeared very suddenly in Europe in its current, fully-developed form.[71] The Mamlūk suits of Swords, Polo-Sticks, Cups and Coins translated into the corresponding Italian suits with the exception of Polo-Sticks which became Batons, probably because polo was not popular in Europe at that time.[72] Following the lead of Antoine Court de Gébelin, prolific tarot author Stuart Kaplan, stated that the card suits represented the four castes along the Nile River in ancient times,[73] but there is scant evidence to support that statement.

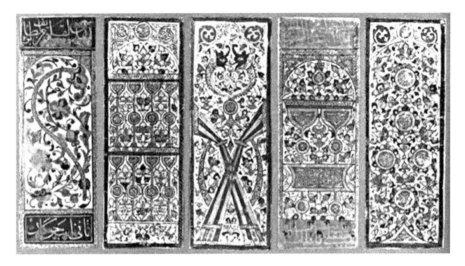

Figure 1: Mamlūk playing cards now housed in the Topkapi Sarayi
Museum, Istanbul.

Ṣūfī writer Sayed Idries Shah and tarot enthusiast Paul Huson proposed a Ṣūfī origin for the deck, while still acknowledging the Mamlūk deck as the immediate progenitor of the European pack.[74] Huson theorised that the game of polo formed the link between Ṣūfīsm and tarot. In support of his hypothesis, he traced the movement of the popular game from Persia before King Darius I established the Persian Empire in the sixth century BCE.[75] He claimed that from Persia, the game travelled to Constantinople, Turkestan, India and the Far East. The Arab conquests took it to Egypt where it became a popular pastime; the polo stick being incorporated into Islamic heraldry and also among those Shi'ah Muslims that came to be known as Ṣūfīs.[76] Huson argued that polo became so entrenched in the Ṣūfī consciousness that Arifi of Heart, a fifteenth century Ṣūfī poet, wrote *The Ball and the Polo Stick*, a narrative about self-sacrificing love where the game of polo was used as an allegory for his teachings. He further offered *The Rubaiyat of Omar Khayyám* quatrains of the eleventh-century *Ṣūfī* poet as evidence. Here also, the game of polo illustrated the helplessness of mankind.[77]

> The ball no Question makes of Ayes and Noes,
> But Right or Left as strikes the Player goes;
> And He that toss'd Thee down into the Field,
> *He* knows about it all – He knows – HE knows![78]

Images resembling the other suit signs can also be found in the verse. Allusion was made to the magic, seven-ringed cup of the legendary Persian king Jamshid, in which the past, present and future were revealed to him. Coins can be visualised when the poet talked of 'money, better than a thousand promises'. Further, Khayyám equated coins to 'a cup, a lover, and music on the field's verge' to be relished today rather than exchanged for the vague promise of Heaven later, with actual money better spent on friends rather than hoarded and left behind for one's enemies.[79]

In a purely speculative and unsubstantiated fashion, Huson further linked the four Cardinal Virtues of Fortitude, Prudence, Temperance and Justice to the suit signs of playing cards. He traced the allegoric representations of the Virtues through Apuleius of Madaura, author of *The Golden Ass*, to Plato and spuriously back to Persia.[80] He quoted a seventeenth-century Persian text, *Dabistān-ul-mazahab*, a translation of which was published under the title *The School of Manners*. The work described the beliefs and practices of the extant religions of that period. The author was believed to be Muhsin Fani, a *Ṣūfī* of Persian extraction living in India and born around 1615. However, Internet esotericist Joseph H. Peterson has ascribed the book to a Shi'ah mullah named Mir Du'l-fequar Ardestani, believing he based the book on the teachings of Azar Kayvan, a sixteenth-century Zoroastrian high priest.[81]

The *Dabistān-ul-mazahab* described the religion of the Magi or Zoroastrianism, which had been practised in Persia since the sixth century CE. Fani described the exploits of the folk hero Mahabad who, according to legend, was responsible for the organisation of cities, villages, streets, colonnades, and palaces, the introduction of commerce and trade, and the division of humankind into four castes.[82] These were:

> Class 1: The priestly class of Magi. This was divided into *Hirbeds* (disciples), *Mobeds* (masters), and *Destur Mobeds* (master of masters). This caste is described as consisting of ascetics and learned men, responsible for maintaining the faith and enforcing

the laws. They are also referred to as *Húristár, Birman* and *Birmun.*[83]

Class 2: Kings and warriors. These men were chosen to devote themselves to the responsibilities of government and authority, to ensuring equity, policing, and curbing aggression. Members of this caste are named *Núristár, Chatraman* and *Chatri.*

Class 3: Farmers, cultivators, artisans, and skilful men. This caste is styled *Súristár* or *Bas,* reported to imply 'cultivation' and 'improvement'

Class 4: The *Rúzistár* or *Sudin.* This last caste was composed of people destined for 'employment' and 'service'.[84]

Huson claimed that the priestly caste officiated as clergy in the Persian Empire. Referred to as *Húristár* by the *Dabistān,* they allegedly prophesied the future, made sacrifices to the god Ahuramazda and prayed. They wore white robes, with fur caps peaked forward, and carried bundles of rods in their hands as symbols of office.[85] Huson theorised that these rods came to be represented in playing cards mistakenly as 'polo sticks' or 'batons' and became linked to the Cardinal Virtue of Fortitude, often represented as a column.[86] Huson carried this idea further:

> ... might it be that the *Núristár,* who promoted equity, were represented by a sword or scimitar; that the *Rúzistár,* who served, by a coin? Do these classes of Persian society constitute the origins of the four virtues in which the young kings of Persia had to be schooled? Have we found, in fact, the origins of the Four Cardinal Virtues? If so, then the four Italian suit signs might well acquire a fairly ancient provenance, ironically of a quite literally Magian, and therefore 'magical' origin.[87]

Hence, he associated the swords of the *Núristár* with the Cardinal Virtue of Justice; the coins of *Rúzistár* mistakenly represented as the mirror of Prudence and the *Súristár* supposedly with cups and also associated with the Virtue of Temperance.[88] Even a superficial glance at this scheme reveals that these associations were somewhat spurious with the symbolism supposedly associated with each of the castes being forced to fit into this somewhat arbitrary system. Further, to forge a connection between these symbols and the Cardinal Virtues was mere fantasy, undocumented and unreferenced. These symbols never existed in their own right to represent the Cardinal Virtues, but rather appeared as part of a larger allegorical schema, usually featuring women and with other characteristic symbols appearing with them, such as with Justice who usually held a set of scales as well as a sword.[89]

Huson's fantastical theory was completed with the Persians having substituted the four suit signs of Chinese money cards, used by the Mughals, with the suits mentioned above. The cards were carried to the Mamlūk Empire where the Mamlūks changed the 'batons' or 'rods' suit to polo sticks in line with their spiritual beliefs. It was not until the cards reached Europe, that the suit was returned to its original form of 'batons'.[90] Huson's theory, though intriguing, must be abandoned in the absence of documentary sources, extant Persian decks displaying this symbolism and even basic referencing in support of his ideas.

To properly explain the symbolism of the Mamlūk suit signs, it is necessary to examine the structure of Mamlūk society itself. The Mamlūks were rulers of Egypt, Syria, and Palestine from 1250 until 1517. The word 'mamlūk' derives from the root 'to possess' in Arabic and referred to slaves, particularly military slaves.[91] The highest members of the government, including the sultan, were all former mamlūks.[92] The 'slavery' of a mamlūk, far from being degrading, was the first stage in a career that could culminate in the highest offices in the state.[93] Children, primarily from the northern Caucasus and Qipchaq steppes, were brought to Cairo where they received military training before being sent to work as pages for *amírs* (commanders) in the government.[94] Mamlūk pages eventually were freed and served in the sultan's citadel as bodyguards, equerries and pages in his élite core, the *khāṣṣakiyah*.[95] It was from this last group we see the emblems which became the suit-signs within the Istanbul pack of cards.[96]

The *khāṣṣakiyah* were a privileged assemblage who were raised and educated at the sultan's court. They occupied traditional posts such as cupbearer, keeper of the polo sticks, sword-bearer and keeper of the wardrobe, but they could also become provincial governors, major-domos of the royal household or treasurers.[97] At formal occasions they displayed the specific objects belonging to their posts. These objects were both prized attributes and possessions of the sultan; they were symbolic of his power and wealth, as were the mamlūks who bore these devices.[98] The *khāṣṣakiyah* were eventually freed by the sultan, granting them important military commands or prestigious appointments in outposts of Mamlūk territory. It became practice for these former mamlūks to retain the use of their emblems even after leaving their official posts. Beginning in the early fourteenth century, sultanic devices appeared on monuments and precious goods commissioned by *amírs* who had previously served as mamlūks to the sultan. Former mamlūks advertised their former posts by wearing its prestigious emblem on their person and labelling their possessions and servants. There were many more offices and attendant objects within the *khāṣṣakiyah* than the four symbols of the Istanbul deck, but all of the Istanbul deck's suit signs were well-known sultanic devices.[99]

Once the Arabic cards had been imported into Italy in parallel with spices, silk and other valuable commodities, they were adapted to reflect the nuances of the local culture by card-makers.[100] The most obvious change was the transformation of the suit of polo sticks into batons as polo was not well-known in Europe.[101] Also, the suit signs abstract in form on the Istanbul deck become less so on the European cards.[102] The slender cups of the Arabic pack become stout and gilded on the Italian cards, often with covers and more resembling liturgical chalices than everyday drinking vessels.[103] The stylised coins of the Muslim deck, depicted as circles with floral emblems, were transformed into heavily textured coins of gold on the Italian cards.[104] Thus the Arabic deck, though retaining its basic structure, macro-symbolism and function, became adapted to the culture which so readily adopted it.

Some Theories of Tarot Origin

After examination of the documentary evidence, it is certain that the arrival of the ordinary playing card deck in Europe predated the appearance of tarot by about fifty years. The oldest extant tarot decks were from northern Italy and were dated to the first half of the fifteenth century. Speculation was rife as to whether or not these decks were in fact the first tarot decks created, pointing to an Italian provenance for tarot, or whether they were simply the oldest surviving examples of a long line of such decks dating back to an indeterminate time. An identification of the correct theory of tarot provenance will definitively pinpoint where and when tarot was invented, making it possible to ascertain the significance of the symbolism displayed on the cards.

Though it has been established that the tarot known as the Visconti di Modrone deck is the oldest extant tarot pack, for nearly 150 years another deck vied for the title.[105] In the seventeenth century, Père Menestrier found an intriguing reference while searching through the records of Charles VI of France, authored by his treasurer, Charles Poupart. Dated 1392, the entry read: 'Paid to Jacquemin Gringonneur, painter, for three packs of cards, gilded, coloured, and ornamented with various designs, for the amusement of our lord the king, 56 sols of Paris.'[106] Menestrier wrote in a memoir in 1704, that these cards were tarot packs and if this were true, it could be that Gringonneur was in fact the inventor of the tarot deck.[107] By 1842, M. C. Leber in his book, *Études historiques sur les cartes*, managed to link this entry with some seventeen extant cards in the Bibliothèque Nationale; claiming these cards had been painted by Gringonneur. This opinion garnered wide acceptance, the cards becoming known as the 'Tarots de Charles VI' or sometimes, the Gringonneur deck.[108] A story soon arose that the cards had been created as a diversion for Charles VI as he struggled to retain his sanity.[109] Artist Basil Rákóczi augmented the story, claiming that Gringonneur was also a kabbalist and that the cards were intended as an occult cure for the mental illness of the monarch.[110]

Because of the absence of coats-of-arms or mottos on the cards, it is improbable the seventeen specimens housed in the Bibliothèque Nationale were from the courtly milieu of circa 1400.[111] In fact, a close examination of the costumes worn by the figures on the cards revealed them as belonging to the last quarter of the fifteenth century and probably of Venetian rather than of French origin.[112] It is therefore unlikely that they were the cards painted for Charles VI by Jacquemin Gringonneur in 1392. Further, there was no reason to believe that the entry made by Charles Poupart related to tarot cards at all as there was no mention of the trump cards that distinguish tarot from ordinary playing cards.[113] It is interesting that even though the truth of this matter has been acknowledged for some 150 years, contemporary writers still perpetuate this myth of tarot as the amusement of a mad king and of Gringonneur as the creator of tarot.[114]

An alternative theory of French derivation for the tarot trumps was propounded by an American scholar of English, Charlene Gates. Gates proposed in her doctoral dissertation, that the symbolism of the tarot trumps was derived from a common pool of medieval iconography which arose in southern France in the twelfth century. This symbolism could be seen in cathedral architecture, art, and literature. Gates lists Norman political and military power, the Gothic cultural movement, Neoplatonism, heretical sects such as Catharism, medieval chivalry and courtly love as the likely sources of this symbolism.[115] Gates readily admitted that there were no extant decks to support her hypothesis yet confidently declared that 'this environment almost certainly would have precipitated the creation of the major arcana.'[116] What confounded Gates' theory was that similar symbolism existed concurrently in England and Italy.[117] If a pool of like symbols was all that was necessary for the spontaneous creation of tarot, there was no obvious reason why it should have arisen in France rather than in England or Italy.

Still with our attention turned to France, perhaps the most persistent and entertaining theory of tarot origin envisioned the deck arising from the mysterious land of Egypt at a time lost in the mists of antiquity. This hypothesis was first promulgated by Freemason, protestant clergyman and esotericist Antoine Court de Gébelin in France just prior to the French Revolution.[118] Court de Gébelin was well-versed in all of the esoteric currents that permeated French culture at that time including Rosicrucianism, Hermeticism, kabbalism, the works of Emmanuel Swedenborg and esoteric Freemasonry. In addition, Basil Rákóczi claimed that Court de Gébelin was also an initiate of the Martinists and that he had been taught about the *Book of Thoth* by Louis Claude de Saint-Martin himself.[119]

Between 1773 and 1782 Court de Gébelin, published his nine-volume opus entitled *Le Monde Primitif Analysé et Comparé avec le Monde Moderne* of which the eighth volume was in part devoted to the origins of tarot.[120] Here Court de Gébelin reported that some time in the last quarter of the eighteenth century, he had come across some ladies playing the game of tarot. In Paris these cards were unusual, and he had not seen them since he was a boy. He was interested in the Hermetic mysteries of ancient Egypt and it occurred to him that he was seeing a sacred Egyptian book, the remnants of the lost *Book of Thoth*.[121] The trump cards he regarded as a disguised assemblage of ancient Egyptian religious doctrines. For example, he identified the Popess as 'the High Priestess', the Chariot as 'Osiris Triumphant' and the Star as 'Sirius' or 'the Dog Star'.[122] This *Book of Thoth*, he supposed, must have been brought to Europe by the gypsies who had been safeguarding it since it had been entrusted to them by Egyptian priests millennia ago. He deduced that the safest way to preserve their ancient wisdom must have been to encode it as a game and to trust that some day an adept would be able to decipher it. This honour he claimed for himself.[123] More recently, Arland Ussher eloquently elaborated this strategy: 'If you intend that a thing shall last forever, do not commit it into the hands of Virtue but into those of Vice'.[124]

Charlene Gates proposed that the Egyptian priests may have been forced to encode their secrets when the Persian king Cambyses invaded Egypt down to Nubia after the death of the Pharaoh Ahmose in 525BCE.[125] This timing would seem appropriate as Egypt was experiencing a cultural revival with a surge of patriotic and religious fervour under the Saite dynasty (664–525BCE). Herodotus described the invasion as both ruthless and sacrilegious. If ever there was a time that would necessitate the encryption of Egyptian wisdom in order to hide it from marauding invaders that would be it.[126]

The theory of tarot's Egyptian provenance was reinforced by other French occultists such as Éliphas Lévi (1810–1875),[127] Paul Christian (1811–1877)[128] and Gérard Encausse (popularly known as 'Papus', 1865–1916).[129] Even within Court de Gébelin's *Le Monde Primitif*, an essay by Comte de Mellet supported the hypothesis of an Egyptian origin for tarot. Egypt was thought to be the source of all esoteric wisdom and the Egyptian hieroglyphics an ancient magical language. Of course, this was before the decryption of the Rosetta Stone by François Champollion in 1822 which enabled the ancient language to be translated.[130]

More recent sources also maintain an Egyptian origin for tarot, an appealing example of which can be found in the obscure books of prose poems written by Mrs Anna M. Fullwood. *The Song of Sano Tarot* published in 1946, stated that the tarot was 'the ancient Egyptian doctrine of Equilibrium.' Mrs Fullwood received all of her information from clairvoyant visions.[131] William Lindsay Gresham in his 1947 novel *Nightmare Alley*, had Zeena a clairvoyant and mystic in a travelling circus, ascribe an Egyptian origin to the tarot.[132] Interestingly, a significant number of contemporary New Age sources, in spite of the speciousness of this Egyptian theory, still maintain that tarot was born in the sands of Egypt and that the tarot deck contains all the wisdom of humankind.[133]

The hypothesis of an Egyptian provenance for tarot can be discounted on several grounds. First, the ancient Egyptians did not have paper or cardboard with which to construct tarot cards. Some occultists explained away this difficulty by insisting that the tarot images were painted on gold or ivory or on wall panels.[134] It is difficult to see how this could be consistent with the idea that the Egyptian priests encoded their wisdom in a card game. Second, if tarot cards were in fact created in Egypt, then we would expect that at least some remnants would have been discovered. In addition it seems likely that the deck would have been adopted by neighbouring countries and some record of them or extant decks would be preserved there. Further, if they did contain Hermetic information, this too would have survived among Muslim esotericists, common in the cities of the Middle East at that time. And we would expect to discover some evidence of their transmission to Italy, in trade logs or inventories.[135]

But the most compelling reason we have to disregard this theory was that Egyptian symbolism did not resemble that of the tarot. As more and more sites were excavated and the images studies and catalogued, it became progressively clearer that Egyptian iconology was radically different from that of the tarot. As tarot scholar Robert O'Neill stated:

> The gods are humans with animal heads. The icons are full of nature figures: chicks, snakes, vultures, hawks, ibises. These natural figures appear as elements of the hieroglyphics but are completely absent from the tarot. None of the most important images or themes of Egyptian knowledge are found in the Tarot. Horus as the hawk, the scarab pushing the sun across the sky, the preoccupation with preparing the soul for the journey to the afterlife.[136]

This theory of an Egyptian origin of tarot gained currency amidst France's pre-Rosetta infatuation with all things Egyptian and placed little reliance on historical evidence. This also accounted for the French occultists' fascination with the *Corpus Hermeticum*. It had been written by Greek writers who believed that Egypt was the repository of a pristine philosophy and powerful magic. The *Hermeticum* took the form of writings supposedly authored by or dialogues with Hermes Trismegistus, who was also supposedly the

Egyptian Thoth.[137] When these documents were rediscovered and translated during the Renaissance, the aspiring philosophers and magi of the period took them literally and assumed they were the works of an ancient Egyptian provenance.[138] It was not until 1614, when classical scholar Isaac Casaubon, unsettled by the idea that pagans had predicted the coming of Christ that doubt was cast on the authenticity of the Hermetic texts.[139] He detected in the writings of Hermes, linguistic proof that the texts had been written at a date much later than originally thought. Further, he found evidence of Biblical Jewish and Christian language and ideas, Greek diction too abstract to be early, Greek puns and etymologies unlikely in a translation from the Egyptian and references to history and doctrinal views consistent with a later date.[140] The discovery of this deception was widely recognised, especially by Protestants, but in largely Catholic France, the enthusiasm for the texts remained unabated.[141]

By Court de Gébelin's time, this Renaissance misconception had become a cornerstone of the occult philosophy that was promulgated by means of secret societies such as the Freemasons of which Court de Gébelin was a member. Moreover, though many works attributed to Hermes/Thoth had been discovered and incorporated into occult lore, there remained the possibility that another work, perhaps even more compelling, remained undiscovered. It was little wonder that Court de Gébelin, on seeing the unfamiliar and overtly symbolic tarot trumps, immediately believed them to be Egyptian.[142]

Intimately connected with the hypothesis of an Egyptian provenance for tarot, was the idea that the gypsies brought the deck to Europe. For many people, the image of the gypsy card reader is their strongest association with tarot, and one that is constantly reinforced by popular culture.[143] Bizet's opera *Carmen* was a stereotypical representation of this fantasy – the fiery Andalusian gypsy girl Carmen reads her cards, turning them over one at a time until she reveals the Death card in the climax of the scene.[144] More recently, in *Last Love in Constantinople* (*Poslednja Ljubav u Carigradu*), an unusual novel by Mildorad Pavic, tarot was described as being in use among the gypsies.[145]

Many mistakenly believed the gypsies had come from Egypt, and that 'gypsy' was in fact an abbreviation of 'Egypt'.[146] Even though gypsies had been resident in Europe for around 400 years, it was not until 1781, when Antoine Court de Gébelin espoused the idea that tarot was from Egypt, did people link tarot with this wandering people.[147] Court de Gébelin spoke of the gypsies as having retained the Egyptian mode of divination by cards,[148] and this idea was further elaborated by Comte de Mellet. He believed that once the Egyptian priests had encoded their wisdom in the tarot cards, particularly in the trumps, the deck was given to the gypsies for safekeeping.[149]

This theory was reinforced by several authors who merely repeated the hypothesis with or without further elaboration.[150] In 1854, for example, Boiteau d'Ambly in his book *Les Cartes à jouer et la cartomancie* espoused the theory that tarot, created solely for the purpose of fortunetelling, was transmitted to Europe by the gypsies.[151] Jean-Alexandre Vaillant, erroneously assumed to be the first to espouse a gypsy involvement, published a classic study in 1857, *Les Rômes, histoire vraie des vrais Bohémiens*, in which he detailed his theory of the transmission of tarot by this nomadic people.[152] Vaillant was said to have lived with the gypsies and was reputedly instructed in their traditional lore. Much of the information he obtained was elaborated in *Les Rômes* and reinforced in *La Bible des Bohémien* (1860) and *La Clef Magique de la Fiction et du Fait* (1863).[153]

In 1865, playing card historian Ed S. Taylor published a history of playing cards which attributed a non-specific eastern origin to the tarot with the cards later being transported by the gypsies to Europe.[154] In 1913, Russian occultist Petyr Demianovich Ouspensky claimed that tarot was in common use among the gypsies of Spain in the fourteenth century.[155] Éliphas Lévi also espoused a gypsy provenance for the cards.[156] French playing-card historian Romain Merlin quoted Breitkopf from his book *Versuch den Ursprung der Spielkarten zu Erfrischen* (1784), stating that the gypsies obtained tarot cards from the Arabs.[157] This idea of a gypsy involvement with tarot has also been perpetuated in fiction. The translator of Gustav Meyrink's *The Golem*, Madge Pemberton wrote in a footnote: 'Tarok is possibly the oldest game of cards in Europe. It was probably introduced by gypsies, and dates as far back as the thirteenth century.'[158]

A variation on the theme emerged with the idea that tarot came from the East and probably India, before being brought to Europe by the gypsies. Devey Fearon de 'Hoste Ranking writing in 1908, believed that sixteenth-century author Guillaume Postel may have been obscurely referring to tarot in his work in *Absconditorum Clavis* when he asserted that the gypsies claimed a very ancient acquaintance with playing-cards, referring to the suit signs as *rup, pohara, spathis* and *pal*.[159] He went on to determine an Eastern provenance for tarot by noting that gypsies spoke some words of Sanskrit or Hindustani origin and were therefore probably of Indian ancestry. He examined the Pope card of the trumps, which he believed showed the influence of the Orthodox Eastern Faith as the Pope was depicted as being bearded and carrying the Triple Cross. He went on to explain that the card called 'The King' (I am assuming he meant the Emperor) represented a figure with the head-dress of a Russian Grand-Duke and a shield bearing the Polish Eagle. From this he concluded that the people who used the tarot must have been familiar with a country where the Orthodox Faith prevailed and which was ruled by Grand-Dukes. He deduced that tarot must have originated in the East and was then introduced into Eastern Europe by gypsies. From these eastern parts, tarot was disseminated across the rest of Europe.[160]

Writing in 1962, Indian author Chaman Lal, also correctly assumed that gypsies originated in India and suggested that this people fled from their home during the Moghul invasions. He theorised that these displaced gypsies fled to Persia where they were exposed to Manichaeism and it was the secrets of Mani that Lal believed were encoded in tarot.[161] Swiss author Sergius Golowin offered a variation on this theory. In his book *The World of the Tarot: The Gypsy Method of Reading the Tarot,* he theorised that when the Moghul invaders destroyed Indian culture, the gypsies carried the tarot with them as part of the Hindu cult of Śakti, which they spread all over Europe.[162] Jules Bois, infamous author of *Le Satanisme et la Magie,* claimed that the Albigenses contained the knowledge of the early Gnostic sects and encoded them in the tarot before delivering them into the hands of the gypsies for safekeeping.[163] With no convincing evidence to support their theories, many other authors have similarly claimed either a gypsy provenance for tarot or maintained that gypsies were responsible for bringing the deck to Europe, repeating and sometimes elaborating on already extant theories.[164]

It is necessary to have some idea about the history and origins of the people called 'gypsies' to be able to ascertain the extent of their involvement with tarot. A thorough academic study has been hampered by the unpopularity of gypsies in Europe. They have been persecuted from the time of their first appearance in that continent and even today are often described as 'thieves' and 'pickpockets'. A clan system, based mostly on their traditional occupations and geography, has made them a deeply fragmented and suspicious people, only unifying in the face of enmity from non-gypsies, whom they call *'gadje'.*[165]

The English word 'gypsy' and its European equivalents – the Greek *Gyphtoi,* Spanish *Gitano,* Turkish *Farawni* and Hungarian *Pharao nepe* (Pharaoh's folk) – reflect an early though erroneous belief that the wanderers were Egyptian.[166] It was in 1782 that Johann Rüdiger first compared Hindustani and Romani (gypsy) words and espoused the theory that gypsies came from northern India, near that country's ancient border with Persia.[167] The following year, Heinrich M. G. Grellmann published his *Dissertation on the Gypsies* in which he traced the gypsy language to the Jat tribe located at the mouth of the Indus River in north-western India.[168] Konrad Bercovici noted that Jats and Sudras were of a different stock from the other inhabitants of India and said that when the Hindus invaded India, the proto-gypsies were already there; subsequently becoming enslaved by the invaders.[169] Another theory proposed that the gypsies broke away from the main Aryan invasion before it reached India. However, there were remnants of the indigenous Indian Dravidian language in the Romani language of the gypsies which suggests that Romani must have originated from within India.[170]

There is little consensus among scholars as to when gypsies first arrived in Europe. In 1936, in his book *Gypsies: Their Life and their Customs*, Martin Friedrich Block reported that a Georgian monk first spoke of gypsies at Mount Athos on the peninsula of Alkidiki in Greece around 1100CE. Block further reported that by 1322 there was evidence that gypsies were known in Crete and by 1346 in Corfu.[171] Documentary corroboration indicates that gypsies were established in the Peloponnese and a number of the Greek islands during the fourteenth century. In 1416, Byzantine satirist Mazaris in the *Sojourn of Mazaris in Hades*, cited an imaginary letter dated 21 September 1415 and addressed from the Peloponnese to Holobolos of the Underworld, which described the conditions then existing in the peninsula: 'In the Peloponnese ... live pell-mell numerous nations, of which it is not easy nor very necessary to retrace the boundaries, but every ear can easily distinguish them by their language, and here are the most notable of them: Lacedaemonians, Italians, Peloponnesians, Slavs, Illyrians, Egyptians [*Aigúptioi*], and Jews (and among them are not a few half-castes) in all seven nations.' It seems likely that the 'Egyptians' referred to were in fact gypsies, especially as other sources indicate that they were resident in the Peloponnese at that time.[172] Gypsies chose to reside in Venetian territories, both in the Peloponnese and in the neighbouring islands, as these territories were deemed to be more stable; other areas suffered because of frequent Turkish incursions.[173] There was a large gypsy settlement located at Jaffa, part of modern-day Tel-Aviv, which formed a convenient resting place for pilgrims halfway between Venice and the Holy Land. Several of the pilgrims' diaries mentioned gypsies resident there.[174] Lionardo di Niccolò Frescobaldi, who visited the Medieval Greek city of Modon in 1384, reported seeing a number of *Romiti* outside the city walls. He believed they were penitents, though the testimonies of subsequent travellers indicated that they were gypsies.[175] By the end of the fourteenth century, gypsies had established themselves in the Balkan territories.[176] It is not difficult to imagine that from these territories, it would be a relatively simple matter for at least some gypsies to make their way to Venice and gain access to the rest of Europe.

Many authors have renounced a gypsy provenance for tarot on the basis that the appearance of the deck in Europe predated the arrival of gypsies. As previously argued, this was clearly not accurate. Gypsies did arrive in Europe before the advent of tarot and even before the introduction of ordinary playing cards. It must be conceded however, that even though the gypsies were well-established in Europe by the beginning of the fifteenth century, there was no other evidence of their early involvement with tarot cards.[177]

Though the hypothesis of a gypsy provenance has no currency in the academic milieu, New Age tarotists still espouse the theory. This theory is similarly espoused in popular books about the Romany.[178]

The idea that tarot contained the spiritual and magical secrets of a persecuted population is an enduring one, and a variation on this theme has been given currency by Dan Brown's bestselling novel, *The Da Vinci Code*. In this fictional account, tarot was created to conceal the heretical ideas of one or more sects in medieval Europe. Brown does not specify an ideology, instead stating: 'Originally, Tarot had been devised as a secret means to pass along ideologies banned by the Church. Now, Tarot's mystical qualities were passed on by modern fortune-tellers.'[179] In a hypothesis somewhat similar to that espoused involving an Egyptian provenance, tarot was supposedly created when a heretical group was threatened or persecuted, usually by the Catholic Church. Depending on the author, the sect is described as being Albigensian, Waldensian, Cathar, Manichean or Gnostic.[180]

Sir Steven Runciman suggested that the persecuted Cathars may have been the originators of tarot.[181] For playing card historian, Roger Tilley, the most likely candidates were the Waldenses. Excommunicated by Lucian III in 1183 and pressured by the Inquisition, many of the Waldenses (also known as the Vaudois) took refuge in the Cottian Alps, west of Milan.[182] They were unpopular with the Church, whose clergy they often denounced as being a 'sink of vice' and challenging their right to restrict access to Grace.[183] Initially, the Waldenses sought acceptance from the Church, teaching more or less traditional doctrine. They considered their mission to be important, making up for the deficiency in the ministry of the Catholic clergy.[184] As time went on, certain traditionally important doctrines were downplayed and others amplified until the practices of the Waldenses became unacceptable to the Church and the cry of 'heresy' was raised.[185]

As with all heretics, the Waldenses were forbidden from performing or participating in the sacraments which were seen as essential for eternal life. They were also forbidden from associating with any Christians. Their ministers were known as 'barbe' and they embarked on their missions in pairs, in search of converts or comforting the faithful who could not openly participate in their religion.[186] Of course, they were forced to conceal their identities to escape the vigilant eye of the Inquisition. According to Tilley, they were also forced to conceal their teachings; this they did by disguising their instruction in the symbolism of the tarot pack, to all outward appearances resembling a simple game.[187]

This theory must be discounted due to the lack of documentary evidence. Those who espoused this theory would argue that it was not feasible to document what supposedly was secret, especially when the revelation of those secrets would attract the attention of the Inquisition. Even so, it seems unlikely that there was not even a whisper of such a conspiracy. This theory was rendered yet more dubious by the fact that Waldensian instruction was generally oral.[188] Even in the most favourable of times, the Waldenses did not document their teachings; it is difficult to see why they would do so when they were threatened with persecution. It is unfeasible to divine a role for tarot in this scheme.

Suggestions that were every bit as implausible as a Waldensian involvement with tarot were those that proposed that the tarot deck evolved from a pre-existing game. Just as playing cards supposedly evolved from the Indian game of Ganjifa, there was a corresponding theory espousing that tarot grew from another Indian game, *pachisi*, known mostly in the West in its simplified form, *Ludo*.[189] Contemporary scholar Stephen Franklin claimed that there was a direct relationship between the fifty-six places on the outside track of the pachisi cross-shaped board and the fifty-six suit cards of tarot.[190] Other scholars draw a comparison between tarot and yet another Indian game, *Chaturange*.[191] In the absence of relevant documentation supporting the transition from board game to tarot card deck, an absence of evidence demonstrating a similarity in methods of play and a probable manner by which the game could have travelled from India to Europe, these theories must be discounted. The differences between the nominated games and the deck far outweigh any superficial similarities.

It would be easier to discern the similarities between another card game and tarot than between board games and tarot. Consequently, there has been much speculation as to the precise nature of '*naïbi*', a term associated with playing cards and frequently found in documentary sources from the fifteenth century. If it could be determined that this was a distinct card game, then it becomes feasible that it could be related to tarot in some way and possibly be the progenitor of that deck.

It is difficult enough to distinguish between tarot cards and the ordinary playing card deck in documentary sources. Unless the trump cards that characterise tarot were specifically mentioned, it is unclear which type of deck was being referred to. In most European languages, the term for 'card' was derived from the Latin '*charta*' which means 'paper',[192] but this is frustratingly non-specific. In early modern Italian sources, tarot decks were differentiated as '*trionfi*' or '*tarocchi*'.[193] To further add to the confusion, the term '*naïbes*' or '*naïpes*' was scattered through documentary and literary sources and it is difficult to determine whether this term referred to the ordinary card deck or to another kind of playing card altogether. The term was not in common use in Italy until the end of the fifteenth century but a derivative, '*naipes*' is still used in Spain to denote playing cards.[194]

Several authors have claimed that 'naïbi' referred to a particular kind of deck which consisted of a series of illustrated figures, the purpose of which was to educate children. Alessandro Bellenghi asserted that these decks were in common use in Italy towards the end of the fifteenth century.[195] Romain Merlin, among others, suggested that the famous *Tarot de Mantegna* was a deck of *naïbi* derived from an instructive picture book.[196] He hypothesised that tarot evolved from this deck.[197] Other tarot scholars such as Jean-Pierre Seguin asserted that tarot was created by the combining this educational, picture deck with the ordinary playing card deck.[198]

A number of theories have been posited to explain the etymology of the term '*naïb*'. Stuart Kaplan offered the opinion that the word was derived from 'napa' which means 'flat' or 'even' in the Biscayan dialect.[199] Alfred Douglas noted that '*naipes*' could well be derived from the Flemish '*knaep*' meaning 'paper' at a time during the Early Modern period when trade flourished between Flanders and Spain.[200] Marlene Dobkin claimed that in the dictionary of the Royal Spanish Academy, the term '*naipes*' was said to be etymologically derived from the Arabic '*naib*': he who represents, or '*laib*': he who plays.[201] Perhaps in an attempt to procure an occult derivation for the word, Bellenghi asserted that it was derived from the Arabic word for prophet, which is '*nabi*', the Hebrew '*naibes*' meaning 'magic' or from '*naahab*' (to prophesy).[202]

Tarot historian Michael Dummett proposed that the term '*naïb*' and its derivatives actually arose from the name of one of the court cards of the Mamlūk pack, the *nā'ib*. The entry in the Viterbo Chronicles read in part: 'In this year of such great tribulations the game of cards was introduced into Viterbo, which came from the Saracens and was called "Naib".'[203] Dummett logically assumed that it was unlikely that playing cards were ever called '*naïbs*' in Arabic sources, especially as the plural form of '*nā'ib*' was actually '*nuwwāb*'. It was plausible, however; that Italians or Spaniards unfamiliar with the Arabic term could give all cards of Arabic origin this name.[204] Given such an obvious etymology for the term, along with its direct connection with those Arabic decks resembling the regular European deck, it appears unlikely that the term '*naïb*' ever referred to an educational deck of pictures.[205]

Another theory posits that tarot was derived from the game of *tarocchino*, once popular in Bologna. A *tarocchino* deck was comprised of sixty-two cards of which twenty-two were trump cards; the rest were numbered cards, as with tarot, across four suits but with the 2, 3, 4 and 5 from each suit being dropped.[206] According to Count Leopoldo Cicognara writing in 1831, *tarocchino* ('little tarot') was invented in 1419 by Francesco Antelminelli Castracani Fibbia, prince of Pisa though exiled in Bologna. He based this theory on an inscription from a wide label on a portrait of Fibbia which credited him with the invention of the game and supposedly recorded the privilege granted to Fibbia of placing his arms and those of his wife on the

Queen of Batons and the Queen of Coins respectively.[207] The portrait, tentatively dated to the second half of the seventeenth century, showed Prince Fibbia holding a pack of *tarocchino* cards, some of which were falling to the floor. The inscription appeared to be painted over an earlier version which lacked the sentence describing Fibbia as the inventor of *tarocchino*.[208] As the earliest extant *tarocchino* packs can be dated from the sixteenth century, it seems highly unlikely that *tarocchino*, as a shortened version of tarot, predated the appearance of the seventy-eight-card tarot deck. Further, it seems similarly doubtful that Prince Fibbia, who died in 1419, was the inventor of either tarot or *tarocchino*.[209]

Because of their close structural and symbolic similarities, it seems certain that the tarot deck evolved from the ordinary playing card deck. However, it proves to be impossible to demonstrate the emergence of tarot from other card games such as *tarocchino*, or from pre-existing board games such as *pachisi* or *chaturange*. In the quest to ascertain the provenance of tarot, an alternate methodology must be explored. One approach that has drawn much attention was the close examination of the etymology of those terms associated with the extended deck.

Numerous tarot scholars have attempted to unravel the etymology of the word 'tarot' and associated terms to substantiate a theory of tarot's origin. In the earliest references to the cards, they were called '*cartes de trionfi*' in Italian or 'cards with triumphs', indicating that one card would 'triumph' over another during play. This was an entirely descriptive term to distinguish the tarot deck from regular playing cards.[210] By the sixteenth century, this term was replaced by '*tarocchi*', though the etymology remains mysterious.[211] According to internet tarot historian Tom Tadfor Little, the impetus for the change came with the realisation that an ordinary playing card deck could be used for playing a game with 'triumphs' or 'trumps' in a manner similar to tarot, as long as it was decided which suit would supply the trump cards.[212] The earliest known use of the term '*tarocchi*' (or '*tarocco*', singular) was found in an account book of the Ferrarese court for June and December 1505.[213] Less than fifty years later in 1550, poet Albert Lollio in his *Invettiva Contra il Giuoco del Taroco*, declared that the origin of the word was unknown.[214] The earliest printed reference to *tarocchi* was in *Capitolo del Gioco della Primiera* by Italian poet Francesco Berni, supposedly published in Rome in 1526.[215]

Though no definitive etymology can be discovered for the term '*tarocchi*', Alessandro Bellenghi asserted that the word was probably derived from the name given to a surface gilded with leaves engraved with a stylus which was said to be '*taroccata*'.[216] Though this was plausible given that the hand-painted cards of the Italian courts could have been decorated in this way, there exists no other evidence to support this assertion. Others have suggested that the term instead refers to the tributary of the River Po, called 'Taro' which runs across the northern Italian plains.[217] However, why this would be so in the absence of any symbolism on the deck that denotes a connection to the riverine system remains unanswered.

Archivist Hyacinthe Chobaut, in her book *Les Maîtres Cartiers d'Avignon du XVme siècle à la Révolution*, claimed that she had found a document dated 1507 which referred to a card-maker named Jean Fort in Avignon who made 'cards called in the vernacular *taraux*'.[218] Mme Esther Moench, curator of the Musée du Petit-Palais d'Avignon, encouraged by playing card historian Thierry Depaulis, found the true date to be 1505.[219] The term itself was not in Latin, as was the rest of the document, and it was not Provençal which was the language spoken in Avignon at that time, but was French indicating that tarot was being used and manufactured north of Lyons. Because this date was so close to that of the first appearance of the word '*tarocchi*' in Italy, Depaulis posited that the Italian term '*tarocchi*' was actually derived form the French term '*taraux*' (later 'tarot').[220]

Other theories specifically reference the craft of cardmaking. In 1694, the card-makers of Paris called themselves '*tarotiers*', which in all likelihood was a corruption of '*tarot*'.[221] The term '*tarotée*' was the name applied to the criss-crossing lines that adorned the backs of early cards which were called '*cartes tarotées*'.[222] Further, a border of dots on some old cards was called '*tares*'.[223] The term 'tarot' could have been derived from the expression of these processes but just as readily, the terms specific to these crafts could have been copied from 'tarot'. In addition, these decorations were not specific to tarot cards.

There were numerous theories of etymological derivation with a decidedly esoteric bent. Cynthia Giles spoke of 'tarot' as having possibly being derived from the name 'Tara' which appears in many mystical traditions. For example, in the Hindu tradition, Soma as the god of ecstasy has a liaison with Tārā, one of the forms of the goddess Kali with the Buddha as the resultant offspring. In Mahāyāna Buddhism, Tārā is venerated as one of the *Matrika-devis* or mother goddesses and is the consort of the Bodhisattva of Compassion, Avalokiteśvara, saviour of mankind, who leads all sentient beings to enlightenment.[224] In 1857, Jean-Alexandre Vaillant speculated about the connection between the Assyrian goddess Ashtarot and the Indo-Tartar divinity Ten-tara. This relationship has not been substantiated.[225]

Just as theories of an Egyptian derivation for tarot have proven popular, so have theories supporting an Egyptian derivation for the term 'tarot'. Antoine Court de Gébelin wrote that the word was derived from an Egyptian phrase '*Ta-Rosh*' meaning 'the royal way' or the 'royal road of life'.[226] Gérard Encausse in *The Tarot of the Bohemians* (1889) stated that 'the whole Tarot was based upon the word ROTA, arranged as a wheel.'[227] He equated TARO with INRI (the initial letters of the Catholic monogram, *Iesus Nazaraeus Rec Iudeorum*, and of the Freemasonic formula *Igne Natura Renovatur Integra*), and with YOD-HE-VAU-HE, the Hebrew Tetragrammaton.[228] Another theory held that this Latin word for wheel, '*rota*,' demonstrated an Egyptian link as it was no more than an anagram of the name of the Egyptian goddess 'Ator', a form of 'Hathor'. Some see evidence of this connection in the naming of the tenth trump or 'The Wheel of Fortune'.[229] Others maintained that it derived from '*tarosc*' in which the 't' was the article, the 'a' meant 'doctrine' or 'science' and '*rosc*' represented Mercury or Thoth, thus giving 'the doctrine of Thoth'.[230]

Samuel Liddell MacGregor Mathers, one of the founders of the occult society the Hermetic Order of the Golden Dawn, also saw 'tarot' as being derived from the Egyptian word '*táru*' which allegedly meant 'to require an answer' or 'to consult'; and that the second 't' was added to denote the feminine gender.[231] Mrs John King van Rensselaer claimed that Egyptologist Sir John Gardner Wilkinson stated that 'tarot' was a derivative of 'thror Tahar' which 'were the parchment records kept in the Temple, which are mentioned in the time of the 18th Dynasty [and] that were written on skins.'[232] As expected, closely linked to Egyptian theories of 'tarot' were those hypotheses of gypsy provenance. Basil Rákóczi in 1954 proposed that 'tarot' had its roots in the secret language of the gypsy. The word was supposed to be a corruption of 'Ptah' plus 'Ra', the male gypsies' prevailing deity.[233]

Some see a connection with the Hebrew '*Torah*' and 'tarot', particularly when considering the deck's alleged connections with the mystical kabbalah.[234] This view was reiterated by Gustav Meyrink in his occult novel, *The Golem*.[235] According to Gérard Encausse (Papus) and Guillaume Postel, following the lead of Éliphas Lévi, 'tarot' was derived from the tetragram of the kabbalists, which – variously expressed (*rota*, *tora*, taro etc.) – embraced the meaning of both 'God' and 'Man', a concept inspired by the example of the tetragram of the Hebrew God (*Jeve*) and the tetragram of the alchemists (*Azot*, which means 'mercury' in Arabic). The wheel was seen as an illustration of the Hebrew name for God: Jeve or Javé.[236] Another theory proffered by the magus Aleister Crowley stated that: 'One important interpretation of Tarot is that it is a Notariquon of the Hebrew *Torah*, the Law, and of ThROA, the Gate.'[237] Bellenghi thought that perhaps the word owed its origin to the angelic *théraph* or *théraphim*, the 'figures' through which the priests of Israel asked questions of the oracle.[238] He also posited that the root '*thr*' carried the idea of 'modality', while the root '*reh*' expressed the concept of 'guideline', so that '*tarah*' translated as 'showing the way'.[239]

Aligned with his hypothesis of a *Ṣūfī* origin for tarot, Idries Shah claimed that 'tarot' was derived from the Arabic '*TaRIQ*' meaning 'the course of life or the way'.[240] This theory was echoed by Bellenghi: 'In Arabic *tariqa* again signifies "the way", the way of life, the course of life to follow, which is further developed in the *Ṣūfī tariqat*, meaning the right way.'[241]

There are as many theories as to the derivation of the term 'tarot' as there are theories about the provenance of the cards themselves. In the absence of substantiated etymological evidence, most theories relating to the derivation of the terms 'tarot' and 'tarocchi' tell us more about the prevailing social and intellectual currents at the time that these theories were formulated than about the place and time of the origin of the tarot deck. While we can be certain that tarot evolved from the regular playing-card deck and confidently discount the theories that would have it being created in ancient Egypt to be disseminated by the gypsies or evolving from an extant game, the circumstances surrounding its creation remain ambiguous without the examination of further evidence. The most significant clues to tarot's true provenance are to be found in the documents where '*cartes de trionfi*' are first mentioned, in the correspondence and record books of the courts of Northern Italy. These will be considered in detail in the next chapter.

2

Renaissance Italy and the Emergence of Tarot

Evidence garnered from bureaucratic records suggests that tarot was incubated in the court of either Ferrara or Milan, and a letter written by a Venetian military captain to a distant queen would insinuate the latter. A treatise in Latin described an early version of the game – quite possibly the original version – intermediate in design between the regular playing card deck and that of tarot. Having established where and when the deck came into existence, it becomes possible to view the symbolism in light of the context in which it arose. In this way the tarot images will reveal their earliest meanings, their significance lost and re-imagined as esoteric law with the passage of time and the relentless march of history.

As the principal city of the Po and situated on the marshy plains associated with that river,[1] Ferrara has a history marked by bloodshed and dark deeds as Guelf and Ghibelline factions struggled for control of this northern Italian city.[2] Eventually triumphant in 1208, the Este family, sympathetic to the Papacy and the Guelfs, precipitated a Renaissance in culture and romance through poetry, song and art.[3] Known as the first truly modern city in Europe,[4] Ferrara was ruled despotically by the Este family as an independent commune, though it was nominally a papal fief.[5] Under the rule of Niccolò III (1393–1441), the city enjoyed considerable military success with Rovigo, Modena, Reggio, Parma and briefly, Milan falling under Ferrarese control.[6] Niccolò III was succeeded by his son, Leonello, who was a popular ruler who cherished and maintained peace in the region.[7] Though the citizens were highly taxed to fund the frequent incursions into adjacent territories and defence of the city, they were generally wealthier than most in the region.[8] It was in this milieu, as much renowned for its strife as for its culture, that tarot or *cartes de trionfi*, were first mentioned in the public record.

Though there has been much speculation as to the origins of tarot, the first documentary evidence for its existence did not appear until 1442 in the account books of the Este court of Ferrara.[9] There was a reference in the *Registro dei Mandati* to '*pare uno de carte da trionfi*', and again in the

Registro di Guardaroba, (Storeroom register) of February 10 there was allusion to '*Quattro paia di carticelle da trionfi*'.[10] The Italian word for 'pair' ('paro' or 'paio') was used to designate a pack of cards.[11] Further entries occurred in the records for 1452, 1454 and 1461.[12] But there is reason to believe that tarot was already widely known by this time. The *Registro di Guardaroba* of February 10 1442 indicated that the Este court painter Jacopo de Sagramoro received twenty lire 'for having coloured and painted the cups, swords, coins and batons and all the figures of four packs of trump cards, and making the backs for a pack of red cards and three packs of green ones, embellished with roundels painted in oil, which the Lord has for his use.'[13] Further, an entry of 28 July 1442 referred to packs of *carte da trionfi* intended for Ercole and Sigismondo d'Este (the brothers of Leonello) and purchased for just twelve *soldi* and three *denari* from the shopkeeper, Marchione Burdochi.[14] If cheap packs (less than one eighth of the price of a hand-coloured deck by Sagramoro) were readily available, it seems likely that tarot decks were already in wide use by this time.[15] It also seems probable that the creation of tarot occurred significantly earlier than these dates and consequently, the geographical origin of the deck might be other than Ferrara.

Further evidence of an early Italian provenance for tarot can be found in a Milanese fresco which has been similarly dated to the early 1440s.[16] *The Tarocchi Players* was one of three frescoes on the walls of a small room in the Casa Borromeo in Milan and features five young people playing cards in the outdoors.[17] The fresco has deteriorated to such an extent that it is to see the faces of the cards, yet in earlier photographs these were still evident.[18] The cards were identified as the Two of Coins and the Ace of Coins. Though the cards could have belonged to a tarot pack, they could have just as easily belonged to an ordinary playing card deck.[19] The only suggestion we have that the fresco portrayed tarot players was from its name, long established by tradition, *The Tarocchi Players*.[20] It is possible that the number of cards or even the number of players would have given fifteenth-century viewers a clue as to the games being played and hence, to the composition of the pack.[21] There is not even a consensus as to who painted this evocative work with Michelino da Besozzo,[22] Franceschino Zavattari[23] and Antonio Pisano (Pisanello)[24] being suggested as likely candidates.[25] With both the artist and hence, an accurate dating of this work being unknown, it is difficult to confidently ascribe a provenance older than that of the Ferrarese records. The theory is further confounded by the ambiguous nature of the card game depicted. Though the title does suggest that the game was played using a tarot deck, it is possible that the name had been more recently attached to the fresco by someone other than the artist or patron who had no knowledge of the original intent of its creator.

Figure 2: The Tarocchi Players, Casa Borromeo, Milan.

The First Tarot Deck

The first intriguing hint as to the identity of the inventor of tarot was glimpsed in a letter written by a Venetian military captain, Jacopo Antonio Marcello. Dated 1449, the letter accompanied a gift of tarot cards (*carte de trionfi*) destined for Queen Isabella of Anjou, the consort of King René I, Duke of Lorraine.[26] Marcello claimed the deck had been painted by the famous artist Michelino da Besozzo and invented by Duke Filippo Maria Visconti of Milan.[27] Unfortunately, the deck of cards did not survive but the letter and an explanatory treatise in Latin written by Duke Visconti's secretary, Marziano da Tortono, still do.[28] In his letter, Marcello reported that he had originally secured a pack of tarot cards for the Queen but was disappointed with their poor quality. He had heard of the deck painted by Michelino da Besozzo for Duke Visconti and resolved to locate it.[29] He also described the treatise by Marziano and stated that the secretary had also been an expert in astrology.[30]

Marziano, in his treatise *Tractatus de Deificatione Sexdecim Heroum*, claimed the idea for the deck originated with Duke Filippo Maria Visconti and its creation was realised by the celebrated artist, Michelino da Besozzo.[31] Marziano's work was the first to mention '*trionfi*' in reference to a card game.[32] The pack thus described would have to have been created sometime before 1425, the year in which Marziano died, and probably sometime between 1414 and 1418.[33] If these dates were correct, then Duke Visconti could have been as young as twenty-two when this deck was created, keeping in mind he became the ruler of Milan when he was just twenty, after the death of his brother, Giovanni Maria.[34]

Writing around 1440, Duke Visconti's biographer Decembrio, also described a deck of cards and it seems probable that this deck was the one mentioned in both Marcello's letter and Marziano's treatise.[35] The relevant passage read as follows:

> Filippo Maria from youth was in the habit of playing games of various kinds. Sometimes he exercised with the spear, sometimes with the ball, but chiefly played that type of game which uses painted images, to which he was so immensely attracted that he bought a whole set of them for 1500 gold pieces, the person responsible being primarily his secretary Mariano of Tortona, who arranged for the images of gods, and figures of animals and birds dependent on them, with the greatest intelligence.[36]

Marziano divided his manuscript into two sections: the first was a preface or '*Prohemium*' which detailed the deck's structure and the second described in detail the subject of each of the cards.[37] The deck was described as having 'sixteen celestial princes and barons' (*sexdecim coeli principes ac barones*) and four kings. Though these sixteen cards were organised sequentially, they were also divided into four orders, namely Virtues, Riches, Virginities and Pleasures.[38] The structure was as follows:

Virtues	Riches	Virginities	Pleasures
1. Jupiter	2. Juno	3. Pallas	4. Venus
5. Apollo	6. Neptunus	7. Diana	8. Bacchus
9. Mercurius	10. Mars	11. Vesta	12. Ceres
13. Hercules	14. Eolus	15. Daphnes	16. Cupido

Table 2: The alignment of the 'celestial princes and barons' with the four orders.[39]

Arranged below these cards were four Birds which corresponded with the four orders' meanings, hence the Eagle was associated with Virtues; the Phoenix with Riches, the Turtle with Virginities; and the Dove with Pleasures.[40] Marziano stated that no order of Bird had any power over any other in play, probably inferring that none had any trick-taking power over another during the game.[41] Marziano explicitly mentioned just twenty-four cards but his comments about Birds 'taking power' implied the presence of other cards. He remarked that this power was direct for Eagles and Turtles and reversed for Phoenixes and Doves. He probably intended that cards in the Eagle and Turtle suits ascended in order of value (i.e. a five was ranked above a three) while cards in the Phoenix and Dove suits followed a descending order (i.e. a five was less valuable than a three). This was a common practice in fifteenth-century Italy and Spain.[42] If the Bird suits had a forward or backward order, there must have been several cards in each suit group, not just a single King. On the basis of this evidence, Pratesi believed that the deck possessed numeral cards, although neither Marziano nor Marcello explicitly mentioned them.[43]

In this unique deck, the deities were ranked higher than the orders of Birds and Kings, resembling the trumps of a traditional tarot deck. The deities belonged to one or another of the suits even though they followed a strict order of one to sixteen. Elsewhere in the manuscript, Marziano stated that there were several gods of the same name. For example, he said that there were three Jupiters: two from Arcadia and the other from Crete.[44] The exact meaning of these statements was probably obvious when the treatise was read while having access to the deck, but when considered without it, it is difficult to ascertain the exact composition of the deck. In the second section of Marziano's treatise, he described each of the sixteen classical figures, providing detail about their genealogy, the sphere of human activity governed by each and the attributes which distinguished them. The emphasis on certain attributes such as dress, physique and setting was intended to correspond with the cards painted by Michelino.[45]

There is little doubt that the deck described by Marziano differed markedly from that which became standardised as tarot. However, it could have represented an intermediate stage between playing cards and *cartes da trionfi*. Though the sixteen deities were not represented as trumps in later tarot decks, there was some resemblance between the suits of Virtues, Riches, Virginities and Pleasures with those of both the regular tarot deck and regular playing cards. Pratesi concluded that the *denari* (Coins) corresponded with Riches; *spade* (Swords) inspired Virtues; *coppes* (Cups) inspired Pleasures; and *bastoni* (Batons) inspired Virginities.[46]

In his letter to King René of 1449, Jacopo Marcello admitted he had augmented Michelino's deck with some high cards, seemingly to make it compatible with games played with the seventy-eight card tarot deck. As only high cards were mentioned, Pratesi speculated that the deck already contained pip and court cards, needing only six trumps to equal the seventy-eight-card deck.[47] Interestingly, it was on this basis that Michael Dummett denied that the deck belonged in the genealogy of tarot as it had fewer than twenty-two trump cards and its trump subjects were not those of the later, standardised deck.[48]

The administrative documents of the Northern Italian courts indicated that there were a plethora of hand-painted decks produced between the time of Marcello's letter and the end of the fifteenth century; with about twenty incomplete packs surviving.[49] The earliest extant packs were from the court of Milan. Apart from a general similarity in structure confined to pip cards distributed across four (non-standard) suits and an additional 'suit' of trump cards, they did not closely resemble the pack described in Marziano's treatise or Marcello's letter. Of the twenty fragmentary packs, three are of particular interest, being the oldest and most complete. All of these decks featured pip cards distributed through the traditional Latin suits of Coins, Swords, Cups and Batons, though the depiction of the suit signs varied between the decks. All were believed to have been painted by Bonifacio Bembo though other artists have been nominated.[50] Two of the decks were created for Duke Filippo Maria Visconti and the other for Francesco Sforza, who subsequently ruled Milan and married Filippo's illegitimate daughter, Bianca Visconti.

The first of these, the Visconti di Modrone pack named for a former owner, is believed to be the oldest extant deck.[51] Its structure differed markedly from the newer, standardised tarot decks so that it can be supposed that a regular form had not yet been established. Sixty-seven cards survived including eleven trumps: the Empress, the Emperor, Love, Fortitude, Faith, Hope, Charity, the Chariot, Death, the Angel and the World.[52] The Theological Virtues of Faith, Hope and Charity were not usual subjects for tarot trumps. It is also reasonable to suppose that as the sequence contained the Cardinal Virtue of Fortitude, it may have also contained Temperance, Prudence and Justice as the remaining Cardinal Virtues.[53] Though fifty-six pip cards survived, they were somewhat unusual in that there were male and female counterparts for each court rank, resulting in six court cards for each suit.[54] This deck featured straight blades on the cards of the Swords suit, arrows replaced the Batons on some of the cards of that suit and imprints of Filippo Maria's gold florin were seen in the Coins suit.[55] The second deck made for Duke Filippo Maria Visconti is known as the Brambilla pack after a former owner, and was thought to have been painted between 1442 and 1445.[56] Of the trump cards, only the Emperor and the Wheel of Fortune have survived. This deck featured arrows rather than Batons on the court cards and imprints of Duke Visconti's florin on the Coins suit.[57]

The third pack, known as the Visconti-Sforza deck, was painted for Francesco Sforza and his wife Bianca. It is the most recent and most complete of the three decks.[58] The Fool, nineteen trump cards and fifty-four pip cards survive. The Devil and the Tower were missing from the trumps and six cards were obviously later additions. These were Temperance, Fortitude, the Star, the Moon, the Sun and the World.[59] The suit of Swords in this deck featured weapons with straight blades as with the Visconti di Modrone pack.[60] As with the Brambilla pack, the Visconti emblems were found on the Cups and Coins suits but the Sforza emblems were found on the other two suits.[61] It was thought that the original deck was painted by Bonifacio Bembo, though the identity of the artist who painted the later cards remains unknown.[62] Interestingly, it was the Visconti-Sforza deck that has been the model for most subsequent decks.

It seems probable that tarot was invented at the Court of Milan either for or by Duke Filippo Maria Visconti as stated by Jacopo Antonio Marcello in his letter to Queen Isabella.[63] It is unimportant that the identity of tarot's creator cannot be confirmed. The deck, if not invented by Duke Visconti, was certainly crafted for him and the symbolism displayed on the trump cards undoubtedly was devised to be of particular relevance to him. The oldest extant tarot decks come from Milan and the earliest documents that mention the pack also come from the court of that northern Italian city as well as Ferrara.[64] The progenitor of the standard tarot deck was that painted by Michelino da Besozzo depicting gods and birds, described by Marcello in his letter and detailed in Marziano da Tortona's explanatory treatise. The Visconti di Modrone pack, again from the Milanese court, was a further experimentation with an ordinary playing card deck augmented by trump or 'triumph' cards, before the tarot pack became standardised as the Visconti-Sforza deck with the familiar trump subjects.[65]

The Viscontis and the Italian Renaissance

The history of the Visconti family and later the Sforzas, was set against the cultural currents which characterised Renaissance Europe and in particular, the Italian peninsula. The Visconti di Modrone and Brambilla packs were specifically made for Duke Filippo Maria Visconti, whereas the Visconti-Sforza deck was created for Francesco Sforza and his wife, Bianca Maria Visconti. A detailed knowledge of the history of these families will afford some insight concerning the significance of the symbolism displayed on these decks.

The common perception of the Italian Renaissance is one of gentility, opportunity and a religious devotion to art and culture. History books speak of grand battles fought with honour and courage, and galleries and museums the world over are crammed with works of art deriving from this epoch. The names of Renaissance artists are familiar to labourers and academics alike, even if only through best-selling novels such as *The Da Vinci Code*[66] or through the cartoon exploits of the Teenage Mutant Ninja Turtles.[67] These associations have given the Italian Renaissance a preternaturally rosy reputation which misrepresents the complex social and cultural factors which shaped the period.

To think of the Italian Renaissance as life-affirming and unequivocally optimistic is to seriously discount the effects of constant war, widespread famine and the devastating economic and social ravages of repeated outbreaks of plague.[68] In truth, these factors made possible the cultural flowering for which the Renaissance is best known. The industries of the Italian cities were in rapid decline, unemployment skyrocketed and the wealthy pillaged the countryside to maintain their fortunes.[69] Wealth became even more unevenly distributed and the urban aristocracy were able to spend large sums on art and country estates as investment opportunities within industry dwindled.[70] Milan was to some extent insulated from this economic depression due to the sensible fiscal policies of the Visconti and agriculture remained viable in this region.[71] Even so, the city was frequently at war and its citizens were heavily taxed to support these campaigns. Far from the modern perception of the Renaissance as a time of art and beauty, this was an exceedingly pessimistic period characterised by a morbid preoccupation with death.[72]

The enduring strain of economic depression, the unremitting proximity of death and the difficulties inherent in maintaining even a modest existence began to erode religious faith.[73] The Church was riddled by internal strife as factions battled for power, wealth and territory, resulting in the Western Schism which saw two popes battling for the loyalty of a divided Europe.[74] This perceived fallibility of God's representatives exposed them as ambitious political contestants rather than spiritual leaders, and this realisation manifested in society as an increasing secularisation.[75] In tandem with this came a rediscovery of the classical world and in fact, the term 'Renaissance' refers to this revival.[76] The epic stories describing the feats of the pre-Christian pagan gods fell under particular scrutiny. Paganism was not seen as a replacement for Catholicism, rather the emphasis was placed on the similarities between Christianity and the ancient religions. This shift saw the moral content of religion accentuated at the expense of the sacraments and the clergy.[77] A pertinent example of this fascination was evidenced by the depiction of the pagan gods on the trump cards of Marziano's deck as described by Jacopo Antonio Marcello in his letter to Queen Isabella of Anjou.

The revival of classicism promoted the philosophy of secularism. There was a greater enjoyment of mundane pleasure and a rising sense of personal independence and expression.[78] Through the revival of classical learning, first Roman and later Greek, the idea of humanism arose which manifested as a celebration of the dignity of man and his place in the universe.[79] The humanists celebrated the scholarly disciplines of grammar, rhetoric, history, poetry and moral philosophy as espoused in the writings of the classical authors, each word read, reread and carefully studied so as to assimilate every nuance of meaning.[80] Such concepts were exemplified by celebrated authors such as Manetti[81] and Petrarch,[82] who for some time were resident at the Visconti court.[83]

The Visconti family had been associated with the history of Milan from the thirteenth century when Pope Urban IV appointed Ottone Visconti as archbishop, in an attempt to balance the power of another dominant Milanese family, the della Torres.[84] Through intrigues, manipulations and strategic marriages, the Visconti secured their place in Milanese history, their rule characterised by ruthless cruelty and devious machinations. Bernabò Visconti, who ruled Milan from 1349, typified the family's administration. He taxed his subjects to breaking point and forced them to feed and care for the five thousand hounds he used in the chase.[85] During the outbreak of plague in 1360, affected houses had their doors sealed and guarded until all inside had either died or recovered. Bernabò himself escaped into the countryside until the danger had passed.[86]

This ruthless autocrat married his legitimate daughters into useful European monarchies and his illegitimate daughters to *condottieri* for the protection and advantage of Milan. Bernabò's despotic tyranny came to an end when he was ambushed, arrested and later poisoned by his equally treacherous nephew, Gian Galeazzo Visconti, in 1385.[87] In 1392, this ambitious despot purchased the hereditary title of Duke of Milan from Emperor Wenceslas of Germany, cementing his status and endowing him with the imperial eagle that was to become part of the Visconti coat of arms.[88] In turn, he fathered two sons, Giovanni Maria and Filippo Maria,[89] and his daughter was married to the younger brother of Charles VI of France, Louis, Duke of Orléans. Such a marriage was testimony to the power and wealth attained by the Visconti.[90]

Giovanni Maria, at the age of thirteen, succeeded his father as duke on Gian Galeazzo's death from the plague in 1402.[91] Continuing the family tradition of treachery and tyranny, he was purported to have trained his dogs to eat human flesh, enjoying the spectacle of the grizzly deaths of political prisoners or social criminals. It is unsurprising that he was stabbed to death by three nobles in 1412.[92] His younger brother, Filippo Maria, became Duke of Milan at just twenty years of age; the last of the Visconti rulers.[93]

Filippo Maria Visconti was somewhat of an enigma. He ruled Milan with an iron fist, aligning himself to power and protection with carefully engineered strategic marriages. Through such machinations, he regained much of the Milanese territories lost by his incompetent brother. He considered himself to be so ugly, with a large mouth and a low forehead marked by deep lines, that he declined to be painted or drawn.[94] In contrast to the rest of the Visconti who were blonde and athletic, he had dark hair and an unattractive sallow complexion.[95] Nevertheless, he was also known as a gentle and sensitive scholar, interested in astrology, pious and introverted. His shyness was extreme and later in life he became obese, rarely being seen outside of the Castello di Porta Giovia.[96] His home was surrounded by extensive gardens and for years he never set foot in the actual city of Milan.[97] Emperor Sigismund visited in 1432, but the Duke would not meet with him, though he was happy to have the Emperor accommodated.[98] In addition, he had an extremely nervous disposition and always suspected plots against him, which given the history of his family was unsurprising. He had guards watch over him as he slept and these were changed several times a night.[99] Whoever entered the Duke's castle was carefully watched and no one was permitted to stand near a window lest they signal to someone outside.[100] He even distrusted the military generals sworn to protect him, constantly playing one off against the other.[101]

Filippo Maria disliked music and theatrical entertainments, preferring instead to play chess.[102] As was common at that time, he was fascinated by astrology and would not make a move without consulting the stars.[103] He was exceedingly superstitious and was mortally afraid of putting his shoes on the wrong feet, easier to do in those days as the left and right shoes were not much differentiated.[104] His piety showed itself in his generous endowments to the Church and he was said to rise two or three times a night to pray near the window, in the light of the moon and stars which he adored.[105]

As gentle and as studious as he could be, Filippo also retained the ruthless political nature of the Viscontis. In order to avert an attack from the troops of his former *condottiere*, Facino Cane, he married the general's widow Beatrice Tenda, twenty years his senior. This strategic marriage annulled the threat of insurrection and Beatrice also brought with her a much needed dowry of 40 000 florins to replenish Milan's coffers after the misrule of Giovanni Maria.[106] When Beatrice had outlived her usefulness, trumped up charges of infidelity were levelled at her and a teenage pageboy, who had done nothing more than play the lute in the company of his mistress and her maids of honour. The latter were tortured until they supported the accusations and both Beatrice and the pageboy were executed.[107] Filippo probably did not intend to marry again but the threat of attack from the north forced him into another strategic marriage, this time with Maria of Savoy. In spite of her greatest efforts to effect a genuine union, Filippo Maria refused to be even within the same house as his bride.[108] Apparently, the superstitious duke heard a dog howling as the couple were about to retire to their wedding bed and this he interpreted as an ominous sign.[109]

His one genuinely romantic attachment was with his mistress, Agnese del Maino.[110] He remained faithful to her and she was the mother of his only child, Bianca, who he adored.[111] As with all the Visconti, Filippo sought to strengthen his position by strategically marrying of his offspring. Bianca Maria Visconti, as precious as she was to him, was promised to the *condottiere* Francesco Sforza, twenty-two years her senior, when she was just nine years old.[112] Sforza was a man of humble birth who, in the true spirit of the Renaissance, rose to great heights with a combination of wit, patience and luck.[113] Sforza had fought both for and against Milan. Cosimo Medici of Florence had hired him to repel an invasion by Milan in both 1437 and again in 1438 and only his hopes of marrying Bianca Visconti prevented him from entirely routing the Milanese.[114] Most of his career he worked for the perennial Milanese enemies of Florence and Venice, earning the ready distrust of Duke Visconti.[115] Francesco Sforza and Bianca Maria Visconti eventually wed in 1441, their marriage being long and happy.[116] But once Sforza had actually married Bianca, Filippo became increasingly jealous and suspicious of him. Sforza could now claim a legitimate right to the throne; that was until Filippo explicitly excluded him from the succession.[117]

When Duke Filippo Maria Visconti died without leaving an obvious successor, Milan proclaimed itself the Ambrosian Republic, named for the patron saint of the city, St Ambrose.[118] Opportunistic aggressors assailed Milan and soon the citizens begged Francesco Sforza to defend them. This he did but turned from being their defender to their foe when the republic negotiated a peace with Venice without consulting him. He laid siege to Milan and drove its inhabitants to the point of starvation until they capitulated in 1450 and accepted him as the new Duke of Milan. He ruled the Duchy effectively and peacefully for sixteen years.[119]

The Purpose of the Deck

Although tarot is best known as a fortune-telling device, there is no evidence to suggest that it fulfilled such a role before the end of the eighteenth century.[120] There was only one spurious reference that linked divination to tarot and that was recorded in a work of fiction, *Il Caos dell Triperuno* by Merlin Cocai.[121] This work was first published in Venice in 1527. The trump cards of a tarot pack were divided between four people and the character of Limerno composed a sonnet for each person by referring to the symbolism on the trump cards. The sonnets described the character of the individual concerned.[122]

Because tarot is most familiar as a divinatory device, it is difficult to believe it did not serve this function from the beginning. An explanation can be found in the Renaissance attitudes to divination and magic. It was believed that clues were planted in nature that had only to be deciphered by an astute observer in order to know the mind and will of God.[123] Thus the causes of tempests, misfortune and famine could be discerned by a close examination of omens, the movements of stars or even an interpretation of the physical attributes of the human body.[124] Divination which required invocations, written petitions or the use of signs or sigils was deemed to be devilish and was likely to attract the unwelcome attentions of the Inquisition.[125] Using tarot for divinatory purposes would have been considered analogous to collaborating with the Devil.

Another theory which sought to explain the original purpose of tarot purported it was used as a form of a*rs memoria* or *ars memorativa.*[126] This popular medieval occupation was greatly valued as revealed by the ardent recommendations of Thomas Aquinas.[127] Though the deck no longer survives, precluding a close examination of the type of symbolism displayed, there is reason to believe from Marziano's detailed descriptions of the pantheon of gods and goddesses, that this deck was probably was used as an aid to memorising a collection of classical stories as well as for playing a game.[128] There were other decks that have been used thus including a deck by Franciscan monk, Thomas Murner, in 1502. The deck he devised to teach logic consisted of mnemonic pictures and was also used as a game.[129] His method was so successful, he was suspected of employing witchcraft.[130]

Modern authors acknowledge that certain imagery is more effective to aiding memory.[131] Though the trump imagery was appropriate to this purpose, there are compelling reasons which render this explanation improbable. First, there was considerable variation in both the composition of the tarot trumps and the depiction of those trumps between decks. It seems unlikely that the differing symbolism could have referred to the same body of knowledge, irrespective of what that might have been. Second, the order of tarot trumps varied between regions. As the order of the imagery was usually as important as the imagery itself, it is improbable that the trumps were following such a scheme.[132] The order of the trump cards was important for the game of tarot. Certain cards could trump or triumph over others, so the agreed order was important during a game, but as long as everyone playing agreed on an order, the absolute order could not have been important.[133] Most compellingly, no references have been revealed which would indicate a body of knowledge to which tarot symbolism could have been a key. A system of knowledge complicated enough to require a complex key such as found in the tarot deck must surely have been recorded, if only as an aid while learning the associations connected with a particular image. Consequently, it is improbable that tarot symbolism was designed as a memory aid.

As intriguing as these theories are, there is substantial evidence to suggest that the tarot deck was primarily used to play a game. In fact, Marziano's treatise spelt out some of the rules and method of play for that first pack, though not sufficiently to enable the game to be played. And though documents indicate that the tarot deck was used for game playing from the fifteenth century, there were no records that specifically detailed the rules of play until the following century.[134]

Tarot Imagery

Librarian Gertrude Moakley was the first to envisage a comprehensive source of imagery for tarot.[135] Writing in the mid-1960s, she saw in the tarot trumps a depiction of the medieval passion for carnival, that period of seven or eight days before Ash Wednesday and drawing to a close with Shrove Tuesday. This was a period of chaos and revelry to be followed by the abstinence that characterised Lent. The social order was upturned, scores were surreptitiously settled and those who were seen to have acted outside of societal norms were mercilessly humiliated. Cuckolds, cradle snatchers and wife beaters were humiliated with rough music and ribald costumes.[136] Amid the revelry wound a procession made up of carnival floats upon which sat allegorical figures variously representing the Cardinal Virtues, the four Elements, figures from the Arthurian legends or sometimes scenes from classical mythology.[137]

Petrarch had used this theme in his poem, *I Trionfi*, written between 1340 and 1374, where six allegorical figures took part in a triumphal procession, each overcoming the previous one.[138] The Triumph of Love was overcome by the Triumph of Chastity, then Death, Fame, Time and finally Eternity, representing the triumph of eternal life.[139] Moakley argued that this sequence was represented in the game of triumphs. *I Trionfi* was the favourite poem of the early Renaissance and outshone Petrarch's other works and Dante's *Divine Comedy*.[140] The poems became a favourite subject for artists and their patrons, the *Triumphs* depicted on panels, canvasses, woodcuts, engravings, stained glass and tapestries. Certainly, Petrarch was resident at the Visconti court from 1353 until 1374 and his work was well-represented in the Visconti library.[141]

Though this is an appealing theory, it is very difficult to make the details fit.[142] Moakley crafted a narrative recreating the carnival procession. The Duke of Milan was in attendance at the procession but the Duke she has chosen was actually Francesco Sforza with his wife, Lady Bianca Maria.[143] As discussed earlier in this chapter, the Visconti-Sforza tarot deck was the most recent of the three we are considering and was clearly derived from the Visconti di Modrone and the Brambilla packs. These first two decks were made for Duke Filippo Maria Visconti but Filippo Maria was a recluse who rarely ventured beyond the walls of his residence.[144] In addition, he disliked crowds and theatrical entertainments.[145] Consequently, carnival was not the lavish and exciting event in Milan that it was in other Italian cities such as Venice.[146] Given that his preferences did not extend to such diversions, it is improbable that he would have sought to reproduce them on the tarot trumps.[147]

Examining the details of Petrarch's poem, it becomes yet more difficult to find support for Moakley's theory. Only one trump – The Chariot – was depicted as a triumphal car, yet, wherever we find visual interpretations of Petrarch's *Triumphs*, the allegorical figures were always portrayed riding on cars. If this were truly a representation of Petrarch's *I Trionfi*, all the trump figures should have such transport. Even the presence of Death in this procession was controversial. Death did not participate in the triumphal procession until 1511, a considerable time after the invention of the cards and even then the propriety of Death's presence was questioned.[148] Although clear correspondences can be seen between Petrarch's triumphs and some of the tarot trumps, for example Cupid can be seen as Love, and the Hermit could represent Time, there were many more tarot trumps than those explored in *I Trionfi*. It is difficult to see a place for the Hanged Man or the Female Pope in such a scheme.[149]

Petrarch's *I Trionfi* was a common theme for Renaissance artists and the triumphs were depicted in a characteristic manner.[150] Unfortunately, the trump cards which could be said to have corresponded to these triumphs did not resemble those depictions. Cupid, representing love, stood on his car drawn by goats or horses shooting arrows.[151] On the Love card of the Visconti tarot trumps, Cupid stood blindfolded on a pedestal. In the foreground a couple held hands.[152] Petrarch's triumph of Chastity featured Cupid kneeling before a maiden with his bow broken.[153] Chariot cards survive from the Visconti di Modrone and Visconti-Sforza decks yet neither feature the traditional iconography of this figure. Later decks often feature a soldier riding the chariot.[154] The Triumph of Death was represented by the form of a skeleton with a scythe. He rolled over the dead and dying in his car drawn by black oxen.[155] Death from the Visconti-Sforza deck was simply a skeleton holding a bow. The corresponding card in the Visconti di Modrone deck rode a horse.[156] Fame was winged and rode a car drawn by elephants.[157] Sometimes the figure was accompanied by angels blowing trumpets. This relationship has led to the Angel (Judgment) trump being associated with the triumph of Fame.[158] Other authors posit a relationship with the Star card.[159] The triumph of Time from Petrarch's poem was generally played by an old man with wings. He carried a scythe and hourglass as he hobbled along on crutches.[160] The Hermit (Old Man) of the Visconti-Sforza deck fairly closely resembled this figure except for the wings and crutches.[161] Christ featured in Petrarch's triumph of Eternity, his car drawn by apocalyptic beasts or angels.[162] O'Neill associated this triumph with the World card,[163] yet the symbolism displayed on the cards from both the Visconti di Modrone and the Visconti-Sforza decks contained none of the established visual characteristics of this triumph as depicted in Renaissance art.[164]

Moakley's theory that attempted to tie trump symbolism to Petrarch's poem, *I Trionfi*, was the first comprehensive supposition to account for the symbolism of tarot trumps and from that viewpoint it is significant. However, there are too many problems to make this theory viable in spite of some superficial correspondences. It seems most likely that triumphal processions were part of the cultural milieu and as with tarot; the themes were drawn from a common pool of symbolism, thereby accounting for any apparent similarities.

Another theory, posited by Paul Huson, suggested that the symbolism of the tarot trumps could be directly traced to the imagery of medieval theatre especially from mystery, miracle and morality plays; in particular the Dance of Death or *Danse Macabre*.[165] Gregory the Great, elected Pope in 590CE, had sought to take the Christian message to his illiterate subjects by means of the theatre.[166] Mystery plays were originally created by setting the Christian liturgy to music, to be sung as a dialogue between two sections of the choir and known as Gregorian Chant. By the early fourteenth century these productions were performed by specialist tradespeople as well as by the clergy. These secular productions were loaded into pageant carts and taken to large open areas such as marketplaces. Once there, the plays would be acted out sequentially beginning with the stories of Genesis and concluding with the Last Judgment.[167] Elements from these plays can be discerned in tarot symbolism. For example, the Last Judgment, often known as the Angel, played a role in the trump sequence.

From the beginning of the fifteenth century, morality plays became increasingly popular. Though not specifically linked to the liturgy, they often depicted humankind's fall from grace.[168] The Christian concept of sin was often linked to allegorical figures from pagan mythology. For example, the sinful notion that fate controlled humanity rather than the will of God was associated with images of the goddess Fortuna who, as Huson argued was represented in the tarot trumps by the Wheel of Fortune.[169] The theme of the *Psychomachia* proved to be particularly popular in this context. The term came from a poem written by the Spaniard Aurelius Clemens Prudentius in about 400CE and described the battle fought between the Virtues and Vices for a person's soul.[170] The poem directly influenced many writers including the Carolingian poet Theodulf of Orleans, the theologian Alanus de Insulis and Isidore of Seville.[171] According to Huson, this was also the source of the imagery depicted on the trump cards of Fortitude, Justice and Temperance.[172]

Huson identified the morality play known variously as the *Dance of Death, Danse Macabre* or *Dodentantz* as the original inspiration for many of the trumps. The theme of this play alluded to the indiscriminate power of death made explicit in medieval Europe by way of the Black Death.[173] The earliest depiction of the *Danse Macabre* dated from 1424 on a cloister wall of the Cemetery of Innocents in Paris. The scene depicted members of all social classes from the pope and emperor to the fool, dancing with skeletons and corpses. The dead escorted the living to the tomb. Hans Holbein the younger also represented this theme in his drawings which were published in 1538.[174] Huson believed the symbolism of the tarot trumps I though to XIII adhered to this theme.[175] Finally, Huson posited that Catholic doctrine supplied the imagery for the trumps depicted as

Figure 3: The Bishop by Hans Holbein, first half of the sixteenth century.

the Devil, Judgment and the World (representing Heaven). He also included Death to complete the grouping of the Four Last Things.[176]

Without a doubt, many of the symbols displayed on the tarot trumps can be found in the imagery of medieval theatre, yet as with Moakley's hypothesis, the visual correlations were not close. Medieval theatre comprised a vast and diverse corpus of works. Huson gave no explanation as to why some themes were adopted when so many others were passed over. For example, historian Glynne Wickham significantly emphasised the point that in Italy, medieval theatre made particular use of the stories of saints and these were as popular as plays about the Magi, the Virgin or even Christ himself.[177] Since the Milanese so revered their patron, Saint Ambrose, who converted and baptised Saint Augustine, his likeness would probably have been included in the trump sequence. If, as Huson suggested, medieval theatre was genuinely the source of tarot symbolism, why was this important figure overlooked? Perhaps most convincingly, Filippo Maria Visconti was an antisocial recluse who disliked theatre and music.[178] It is inconceivable that he would use the symbolism of something he disdained to decorate his cards. The superficial commonalities between the symbolism of the tarot trumps and the themes of medieval theatre can be explained by the fact that both arose in a similar time and place and were informed by similar cultural and historical currents; both drawing from a common pool of symbolism.

A similar theory was posited by movie industry lawyer William Marston Seabury, who wrote a short treatise – just twenty-eight pages – linking tarot with Dante's works.[179] Dante Alighieri (1265–1321) was a Florentine poet whose *La Divina Commedia* (*The Divine Comedy*) was considered by many to be the greatest literary work of the Medieval period. Seabury wrote that in 1947, while reading *The Divine Comedy* and some other of Dante's works including *La Vita Nuova* (*The New Life*), *Il Convito* (*The Banquet*) and *De Monarchia* (*On Monarchy*), it became apparent that if the order of the tarot trumps were rearranged, correlations could be found with the themes and characters depicted in these works.[180] Unfortunately, Seabury died before he could complete his investigation and the book was printed privately by his surviving friends.[181] Popular mythologist and writer, Joseph Campbell revived this hypothesis some thirty years later. Campbell in part justified his assertion by stating that Dante lived about the same time as the first tarot deck was invented. Unfortunately, Campbell believed that the Gringonneur deck, which was erroneously dated to 1392, was the oldest extant deck even though this information had been known to be incorrect for about 150 years.[182] Dante's *La Divina Commedia* was an expansive work that incorporated a myriad of characters and themes. The correlations suggested by Seabury and Campbell were not overt and it seems likely that tarot and Dante were informed by the same cultural currents and therefore utilised a similar pool of imagery.

Though none of the schemes so far posited can convincingly explain the source of Renaissance tarot symbolism, collectively they infer that the imagery displayed upon the tarot trumps was common in Medieval and Early Modern literature, theatre and art. There is no need to look to esoteric themes or to ancient origins for a suitable exposition. If the symbolism contained the keys to occult understanding, these same keys were extensively embedded in almost every aspect of northern Italian culture. It is more likely that the imagery so prominently displayed on the *cartes da trionfi* related to matters more mundane. The possible constitution of such a scheme forms the basis of enquiry for the following chapter.

3

An Alternative Explanation of Tarot Symbolism

Filippo Maria Visconti's first tarot pack, illustrated with images of 'deities' and birds, was crafted when the new Duke was in his early twenties. He was the ruler of Milan subsequent to the ruthless assassination of his brother, Giovanni Maria. By the time the cards known as the Visconti-Sforza decks were crafted, Filippo was at least ten years older and his circumstances were in flux. He was struggling to hold Milan against his hostile neighbours; his first wife had recently been executed for adultery and his illegitimate daughter had just been born. The symbolism depicted on that first deck was replaced by something altogether more indicative of the forces affecting the Duke's troubled passage through life.[1]

It is not surprising that Filippo Maria should choose a game as an allegory for his life. Like life, a game is a mixture of chance and careful calculation; as circumspectly as it is planned with every conceivable contingency planned for, the unexpected can derail or divert its progress. Robert Burns expressed this idea eloquently: 'The best-laid schemes of mice and men gang aft agley.'[2] The element of chance is preserved in all games where cards are blindly distributed to players. But in tarot, the indiscriminate nature of chance was emphasised; being made explicit again and again in the trump symbolism.

As with life, skill is an integral part of the game of tarot. Though the precise nature of the games played remains unknown – rules of play were not documented before the sixteenth century – there were a few indications as to how the game proceeded.[3] From Marziano's treatise, it was evident that the order of two of the suits was reversed as was the case in games documented at a later date.[4] It is a reasonable assumption that they would have been reversed in games played with those first decks and astute players would have factored this complication into their overall strategy. In addition, the order of trumps had to be committed to memory as they were not numbered or otherwise labelled until some later time.[5] Tarot was undoubtedly a game requiring skill and intelligence, yet the player was still subject to the vagaries of chance introduced by the other participants. A game is a reflection of life and the game of tarot, with its evocative symbolism, made this relationship explicit.

Two of the three decks under consideration were specifically crafted for Duke Filippo Maria Visconti and so the allegory described there would pertain to his life. Evidence for this theory can be seen in the colouring of the figures on both the court cards and trumps of these early hand-painted decks. The majority of the figures were painted with blond hair, an allusion to the Frankish heritage of the Visconti family.[6] Their fair colouring stood out in contrast to the darkness of most Italians, even in the north of the country. The exception in the family was Filippo Maria who had dark hair and a dark complexion, which suggests that the tarot trumps depicted the fortunes of the Visconti family as a whole rather than just of Filippo Maria.[7] This theory was reinforced by the presence of the Visconti coats-of-arms on several of the cards. Francesco Sforza aligned his destiny with that of the Viscontis when he added his own insignia to the deck. The challenge lies in correctly describing and positing a location in this schema for the tarot trumps and the Fool. When considering the trumps, I will be following the sequence as described by the poet Giovanni Battista Susio in the sixteenth century with two exceptions: the Emperor, Empress, Pope and Popess will be considered as a group, as will the cards depicting the Cardinal and Theological Virtues.[8]

The Magician/Il Bagatella

The trump sequence began with a street performer, dressed in bright red and seated behind a table. Though this card has come to be known in modern tarot as the Magician, in early decks it was known as *il Bagatella*.[9] The word was probably a diminutive form of the root 'baga' meaning to 'truss' or 'tie up' and subsequently it came to denote a trifle,[10] though this may have referenced the trump's low trick-taking capacity in the game rather than the figure on the card.[11] Christina Olsen believed that the term could also be interpreted as 'quarterpenny', referring to a small coin.[12] The Visconti-Sforza deck was the only one of the three under consideration with a surviving example of this card.

In modern decks this figure is depicted as the magus, a keeper of esoteric knowledge, but in these early decks he was a juggler, entertainer or stage magician. Bearded and holding a wand or stick, he sat before a table with some objects arranged in front of him.[13] In later decks, the figure was more explicitly a conjuror, yet in the Visconti-Sforza deck his role was more ambiguous and he could have been a merchant or artisan.[14] Such a figure was common in Renaissance art and a close similarity can be seen between this tarot trump and illustrations from the thirteenth-century treatise on astronomy by Sacrobosco, *De Sphaera*.[15] The low status of this conjuror was evidenced by his early entry into the trump sequence. Even though this order was not recorded until the last quarter of the fifteenth century, it is reasonable to assume that it would at least approximate an earlier one.[16] If *il Bagatella* was not the first trump, it probably was one of the first. The low status of the card was reinforced by *il Bagatella's* red garb which distinguished him from all other figures in the deck.[17] Red was only deemed appropriate for disreputable members of society such as foot soldiers, executioners, gamblers and dandies.[18]

The role for this card in the scheme of Visconti history is not obvious. Certainly, merchants, artisans and entertainers were common in the cultural milieu of Renaissance Milan and were often depicted in the art of the period. The figure may have been a reference to a theme common in the tarot deck, that of all people being equally susceptible to the vagaries of chance; *il Bagatella* represented chance in its most innocuous and impotent form. In addition, the card would have been an indictment on the cards that immediately followed it: the Popess, Emperor, Empress and Pope. The inference would have been that these figures were only marginally better than a common conjuror; a view not difficult to understand given the uneasy relationship the Viscontis shared with both the Papacy and the Holy Roman Empire.

Temporal and Spiritual Power: The Emperor and Empress, the Pope and the Popess

The next four cards of Emperor (*l'Imperatore*), Empress (*l'Imperatrice*), Pope (*il Papa*) and Popess (*la Papessa*) will be considered as a group representing spiritual and temporal power in northern Italy in late Medieval and Early Modern times.[19] The Pope was considered the spiritual leader of Western Christendom with the interests of the Church protected by the Holy Roman Empire.[20] The Emperor was elected from among the kings of Germany and took office when he was crowned by the Pope. The Emperor and his Empress were crowned in Rome and housed in chambers called 'Livia' and 'Augustus'.[21] Originally, the Emperor appointed the Pope and in turn the Pope crowned the Emperor. Relations became strained when, in the eleventh century, there was a dispute over who could appoint Church offices. This was usually conducted by a secular authority that derived a great deal of income from selling these appointments. A group within the Church wanted this sin, known as simony, expunged and sought to remove the ability of the Emperor to appoint a pope. This change was effected in 1059 when the ability to appoint Church offices was restored to the Church and the College of Cardinals was created to elect the pope. This transfer of power created a rift between the Holy Roman Empire and the Papacy. In this dispute, supporters of the Church were known as Guelfs and supporters of the Empire were known as Ghibellines.[22]

When the Holy Roman Emperors did come down into Italy to assert their rights, the city states had to defend their territories against them, as they rarely had titles to these new acquisitions which in theory remained with the Empire.[23] Cities with Guelf sympathies were particularly vulnerable and their leaders were often replaced by those sympathetic to the Ghibellines. In 1311, the ruling della Torre family of Milan were Guelfs who, tired of maintaining the excessive costs of the entourage of Emperor Henry VII, unsuccessfully rebelled against the Empire; the recriminations against the family were harsh.[24] Originally, this Emperor was seen as the hope of both Guelfs and Ghibellines, yet he showed his favour to the latter; dying in shame, failing to reconcile the factions.[25] By the middle of the fourteenth century, the Emperors stopped coming into Italy as enemies of the Pope but came to confirm and legitimise appointments in return for large sums of money. Charles VI of Bohemia came south in 1354 to be crowned in Rome and the Viscontis thought it prudent to donate 50 000 florins towards his coronation expenses and a further 150 000 to confirm their vicariate.[26] Originally, the Emperors only appointed the office of vicar, but in 1395, Wenceslas went a step further, promoting Gian Galeazzo Visconti to a hereditary prince of the Empire thereby making him Duke of Milan.[27]

By the fourteenth century, the Church was losing its power and absolute dominance of Europe. Seeking to escape the infighting between the powerful Italian families that supplied former popes, the Papacy was removed to the relative safety of Avignon in France in 1305.[28] While the Papacy remained there, all of the popes were French. With Pope Clement VI (1342-1352), French interests began to dominate the affairs of the Holy See.[29] Pope Gregory XI (1370-1378) eventually restored the Papacy to Rome in order to settle the disputes that threatened the interests of the Church in Italy.[30] Upon the death of this pontiff, riots ensured that an Italian pope was elected. Unfortunately, Pope Urban VI was unstable and suspicious, and the very cardinals who had elected him, elected another pope and set up a rival papacy in Avignon. This division became known as the Western Schism and Italy, and indeed Europe, became bitterly divided.[31] Milan sided with the Avignon pope because of their strategic family ties to the French.[32] The schism was not finally resolved until the Council of Constance in 1417 elected one pope, a friend of the Visconti family, Pope Martin V.[33]

The Visconti family had been growing in status since the appointment of Ottone Visconti as Archbishop of Milan by Pope Urban IV (1195-1264) in 1262.[34] Control of the city was finally wrested from their archrivals, the della

Torre family, in 1277 with Wenceslas of Bavaria confirming them as hereditary rulers towards the end of the fourteenth century.[35] The Viscontis had prevailed against the whims and fancies of successive popes and emperors. They had survived the hardships of political strife and repeated wars to become the rulers of a strong and wealthy city state that few dared oppose. It is little wonder that the Pope, Emperor and Empress should be so lowly ranked in the trump order; they were perceived to be corrupt and ineffectual, certainly no match for the might of the Viscontis.

The Emperor

The Emperor card was found in all three of the hand-painted decks under consideration with the figures of those cards in the Visconti-Sforza and Brambilla decks holding an orb which sat beneath a cross, symbolising the triumph of Christ over the sins of the world, but also alluding to the Empire's role as protector of the Church.[36] Emperors from all of the decks were seated on a throne and wore the eagle of the Holy Roman Empire on their dalmatics, making the identity of the figure unmistakeable.[37] There was no feature on any of the cards that would indicate a particular emperor and the image probably referred to the office.

The Empress

On the third trump, the Empress was represented as the consort of the Emperor. This trump survived from the Visconti di Modrone and the Visconti-Sforza decks. In both cases, the Empress wore the imperial eagle of the Holy Roman Empire.[38] In the Visconti di Modrone deck she was also accompanied by two ladies-in-waiting.[39] Again, as a low-ranking trump she represented the low status of the Holy Roman Empire in the eyes of the Viscontis; this opinion reflected in Duke Filippo Maria's refusal to grant Emperor Sigismund an audience when he came to Milan in 1432.[40]

The Pope

Representing spiritual power, the Pope trump from the Visconti-Sforza deck was the only one to have survived. He held his right hand in a sign of blessing, his status confirmed by the papal tiara.[41] The third crown was added to the tiara in 1315, the number alluding to the Trinity or to the Three Estates of the Kingdom of God.[42] Paul Huson posited that the figure specifically represented Pope Nicholas V who supposedly held office when the decks were painted.[43] In fact, Nicholas V held office between 1447 and 1455 some time after the creation Visconti-Sforza deck; hence Huson's identification was probably wrong. If the figure represented an actual figure at all, it would more likely be Martin V who was not only a great friend of the Visconti family but also effectively ended the Western Schism.[44] It seems unlikely that the presence of this card would have been tolerated closer to Rome and it owed its existence to Milan's relative isolation from the Holy See.

The Popess

The Visconti-Sforza deck was the only one of the hand-painted decks to boast the Popess. Robert O'Neill posited that the card represented the deity of a sect of witches who Godfrey Leland claimed existed outside of Florence, though the theory was not well argued.[45] A popular hypothesis identified the figure on this card as Pope Joan.[46] Certainly, the story was popular at the time that these tarot decks were painted and there was even a version of the story written by Petrarch.[47] The legend told of Pope John Anglicus who was pope for two years, seven months and four days.[48] This pope was really a woman who had been led to Athens, disguised as a man, by her lover. Once in Athens she mastered all manner of learning before going to Rome to teach the liberal arts. She eventually became pope but became pregnant by her lover. Unsure of the exact time of the upcoming birth, Pope Joan gave birth to the child while in procession from St Peter's to the Lateran.[49] She was said to be excluded from any lists of pontiffs as she was a woman and her impersonation of a pope was sordid.[50] In some accounts, she was bound by the feet to a horse's tail and dragged and stoned by the people for half a league, before being buried where she died.[51] Though this legend had sufficient currency in the fifteenth century, there is no obvious reason why such a subject would have been depicted in the Visconti-Sforza deck. Further, the image on the Popess card did not resemble traditional representations of Pope Joan who was usually illustrated suckling or holding a baby.[52] Furthermore, unlike the figure on the Visconti-Sforza card, Pope Joan had never been a nun.[53]

Upon closer scrutiny, Pope Joan was not the only woman to claim the title of pope in the Middle Ages.[54] A close relative of the Viscontis, Sister Maifreda da Pirovano, a member of a heretical sect called the Guglielmites, also earned that title among her admirers. The first to make this connection between *la Papessa* and Sister Maifreda was Gertrude Moakley and this identification has gained wide acceptance.[55] The woman on the card was dressed in a nun's habit and sat on a throne. She wore the triple tiara usually associated with the office of pope. In her left hand she held a book and in her right, a staff.

Around 1260, a woman named Guglielma arrived in Milan, choosing to live as a *pinzochera* – a religious woman who lived independently in her own

home.[56] It was not clear where she arrived from, though it was rumoured that she was the child of the King of Bohemia.[57] She practised good works and preached piety, going about her work without special austerity.[58] She died in 1281, leaving behind a devoted *famiglia;* its membership included a layman Andrea Saramita, Sister Maifreda da Pirovano of the Umiliate order and nearly forty upper-class citizens of Milan.[59] The *famiglia,* in accordance with a prediction by Joachim of Fiore, believed that Guglielma was the Holy Spirit incarnate in spite of her own vehement denials.[60] Her devotees preached that Guglielma had come as the Holy Spirit to found a new church, replacing the old corrupt establishment and that Jews, pagans, and Saracens would be saved. After Guglielma's resurrection and ascension, the new Church would be led by Sister Maifreda, who would be the new Pope or more correctly, *la Papessa.*[61]

Figure 4: The Popess from the Visconti-Sforza deck housed in the Pierpont Morgan Library, New York.

The Guglielmites spent large sums of money on altar frontals, liturgical vessels and ornate vestments.[62] The convent of the Umiliate nuns of which Sister Maifreda was a member at Biassano became the centre for another cult, this time centred on the would-be popess.[63] She anointed devotees with Holy Water in which the relics of Guglielma had been washed, and blessed hosts that had been consecrated at her tomb.[64] Many honoured Sister Maifreda as the popess by kissing her hands and feet and addressing her as 'Lord Vicar' or 'Lady by the grace of God'. An altarpiece at the convent showed the Trinity with Guglielma as the third person in an allusion to the Harrowing of Hell, with Jews and Saracens to be saved by the Holy Spirit as Christians were by Christ.[65] Naturally, these activities were considered heretical by the Church and the actions of Saramita and Sister Maifreda soon attracted the attentions of the Inquisition. In 1284, the Dominican tribunal symbolically punished them after they had repudiated their errors but in 1300, both were sentenced to death and burnt at the stake as relapsed heretics.[66]

Sister Maifreda was the first cousin of Matteo Visconti who by 1300 was the lord of Milan.[67] In 1311, Matteo was appointed Imperial Vicar of Milan by Henry VII and he celebrated by expelling the Inquisition from the city.[68] The Inquisition was unpopular in Milan, possibly because so many upper-class families were Guglielmites.[69] Pope John XXII took advantage of Henry's death to strip Matteo of his title and called him to answer charges at the seat of the papacy in Avignon. Matteo refused to go, risking excommunication, and went to war with the papal troops who were defeated by his armies.[70] In 1321, Matteo was summoned once more to Avignon, this time to answer charges of sorcery and heresy. The pope declared a crusade against Matteo Visconti who once more was declared a heretic.[71] He was accused of denying the Resurrection while his son was accused of refuting that fornication was a sin. Both were accused of violating nuns and their position was compromised due to their association with 'the heretic Maifreda' and her followers.[72]

By 1420, the cult of Guglielma had been revived. The Viscontis were proud of their relative and kept her memory alive by secreting the trial records from the Dominican tribunal in their library at Pavia.[73] In 1425, Antonio Bonfadini, a friar of Ferrara, wrote a biography of Guglielma thereby demonstrating that the cult had spread beyond Milan, possibly taken to Ferrara by Galeazzo Visconti who was exiled there from 1302 until 1310.[74] The story was recast and given greater currency by Antonia Pulci (1452–1501), ensuring the legend was known well into the Early Modern period.[75]

Bianca Maria Visconti, wife of Francesco Sforza and daughter of Filippo Maria Visconti, was an ardent admirer of both Guglielma and Sister Maifreda, her interest encouraged by Maddalena Albrizzi who entered the nunnery of San Andrea in Brunate in 1420.[76] The nunnery was generously patronised by the duchess. It subsequently became a church and in 1826, workmen uncovered a painting of Guglielma which had been one of a narrative cycle depicting her life.[77] It seems that about 150 years after the deaths of both Saramita and Sister Maifreda, a painting had been commissioned of Guglielma and her most ardent followers. This painting is interesting because it showed Sister Maifreda in a nun's habit resembling that depicted on the Visconti-Sforza Popess card.[78] Also, this identification seems logical given the Visconti pride in their pious relative. It also seems likely that the Popess card was not a part of the earlier Visconti decks and was probably included in the later deck because of Bianca's special affection for Sister Maifreda. There was also some similarity between the Popess card and Giotto's *Fides* (*Faith*) painted in 1306.[79] The artist of the Visconti-Sforza deck probably referenced the earlier painting as a means of highlighting Sister Maifreda's piety.[80]

The only mystery that remains is why was the card such a low-ranking trump? It could be that form triumphed over familial pride so that the Emperor and Empress cards were matched to the Pope and Popess, but it probably says more about the Viscontis' attitude to the Inquisition. The Visconti family were firmly Ghibelline in opposition to the papacy. Matteo Visconti expelled the Inquisition and fell foul of Pope John XXII. In this position, the Popess probably represented the Inquisition and the troubled relationship that the Viscontis had with that institution, much exacerbated by the execution of Sister Maifreda. Not only was the Holy Roman Empire represented in the tarot trumps by the Emperor and Empress, but so were the Church and its disciplinary instrument, the Inquisition as administered by the Dominicans.

There was some thought that the trump sequence depicted the historical tussle between the Guelfs and Ghibellines. Samuel Weller Singer, a nineteenth-century playing-card historian, repeated such an assertion, though he doubted its veracity.[81] It is unlikely that the tarot trumps comprehensively depicted this theme, though undoubtedly the dispute played some small part with the opponents placed together as the low-ranking trumps.

Love

The sixth card in the trump sequence was invariably called 'Love' (*l'Amore*) in the old Italian sources, though it is difficult to determine the original title of the card as there was no record of the trump names until at least fifty years after their invention. Only in more recent decks has the name of this trump become 'Marriage' or even 'The Lovers'. Examples of the card survive from both the Visconti di Modrone and the Visconti-Sforza decks. The Love card from the former deck showed a man and a woman clasping hands, standing under a pavilion edged with coats-of-arms. The figure of Cupid blindfolded lay across the top of this scene.[82] The card from the Visconti-Sforza deck was very similar except there was no pavilion and the figure of Cupid, while still blindfolded, stood upright and held a bow in one hand and a long arrow in the other.[83]

This card is thought to have depicted a wedding though the identity of the participants remains controversial, even after examination of the coats-of-arms from the card of the Visconti di Modrone deck. All agree that the serpent represented the Visconti dynasty, but the identity of the owner of the red shield bearing a white cross is in dispute. Robert Steele identified the arms as belonging to the House of Savoy and concluded that the marriage was that of Duke Filippo Maria Visconti to Maria of Savoy.[84] Perhaps some support for this theory can be taken from the presence of a small dog at the feet of the bride. On the couple's wedding night, when the newlyweds retired to bed, the exceedingly superstitious Filippo Visconti heard a dog barking and considered it a bad omen. From that night on, he resolved never to spend a night under the same roof as his new bride.[85] Giuliana Algeri also believed that coat-of-arms was that of Savoy but thought the wedding was a more recent one. She believed that the trump cards of the Visconti di Modrone deck – including the Love card – were painted at a later date and that the card represented the marriage of Francesco Sforza and Bianca Visconti's son Galeazzo Maria to Bona of Savoy in 1468.[86] Leopoldo Cicognara, writing in 1831, suggested that the arms represented Pavia, a province ruled by Milan.[87] They were also said to be those of Pisa and of Beatrice Tenda, the widow of Facino Cane who Duke Filippo Maria Visconti married in 1413.[88]

Though the identity of the couple is in dispute, the most interesting figure on this card was Cupid and on both extant examples he was blindfolded. In classical sources Cupid was rarely seen with his eyes covered,[89] but from the thirteenth century on, love as Cupid was depicted as one of the three great blind powers controlling human affairs, along with Fortune and Death which significantly, were also depicted on the tarot trumps.[90] Under the influence of Christian thought, the blindness of Cupid came to represent the profane component of love and was a caution against the temptations of the flesh.[91] Certainly, Erwin Panofsky wrote that any positive view of love required that it not be blind.[92] This view was not shared by the Florentine Platonists Marsilio Ficino and Pico della Mirandola who believed that love was blind because it was above reason.[93] Even so, Renaissance writers were well aware that Cupid was not blind in classical art.[94]

It is difficult to be certain about the most appropriate interpretation of the Cupid figure on the extant Love cards. Without a doubt, love rarely entered into the contractual marriages of the Viscontis; instead marriage was a means of securing wealth, power or military loyalty. Both of Filippo Maria's marriages were of this nature, as was the marriage of his only daughter to Francesco Sforza. Even his father's marriage was one of strategy: Gian Galeazzo married Isabella, daughter of the King of France when he was just nine years old.[95] The French gave the county of Virtú as a dowry and Gian Galeazzo's father gave 100 000 florins to boost the French coffers, depleted after their disastrous war with England.[96] Gian Galeazzo's sister, Violante, married the son of Edward III, and his daughter Valentina – Filippo's sister – married Louis of Orléans. And these were just the more recent alliances in the House of Visconti. Because of their enormous wealth and power, the family had managed to marry into nearly every royal house of Europe.

The couples on the cards did not look amorous which surely was not beyond the skills of the artist, if that was his intent. The man and woman were not looking longingly into each other's eyes. They were not clinched in a passionate embrace. Instead, they looked like business associates shaking hands over a deal. Could it be that the blindfolding of Cupid was intended to portray that love played no part in these alliances? Cupid was not aiming his arrows at the couple; instead, he adopted a passive stance. This was the milieu in which the ideal of courtly love flourished and that love was rarely found within a marriage.[97] Marriage had far more pragmatic aims, and love was usually reserved for a woman who was unobtainable and remote.[98] It was exemplified in the legends featuring King Arthur and his knights which were popular across Europe, particularly in Italy.[99] The great love of Duke Filippo Maria Visconti and the mother of his only child was his mistress, Agnese del Maino, who he remained faithful to though he never married her.[100] This entirely pragmatic view of marriage was reflected in the low status of this trump, ranking just above those four cards representing temporal and spiritual power.

The Chariot Misidentified

The Chariot card, usually called *il Carro* (the Car), at first appears the most difficult to fit into the scheme of tarot as a reflection of Visconti history and life. The card was present in both the Visconti di Modrone and the Visconti-Sforza decks. On both cards, a queen was seated on a car drawn by two white horses. The card from the Visconti-Sforza pack featured horses that were also winged. In later decks, the figure was usually a soldier or conqueror.

Many authors believed this card represented a car from a triumphal procession like those usually celebrated after a victory or conquest.[101] If this were the case, it seems more likely that the seated figure would have been a man, specifically Duke Filippo Maria Visconti or Francesco Sforza in the case of the card from the later deck. But Duke Filippo Visconti was reclusive, making him an unlikely participant in such an event.[102] Further, it was well known that Francesco-Sforza refused the honour of a triumphal procession when he entered Milan after its surrender in 1450.[103] Instead, he distributed bread to the populace, starving after a lengthy siege.[104] If this card was intended to represent victory or conquest, the allusion could have been made more obvious by the presence of the traditional allegory of winged victory driving the chariot. It was therefore unlikely that such an attribution was intended.

Gertrude Moakley hypothesised that the Chariot represented a carnival float. As discussed in the previous chapter, she believed all of the tarot trumps owed their symbolism to such a scheme particularly as described by

Petrarch. Carnival was burlesque and frivolous; roles were reversed and scores settled, yet there was nothing in the demeanour of the queen to signal such an irreverent attitude.[105] Instead she sat serenely, resplendent in a sumptuous gown and with a globe in her left hand. Internet tarot historian Tom Tadfor Little theorised that the queen represented Bianca Maria Visconti and Count Emiliano di Parravicino suggested that she was Beatrice Tenda, Filippo Maria's first wife, yet neither author ventured a hypothesis as to what these figures were intended to portray.[106]

It could be that this card, in contrast to the previous trump in the sequence, could have represented idealised or courtly love.[107] As discussed previously, love rarely figured in the strategic marriages of the Viscontis. Matrimony was generally politically or economically motivated, and love itself was usually reserved for another woman who was unobtainable and remote.[108] Certainly, the queen on these cards sat remote from any lover and her serene facial expression radiated purity and equanimity. It was usual in Renaissance art for the intentions of the driver to be represented by the team pulling the chariot and the white horses would have signalled her purity. The winged horses, such as those on the Visconti-Sforza card, generally symbolised divine mission or more generally, spirituality.[109]

The theory that this card represented idealised love must surely be discounted because of the presence of the crown signifying the status of queen which, in itself signals marriage to the ruler. Both of Filippo Maria's marriages were devoid of love, let alone idealised love, and though the same was not true of the marriage of Bianca Maria Visconti to Francesco Sforza, this fact does not explain the presence of *il Carro* in the Visconti di Modrone deck. There would have been more obvious ways of representing idealised love. For example, in contrast to the previous trump, Cupid could have been present but this time without the blindfold or a pining lover, his affections unrequited, could have been skilfully drawn.

In light of the unsatisfactory arguments presented thus far, an alternative explanation of the symbolism of this card becomes necessary. I believe that the evidence suggests that the figure of the queen in the chariot or cart was a personification of the Church. The presence of wings on the white horses of the Visconti-Sforza card suggested that its subject was probably intended to be allegorical rather than historical. The chariot or cart was often used to symbolise the Church, acting as the vehicle to convey the faithful to Heaven.[110] Dante used this allegorical device in his *Divine Comedy*.[111] In a similar manner, Saint Jerome likened the gospel to a chariot, drawn by horses representing the four evangelists. J. C. Cooper wrote that the wheels of such a vehicle represented desire and will, yet other authors suggested they stood for the Old and New Testaments.[112] Further, it was also common for the Church to be personified as a woman as with Lady Holy Church in

William Langland's *Piers Plowman*, which was written late in the fourteenth
century.[113] The allegorical significance of the queen in the chariot was
strengthened by the presence of the white horses indicating purity, which
were also winged in the Visconti-Sforza card denoting divine mission.[114] The
queen also held an orb crowned with a cross in her left hand, signifying the
triumph of Christ over the sin of the world.[115] It was not unusual in the
Renaissance, for artists to combine two allegorical themes to reinforce the
meaning of an image.[116]

It is not surprising that the title of the card did not match the subject
matter depicted as titles were not ascribed to the trumps until some fifty years
after the invention of the game. It could be that by the time specific titles
were ascribed to tarot trumps, the original significance of the card had been
forgotten or lost. There is evidence to suggest that this happened with other
tarot trumps as well. If this card were to be renamed the 'Church', its place
within the schema of the tarot trumps as a reflection of the life and history of
the Viscontis becomes more obvious. Though this powerful family were
contemptuous of the papacy and its acquisitive ambitions, Duke Filippo
Maria was deeply religious and was often seen silently praying to himself.[117]
Certainly, during his rule he was generous to the Church, giving large
amounts of money to continue the construction of the great Gothic Duomo,
the building of which was instigated by his father, Gian Galeazzo Visconti.[118]
Hence, the Chariot or more correctly, the Church ranked higher than the
Pope in the sequence of trumps.

The Virtues: Fortitude, Justice and Temperance

Jules Michelet was the first to use the term 'Renaissance' in 1855, but it was
popularised by Swiss historian Jacob Burckhardt through his famous book
The Civilization of the Renaissance in Italy. The term literally means
'rebirth' and referred to the revival of classical antiquity which occurred
initially in Italy and then across the rest of Europe from the fourteenth
century.[119] New translations of Latin poets were commissioned and libraries
were formed from copies of translations of ancient Greek works.[120] Classical
architecture was revered and the language of Latin was favoured by poets and
administrators alike. Like Poliphilo, erecting palaces and theatres in his
dream as described by Dominican monk Francesco Colonna in the
Hypnerotomachia, the Renaissance Italians were besotted by antiquity.[121]
This was especially so in northern Italy where the universities of Padua,
Pavia, Bologna and Ferrara had been the centres of secular learning for
centuries. In addition, the Viscontis had brought stability to the city-state of
Milan and established a court with a secular focus. Relatively free from the

intellectual restraints of the Church, archaeologists, painters and humanists worked closely together and the classical revival flourished.[122]

This acquaintance with classical literature familiarised the artists, authors and poets with the device of allegory.[123] Almost any quality was regarded as a separate and distinct entity and was almost automatically personified.[124] Associating a quality with a characteristic personage or figure lent it a deceptive simplicity, clarifying what may otherwise have been difficult and complicated to understand fully.[125] This device was used extensively in literature.[126] For example, Petrarch's *I Trionfi* which utilised almost entirely allegorical characters to populate its narrative has already been discussed, and Dante's *Divine Comedy* was another example employing such a literary style.

Allegory was also exploited by the artist of the tarot trumps. Whereas the allegory used in the trump of the Chariot was subtle and ambiguous, that employed in the depictions of the Cardinal and Theological Virtues was overt and well-recognised in the art and literature of Early Modern Europe. The four Cardinal Virtues could be traced back to classical rather than Biblical sources, and were attributed to Aristotle.[127] The Theological Virtues of Faith, Hope and Charity were listed by St Paul. Typically, they were represented as long-robed women bearing symbolic objects or frozen in characteristic gestures which would clarify their nature and function.[128] The seven virtues were in direct opposition to the Seven Deadly Sins of Lust (*luxuria*), Gluttony (*gula*), Avarice (*avaritia*), Sloth (*acedia*), Wrath (*ira*), Envy (*invidia*) and Pride (*superbia*).[129] Under the influence of St Augustine's *City of God*, Heaven and Hell were seen as hierarchically structured, each rank taking orders from those superior to it. Eventually, ranks of angels and demons were boosted by their agents on earth who fought for control of human souls, namely the Cardinal and Theological Virtues and the Seven Deadly Sins.[130]

Modern tarot enthusiasts would be aware that the tarot deck boasts three of the four cardinal virtues: Fortitude (Strength), Justice and Temperance, but would be unaware that in medieval times, the virtue of Prudence completed the quaternary. The Visconti-Sforza deck likewise featured the same three virtues, again with Prudence missing. In the earlier Visconti di Modrone pack, only Fortitude was represented from the four, yet the Theological Virtues of Faith Hope and Charity were also present.

Fortitude

Fortitude (*la Fortezza*) was represented in both the Visconti di Modrone deck and the Visconti-Sforza deck yet the cards bore no resemblance to each other except in name. In the former, a crowned woman with flowing hair and flowing robes held open the mouth of a lion.[131] This representation of the virtue of Fortitude was common in the art of the period.[132] For example, a similar figure was seen in a relief from the Tomb of Clement II at Bamberg Cathedral in Bavaria dating from 1237.[133] The woman lacked a weapon because, according to St Thomas Aquinas, fortitude implied the ability to endure rather than to be on the offensive.[134] In this manifestation, Fortitude can be likened to courage and in fact was often listed as such.[135] This concurred with Aristotle's original conception of this virtue, whereby a person should neither seek out danger nor avoid it.

The card in the Visconti-Sforza deck was quite different and was probably painted at a later date, possibly to replace a lost card. The most significant divergence was that the figure on this card was male. He held a club and looked set to strike a cowering lion. Many authors, including Michael Dummett, identified this scene as Hercules attacking the Nemean lion.[136] But according to legend, the lion that terrorised the citizens of Nemea was invulnerable to weapons, forcing Hercules to strangle it with his bare hands. When this scene was represented in art, it usually showed Hercules holding the lion in a headlock or more usually, with a knee in its back and forcing its jaws open with his hands.[137] Another version of this story had Hercules chasing the lion into a cave with his club before he strangled it and possibly it was this version of the story that was illustrated on the card.[138] Interestingly, the depiction of the Nemean lion was not usually associated with the virtue of 'Fortitude'. It was very rare for a Cardinal Virtue to be depicted with a male figure as it flouted both iconographical convention and the gender of Latin nouns.[139]

Robert O'Neill offered an alternative explanation, half-heartedly conjecturing that the figure represented Samson.[140] According to this legend, Samson was on his way to visit his Philistine lover when a young lion attacked him. The Spirit of the Lord came upon him and Samson tore the lion apart before continuing on his way to see his lover. While he was gone a swarm of bees had built a nest inside the lion and when Samson returned, he ate honey from the carcass of the lion.[141] This story was a favourite subject for artists, prefiguring Christ 'who overcame our enemy, the infernal lion'.[142] However, it was not usual to depict Samson using a club; he tore the lion apart with his bare hands. Hence, it was implausible that this legend supplied the subject matter for this card.

It should be remembered that this card was painted for another Duke of Milan, Francesco Sforza. This accomplished soldier was the illegitimate son of a mercenary military leader or *condottiere* and succeeded his father in his command, gaining the reputation of Italy's greatest military leader.[143] The family had adopted the name 'Sforza' meaning 'force', as a reflection of their great military prowess.[144] While he was still alive, Duke Filippo Maria Visconti promised his daughter, Bianca, in marriage to Francesco Sforza in order to secure his loyalty.[145] Sforza was too dangerous an enemy to leave unchecked. Duke Filippo Visconti died in 1447 and refused to name Sforza as his heir.[146] Milan proclaimed itself the Ambrosian Republic, named after the patron saint of the city, St Ambrose.[147] Factional infighting divided the city, leaving it vulnerable to attack from either Venice or Florence.[148] The Milanese rejected Sforza as the successor to Filippo Visconti as he was on close terms with Cosimo Medici of Florence and the prominent families feared undue Florentine influence on their af-

Figure 5: Fortitude from the Visconti-Sforza deck housed in the Pierpont Morgan Library, New York.

fairs.[149] However, with their enemies poised to attack, a deputation from Milan begged Sforza to defend them in return for Brescia, which he did, inflicting two crushing defeats on the Venetians.[150] In spite of his successful defence of the city, the Milanese went behind his back to secure a peace with Venice and with the support of their new ally, they turned against Sforza.[151] In response, the *condottiere* laid siege to Milan, bringing the populace to the brink of starvation before they surrendered.[152] Though Venice was subdued for the moment, they remained a future risk, having aligned with the Kingdom of Naples. Sforza tempered the menace by aligning with Florence until a treaty was negotiated which also included the Papal States in 1455.[153]

Perhaps the figure on the Visconti-Sforza card of Fortitude or Courage was really none other than Francesco Sforza, whose name meaning 'force' was close to the original name of the card. Certainly, the man on the card resembled some paintings of Francesco Sforza. This would explain why the

card was so different from that of the Visconti di Modrone pack. Though the
trump subjects from the two decks varied in detail when both were present,
this was the only card that was markedly different. If the man on this card did
represent Sforza, then the lion cowering in the foreground was sure to have
represented Venice; the symbol of the lion being associated with St Mark,
the Patron saint of that city.[154] The scene spoke of the humiliating Venetian
defeats at the hands of the military captain and later Duke of Milan,
Francesco Sforza. The *condottiere* commonly linked himself with important
Biblical and historical figures in artworks. For example, he was portrayed as
talking to Julius Caesar and other Roman soldiers in a painting by Giovanni
Pietro Birago at the Uffizi, and his profile was recognisable among the reliefs
of Emperors on the façade of the Certosa of Pavia (where his son also
appeared as Alexander the Great).[155] Francesco Sforza obviously took great
pride in his military prowess and it would not have been uncharacteristic of
him to have associated himself with the legendary Hercules. Certainly, this
interpretation of the card is consistent with the overarching theme uniting the
tarot trumps, that of Visconti (and later Sforza) history.

Justice

Justice was present only in the later Visconti-Sforza deck and her allegorical
depiction was fairly typical.[156] A woman in long robes held a set of scales in
her left hand and a sword poised in her right.[157] Above her head, a knight
brandishing a sword rode a white horse caparisoned in gold and red. In
Plato's 'ideal city', Justice regulated both the social and personal actions of
the citizens, therefore making her the leader of the four Cardinal Virtues.[158]
The scales signalled her impartiality and her sword signified power. In
modern times, Justice is often seen blindfolded outside courthouses and
other public buildings. However, this depiction of blind Justice did not occur
before the sixteenth century and in fact, Justice was known for her clear-
sightedness.[159]

     The identity of the knight is in some question. He could have signified the
administration of justice. The white horse would have symbolised the purity
of his intent.[160] More specifically, he may have denoted Francesco Sforza as
the saviour and protector of Milan, though the caparison lacks the typical
Sforza emblems. But the allegory of Justice was frequently associated with
Trajan, Emperor of Rome from 98 to 117CE, who was renowned for his
generosity, fairness and administration of justice. His campaigns in Dacia and
Parthia were highly successful and he extended the Roman Empire with the
annexation of Arabia and Armenia.[161] Trajan was often depicted riding a
white horse so it seems likely that this was the true identity of the rider on the
card.[162]

Temperance

The depiction of Temperance in the Visconti-Sforza tarot deck was fairly standard.[163] A young woman held two jugs as if pouring liquid from one to the other. Temperance often indicated abstinence from liquor and so this figure was diluting wine with water.[164] Marie-Louise D'Otrange wrote that it symbolised the tempering of human justice with divine mercy.[165] Because no virtue could be sustained in the absence of self-control, St Thomas Aquinas considered it to be a special virtue, with three other virtues subordinate to it: abstinence, chastity and modesty.[166] In classical philosophy, temperance was associated with the subordination of physical desire to higher, rational ideals.

And Prudence?

Though the three other Cardinal Virtues of Strength, Justice and Temperance were represented in the tarot sequence of the Visconti-Sforza deck, the fourth, Prudence, was mysteriously absent. There is no obvious reason why this should be so and it seems most likely that the card was originally located in the sequence but was subsequently lost. The fact that six of the trumps were obviously painted at a later stage (including Temperance and Fortitude) probably to replace lost cards, makes such a scenario feasible. Prudence was represented in the Mantegna tarot thought to date from 1565, and also in the ninety-seven card minchiate deck also formulated in the fifteenth century.[167] Prudence typically had two faces: one looking forward into the future and the other looking backwards, remembering and learning from the past.[168] She held a mirror which symbolised circumspection.[169]

Theological Virtues

Though the Visconti di Modrone pack boasted only one of the four cardinal virtues (Fortitude), the Theological Virtues of Faith, Hope and Charity with their typical attributions were represented. Faith held a cross in her left hand and her right hand was raised in benediction. This portrayal was consistent with other Early Modern depictions of the virtue in art.[170] At her feet was the allegorical figure of Heresy. The virtue of Hope knelt in prayer, a rope tied around her wrists and tied at the other end to an anchor.[171] The anchor, as a disguised cross, was an early Christian symbol of hope.[172] A bearded male, with a rope around his neck, crouched at her feet. In Renaissance art, this figure was usually identified as Saint James, but in this case was more likely to be Judas.[173] Tarot trumps using this theme in the fifteenth century specifically identified the man as Judas by inscribing 'Juda traditor' on his purple garment.[174] The trio of Theological Virtues was completed by Charity, represented as a woman suckling a child, and holding a vase with a flame in her right hand.[175] A male figure was at her feet, usually identified as Saint John the Evangelist in Renaissance art,[176] though Stuart Kaplan suggested the figure represented King Herod.[177]

The prominence given to the allegorical virtues in the trump sequence eloquently demonstrated the Renaissance infatuation with the classical world, but also expressed the rising secularism and diminished importance of the Church and clergy. There was an emphasis on the commonalities between classical philosophies and Christian doctrine which stressed the moral content of Christianity while playing down the sacraments and the role of the clergy.[178] A person could secure salvation through righteous conduct alone.[179] This trend was further evidenced by the growing popularity of classical mythology and sagas which placed profane and sacred history on the same plane.[180] The sequencing of the tarot trumps made this changing accent explicit. The virtues ranked higher than the Popess, Pope and Church (here designated as the Chariot), though still below the trump of the Angel, depicting the Resurrection before Judgment. Though the presence of the Theological and Cardinal Virtues in the trump sequence did not specifically refer to Visconti history (with the exception of the Strength card in the Visconti-Sforza deck), it did underpin the importance of personal piety and righteous conduct in Filippo Maria's life.[181]

The Old Man as Time

Modern tarot enthusiasts would know the trump occupying the ninth position as the Hermit, yet this label tells us very little about the card's original symbolic meaning. In Renaissance tarot packs, this trump was variously known as the Old Man (il Vecchio), the Hunchback (il Gobbo) or Time (il Tempo), and it is this last moniker that belies the original meaning of the explicit symbolism.[182] Time, personified as an old man, featured in Petrarch's I Trionfi, triumphing over Fame and representations of the theme followed this imagery.[183] He leant on a staff or crutches to suggest extreme old age, and in his right hand he held an hourglass, symbolic of time running out and approaching death.[184] In subsequent decks, the hourglass was mistaken for a lamp. This card as Time was found only in the Visconti-Sforza deck where the old man, with a long white or grey beard, was dressed in blue and wore a large hat.[185] The personification of Time as an old man, which first appeared in the Renaissance, survives to this day as the familiar figure of Father Time often seen at New Year's Eve celebrations.[186]

The implications of the symbolism of this card are obvious: time marches on irrespective of circumstance and death comes ever closer. For Duke Filippo Maria Visconti, death was a constant companion. He came to power after the brutal murder of his brother and remained distrustful, suspecting conspiracies against him at every turn.[187] He was a hypochondriac, obsessing about his health until time and death triumphed over him in 1447.[188] As Niccolò Machiavelli wrote in his masterwork *The Prince*: 'Time sweeps everything along and can bring good as well as evil, evil as well as good.'[189]

The Wheel of Fortune

The concept of the wheel of fortune had a Greek provenance being first described by the lyric poet Pindar (518–438BCE), though many erroneously ascribed primacy to the writings of Cicero (106–43BCE).[190] The Romans were the first to link the wheel with the goddess Fortuna, her equivalent was Tyche in the Greek pantheon.[191] Ancius Manlius Severinus Boëthius (480–524BCE) in his *De consolatione philosophiae* described the wheel as raising the fallen and debasing the proud:[192] 'We turn the wheel on its flying orb, we rejoice to change the lowest for the highest, the highest for the lowest.'[193]

Fortuna proved to be the most persistent pagan deity, maintaining her dominion up until the dawn of science.[194] The Church fathers railed against her authority. Saint Augustine in his *City of God* stated that what does occur does so by God's hidden plan or by our own free choice between good or evil; Saint Jerome and Saint Thomas Aquinas concurred.[195] Renaissance thinkers granted fortune a prominent place in their philosophies. Florentine strategist Niccolò Machiavelli spoke eloquently about the role of fortune in politics, declaring that 'fortune is the arbiter of half the things we do.'[196] References to the wheel of fortune were plentiful in Medieval and Early Modern literature, art and morality plays of that period. King Arthur dreamt he was cast from the highest peak of the wheel of fortune in the French text of unknown authorship, *Mort le roi Artu* which inspired Sir Thomas Malory's *Le Morte d'Arthur*.[197] The goddess Fortuna spinning the wheel featured in *Roman de la Rose*, Dante's *Inferno*, and the works of the Florentine humanist Boccaccio.[198] At different stages of his life, Petrarch held varying opinions on the subject of fortune. Towards the end he held with the views of Saint Augustine and Saint Thomas Aquinas, that whatever occurs does so in accordance with God's divine plan. Yet in his sonnets he complained about the vagaries of fortune. In the prologue to the first book of *De Remediis,* he distinguished between good and bad fortune, considering each to be equally formidable.[199]

The Wheel of Fortune was present in both the Brambilla and Visconti-Sforza tarots and the representations were typical of those found in Renaissance art.[200] The winged goddess Fortuna stood at the middle of the wheel. She was blindfolded, not wanting to discriminate between kings and peasants, man and woman, rich or poor.[201] A figure was carried up one side of the wheel.[202] Another sat on the top with the ears of a donkey to signal ignorance,[203] a third with a tail to indicate his degradation was turning headfirst down the other side and an old man was caught under the wheel.[204] In the Visconti-Sforza deck, the figures were each accompanied by an inscription: '*Regnabo*', '*Regno*', '*Regnavi*' and '*Sum sine regno*' – 'I shall reign', 'I reign', 'I have reigned', 'I am without sovereignty.'[205]

Fortune had been grouped with both Love and Death, depicted as personifications of an active force behaving like a blind person, choosing people at random irrespective of age, sex or social position.[206] French poet Pierre Michault wrote a poem entitled *La Danse aux Aveugles* where love, fortune and death – all blind – made humankind dance to the tune of their wanton decrees.[207] To the Visconti and Sforza families this view of fortune would have seemed particularly pertinent. The Visconti rule of Milan was largely shaped by fortune, good and bad. Conspiracies, strategic marriages, unstable military alliances and the vagaries of the Church – both temporal and spiritual – were all beyond the control of the Milanese despots, both aiding and hindering their cause. From humble beginnings, the family rose to prominence, peaking with the achievements of Gian Galeazzo Visconti, squandered by Giovanni Maria, partially reclaimed by Filippo Maria, until without a whimper, the Visconti rule of Milan ended with the death of the Duke who had refused to name an heir.[208] Francesco Sforza, an illegitimate mercenary fighter, a *condottiere*, who could himself have been a personification of fortune, took control of the city and founded another dynasty.[209]

The Hanged Man

The Hanged Man is one of the most controversial cards in the modern tarot deck, probably because the image of the man suspended by a foot from a gallows has no counterpart in modern culture. The card was found only in the Visconti-Sforza deck of the three under consideration. A man was suspended from a timber frame by a rope tied around his left ankle. His right leg was crossed behind the left and his arms were held or tied behind his back. He had a serene expression on his face in spite of his inversion. To Renaissance society, this was a familiar sight and a clue was concealed in the traditional name of the card, the Traitor (*il Traditore*).[210] The card was an example of an art form called *pittura infamante* or 'shame painting' in which a person was depicted as a traitor, particularly when beyond the reach of legitimate legal recourse; typically bad debtors, those guilty of bankruptcy, fraudsters or turn-coat *condottieri*.[211] In 1440, Andrea del Castagno earned the descriptive nickname of 'Andrew the Rope' ('*Andrea degli impiccati*') by painting images of rebels suspended by their feet on the façade of the gaol in

Florence.[212] Botticelli painted the images of the Pazzi conspirators on the wall of the Bargello after their unsuccessful coup against Lorenzo Medici in

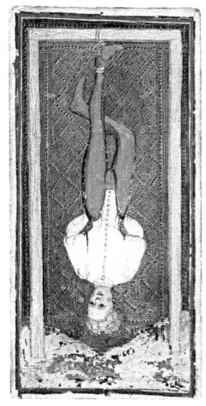

Florence in 1478.[213] In the first part of the sixteenth century, Andrea del Sarto painted inversed images of the captains that had fled after the siege of Florence in 1530.[214] The *pittura infamante* were a means of trying to regulate human behaviour by using shame and it is no surprise that the Renaissance Italians also invented other means of exploiting this emotion including the dunce cap, stocks and charivari.[215]

There is some speculation as to how the image of the hanged man came to be associated with traitors. Paul Huson hypothesised that Boëthius was the indirect source of this practice. In his *De consolatione philosophiae*, Boëthius described the human race as holding its head high to seek the divine and warned against letting the head sink lower than the body and consequently, away from what is holy.[216] Hence, to depict a person as hanging by a foot was to show that they have turned from God. Another theory held that the apostle Peter wanted to be crucified with his head down as he was unworthy to die in the same man-ner as Christ. Peter denied Jesus

Figure 6: The Hanged Man from the Visconti-Sforza deck housed in the Pierpont Morgan Library, New York.

three times in the Garden of Gethsemane and was thus known as a traitor.[217] To be hung by the feet with the head closest to the ground was also known as the 'Jewish execution' and as the name suggests, was mostly reserved for the execution of Jews.[218] The shame of the victim was heightened by simultaneously hanging two dogs from the gallows. The purpose was to try and force a pre-mortem conversion and the new Christian would be humanely beheaded for his trouble. As Jews were thought to have betrayed Christ resulting in his crucifixion, this practice became associated with treachery. It was subsequently used for witches found guilty by the Inquisition, and for Christians who had committed perfidy.[219]

The history of both the Visconti and the Sforza families featured treacherous plots of Machiavellian proportions that would have been suitable subjects for *pittura infamante*. Francesco Sforza's father, Muzio Attendolo, was depicted thus on the walls of Rome by order of the Pope.[220] In addition, hostilities between Milan and Florence escalated through the 1380s and much use was made of *pittura infamante* by both sides. Not even Milan's famous patriarch, Gian Galeazzo Visconti, escaped the infamy.[221] In 1392, the Duke offered a peace treaty to Florence on the condition that all the *pittura infamante* be removed from the walls of the Bargello. So offended was Gian Galeazzo by these portraits, that he even forbade their use in Milan. In 1396, he issued the following decree:

> Concerning the removal of pictures of infamy on the walls of the palazzo and the registration of the names of the defamed. Since certain images are painted on the walls of the Palazzo Nuovo of the commune of Milan, representing false witnesses and corrupt notaries, merchants and money changers, and although they seem to be made for the purpose of confounding and defaming frauds, yet they disgrace and defame not only the authors of the deceits themselves, but also the whole of the city in the eyes of visitors and foreigners; for when the latter see these images, they imagine and are almost convinced that the majority of citizens can barely be trusted, and are involved in great falsehoods; and so it is decreed that all these pictures be removed, and that no one should be painted in future. Rather, let him be strictly and firmly punished; and as for those who are already painted, and those who will in future be condemned for falsehood – let them be registered in a book in the Communal Chamber of Milan.[222]

In 1470, the Sforza leadership of Milan, by this time friends and allies of the Medici and great admirers of Florentine culture, once more made use of the *pitture infamanti*.[223] Ludovico Sforzo ('*il Moro*') ordered one to be made of Barnardino da Corte, who betrayed him to the French.[224]

It is difficult to link the Hanged Man to any specific event in Visconti history. Francesco Sforza fought both for and against Milan but it seems unlikely that he would have tolerated a depiction of himself as a traitor to be perpetuated in the tarot deck. I therefore favour the source of the image as being from the war between Florence and Milan, ironically the event which inspired Gian Galeazzo Visconti to discontinue the use of shame paintings. This becomes feasible given the Sforza infatuation with all things Florentine and Francesco's friendship with Cosimo de' Medici.[225]

Interestingly, as the significance of the Hanged Man became lost to European society, some authors turned the card around so that the figure appeared to stand on one foot. Antoine Court de Gébelin made such an inversion, believing the original to be a printer's error. Once righted, he thought the card represented the Cardinal Virtue of Prudence which was otherwise absent from the deck.[226] More recently, a painting by Filippino Lippi (c.1457–1504) was incorrectly identified as a dancer with his hair flying and garments swept upwards. It was not until Keith Richardson, familiar with *pitture infamanti*, saw the painting, that a correct identification was made.[227]

Death

To say that Renaissance Europe had a particular preoccupation with death would not be an overstatement.[228] Jean Delumeau attributed the pervasiveness of this attitude to two factors: first, to a culture of religious 'culpabilisation' that originated in the monasteries and resulted in the widespread belief that humankind deserved punishment, and second, from a profound pessimism founded in the relentless onslaught of the Black Death and ending with the French Wars of Religion in the sixteenth century.[229]

Milan escaped the first three waves of plague that hit Italy from 1347, finally succumbing in 1360.[230] As if making up for lost time, the city was stricken seven times between 1361 and 1485.[231] This pattern was fairly typical of many regions in Italy, though the port cities such as Venice were most susceptible because of their brisk trade with the near east.[232] Humans do not form a lasting immunity to plague and so populations remained susceptible to repeated outbreaks.[233] In spite of rigorous efforts, the plague could not be arrested and outbreaks recurred, particularly in densely populated places.[234] The impact of this terrible disease was felt across Europe, a third of the population falling prey and preplague numbers were not regained until well into the sixteenth century.[235] The Milanese administration kept records of morbidity and mortality from the end of the fourteenth century in an effort to determine the impact of such a high mortality rate on production and industry. Milan possessed a strong economy founded on trade and agriculture and every precaution was taken to ensure its continued viability.[236]

In an effort to minimise the effects of the Black Death, the Viscontis and later the Sforzas, instituted one of the first public health systems in Europe. Successive rulers were kept informed of the occurrence and prognosis of cases and the cause of every death had to be verified. Hospitals were built and provision was made to care for the poor.[237] Their concern was evidenced by the number of books pertaining to pestilence housed in the Visconti library, including works by Antonio Guainerio of Pavia, Petrus Codazzo and Ugo Benzoi.[238] In 1398, Pietro Curialti da Tossignano dedicated his *Consilium pro peste cvitanda* to Gian Galazzeo Visconti. The book was to become the most famous tractate on pestilence produced in the fourteenth century and was reprinted several times.[239]

Strict quarantine measures were instituted by the Viscontis, severely restricting communication and causing wealthy families and employers to flee from the city.[240] Villages and small towns, already suffering due to heavy taxation and migration to the cities, became completely denuded of people.[241] Petrarch speculated as to whether or not posterity could believe that there were so many corpses, vacant houses, deserted towns and neglected countryside, when it seemed dreamlike even to those who had witnessed it.[242] The Milanese administration attended to the physical needs of the population as well as they could, yet their spiritual concerns were not so readily addressed.[243] The Western Schism had torn apart the Church and divided loyalties all over Europe. The subjects of those princes who did not support the Pope were excommunicated, leaving the souls of its citizens in peril.[244] Not only did these people have to face the possibility of death from plague but also eternal damnation *post mortem*. This religious aspect of death was emphasised by the Church and its descriptions of Hell were frightening and graphic.[245]

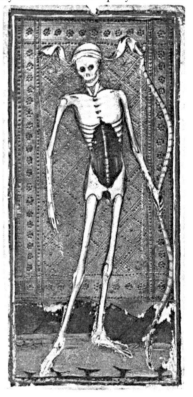

Figure 7: Death from the Visconti Sforza deck housed in the Pierpont Morgan Library, New York.

No one remained untouched by the effects of plague. Each had lost a family member, a partner, a child or an employer. French writer Michel Eyquem de Montaigne in the first volume of his *Essays*, summed up the Renaissance familiarity with death by declaring that men must be taught to die in order that they may learn to live: 'One must always be booted and ready to leave.' He advised thus: 'Let us remove [death's] strangeness and practise it instead. Let us grow accustomed to it, having no thought in mind as often as that of death.'[246] When death could come at every turn, each citizen had to be prepared. First appearing in the fifteenth century, the *Ars moriendi* or *Art of Dying* was a small instructional book that gave precise instructions detailing how to die 'well'. The drama was played out at the foot of the bed of the dying person; where angels and demons battled for possession of the soul of the victim.[247] Wood engravings increased the popularity of the work which retained a strong following until the sixteenth century.[248] The Black Death also made its mark in literature, most famously in Boccaccio's *Decameron* whereby ten young people tell one hundred stories in ten days while in the country in order to escape the effects of plague in Florence.[249] A manuscript of 1427 showed Death mounted on a pale horse, a theme that was to become common in Renaissance art.[250] Death was one of the Four Horseman of the Apocalypse; he rode a pale horse, its colour an imitation of the paleness of skin in death.[251]

Death and the corresponding transience of life were never far from the minds of the Renaissance Italians. The *memento mori,* an object kept as a reminder of death, also echoed this grave sentiment; life was fleeting and death inevitable.[252] The skull became the focus of this preoccupation. It was all that remained once the body has decayed. Once it had been the receptacle of life and thought, now its empty eyes stared out into nothingness.[253] Sermons and religious pictures kept the focus of the congregation on the inevitability and proximity of death.[254]

Already in the Middle Ages, this fixation with mortality was evident in the frequent depictions of the legend of the *Three Living and the Three Dead.*[255] According to this tale, three men, merry and laughing, skirted a cemetery on their way home. Three skeletons appeared and said to the men: 'We were once like you, happy and rich. See what happened to us!' The three men ran away terrified.[256] This legend prefigured what was perhaps the most persistent representation of death seen in the fifteenth century, that of the *Totentanz* or *Danse Macabre*, where Death indiscriminately swept away people of any age or status.[257]

The *Danse* was frequently enacted as a pantomime with gravediggers in skeleton costumes leading all of humanity in a dance to the grave.[258] Originally, it was a procession of living figures each with a dead counterpart. Popes and paupers, the young and the old, man and woman were inexorably drawn into the dance.[259] In another variation, the spectre of death would appear among a group of revellers who would then stop in horror and grief.[260] The messages were clear: divine retribution was at hand, death was brutal and it did not discriminate.[261] The *Danse* was frequently the subject of commissioned art, sometimes in response to an outbreak of plague as happened at Basel in 1439 or at Lübeck in 1463, but usually no such incentive was necessary.[262] The theme appeared in stained glass, ecclesiastical artworks, on parochial registers, miniatures, frescoes, woodblock prints and tapestries.[263] It was famously depicted in the lost drawings of Hans Holbein the Younger published in 1538.[264]

The Death card, represented in both the Visconti di Modrone and the Visconti-Sforza decks, reflected the Renaissance obsession with death. The figures from both cards were not anatomically correct as was typical of depictions of Death from this period. Instead, the artist tried to make the figures appear more frightening and grotesque.[265] The card from the later deck featured the skeletal form of Death holding a bow which represented power.[266] Death from the Visconti di Modrone deck rode a horse and carried a scythe which signalled the cutting short of life.[267] His victims, trampled beneath the horse's feet, included a well-dressed man as well as a pauper and a disreputable figure in red.[268] The message was clear: death does not discriminate, all are his potential victims.[269] Death completed the trio of great blind forces that controlled human affairs and nowhere was its presence felt more than Milan in the fifteenth century. All of Duke Visconti's riches and power were poor protection when Death came to call.

The Star, Moon and Sun: Astrology in Renaissance Italy

Though astrology was universally popular all over Renaissance Europe, it was particularly so in Italy.[270] The revival of interest in classical literature saw a revival of interest in astrology through the works of Ptolemy, Manilius, Firmicus Maternus and other writers. Furthermore, the interest in Greek mythology and its association with the constellations also enhanced this fascination. Propitious times for new enterprises were determined by official astrologers in the employ of almost every Italian government and many university professors would annually issue *iudicia* or astrological predictions.[271] Lorenzo de' Medici was forced by students to provide a course in astrology when he opened the University of Pisa.[272]

Astrology permeated many spheres, even the newly emerging science of medicine. Many works were written on 'iatromathematics', the influence of astrological bodies on medicine. One such treatise, *Amicus Medicorum*, written in 1431 by Jean Ganivet, remained popular for two centuries.[273] Many diseases were thought to be under the direct control of the stars, for example, syphilis was thought to have been caused by the conjunction of the four great planets in Scorpio which occurred in 1484. Gaspar Torella, physician to Pope Alexander VI and Cesare Borgia, predicted the disease would go away in 1584, when a different conjunction would occur.[274] Even Augustinian friar Agostino Trionfo, author of *Contra divinatores et somniatores*, who spoke out vehemently against magic and divination, accepted astrology as valid, asserting it was irresponsible for doctors to treat a patient without reference to the phases of the moon.[275] The Renaissance saw no contradiction between astrology and science; the influence of astrology was all pervasive.[276]

Duke Filippo Maria Visconti was a man typical of his time. His secretary, Marziano da Tortona, was well versed in current astrological thought. The representation of the classical pantheon in that first tarot deck may have been a reflection of this knowledge. Before he was thrust into the limelight after his brother's untimely assassination, Filippo preferred to spend his time playing with games or studying astrology. As Duke of Milan, he retained his interest in this pseudoscience, some suggesting that it became an obsession.[277] He would consult the astrologers before taking any political action, though this may have been a useful delaying tactic.[278]

The pervasiveness of astrology in Renaissance Italy and Duke Visconti's love of the discipline was reflected in the cards of the Star, Moon and Sun which were only represented in the Visconti-Sforza deck. Though the cards were missing from the decks specifically crafted for Filippo Maria, it is reasonable to assume that they were probably lost from the earlier decks. Even if this was not the case and the cards were only ever present in the Visconti-Sforza deck, the cards would still echo the Renaissance infatuation with astrology. Francesco Sforza kept three astrologers in his employ and preferred to take a new fortress on the waxing moon.[279] His son, Gian Galeazzo (1444–1476),[280] and his grandson, Ludovico,[281] also shared his belief in the validity of astrology.

In some later tarot decks, the cards of the Star, Moon and Sun featured astrologers among their symbolism. For example, the Moon card from a fifteenth-century Venetian pack, once wrongly ascribed to Jacquemin Gringonneur, featured two astrologers with dividers and a textbook.[282] The Star card from a deck painted for Ercole d'Este (1431–1505), Duke of Ferrara, likewise featured two astrologers pointing skywards and holding an astrological book (a picture of the moon was clearly visible on its pages).[283] The Moon from the same deck displayed a seated astronomer with dividers and a text. Next to him stood an armillary sphere which served as a model of the heavens. The signs of the zodiac travelled across the sky represented by the large band which was clearly visible around the middle of the sphere on this card.[284]

The symbolism on the corresponding cards of the Visconti-Sforza deck was not so elaborate. On the Star card, a woman held a star in her left hand, above her head. She wore a long blue dress that came to her shoes, with a red cloak patterned with small stars draped over her shoulders.[285] Her stellar cloak probably marked her as a personification of astrology. A similar device occurred in the so-called Mantegna tarot, though that figure was winged and wore a crown as 'Astrologia'. In addition, the star was frequently seen as a symbol of divine guidance and here may link the themes of religion and astrology.[286]

A woman very similar in appearance to the one on the Visconti-Sforza Star was found on the Moon card. This time she was holding a crescent moon in her right hand, just above her head. She was dressed in a red dress with blue sleeves that were gathered in by a rope at the waist. This time, the woman had bare feet. It seems likely that this figure was a composite of two ideas. Again, I think she was a personification of astrology but this time she existed in combination with some of the iconographical features of the Virgin Mary. Mary was often associated with the Moon and her humility was frequently made explicit by her bare feet.[287] In some traditions, the moon was linked with the Old Testament.[288]

The card depicting the Sun was quite different to those that immediately preceded it in the trump sequence. This time a winged and naked *putto*, standing on a black cloud floating above the ground, held an orange Sun with both hands above his head.[289] The Sun had an upturned face from which four sets of rays emanated. An orange length of material like a scarf curled around the *putto's* neck and between his legs to form a large 'C'.[290] The Sun was frequently associated with Christ in Renaissance art, and also with the New Testament.[291] This association was derived from the prophecy in the *Book of Malachi* (4, 2): 'But unto you that fear My name shall the Sun of Righteousness arise with healing in His wings.'[292] Given this association, it would seem that that the letter 'C' formed by the scarf probably stood for 'Christ' or 'Christos'. The elevation of the *putto* probably symbolised proximity to God and demonstrated that the figure was of a higher status than the cards that preceded it; having said that, I believe that this card primarily depicted astrological ideas. In astrology, the most influential heavenly body is the Sun, followed by the Moon and then the planets as they move through the zodiacal constellations, accounting for the trump sequence. However, the artist also wanted to acknowledge the significance of Christ and the Virgin Mary. This mixing of sacred themes with secular ones was common, and was characteristic of the increasing secularism in the Early Modern period.[293] Religion and astrology were not mutually exclusive as evidenced by the large proportion of popes that employed astronomers.[294]

Angel

This card is usually known as Judgment in modern tarot decks, yet early sources invariably labelled it the Angel. The scene inscribed actually referred to the Resurrection of the Dead rather than the Last Judgment. The principal Biblical authority was from Christ's discourse to the disciples as related by Matthew (25: 31-46).[295] The Angel was found in both the Visconti di Modrone and the Visconti-Sforza decks.

The theme of Judgment after death attracted urgent interest as the ravages of war and the Black Death swept through northern Italy. People saw their neighbours and family members dying around them, unprepared and unshriven. The morality plays and sermons became especially relevant and much money was directed towards the celebration of the promises made to penitent sinners and to all of humanity.[296] The fear of Judgment was a principal feature of the *contemptus mundi* characteristic of the time.[297] This theme was well-represented in literature; medieval chroniclers writing about world history frequently closed their works with a detailed description of the Last Judgment and the fate of those destined for Heaven or Hell.[298] Dante's *Divine Comedy* provided one such florid description, locating many recent celebrities in Hell, and consequently being well-received.[299]

The Angel cards, from both the Visconti di Modrone and the Visconti decks, featured fairly typical representations of the Resurrection preceding Judgment. Both cards included two angels with long horns summoning the dead from their tombs.[300] The inclusion of angels with horns was almost obligatory for depictions of the Last Judgment from this period.[301] The dead were naked, except for one figure from the earlier card, to pictorially represent the idea of judgment without reference to rank, status and calling.[302] An inscription at the top of the Visconti di Modrone card read: '*Surgite ad judicium*', meaning 'Rise for Judgment'.[303] The Visconti-Sforza card also boasted a depiction of a white-bearded and crowned God.

This card was the penultimate in the trump sequence and was therefore a high-ranking card signifying the importance of *post mortem* Judgment before God. It is interesting to contrast the low ranking cards representing the machinery of the Church, namely the Pope and Popess (representing the Inquisition), with the higher ranking personification of the Church as the Chariot, and finally outranking all is the Angel representing Judgment. Though Duke Filippo Maria Visconti disdained the Church, he maintained a high regard for religion and valued his relationship with the Divine. It is also interesting to note, that this card also featured the recurrent theme of equality irrespective of rank, age or sex as with Love, Death and Fortune.

The World

The World card, the highest ranked card in the trump sequence, was represented in both the Visconti di Modrone and the Visconti-Sforza decks. Though there was a general similarity between the cards, they were quite different in detail and so will be considered separately. The bottom half of the Visconti di Modrone card was comprised of a scene with four walled cities with the sea in the distance.[304] A river ran across the foreground with a boat being rowed across it. A knight on a white horse was on one side of the river and a fisherman on the other. This was probably a pictorial representation of the major powers of northern Italy in the early fifteenth century. Without a doubt, the city on the left of the scene was Milan, famous for its rose-red brick.[305] The river that ran across the foreground was most likely to be the Po, the major river of this area. It is 650 km long rising in the Cottian Alps and flowing to the Adriatic Sea near Venice. The city across the river from Milan was Bologna and the one between Milan and Bologna but behind them was Florence. The city next to the sea would be Venice. These cities were depicted on this card as they were the major powers of northern Italy and Milan frequently battled for power and territory with all of them. A map of Italy shows these cities and the River Po in the relative positions as depicted on this card. The significance of the fisherman is unknown. His proximity to Milan could have indicated the piety of its inhabitants as the Greek word for fish, *icthus*, is an acronym for Jesus Christ Son of God Saviour in Greek. The connotation of the knight, apparently having come from Florence, is unknown, as is the boat crossing the river.

The scene was bounded by an arch with a crown at its pinnacle. The crown would have represented the independent sovereignty of the city states. Each remained independent from both the Emperor and the pontiff (with the exception of Bologna that was sometimes independent but at other times was ruled by the Viscontis or the Pope). Above the arch was a richly dressed woman holding a crown in her left hand and a sceptre in her right, again the crown represented sovereignty and the sword depicted military might in a personification of punishment and reward, a kind of distributive justice.[306] This card illustrated the pinnacle of Visconti history. Milan acquired vast tracts of territory and wealth through considered conquest, cunning and politics. This was where the trump sequence had been leading: to the Viscontis' dominance of northern Italy and as such, this card can be viewed as an allegory of glory.

The World card in the Visconti Sforza deck was quite different. Two *putti* held a globe above their heads that contained a walled city. Representations of the walled city in Medieval and Renaissance art were frequently linked to Jerusalem as the 'City of God'. Here it represented a scaled-down cosmos and an image of the wider Christian world.[307] Hence, the microcosm of the city symbolically linked the earthly (human) body with the heavenly (cosmic) 'body'.[308] This characteristic iconography was derived from *De civitate Dei* (*The City of God*) written by Saint Augustine in the fifth century.[309] He wrote of a new empire centred around Christian Rome and indebted to Plato and Virgil. This conception laid the foundation of the Holy Roman Empire in Christian imagination, whereby the link between God in Heaven and the Emperor on Earth was to be the Bishop of Eternal Rome. A chain of being was created with its corresponding hierarchies of ministers, servants and subjects. The link between God and the entirety of mankind was to be the Mass.[310] *De civitate Dei* remained popular in Milan as Saint Augustine had lived there from 384 until 387CE, being baptised by Saint Ambrose in 386CE.[311]

The artist has cleverly linked Augustine's *City of God* with Milan by giving the walled city some characteristics associated with that Italian city. It was significant that the city depicted was of a reddish hue. Chamberlin described Milan as 'a city curiously regular in both shape and colour, a polygon of rose-red brick, born of the Lombardy clay; a city of the plain whence mountains were eternally visible,' and this description corresponded closely to the city shown on the card.[312] In addition, Russian iconography often featured monks or saints holding a model of their monastery to recommend their work to the protection of God.[313] A similar theme was also apparent here with *putti* lifting the model to secure divine protection. Further, the city was painted as if on a separate island apart from its surroundings. This was generally indicative of the idea of a healthy island in a sick world; the City of God, eternal and mysterious.[314]

In the middle of the city walls on the card was a prominent fort which could have been a replica of that built by Francesco Sforza when he returned to Milan as its duke. The Castello di Porta Giovia (now known as the Castello Sforzesco) was described as 'the proudest and strongest castle existing on level terrain in the whole universe.'[315] When Duke Filippo Maria Visconti died, the people tore down his citadel as a symbol of their hatred of him.[316] The Milanese people had begged Sforza not to rebuild the fortress as such a building was associated with tyranny and fear.[317] For Francesco Sforza it indicated his possession of the territory and was a potent symbol of his dominion over the Milanese. His contemporaries described the act as 'the ultimate suppression of our nation.'[318] This idea linking Milan with the City of God was reinforced by the appearance of four crosses topping four of the city's towers, probably representing the four evangelists. Further, Saint Augustine described the City of God as containing those who would be saved after the Resurrection of the Dead and Judgment.[319] It was no coincidence that this card would immediately follow the Angel (representing Judgment) in the trump series.

The Visconti-Sforza version of the World card fulfilled a similar role as that of the Visconti di Modrone deck. Both showed a great pride in the achievements of Milan and the prominence of the city state in temporal affairs. In the Visconti di Modrone card, spiritual prominence was indicated by the card's ultimate position in the trump sequence, yet in the Visconti-Sforza card, that religious status was made explicit by linking Milan with Saint Augustine's *City of God*. This card represented the climax of Visconti history as evidenced by the power, wealth and status of Milan. The story of the Viscontis which began with a common street magician, ended with a divine city.

Not a Tarot Trump but still the Fool

Many playing-card and tarot enthusiasts have assumed that the ordinary playing card deck devolved from the tarot deck and that the Joker was all that remained of the trump cards. This theory can be discounted on three main grounds. First, the Fool was not a tarot trump and consequently cannot be a remnant of the trump sequence. Second, the ordinary playing card deck was recorded in Europe several decades before the first appearance of tarot and those decks did not feature a Joker.[320] And finally, the Joker of the ordinary playing card deck and the Fool play quite different roles in the games they are associated with.[321]

The Joker of the ordinary playing card deck first appeared around 1857 in the United States, as the highest trump in Euchre.[322] Cards had served as 'wild cards' in particular games before but this was the first time that a special card had been created specifically for that purpose.[323] In contrast, Joyce Goggin claimed that the history of the 'Joker' began in the fourteenth century when it was common practice for artists to draw their portrait on a blank card as a sort of signature. This unusual card would be used as a 'wild card' in play. According to this theory, Emmanuel Juker of Utrecht eventually became associated with the practice and the cards took their name from him. When these decks reached England, the name was apparently mispronounced as 'joker'.[324] I have found no other evidence to support this claim.

The card of the Fool was found only in the Visconti-Sforza tarot deck. It was not part of the tarot sequence though most modern creators of tarot will classify it as a trump card. In the original game played with the deck, the Fool functioned as a 'wild card' which could be played at any time, excusing a player from having to play a trump or follow suit.[325] Consequently, it was frequently called *l'Excuse* (the Excuse) or *der Sküs* in Germany.[326] In early

Italian sources, the card was called *il Matto* (the Madman). In modern times it is also called *il Folle* (the Fool) or *il Fuggitivo* (the Fugitive).[327]

The figure on the card was a beggar in tattered clothes with feathers in his hair.[328] In his right hand he held a long club commonly known as a foolstick.[329] His ragged clothes covered only his top half and just met across his middle.[330] His thighs and feet were bare and his stockings were rolled down to his calves. The portrayal of clothes exposing the bare skin of the stomach, navel or buttocks was a common device used to suggest indecent exposure.[331] Fools were expected to be indecent and crude as they were viewed as being irresponsible and antisocial.[332] They frequently appeared in Renaissance art as a means of stripping away pretence and revealing the true sentiments at the root of human endeavour.[333]

A large lump on the neck of the Fool was probably goitre.[334] Iodine deficiency was extremely common in Europe in Early Modern times as iodine-rich foods are found predominantly near the sea.[335] The populations of inland and mountainous regions frequently exhibited deficiency symptoms. The figure of the Madman was clearly affected. He had goitre, a gross swelling of the thyroid gland, and he exhibited some of the signs of neurological cretinism. People thus affected are often extremely mentally retarded and are often deaf mutes. Further, their hands and feet can be in a spastic state and cretins frequently have a characteristic stance, similar to that of the figure on the card. The Madman also exhibited strabismus, a condition

Figure 8: The Fool from the Visconti Sforza deck housed in the Pierpont Morgan Library, New York.

which is also associated with cretinism.[336] People who exhibited bodily imperfections such as goitre and cretinism were frequently judged to be morally corrupt, hence the expression 'as ugly as sin'.[337]

The figure of the Fool or Madman was common in Renaissance and Medieval art. In the twelfth century, Giotto painted *Stultitia* (Foolishness) among the Virtues and Vices of the Scrovegni chapel in Padua.[338] The figure of the Visconti-Sforza Fool and the allegory of Foolishness shared several characteristics: both wore tattered clothes, both carried a club and both had

seven feathers in their hair, perhaps signalling foolishness as one of the
Seven Deadly Sins.[339]

Gertrude Moakley hypothesised that the Fool was the personification of
Lent so that the card would fit in with her scheme of the trump sequence
representing carnival.[340] Superficially, this theory had some merit.
Personification was common at this time and well represented in the trump
sequence.[341] Further, the seven feathers could have represented the seven
weeks of Lent.[342] Yet, Moakley's overall scheme has been discussed and
dismissed in the previous chapter. If the trump sequence was a narrative of
Visconti history, there was no obvious role for a personification of Lent.

Instead, the Fool represented the idea of randomness or chaos, a theme
frequently alluded to in the trump sequence. He turned his back on God
and civilisation and made fun of the laws of his country.[343] The Fool was often
promoted to the role of King during carnival, and under his reign, the world
order collapsed.[344] The card of the Fool existed outside of the game just as its
human counterpart existed outside of normal life. He had always been
considered different; his physical characteristics and clothing differentiating
him from the other members of society.[345] As such he was an allegory of the
foolishness of mankind, a commentator on the sphere of human activity.[346]
He was not subject to the rules of life just as he was not subjected to the rules
of the game. His iconographical significance corresponded to the card's role
in the game rather than to the trump narrative of Visconti history.

The Tower: Absent or Lost?

The Visconti-Sforza tarot was the most complete of the early decks and was
obviously the one from which most subsequent decks were conceptually
derived. The trump sequence and the subjects depicted on the trumps were
quickly standardised with two notable exceptions: subsequent decks included
two additional trumps, namely the Tower and the Devil.[347] The first reference
to the card that came to be known as the Tower was believed to be in a late-
fifteenth-century Italian manuscript, *Sermones de Ludo Cum Aliis* where it
was called *la sagitta* (The Arrow).[348] The oldest extant example of the card
was from the misleadingly named Gringonneur deck, tentatively dated to
around 1475.[349] Among the names used to designate this card in subsequent
packs were 'the Fire', 'the Thunderbolt' and 'the Lightning'.[350] In later decks
it was called 'the House of the Devil' or 'the House of the Damned'.[351] In the
Tarot de Marseille it was called *la Maison Dieu* (the House of God).[352] Tom
Tadfor Little and Robert O'Neill hypothesised that the Tower and the Devil
cards were omitted from the early decks as they were considered distasteful
to the nobility.[353] It is difficult to imagine the nobles of the northern Italian
courts, comfortable enough with the Death and Hanged Man cards, would

be too sensitive to endure the implications of the Devil and the Tower. The Tower from the Gringonneur deck corresponded to images found on many subsequent decks. A castellated tower was crumbling; fire struck it from the sky and was also evident within the tower itself. Many examples of this card included people falling headfirst to the ground. In order to confidently state whether or not this card belonged in the Visconti tarot sequence, I would need to formulate a place for it in the narrative of Visconti history.

There have been several hypotheses posited to explain the symbolism of this card. Gertrude Moakley suggested that the card represented the 'Hellmouth' or 'Gates of Hell' that were frequently recreated in medieval morality plays. Yet another theory posited that the tower was derived form the story of Merlin and Vortigern as part of the lore surrounding King Arthur and his court. Merlin agreed to make a prophecy concerning the great king's end, predicting that he would die in a burning tower which he did in various versions of the legend.[354] Though these stories were enormously popular during the Italian Renaissance and many copies of books pertaining to them existed in the Visconti library, there was no obvious connection in this story to the broader themes illustrated in the tarot trumps.[355]

One of the most popular theories imagined the symbolism of the Tower as the artistic representation of the Tower of Babel as described in the Bible.[356] The Tower of Babel was built by the descendants of Noah in an effort to reach Heaven. God was so angry at the presumption that he punished humankind by confounding their language and hence communication between peoples became difficult.[357] In the Talmud, the story was told slightly differently: during the construction of the tower, a man fell to his death but the builders were too busy to pay much attention and it was this that raised God's ire.[358] This would account for the images of falling people seen in some depictions and the fire coming from above could suggest Divine punishment but it was improbable that the Christian Viscontis would be influenced by the Talmud. As beguiling as this theory remains, it seems unlikely that the tower illustrated on the card would represent the Tower of Babel. That tower was so broad it appeared wider than it was high and seven-stepped and was usually depicted as such in art.[359] Further, there is no obvious reason why this Bible story should be chosen above the hundreds of others available to Renaissance artists.[360]

A probable explanation for the symbolism displayed on the tarot card can be accommodated within the framework of the tarot trumps as Visconti history. When Tom Little hypothesised that the Tower symbolised the power and permanence of the noble dynasties, he may have been closer to the mark than he realised, though I would disagree that the symbolism made the nobility uncomfortable enough to omit the card from the deck.[361] The name for the tower in Italian is 'torre' and this was also the name of the main rivals of the Visconti family in Medieval and Early Modern Milan. They were an old family of Frankish descent who belonged to the rural nobility.[362]

The Della Torre family looked likely to form a *signoria* in Milan in the last half of the thirteenth century.[363] Martino della Torre was captain of the people in 1247, and from November 1263, he became 'perpetual lord of the people of Milan'.[364] Able to capitalise on Milanese success to spread his influence, he became '*Podestà* and lord of the communes of Bergamo, Como, Novara and Lodi'.[365] Martino's cousin, Raimondo della Torre, was the successful candidate for the Archbishopric in 1262 but Pope Urban IV intervened and secured the vacancy for Ottone Visconti. Martino was incensed and with his ally Pellavicino, occupied the lands of the Archbishopric so that Ottone could not take possession of them.[366] Further, the della Torre family had Guelf sympathies (as opposed to the Visconti who were pro-Ghibelline) such that the Pope would not wholeheartedly back his own candidate.[367] In fact, by way of compensation to the della Torres, Raimondo was appointed by Gregory X in 1273 to the immensely rich Patriarchate of Aquileia.[368] Napoleone (Napo) della Torre succeeded Martino as lord of Milan in 1265 after the death of Martino and in quick succession his brother Filippo, adding titles including *anziano perpetuo del Populo.*[369] By 1272, the aim of the *Podestà* was not to secure obedience to the statutes of Milan but to Napo della Torre.[370] Napo was a despot typical of the time who entertained lavishly but who also built the Grand Canal and paved the streets of the city. He managed to raise an army of 28 000 from 19 000 families by requiring each household to provide an armed soldier to his forces.[371]

Ottone Visconti remained in exile for fifteen years but did not abandon hope of returning to Milan.[372] He administered his diocese as best he could from outlying fortresses and sent his agents to collect revenue from various parts.[373] In 1276, he became leader of those Milanese who had also been exiled.[374] In the meantime, the della Torres had quarrelled with many of the prominent families who had previously supported their ambitions thereby narrowing their support base.[375] Ottone Visconti enlisted the help of many of the powerful country landlords such as the Marquesses of Monteferrato and the Counts of Langosco, to inflict defeat on the della Torres at the battle of Desio in 1277.[376] Napo was imprisoned in a cage where he died and Ottone became Lord of Milan.[377] At last, he was able to exert effective control over Milan, however he was compelled to rely on the Marquess of Monferrato as Captain-General until the della Torres were decisively defeated on the banks of the Adda River four years later.[378] The great wealth of the Archbishopric sustained Ottone's rule over the city. He erected a *Consiglio delle Provisioni* of twelve deputies to coordinate the city's government which became the mainstay of Visconti rule through the fourteenth century.[379] Ottone practised the nepotism that became so much a part of Visconti rule, with his young relative Matteo Visconti becoming *Capitano del Popolo* in Novara and Vercelli as well as in Milan.[380] Emperor Adolf of Nassau appointed Ottone as Vicar of Lombardy, thus beginning the close association of the Holy Roman Emperors with the Viscontis, an alliance which would prove both useful and troublesome in the future.[381]

Ottone died in 1295 and Pope Boniface VIII intervened to prevent the see from becoming the hereditary preserve of the Viscontis.[382] Archbishop Francesco Fontana of Parma ruled the see from 1296 until 1308, only to discover that the family had infiltrated the administration of the diocese. He sought an alignment with the enemies of the Viscontis; a threat Matteo tried to neutralise by appointing his son, Galeazzo, *Capitano del Popolo* and by arranging strategic marriages with the houses of potential enemies such as the della Scala of Verona and the Estensi of Ferrara, Modena and Reggio.[383] In spite of these elaborate precautions, the della Torres were restored to Milan from exile in 1302 by a confederation of cities fearful of the influence of Milan.[384] The della Torres had formed a league with other parties sympathetic to the Guelfs and managed to make the position of the Viscontis untenable. Matteo retired to the country and Galeazzo moved to his wife's family in Ferrara.[385] In 1307, Guido della Torre was elected captain of the popolani for life, with full power to alter the statutes of the city.[386] His cousin, Cassone della Torre, became Archbishop in 1308 but factional strife within the family ensured that the family lacked the cohesion to keep them in power.[387] Cassone and his supporters thought that he should rule the house but Guido, disagreeing entirely, had Cassone and his supporters arrested.[388]

The appearance of the Emperor-elect in Italy only served to complicate the situation.[389] Henry VII restored the Viscontis to Milan as private citizens. Guido della Torre was removed from his post of *Capitano del Popolo* and Henry installed his own vicar. The statutes of the commune were handed over to lawyers in order to 'cleanse' them of all the marks of della Torre rule.[390] The della Torres, who felt they were suffering excessively at the hands of the Emperor, engineered an unsuccessful uprising against him in 1311 and rejected the peace terms offered to them.[391] Henry VII lacked the money to quell the uprising himself so had to fall back on the assistance of those who had demonstrated Ghibelline sympathy in the past. Matteo Visconti became his vicar in 1311 in return for a payment of 50 000 florins and an annual tribute of 25 000 florins.[392] Pope John XXII demanded that Matteo surrender his post on the death of Henry VII, but he managed to hold onto the office.[393] The Viscontis capitalised on their success in Milan by spreading their influence to neighbouring cities. Galeazzo Visconti became lord in Cremona and Piacenza. Marco Visconti held dominion over Tortona and

Alessandria. Luchino held a similar position in Pavia, Stefani in Lodi, Como and Bergamo.[394] The della Torres were never to regain the power and prestige they had lost at the hands of the Viscontis and of Henry VII.[395] The bitter rivals of the Viscontis had been successfully silenced.

If the Tower card had been a part of the original hand-painted Visconti decks, it is not difficult to explain its significance within the context of Visconti history. The della Torres were bitter rivals of the Viscontis for some fifty years. The coats-of-arms of various branches of the della Torre family often bore towers of the kind illustrated on the Tower card, some even with flames licking from the windows.[396] In addition, the flames could have also symbolised the ultimate ruin of the della Torres which could be interpreted as being the result of Divine intervention, hence the fire blazing down from the sky. For these reasons, I am confident the Tower was a part of the original trump sequence, its name soon forgotten just as the exploits of the family were all but erased from the annals of Italian history.

The Devil in the Deck

The Devil trump was the only card not represented in any of the fifteenth-century hand-painted decks though Michael Dummett believed the trump had originally been present and was subsequently lost.[397] Stuart Kaplan erroneously wrote that the first example of the card was in the Gringonneur deck, but in fact the Devil first appeared in woodblock decks dating from late in the fifteenth century.[398] Yet another opinion was proffered by Robert O'Neill (among others); stating that the Devil card was deliberately left out of those early decks as it considered too distasteful for the nobility.[399] Unless a hand-painted example of the Devil card comes to light, the only way to determine whether or not such a card possibly existed is to examine Renaissance attitudes to the Devil and to re-examine more modern interpretations of the symbolism on that card. The presence of the Devil card as a personification of evil would sit comfortably enough within the framework of Visconti history and Renaissance life as represented in the Visconti decks. The problem remains: was evil personified in this way in Renaissance art and if not, what did the 'devilish' figure represent?

From the ninth until the sixteenth century, depictions of the Devil in art were rare.[400] Rather than portray the Devil, medieval artists preferred to depict the contest for a person's soul as a battle between the Virtues and Vices.[401] Those representations of the Devil that did exist usually expressed neither personality nor feeling.[402] Artists did not consider the subject worthy of their attention as the Devil was not viewed as having a real, personal presence.[403] Until the middle of the fifteenth century, the Devil was usually portrayed as a microbe; hardly a worthy adversary of God.[404] There was no literary tradition that portrayed the Devil and there was no pictorial tradition at all.[405] The Devil was frequently confused with Satan, Lucifer and the demons which led to a lack of consistent iconography.[406] Artists appeared to have forgotten the Christian origins of the Devil as a fallen angel.[407] Saint Augustine described the angels who were ejected from Heaven as impure and unclean spirits. He wrote: 'Evil has no positive nature; what we call evil is merely the lack of something that is good.'[408] The Devil was only an abstraction and could not be viewed as an individual capable of being represented artistically; as such he could claim no fixed iconography.[409] He was rarely mentioned in the Old Testament and there was no hint of a conspiracy between demons and humans.[410] Evil was real but the Devil was not.[411]

When the Devil was portrayed, artists looked for clues of his appearance from among classical sources.[412] The Greeks lacked a god that was perceived as being inherently evil so artists borrowed iconographical motifs from Pan including horns, hoofs, ears, tail and a hairy lower body.[413] The Wild Man, with his human body covered with thick hair and his aggressive attitude to sexuality, also was influential upon the iconography of the Devil.[414] This influence was made explicit with the northern German word for the Wild Man, namely '*schoduvel*' which literally meant a 'frightening devil'.[415] In addition, the Devil was portrayed not quite stark naked but with a distinctive skirt which was tattered indicating that he was outside of society.[416] We see a similar device used in representations of the tarot Fool. The supplementary head on the stomach or chest of Renaissance depictions of the Devil, demons and monsters was thought to derive from representations of a race of monsters that were believed to inhabit India and were thought to possess a face on their chest instead of one on their shoulders.[417] By the fourteenth century, the Devil was often depicted with the ribbed wings of the bat in contrast to the beautiful, white feathered wings of angels. He often wore talons instead of hooves and this iconography was thought to have been derived from illustrations of harpies.[418] Characteristically, the Devil carried a prod identical to the grapnel commonly used by jailers.[419]

In this guise, the Devil appeared as an essentially harmless and even comic creature.[420] Those whom he dragged down to Hell were usually seen as immoral and deserving of their fate. As such, the Devil appeared to be an ally of good, dealing with that which was too distasteful for God to consider.[421] In this role he was not the source of evil, only the unfortunate soul that dealt with humanity's flotsam.[422] Sometimes the Devil could play the role of tempter, inciting a person to do wrong, but still he was not perceived as the adversary of God.[423] The Devil could only represent evil as defined by the Church for its own self-interest. With the advent of the Reformation, Martin Luther identified the Pope as the Devil and *vice versa*.[424] It was not until after this time, when the Devil was not strictly defined by the theology of the Church that he could be associated with a more general image of evil.[425]

Throughout the sixteenth and seventeenth centuries, there was a well-established tradition of defining the Devil as a monstrous animal, possessing both animal and human traits.[426] Though generally resembling a man, he could also have cloven feet and long arms in the shape of wings.[427] These depictions assigned a physicality to the Devil and located him in specific places and times.[428] He was transformed from an incorporeal abstraction to an actual physical manifestation which could grab hold of men or women and kill them with his bare hands.[429] The European witch trials which intensified in the last quarter of the sixteenth century were the direct result of the increasing dread of the Devil.[430] This did not occur until well after the first appearance of the 'Devil' in the tarot trump sequence and renders it unlikely that the Devil was portrayed in those early tarot decks. The idea of the Devil as the manifestation of evil simply did not exist at that time. Even the identification of the figure on the late-fifteenth-century trumps as the Devil is problematic; such depictions were not common until well into the next century.

Another possible source for the images on the Devil card was that of the 'monster' or 'prodigy'. Monsters were highly visible in Early Modern Italy and monsters, demons and the Devil, frequently resembled each other in Renaissance art.[431] The popularity of prophecy by the appearance of monsters or prodigies was another borrowing from classical culture.[432] In the late Middle Ages, increasing attention was paid to infants that had been born deformed.[433] Even Machiavelli, entirely sceptical of religion, stated in his *Discourses* that 'the air is peopled with spirits' and that great events were heralded by prodigies, prophecies, revelations and signs in the sky.[434] These prodigies differed markedly from those monstrous races that had been described in previous times as inhabitants of the Antipodes.[435] Instead, these infant 'monsters' were entirely human and usually died early, either as a result of their deformities or because maternal care had been withdrawn from them. These unfortunate children were often displayed publicly either alive or embalmed, as was the case with the conjoined twins born outside of Verona in 1475.[436] Monstrous births were taken as portents of wars and destruction or as evidence of God's anger with human worldliness.[437] It was generally believed that God allowed these corruptions of nature to occur in order to instruct humankind. Monsters were never viewed as the bastard progeny of the Devil subsequent to his coupling with a human woman; the difference between species was seen as being too great.[438] In addition, the idea that the Devil could procreate violated the belief that only God could create life and was therefore untenable.[439] Several causes were cited for monstrous births including divine judgment,[440] the 'heated and obstinate imagination of the woman' while she conceived,[441] 'superabundance, or defect and corruption, in the seed,'[442] double impregnation, narrowness of the womb, a defect in nourishment of the foetus or some other such natural circumstance.[443]

The appearance of monsters corresponded with the end of the fifteenth century and the beginning of the sixteenth century, coinciding with the first appearance of the 'Devil' card in the tarot trump sequence.[444] San Antonio di Firenze was the first to describe monsters and monstrous breeds in his *Chromicom*, printed in Venice in 1474 to 1479.[445] Other authors soon followed suit including Filippo di Bergamo in his *Supplementum Cronicarum* (1483) and Hartman Schedel in his Nüremberg Chronicle (1493). By the middle of the sixteenth century, the interest in monsters and prodigies had reached fever pitch.[446] Boaistuau published his *Histoires prodigieuses* in 1560, a work that was to gain exceptional success as evidenced by the large number of reprints and editions.[447] The popularity of these works extended well into the eighteenth century.

Folklorist Juliette Wood remarked on the similarity of the figures displayed on the Devil card to depictions of Renaissance monsters.[448] The images had much in common; for example a prodigy was described thus: 'A portrait of a monster said to have been born at Cracow either in 1543 or in 1547 on the day of St Paul's conversion. The eyes were fiery, the mouth and nose ox-like; there was a horn like an elephant's trunk; the back was hairy; monkeys' heads substituted for teats; there were cats' eyes above the navel and dogs' heads at the elbows and knees; the hands and feet were a monkey's.'[449] The monster was reported to have lived for only four hours. Several people claimed that before he died he said: 'Watch, for the Saviour comes.'[450] Likewise, the Monster of Ravenna, born in 1512, shared many characteristics with the tarot 'Devil'; both had talons, horns and bat wings.[451]

In conclusion, I believe that the Devil card was absent from early hand-painted tarot decks as the idea of the Devil as a physical manifestation of evil had not yet formed in the Renaissance psyche. Instead, God was assumed to have dominion over all of His creation including the Devil. The Devil did not assume a physical form in the Renaissance consciousness until the middle of the sixteenth century. Hence, given the similarities between representations of the Devil, monsters and demons it seems likely that the first 'Devil' cards were in fact representations of monsters or prodigies, especially given the Italian fascination with prophecy at that epoch. It was only in later times, when the fashion for prodigies had waned and fear of the Devil had increased, that the identity of these figures became confused, exacerbated by the absence of labelling on the trump cards.

The game of tarot functioned as an allegory for life in which both skill and chance played a part. The trump cards of the three decks of Visconti tarot cards formed a particular narrative of Visconti history, culminating in the glory of Milan as evidenced in the World trump. Historical events were tempered by the indiscriminate forces of Fortune, Death and possibly Love, which lay beyond human control, but also by human forces as administered by the Church and the Holy Roman Empire, and human personality as indicated by the presence of the Cardinal and Theological Virtues. Ultimately, any soul was naked before God as he or she awaited Judgment. The Tower card, representing the misfortune of the della Torre family and corresponding success of the Viscontis, probably took its place in the sequence as a part of Visconti history however, the Devil card probably did not. That particular depiction of evil incarnate was not commonly represented until the middle of the sixteenth century.

Though the symbolism of the tarot deck was readily understood within a fifteenth-century, Milanese context, the success of the game and its subsequent wide distribution, meant that the symbolism was no longer relevant or comprehensible to new users of tarot. Left to interpret the symbolism with little or no knowledge of the original meaning and sometimes the original use of the deck, several theories were formulated which described mysterious though erroneous origins; usually including some esoteric interpretation of the trump symbolism. These esoteric interpretations and subsequent redesigns, re-imaginings or 'rectifications' of the deck will form the basis of the next two chapters of this study.

4

The Transformation of Tarot into an Esoteric Device

Tarot in fifteenth century Milan reflected the predominant currents of Renaissance thought and elaborated them through the narrative of Visconti history. All were presented there: the preoccupation with death and the corresponding desire for eternal life, the importance of religion contrasted with the corruption of the Church and Holy Roman Empire, but also the specifics of Visconti history as seen in Francesco Sforza's representation on the Strength card and Sister Maifreda's on the Popess. In eighteenth century France, tarot symbolism was still a lens through which to view prevailing attitudes and beliefs but this time Christianity lost some ground to exotic religions such as Hinduism and esoteric streams became overt with the assignation of Hebrew letters and astrological correspondences to tarot trumps. Whereas the Christians of the fifteenth century looked forward to securing a place in Heaven, Enlightenment occultists looked nostalgically back to a lost Golden Age of humanity and the hope that Egyptian lore, as encoded in the hieroglyphics and tarot symbolism, could help them recreate the idyll.

From Milan, the game of tarot spread quickly to Ferrara and Bologna. The deck in each centre acquired a characteristic trump order with a differing ultimate trump and sequence of Cardinal Virtues. Though tarot was disseminated from all of these centres to the rest of Italy, it was from Milan that the game spread to the rest of Europe, after the city succumbed to the forces of France and Switzerland in the sixteenth century and tarot subsequently became established in those countries.[1] By the eighteenth century, the game had become popular in Germany and the rest of Europe, carried there via routes that are difficult to determine.[2]

The Tarot de Marseille became the standard pack made by French and Swiss card-makers from about 1700 and probably assumed its definitive form near the beginning of the seventeenth century.[3] The pattern was widely copied by all Swiss, German and Austrian card-makers and from the eighteenth century, even by card-makers in Italy itself.[4] Though the pattern

had a fairly lengthy history, the name was adopted relatively recently, having been applied to the pattern by Paul Marteau of the card-makers Grimaud in the 1930s and named after a typical example produced in the eighteenth century by Nicholas Conver of Marseille.[5] The pattern closely resembled that of a fifteenth-century Milanese uncut sheet of tarot, now housed in the Beinecke Library in New York.[6]

Figure 9: The Moon from a contemporary version of the Tarot of Marseille (© Lo Scarabeo, 2000).

The Tarot de Marseille differed from the original Milanese decks in several ways. First, each trump card was labelled with the name of the card at its base.[7] Second, the trump sequence boasted the presence of a Devil card and a Tower card, any connection to the Milanese della Torre family long forgotten. On the former, the figure of a Devil stood on a pedestal attached to which were two ropes or chains which were also secured around the necks of two smaller, naked figures with tails. The Tower card featured a single edifice struck by fire coming from the sky from which two figures were tumbling headfirst towards the ground.

Finally, the remaining trumps differed in detail from the corresponding cards of the original Milanese decks. There were two kneeling figures before the Pope on that trump.[8] A man was flanked by two women on Love and Cupid had lost his blindfold.[9] A male figure replaced the Queen on the Chariot, giving the image a more martial tone. The horses that pulled the chariot, one blue and one white, also lacked wings. The Old Man had been misidentified and recast as the Hermit, carrying a lantern instead of an hourglass.[10] The goddess Fortuna was lost from the Wheel of Fortune and the human figures were replaced by animals. Instead of a figure holding a star on the Star trump, a naked woman knelt at a stream, pouring water from two pitchers beneath a sky full of stars. She represented the zodiacal sign of Aquarius. The Moon card featured a stylised crab at the bottom of a lake, with two dogs barking beneath the moon. This card represented the zodiacal sign of Cancer.[11] Instead of a *putto* holding the Sun, the trump featured two male figures representing Gemini's twins, who danced beneath the sun in front of a low wall.[12] The World card now featured a naked woman surrounded by a wreath. Each corner of the card occupied by the winged animal associated with each of the four Evangelists.[13] Finally, the Fool carried his possessions in a sack tied to a stick which he slung over his shoulder, seemingly oblivious to the dog jumping up at him.[14] The deck was exclusively used for game playing and there was no evidence that tarot cards or even ord- inary playing cards were used for divination until some four centuries after they first ap- peared. True cartomancy, whereby symbolic meanings were assigned to individual cards, was not evident until the second half of the eighteenth century.[15]

Though the focus of this chapter is esoteric tarot in France, another instance of tarot divination had a claim to primacy. The first substantiation of divinatory tarot reading was contained on a single sheet which gave meanings for thirty-five cards of the *Tarocco Bolognese.* Dating from about 1750, the sheet was found by Franco Pratesi in the Library of the University of Bologna.[16] This form of divination was to remain relatively popular

Figure 10: The Devil from a contemporary version of the Tarot of Marseille (© Lo Scarabeo, 2000).

until the nineteenth century though it bore no similarity to that established in France by occultists and was thought to have risen independently.[17] The first evidence of cartomancy in France was in a book entitled *Etteilla, ou manière de se récréer avec un jeu de cartes* (*Etteilla, or a Way to Entertain Oneself with a Pack of Cards*) which was published in 1770 and subsequently reprinted in 1773 and 1783.[18]

France in the Eighteenth Century

The eighteenth century saw an unprecedented development of Europe, facilitated by the growth of urban markets, long-distance trade and the growth of available capital. It was in this environment, that the pioneers of so-called rationalist thought worked from within to fuel the drive towards less 'fantasy- oriented' ways of thinking.[19] These rationalists believed that the fundamental realities could be determined by using human faculties alone without recourse to metaphysical speculation.[20] They held firm in the belief that what could be uncovered by the increasingly sophisticated scientific instruments was all that was needed to understand the cosmos.[21] Leaders sought to free their constituents from the superstitious beliefs of medieval times; empowering them with the tools of rationality and reason. This period, characterised by the rejection of supernatural beliefs in favour of scientific endeavour, is generally known as the Enlightenment and is said to have incorporated the Age of Reason. Though this philosophy was evident across

Figure 11: The World from a contemporary version of the Tarot of Marseille (© Lo Scarabeo, 2000).

Western Europe, France was usually seen as its home; the French Revolution saw the rejection of both the *Ancien Régime* and of organised religion.[22] The Nation became the new focus of devotional fervour. *La commune de Paris*, governing the city during the Revolution, instigated the Festival of Reason during which cathedrals were desecrated. Journalist Jacques-René Hébert led the people in the worship of a new deity, the Goddess Reason.[23]

In French society, the Church had been immensely powerful with its leaders being members of the *élite*. During this time, they had preferentially served the interests of the privileged few, for the most part ignoring the needs of their greater constituency. Consequently, the significant movements afoot at that time had an anticlerical and an antireligious focus. The Church had to compete for the nation with liberal nationalism.[24] In an increasingly secular society, each individual became empowered to pursue different forms of belief. The Church could no longer dictate patterns of faith.[25] Christianity was not necessarily rejected outright but heterodox and Universalist readings of the Bible became common, often overlaid with borrowings from other religions and traditions.[26] Sometimes the Christian component was pared away from the various esoteric currents, as a response to the disenchantment with the secular world or as an attempt by esotericists to come to terms with a disenchanted world.[27]

Deprived of the solace of the Church in such tumultuous times, people reacted against the thorough rationalism that characterised the period.[28] It was in this difficult philosophical climate that Romanticism appeared, promoting a heterodox religious view of the universe that placed humanity at its centre.[29] Behind Nature was God who cared for and secured the interests and wellbeing of humanity as well as those of the individual.[30] In addition, this philosophy also promoted the idea of the Great Chain of Being, an unfolding of the great creative power coupled with an evolutionary process of change.[31] Nature was immanent, with God beyond this world and hence, beyond immediate discernment.[32] Deeper realities could be fathomed by unleashing the imagination to perceive hidden connections between all things; investing the cosmos with unity and significance.[33] This freedom of belief cleared the way for the rediscovery of occultism embracing astrology, prophecy, alchemy, divination and spiritism.[34] The renewed interest in the occult arts developed as a response to the upheavals and dislocations in the maturation of modern France.[35] The French Revolution and its repercussions convinced many that life was out of balance and these disturbed souls sought solace in an erroneous but nevertheless appealing history, where life was simpler and humankind lived in harmony with nature and the elements.[36]

As a direct consequence, the years between 1770 and 1815 were engulfed by the phenomenon of Illuminism. Scientist, philosopher, theologian and mystic Emmanuel Swedenborg (1688–1772) had abandoned his scientific pursuits subsequent to his dreams of a spiritual world populated by angels and spirits.[37] Formulating a descriptive geography of celestial spheres and spiritual worlds, he popularised the concept of correspondences: the idea of universal relationships from Nature to Man and from Man to God which were presented hierarchically.[38] In his wake, alternative forms of spirituality and spiritual endeavour were embraced and editions of books discussing occult themes such as the works of Albertus Magnus, the French translation of Agrippa's *De occulta philosophia*, the Abbé Villars de Montfaucon's best-seller, the *Comte de Gabalis* and all sorts of books on magic, the divining rod, witchcraft and astrology proved popular.[39] French occultists saw their role as disseminating esoteric knowledge to the rest of the world rather than dominating and ruling. The movement grew in tandem with those artistic and literary movements which fostered an elective interest in the occult such as Romanticism and Symbolism.[40]

Three occult movements became particularly important in France at this time. First, spiritism or communication with the dead through mediums, table rapping or ouija boards became enormously popular; its first major proponent in France being Allan Kardec (1804–1869).[41] Second, the Theosophical Society with its jumbled mix of eastern doctrine and spiritualism, and founded by Henry Steele Olcott and Helena Petrovna Blavatsky in America, reached France during this period.[42] Finally, the French-born Martinism, which was promulgated by Martines de Pasqually and Louis-Claude Saint-Martin, was also destined to play an important role.[43]

Occult Philosophies

By the beginning of the nineteenth century, all of France was enraptured with
the exploits of their new leader, Napoleon Bonaparte. He had secured
victory for France across Western Europe and had consolidated French
power in Egypt. In the true spirit of the Enlightenment, Napoleon had taken
a bevy of scientists and archaeologists with him to this ancient land and they
ensured a steady stream of Egyptian artefacts found their way back to
France.[44] Occultists were quick to incorporate Egyptian lore into their
schemes. There was a common belief that the land of the Nile was the
stronghold of Hermetic wisdom.[45] The French fascination with all things
Nilotic fuelled their obsession with hieroglyphics, at that time still
untranslated. Investigators laboured under the belief that these intriguing
inscriptions concealed ancient magical knowledge.[46] Horapollo's
Hieroglyphica was a major source of inspiration for these occultists even
though the work had long been shown to have little basis in fact.[47] Jean-
François Champollion's translation of the Rosetta Stone in 1822, enabled the
translation of hieroglyphics but occultists were slow to accept that they did
not spell out great wisdom.[48] Even so, occultists still believed that alchemy
was born in an Egypt masked in antiquity; their Egyptomania fanned by abbé
Jean Terrason's successful novel, *Life of Sethos, Taken from Private
Memoirs of the Ancient Egyptians*, written in 1731.[49]

But the French curiosity about the world stretched further than Egypt. By
the eighteenth century, many scholars sought out the similarities between
Christianity and other religions and many became fascinated with the
mysterious land of India and with 'Hindoos'.[50] These scholars included
Giambattista Vico (1668–1744), Constantine Francis de Volney (1757–
1820), Richard Payne Knight (1750–1824), Godfrey Higgins (1772–1833)
and Sir William Jones (1746–1794), the pioneer of research into Sanskrit in
the West.[51] This infatuation was in part fuelled by the reaction against science
and rationality but also with the disenchantment with institutional
Christianity.[52] With the collapse of the Moghul Empire in the second half of
the eighteenth century, India became increasingly accessible to European
interests both commercially and intellectually.[53] Concurrently, there was a
growing awareness of the common origins of European and Indian language,
both being a part of the Indo-European language group.[54] Consequently,
India became an essential element of the occultist landscape.

This systematic investigation of other cultures and their esoteric doctrines,
inevitably led to the rediscovery of kabbalah. The term refers to Jewish
esotericism, though subsequently it was reinterpreted and Christian kabbalah
came into being. Kabbalah describes the nature of God and his divine
emanations which were represented diagrammatically as the Tree of Life.

God is known as *En Soph* and his presence fills and incorporates the Universe. He justified his existence by becoming active and creative via the medium of the ten *sephiroth* or intelligences which emanate from him. The first *sephirah* encompasses the wish to become manifest and this incorporates the other nine *sephiroth*, each emanating from the one that precedes it. The ten *sephiroth* show how the world developed gradually from nothing but also symbolise primordial man who is but a shadow of heavenly man.[55]

The first body of kabbalistic teachings circulated in Provençe in the twelfth century and was called the *Sefer Yeṣirah* or *Book of Creation*.[56] The book was a discourse on cosmogony and cosmology, illustrating an eastern gnosis and a variety of Neoplatonism.[57] Each word and letter of the Torah was believed to have multiple meanings and a correct interpretation would reveal the relationship between God and the world.[58] It was Rabbi Isaac the Blind (1160-1236) who first wrote of the branches and roots of a mystical tree in his commentary on the book. This tree became known as the Tree of Life and was to assume great importance in subsequent esoteric lore. The *Sefer ha Zohar* (*Book of Splendour*) was the next to be added to the kabbalistic corpus in the last quarter of the thirteenth century.[59] Probably written by Moses de Léon, it appeared in Spain sometime after 1275.[60]

Traditionally, there was a greater emphasis on theogony and cosmogony than on messianism, but after the 1492 Diaspora, salvation history increased in importance.[61] Raised in Egypt, kabbalist Isaac Luria (1534-1572) helped to establish this school within the Jewish tradition.[62] The Diaspora forced many Jews to take refuge in Italy and hence, kabbalah became known in that country. Pico della Mirandola (1463-1494) aimed to provide a methodology drawn from the Jewish commentators to reveal the truths hidden in sacred texts. He asserted that esoteric Judaism was aligned with Christianity and that kabbalah demonstrated the divinity of Christ.[63] Christians were attracted to kabbalism because it formed a commentary of the sacred books of the Old Testament by the Chosen People, even winning the approval of the some of the medieval popes.[64] German theosophist Friedrich Cristoph von Oetinger (1702-1782) helped redirect kabbalah towards messianism in the eighteenth century.[65]

Kabbalistic literature could be divided into two main streams. The first constituted a part of Orthodox Judaism. The second merged the Hebrew texts with others espousing esoteric teachings such as Arabic and particularly *Ṣūfī* texts but also some of eastern origin.[66] It was this second stream that informed the writers of the occult. *Les Vers Dores de Pythagore Expliques* published by Illuminist Antoine Fabre d'Olivet (1767-1864) in 1813, was an attempt to assign a mystical meaning to verses attributed to the Greek mystic Pythagoras. He wrote that the purpose of all religions and all initiations was union with God and hence constituted a part of a lost universal tradition.[67] This was followed in 1816 by the publication of *La langue Hebraique Restituee*, a revitalisation of the Hebrew language with a grammar based on Biblical Hebrew.[68] For many, these works stimulated an interest in kabbalah which had been largely inaccessible before this time.

Incorporating one, some or all of these streams of thought, Freemasonry became the first stop for those scholars intent on beginning a systematic study of occult lore. The organisational structure of Freemasonry became the obvious model for the dissemination of occult knowledge as a religion.[69] From its real origins in seventeenth-century Scotland, Freemasonry became a viable alternative to conventional Christianity.[70] Its rich symbolism and elaborate rituals appealed to its educated followers.[71] With its secret meetings, it provided a social community with which to replace the more conventional affairs of the churches.[72] Women were specifically excluded from any involvement in activities, supposedly because they were indiscreet and incapable of maintaining the necessary secrecy.[73] In addition, it was thought that they would cause disorder and would violate the space based on friendship with the introduction of love between men and women. They were eventually allowed to join some lodges, yet their participation remained unequal; they lacked autonomy and were excluded from many Masonic activities.[74] French Freemasonry spawned a bewildering array of rites, grades and orders which incorporated many of the esoteric currents of the time. The symbolism of ancient architecture, particularly of the Temple of Solomon but also of pyramids, cathedrals and pagan temples, was merged with supposedly alchemical, kabbalistic or Rosicrucian symbolism.[75]

Scottish-born Andrew Michael Ramsay (1686–1743), following the lead of the Welsh Presbyterian occultist Christopher Love (1618–1651), claimed there was evidence of a *prisca theologia* which extended as far as China.[76] In his book *The Travels of Cyrus* (1727), he asserted that builders working on the Temple at Jerusalem discovered an underground chamber upon which arches were superimposed to a depth of nine levels.[77] When workmen reached the bottom, they discovered an engraved plate and two pillars. The text on one pillar recounted the history of the vault and the text on the other codified the principles of the liberal arts, especially masonry.[78] The construction of the vault was credited to Enoch who had survived the Great Flood which he had foreseen in a dream.[79] This story formed the basis for the Royal Arch degree of Freemasonry, recreating the story of the return of the Jews from Babylon and the rebuilding of the Temple. Ramsay also suggested that the Christians had first learnt masonry as Crusaders in the Holy Land and on the foundation of this spurious connection, chivalric orders such as the 'Knights Templar' were founded.[80]

Freemasonry also incorporated the rampant Egyptomania of the time. C. Friedrich von Köppen (1734–1797) and Johann Wilhelm Bernhard von Hymmen (1725–1786) anonymously published the *Crata Repoa* (1778) which told of a fictitious initiation into the Egyptian mysteries, consisting of seven rites enacted in crypts, caves and secret chambers.[81] Freemasons had apparently been the heirs of the geometrical skills of the ancient masters who had inherited their learning from Hermes Trismegistus.[82] In 1784, Count Alessandro di Cagliostro (1743–1795) revealed his Egyptian rite, a Masonic order formulated by the count.[83] Visitors to his 'Temple of Isis' in Paris, were greeted by a servant dressed as an Egyptian and ushered into the séance conducted by 'le Grand Copht' Cagliostro.[84]

It was into this intellectually cluttered milieu that esoteric tarot first made its appearance. The game of tarot was very popular across Europe and was played throughout France in the seventeenth century. But by 1700, the game was completely unknown in Paris, being played only in the eastern parts of the country such as Alsace, Burgundy, Franche-Comté and Provençe.[85] For the inhabitants of eighteenth-century Paris, the Renaissance imagery of the tarot trumps appeared especially exotic.[86] It was almost inevitable that the mysterious card game, its symbolism denied its original relevance once removed from its Renaissance context, should appear to contain promises of forgotten esoteric lore when rediscovered by a people primed to discern such knowledge in every object, sacred or mundane. The first to make this connection between archaic wisdom and the tarot was Antoine Court de Gébelin.

Antoine Court de Gébelin

Antoine Court de Gébelin (1719–1784), the man who could be said to be the originator of occult tarot, was a Protestant pastor and a Freemason.[87] He was a dedicated scholar of many of the esoteric currents that permeated French culture including Rosicrucianism, Hermeticism, kabbalism, Swedenborgianism and esoteric Freemasonry. He began his Freemasonic career in the Lodge of *Les Amis Réunis* in 1776, giving a series of lectures on the allegorical meanings of the Masonic degrees the following year.[88] *Les Amis Réunis* founded the research lodge *Philalèthes* and Court de Gébelin became one of its founder members.[89] As was typical of the time, this order combined many types of Illuminist and occult doctrine including Martinism, Swedenborgianism, alchemy, esoteric Masonry and esoteric Christianity. By 1780, Court de Gébelin had also founded the *Société Apollonienne* which evolved into the *Musée de Paris*; a centre for lectures, readings and discussions.[90]

Not content to merely study the occult, Court de Gébelin sought to assemble his beliefs and philosophies into a single work. Between 1773 and 1782, he published his nine-volume opus entitled *Le Monde Primitif Analysé et Comparé avec le Monde Moderne* which reflected the Enlightenment nostalgia for wholeness.[91] The name referred to the belief that humankind had at one time shared a common language, culture, customs and religion, existing in a kind of Golden Age which later disintegrated.[92] All modern civilisations were thought to be the degraded remnants of this glorious original. Court de Gébelin further claimed that the essence of this lost civilisation could be discerned in the many myths from around the world, if only one knew how to look.[93] He also dubiously employed the study of etymology to search back through history to reveal the primeval language and its sixteen-letter alphabet. Swept up in the Egyptomania of the time, he even asserted that the name 'Paris' actually meant 'Ship of Isis' and that a Druid temple to the goddess originally stood on the site of Notre-Dame.[94] This huge work, still much shorter than was intended, was never finished due to the untimely death of its author in 1784.[95]

Figure 12: The Hanged Man recast as Prudence by Antoine Court de Gébelin in *Le Monde Primitif.*

The eighth volume of *Le Monde Primitif* published in 1781, was in part devoted to the mysterious origins of tarot.[96] Here Court de Gébelin reported that some time in the last quarter of the eighteenth century, he had come across some ladies playing the game of tarot. In Paris, these cards were unusual and he had not seen them since he was a boy. He was interested in the Hermetic mysteries of ancient Egypt and it occurred to him that he was seeing a sacred Egyptian book, the remnants of the lost *Book of Thoth*.[97] He regarded the trump cards as a disguised assemblage of ancient Egyptian religious doctrines. He identified the Popess, for example, as 'the High Priestess', the Chariot as 'Osiris Triumphant' and Typhon as the Devil.[98] This *Book of Thoth*, he supposed, must have been brought to Europe by the gypsies, who had been safeguarding it since it had been entrusted to them by Egyptian priests forced to encode their knowledge as their libraries burned millennia ago.[99] He deduced that the safest way to preserve their ancient wisdom was to encode it as a game.[100] Court de Gébelin believed that tarot had survived precisely because no one suspected it was anything but an amusement and it would take an adept to decipher the esoteric knowledge contained therein; this honour he claimed for himself.[101]

Court de Gébelin's essay was accompanied by engravings, probably by Jean-Marie Lhôte. Because the tarot was supposedly Egyptian, all traces of Christian symbolism had to be removed from the deck. Hence, the Pope became the 'High Priest' or

Figure 13: Isis figures in Court de Gebelin's version of The Star in *Le Monde Primitif.*

'Hierophant' and the triple cross he held was proclaimed to be Egyptian. Likewise, the Popess became the 'High Priestess', apparently correcting the mistake of the German card-makers.[102] The Love card was recast as 'Marriage' with trumps VIII, XI, XII and XIV acting as the Cardinal Virtues. Trump XII was usually named the Hanged Man but again Court de Gébelin blamed the card-makers for misinterpreting the card. The figure, according to Court de Gébelin, should be shown upright and in this configuration represented the missing virtue of Prudence.[103] The Chariot was replaced by 'Osiris Triumphant' and the Old Man (the Hermit in the Tarot de Marseille deck) was replaced by the 'Sage'.[104] The Devil was replaced by Typhon, an Egyptian god associated with Set, the enemy of Osiris.[105] The Tower ('*le Masion Dieu*' in the Tarot de Marseille) became the 'Castle of Plutus'.[106] The Star, trump XVII, was identified as the Dog-Star, Sirius, which appeared with the planets.[107] The woman beneath the star was Isis.[108] The Moon card featured the Nile with the two barking dogs representing the Tropics.[109] The next card to undergo a transformation was that of Judgment which in Court de Gébelin's scheme became 'Creation'.[110] Finally, the World was recast as 'Time' with the symbols of the four evangelists (as Christian symbols) being transformed into depictions of the four seasons.[111] Interestingly, Court de Gébelin associated the twenty-two tarot trumps with the twenty-two letters of the Egyptian alphabet which he claimed was also common to the Hebrews and the Orientals.[112] Unfortunately, there were not twenty-two letters in the Egyptian alphabet but significantly, this was the first time tarot trumps had been linked to the Hebrew alphabet and subsequently kabbalah, an association which was pivotal to esoteric schemes.[113]

This theory of an Egyptian provenance of tarot gained currency because of France's pre-Rosetta infatuation with all things Egyptian and placed little reliance on historical reality. This also explained the French occultists' fascination with the *Corpus Hermeticum*. It had been written by Greek writers who believed that Egypt was the repository of a pristine philosophy and powerful magic.[114] When these documents were rediscovered and translated during the Renaissance, the aspiring magi of the period took them literally and assumed they were the works of an ancient Egyptian provenance.[115] It was not until 1614, when classical scholar Isaac Casaubon, unsettled by the idea that pagans had predicted the coming of Christ that doubt was cast on the authenticity of the Hermetic texts.[116] The discovery of this deception was widely recognised, especially by the Protestants, but in largely Catholic France, the enthusiasm for the texts remained unabated.[117]

Included with Court de Gébelin's *Le Monde Primitif* was an essay purported to be written by M. le C. de M.***, subsequently identified as Louis-Raphaël-Lucrèce de Fayolle, Comte de Mellet (1727–1804), an otherwise unremarkable court noble and military commander.[118] Comte de Mellet concurred with Court de Gébelin's assertions that the tarot pack originated in Egypt, that it contained the teachings of ancient Egyptian masters and that the trump sequence should be considered from the highest number to the lowest.[119] However, his ideas did differ from those of Court de Gébelin in several important ways. First, Comte de Mellet concluded that only the tarot trumps concealed Egyptian lore, the suit cards being added later in contrast to Court de Gébelin who wrote that the entire pack was encoded. Second, Comte de Mellet placed the spread of the deck to Europe much later than Court de Gébelin.[120] Third, he divided the trump sequence into three groups of seven cards representing the different ages of man, again showing this enlightenment fascination with the golden prehistory of humankind.[121] The first grouping contained the trumps numbered from XXI to XV and represented the Golden Age. Trump XXI, traditionally the World, represented the Universe with the figure of Isis upon it.[122] The Angel, instead of depicting the resurrection of the dead, illustrated creation with newly formed humans breaking free of the earth with the figure of Osiris animating them with tongues of fire.[123] The Sun represented the creation of that body as with the Moon.[124] The card also featured a dog and a wolf portraying the creation of domesticated and wild animals respectively. Comte de Mellet's Star represented the creation of the stars and fishes.[125] The Tower was called *la Maison Dieu* (the House of God) as it was in the Tarot de Marseille and illustrated humankind's expulsion from earthly paradise by a comet and hailstorm. Trump XV came as Typhon instead of the Devil, signalling the end of innocence and bringing the Golden Age to a close.[126]

According to Comte de Mellet's scheme, trumps XIV down to VIII corresponded to the Silver Age of humanity.[127] Temperance as an Angel came to show humankind how to avoid death which was only a recent affliction in human history. Death retained its familiar guise as did the Hanged Man. Comte de Mellet kept the Hanged Man hanging to represent the misfortunes that dogged life but still associated it with the Cardinal Virtue of Prudence which was needed to avoid calamity. Strength came to the aid of Prudence and vanquished the lion which was identified with uncultivated and unkempt land. Fortune, still depicted as the Wheel of Fortune, portrayed the fickleness of fate.[128] Next in this inverted sequence was the Sage, traditionally the Old Man but the Hermit in the Tarot de Marseille. His lamp aided his search for Justice on earth, the last card in this section.[129]

The ultimate grouping in this sequence alluded to the Iron Age of humankind. The Chariot of War as trump VII, proclaimed the crimes of this heinous age. Love had a sinister note, with a man caught between vice and virtue. Reason was not his guide as evidenced by the blindfolding of Eros.[130] The Pope and Popess were replaced by Jupiter and Juno as with the Tarot de Besançon pack.[131] Trump IV as the Emperor showed a King with a club. Again, the German card-makers were held responsible for transforming this weapon into an imperial sceptre probably because Comte de Mellet's tarot was obviously derived from the Besançon deck which was widely used in Germany, German-speaking Switzerland and Alsace. Trump III nominally the Empress, was represented as a queen also holding a club.[132] The Popess was replaced by Juno, here representing Pride as evidenced by her peacocks. She was announcing the earthly religion of idolatry. The final trump was the Mountebank who held the rod of the Magi. His purpose was to work miracles in order to deceive the credulous people.[133] Though Comte de Mellet could be following Ovid or even Hesiod in describing the Ages of Man, the sequence also corresponded closely with the Hindu cycle of the *yugas* consisting of the Golden Age (*Kṛta Yuga*), the Silver Age (*Tretā Yuga*), the Bronze Age (*Dvāpara Yuga*) and the Iron Age (*Kali Yuga*) which is the stage of the cycle in which we currently exist.[134] Given the tendency towards syncretism between Christianity, Hinduism and classical sources evident in eighteenth century France, it was likely that all of these schemes served as models for Comte de Mellet.

Significantly, Comte de Mellet went on to state that the trump sequence was more than just a retracing of the history of humankind; each trump was also a letter which when combined in different ways could form sentences.[135] He also stated that the Hebrew alphabet had twenty-two letters and that the Fool, representing Madness, completed the sacred alphabet and corresponded to the letter *Tau* signifying completion or perfection.[136] The Hebrew alphabet begins with *Aleph* which in Comte de Mellet's scheme corresponded with what he considered to be the first trump, the World.[137] He then attributed symbolic meanings to each Hebrew letter and hence, to the associated cards. For example, *Zain* was associated with Typhon (instead of the Devil) and indicated inconsistency and *Lamed* with Fortune signifying law or science.[138] Comte de Mellet referred to the 'science of numbers and the value of the letters' as 'formerly very well known' and this was probably an allusion to the kabbalah, which was enormously popular at the time.[139] Similarly, this was the first reference we have to divination with tarot; a practice that he groundlessly attributed to the Egyptians.[140] In this context, tarot lost its significance as a game and an allegory for life. When the French occultists discovered what they believed to be its true meaning and purpose, its 'disguise' could be shed. It would take another person, however, to fully develop tarot's potential as a divinatory device.

Etteilla

Etteilla was the name adopted by an occultist who had simply reversed his surname: 'Alliette', his given name being Jean-Baptiste.[141] Born in 1738, he was thought to have died in 1791.[142] A long tradition among occultists assigned him the profession of wigmaker, though in reality he was a seed seller and subsequently he sold prints.[143] His book entitled *Etteilla, ou manière de se récréer avec un jeu de cartes* (*Etteilla, or a Way to Entertain Oneself with a Pack of Cards)* which was published in 1770 and subsequently reprinted in 1773 and 1783, constituted the first evidence of cartomancy in France.[144] According to Etteilla, the process required a Piquet pack which was an ordinary playing card deck with the pip cards from two to six removed and with the addition of a thirty-third card called 'Etteilla' which represented the querent.[145] Each card was assigned two meanings depending on its orientation (cards were not yet double-headed).[146] Two years later, he published *Le zodiaque mystérieux, ou les oracles d'Etteilla* (*The Mysterious Zodiac, or Etteilla's Oracles)* which consisted of a series of astrological predictions.[147] Obviously astrology was among this seed merchant's interests.

No record of Etteilla existed for a ten year period but when he did reappear, he did so as a print merchant.[148] In 1783, two years after Court de Gébelin's eighth volume of *Le Monde Primitif* was published, Etteilla released the third edition of his cartomancy book, this time titled *Etteilla ou instrcuctions sur l'art de tirer les cartes. Troisième et dernière édition* with an engraving bearing the name 'Cartonomancie, ou l'art de tirer les cartes. Troisième édition ... Extrait des récréations algébriques d'Etteilla' (Cartonomancy, or the Art of Card Reading. Third Edition ... Taken from Etteilla's Algebraic Entertainments).[149] Etteilla claimed that he had originated the term that would become 'cartomancie' ('cartomancy' in English).[150] By this time, Etteilla was promoting himself as a 'teacher of algebra'; a claim which had no basis in fact.[151]

As early as 1782, Etteilla submitted a work to the royal censors, which was the standard practice at that time, called *Cartonomanie* [*sic*] *Egiptienne, ou interprétation de 78 hierogliphes qui sont sur les cartes nommées Tarots* (*Egyptian Cartonomania, or Interpretation of the 78 Hieroglyphs which are on the Cards Called Tarots*). Unfortunately, the manuscript was banned from being published and there was no indication as to why.[152] Finally, between 1783 and 1785, Etteilla produced *Manière de se récréer avec le jeu de cartes nommées tarots* (*A Way to Entertain Oneself with the Pack of Cards Called Tarots*).[153] In this work, which was published in four parts, Etteilla in common with Comte de Mellet and Court de Gébelin, ascribed an Egyptian origin to the tarot pack which he believed was originally intended to be a book written in symbols or 'hieroglyphs'.[154] According to Etteilla, tarot was designed by a panel of seventeen magi answerable to Hermes Trismegistus. It was originated 171 years after the Flood, some 3 953 years before Etteilla was writing.[155] Again, card-makers took the blame for corrupting the original Egyptian form of the pack. Etteilla claimed that the oval wreath on the World card replaced the original *ouroboros,* a serpent biting its tail.[156] Further, he wrote that five of the 'hieroglyphs' had been rendered completely incorrect by the 'vile card-makers'. These cards were Prudence, the Emperor, Empress, Pope and Popess. As with Court de Gébelin, Prudence was associated with the Hanged Man, except that in Etteilla's depiction of the virtue, a woman holding a caduceus raised her skirt and looked down at a snake at her feet.[157] The Pope allegedly replaced a card showing light dispelling chaos.[158] A naked man surrounded by eleven circles in the air, stood surrounded by a beautiful garden in the card that came to be replaced by the Popess. Etteilla also maintained that all of the cards of the deck, not just the trumps, should be numbered as with other books.[159] He further designated that they should bear Arabic numerals rather than the usual Roman ones, as it was the Egyptians who invented the zero from which Arabic numerals were derived.[160]

Card 1 Etteilla (*Le Questionnant*)

Cards 2 to 8 – Seven days of Creation

2 *La Lumière* (Light)	1st day
4 *Le Ciel* (The Heavens)	2nd day
3 *Les Plantes* (Plants and Herbs)	3rd day
6 *Les Astres* (The Sun and the Moon)	4th day
7 *Les Oiseaux et le Poissons* (Birds and Fish)	5th day
5 *L'Homme et les Quadrupèdes* (Man and Animals)	6th day
8 *Repos* (Repose after Creation)	7th day

Cards 9 to 12 – Four Cardinal Virtues

9 *La Justice*
10 *La Tempérance*
11 *La Force*
12 *La Prudence*

Cards 13 to 21 and 78 – Important conditions of human life

13 *Mariage* (Marriage): The High Priest – union
14 *Force Majeure* (Major Force): Satan of the Devil – superior force
15 *Maladie* (Illness): The Magician – malady
16 *Le Jugement* (Judgment): The Last Judgment – judgment
17 *Mortalité* (Mortality): Death – destruction
18 *Traître* (Treachery): The Hermit – hypocrisy
19 *Misère* (Destitution): The Shattered Temple – imprisonment
20 *Fortune* (Fortune): Fortune's Wheel – augmentation
21 *Dissension* (Discord): African despot – arrogance
78 *Folie* (Madness): Folly or the Alchemist - folly

Cards 22 to 77 – Minor Arcana cards

4 Kings	Numbers 22, 36, 50, 64
4 Queens	Numbers 23, 37, 51, 65
4 Knights	Numbers 24, 38, 52, 66
4 Pages	Numbers 25, 39, 53, 67
4 Tens	Numbers 26, 40, 54, 68
4 Nines	Numbers 27, 41, 55, 69
4 Eights	Numbers 28, 42, 56, 70
4 Sevens	Numbers 29, 43, 57, 71
4 Sixes	Numbers 30, 44, 58, 72
4 Fives	Numbers 31, 45, 59, 73
4 Fours	Numbers 32, 46, 60, 74
4 Threes	Numbers 33, 47, 61, 75
4 Twos	Numbers 34, 48, 62, 76
4 Aces	Numbers 35, 49, 63, 77

Table 3: Structure of the Etteilla tarot deck.[161]

Even though Etteilla gave precise instructions as to how to render the tarot trumps, he also suggested that an ordinary tarot card deck could be readily modified. He directed the user to renumber the cards according to his scheme spelt out in his *Manière de se récréer avec le jeu de cartes nommées tarots*. Then the user was instructed to write the first meaning on the card, reverse it and write the second meaning as directed in his book.[162] Etteilla made frequent references to the *Pimander*, one of the tracts of the *Corpus Hermeticum*.[163] He reasoned that as tarot was the *Book of Thoth*, and Thoth was otherwise known as Hermes Trismegistus whose teachings were to be found in the *Pimander*, then it must be possible to find Hermetic knowledge in the tarot deck.[164] However, he did not elaborate on the nature of this knowledge but focused on creation myths.[165] Following Comte de Mellet, trumps II to VIII described the Creation of the world according to the *Pimander*, though it was likely that description was derived from the one in Genesis.[166] He also linked the first twelve cards in his novel trump sequence to the signs of the zodiac, instructing the user to mark those cards accordingly.[167] In fact, the last part of *Manière de se récréer avec le jeu de cartes nommées tarots* was devoted almost exclusively to astrology, a divinatory method very much out of favour with the other Enlightenment occultists.[168] Etteilla attributed the invention of astrology to the Egyptians and he designated equivalences between the tarot cards and astrological values, enabling the querent to fix a birth chart.[169] The structure of the Etteilla tarot can be seen in the diagram on the next page.

Unfortunately, it was difficult for Parisians to obtain tarot packs as the game had not been played there since late in the seventeenth century. Etteilla fulfilled the demand by buying packs in large numbers from card-makers and reselling them in Paris.[170] He lacked the funds to produce his own pack until 1788, when he formed the 'Société des Interprètes du Livre de Thot', a study group intent on unravelling the secrets of the 'Book of Thoth'.[171] The Etteilla tarot is still produced today by Grimaud-France.[172] There are few extant original packs though those that do exist correspond closely to the descriptions given by Etteilla.[173] The Enlightenment infatuation with creation myths and the belief that society was a corrupted version of a glorious original was obvious in Etteilla's deck, as was the rampant Egyptomania of the time. Though the exact sources of the symbolism are not clear, the deck does not closely resemble the Tarot de Marseille nor does it correspond to Court de Gébelin's descriptions of tarot.[174]

Etteilla Tarot Pack	Tarot de Marseille
1 *Etteilla* (*Le Questionnant* – male)	V *Le Pape* (Hierophant)
2 *Éclaircissement* (Clarification)	XVIIII *Le Soleil* (The Sun)
3 *Propos* (Intention)	XVIII *La Lune* (The Moon)
4 *Dépouillement* (Analysis)	XVII *L'Etoile* (The Star)
5 *Voyage* (Travel)	XXI *Le Monde* (The World)
6 *La Nuit* (The Night)	III *L'Impératrice* (The Empress)
7 *Appui* (Support)	IIII *L'Empereur* (The Emperor)
8 *Etteilla* (*La Questionnante* – female)	II *La Papesse* or *Junon* (The High Priestess)
9 *La Justice* (Justice)	VIII *La Justice* (Justice)
10 *La Tempérance* (Temperance)	XIIII *La Tempérance* (Temperance)
11 *La Force* (Strength)	XI *La Force* (Strength)
12 *La Prudence* (Prudence)	XII *Le Pendu* (The Hanged Man)
13 *Mariage* (Marriage)	VI *L'Amoreux* (The Lovers)
14 *Force Majeure* (Superior Force)	XV *Le Diable* (The Devil)
15 *Maladie* (Illness)	I *Le Bataleur* (The Magician)
16 *Le Jugement* (Judgment)	XX *Le Jugement* (Judgment)
17 *Mortalité* (Mortality)	XIII *La Mort* (Death)
18 *Traître* (Treachery)	VIIII *L'Ermite* (The Hermit)
19 *Misère* (Destitution)	XVI *La Maison de Dieu* (The House of God)
20 *Fortune* (Fortune)	X *La Roue de Fortune* (The Wheel of Fortune)
21 *Dissension* (Discord)	VII *Le Chariot* (The Chariot)
78 *Folie* (Madness)	*Le Mat* (The Fool)

Table 4: A comparison of Etteilla's tarot cards with the Tarot de Marseille tarot trumps.[175]

Jean-Baptiste Alliette died in 1791 at the age of fifty-three but had nominated his Lyonese student C. Hugand or Hugand-Jéjalel as his successor.[176] Hugand disappeared from view just three years later yet the tarots of Etteilla continued to be reproduced, altered and disseminated. Detlef Hoffmann and Erika Kroppenstedt writing in 1972, distinguished three distinct phases in the evolution of Etteilla's tarots otherwise known as 'Egyptian' tarots; these they designated Grand Etteilla I, II, and III. Grand Etteilla I referred to Etteilla's own pack and its immediate descendents.[177] A pack which was especially Egyptianised dates from 1845. In this deck, the King of Coins was represented by the legendary Egyptian king Seostris and the Queen of Coins by the Queen of Sheba.[178] Yet another pack housed in the British Museum boast cards 1 and 8 featuring an ancient Egyptian woman surrounded by divinatory implements. Other cards were labelled Osiris, Apis, Horus, Anubis and Isis. The court cards had acquired an Egyptian appearance and Egyptian names. In 1826, a deck with a Masonic flavour was released.[179] Though made using the original copper plates from which Etteilla's deck was produced, the corner symbols were rubbed off and Masonic names such as 'Hiram's Masonry', 'Solomon' and 'the Cup of Balthasar' were ascribed to the cards, a reflection of the popularity of Freemasonry in France.[180]

Grand Etteilla II alluded to the pack released in 1838 under the name of 'Grand livre de Thot' by Simon Blocquel. This deck did differ in some details from its predecessor but not greatly.[181] Temperance led an elephant and Prudence conformed to the more traditional depictions of that virtue by holding a mirror in her right hand and a book in her left.[182] The Chariot was replaced by a four-wheeled carriage boasting a canopy on which crescents were painted. A bearded man stood menacingly upon it.[183] The 'Grand jeu de l'Oracle des Dames' was known as the Grand Etteilla III in Hoffman and Kroppenstedt's classification scheme.[184] The deck was designed by G. Régamey and published by M.-F. Delarue, who was Blocquel's son-in-law.[185] Etteilla's designs were radically altered in order to produce a deck more in the neo-Gothic style.[186] These decks were purpose-made for divination with no expectation that they would be used for game playing; the restructuring and renumbering of the decks made them unsuitable for such a purpose. For example, the Fool (*Folie*) lost its status as a 'wildcard' and was counted as one of the trumps. Though Etteilla was responsible for making tarot popular as a divinatory device, it was magus Éliphas Lévi who incorporated tarot into his syncretistic schema of occult philosophies.

Éliphas Lévi

Éliphas Lévi (1810–1875) was perhaps the most important figure in the history of tarot in France and was largely responsible for the subsequent association of tarot with esotericism.[187] Born Alphonse-Louis Constant in Paris, he spent his early years attending a school for the poor before being encouraged to enter the junior seminary of Saint-Nicolas du Chardonnet at age fifteen, learning Hebrew, Greek and Latin.[188] Subsequently he entered the major seminary at Issy before continuing at Saint-Sulpice.[189] In 1833, he was ordained sub-deacon, vowing to maintain lifelong celibacy. Unfortunately, this challenge was to prove too great for the young man.

Placed in charge of a catechism class for young girls, he developed an amorous affection for one of his young charges, Adèle Allenbach.[190] Eight days before he was to be ordained a priest, he confessed his affections to his spiritual director who forbade him to continue until he was cured of his inappropriate feelings.[191] Constant left the seminary, never to become a priest.

In response to his departure and abandonment of his aspirations to priesthood, his mother committed suicide. Subsequently, his early career was varied and unstable but he worked as a writer, publishing numerous political and religious tracts.[192] In 1841, he published *La Bible de la liberté* (*The Bible of Liberty*) which was immediately seized by authorities. Consequently tried for sedition and for having travestied the Holy Scripture, he was found guilty and sentenced to imprisonment for eight months.[193] A few years later in 1846, he married Noémie Cadiot and the couple had a child, Marie.[194] The union was not destined to last and in 1853, Noémie left Constant. The blow was especially cruel as later in the year their daughter died.[195] It was not until 1852, when Constant met Paul Christian, Józef Maria Hoëne-Wronski and others interested in the occult, that there was any evidence of his interest in esotericism.[196] The year his wife left him, he adopted the Hebraic version of his name, Éliphas Lévi Zahed, the moniker so well-known to every subsequent generation of aspiring occultists.[197]

Éliphas Lévi undertook an intensive study of occult subjects such that the first book under his new name, *Dogme de la haute magie* released in instalments in 1854 and 1855, was published just two years after his initial interest in matters esoteric. It was soon followed by *Rituel de la haute magie* as the second volume of the two volume work, both being re-released in 1856.[198] Each volume consisted of twenty-two chapters, corresponding with the number of letters in the Hebrew alphabet and also to the number of tarot trumps. Some forty years later, British mystical occultist Arthur Edward Waite translated the works into English, garnering for Lévi the wrapt attention of English-speaking occultists around the world.[199]

Lévi was an advocate of high magic and his work became the channel through which the Western tradition of magic flowed through to the modern era.[200] Franz Anton Mesmer (1734–1815) first proposed the existence of a universal magnetic agent or astral light and Lévi made this belief central to his magical doctrines, though he preferred to attribute its discovery to Saint-Martin and Paracelsus.[201] He sought to amalgamate the work of all significant Western writers on magic to form a cohesive world-view.[202] Though Lévi was almost single-handedly responsible for the surge of interest in occultism in the nineteenth century, he achieved only a modest fame during his lifetime. For the most part, his teachings were consistent with conventional Christianity; therefore it was not necessary for his adherents to abandon their faith.[203] This was certainly one of the factors which made Lévi's teachings so popular. No one could say that his ideas were original yet his synthesis of kabbalah, alchemy, Hermeticism, astrology, magnetism and black magic into a coherent tradition was.[204] Tarot was a core component of this vast synthesis, the inspiration for its incorporation probably resting with Etteilla. Instead of copying the symbolism expressed by Etteilla in a pack that was only suitable for cartomancy, Lévi returned to earlier expressions of tarot, namely the Tarot de Marseille, restoring the symbolism and original order of the tarot trumps.[205]

Lévi expressed contempt for both the cartomancers and their practice of cartomancy.[206] Though he admitted that tarot was a perfect instrument of divination, he believed its most valuable purpose was that of conveying all the wisdom of the universe.[207] He believed it was unsurpassed as a means by which to contact higher intelligences.[208] Magic is resplendent with symbolism but lacks significant doctrinal content thus enabling its secrets to be encoded in a small volume such as a tarot deck.[209] The most significant doctrine is that of correspondences which is the belief that one thing can be used to influence another, based on their relationship to one another.[210] Hence, symbols could be used to alter or manipulate something else and as such, were incorporated by Lévi into the complex fabric of his magical system. Etteilla had associated tarot symbolism with the Hermetic books; Lévi sought to disengage the cartomancer's influence by associating the tarot trumps with the letters of the Hebrew alphabet and hence with kabbalah, something hinted at by both Court de Gébelin and Comte de Mellet.[211]

Éliphas Lévi asserted that tarot had been known to all the nations of the ancient world, yet its association with kabbalah must have necessitated its origins in a Jewish state.[212] This would have been extremely unlikely as Jews were forbidden to use representational images as it contravened the First Commandment.[213] Instead, they would have been more likely to dress the cards with the Hebrew letters or numbers.[214] The seeming improbability of a Jewish origin for tarot was readily overlooked not just by Lévi himself but also by his followers. In Lévi's magical system, it was impossible to separate kabbalah from tarot or to understand one without the other.[215] However, there were two main problems. The first was the difficulty in determining the order of the tarot trumps aligned with the Hebrew letters.[216] Court de Gébelin and Comte de Mellet had reversed the trump order to accommodate their schemes. Lévi however, reverted to the original sequencing with the first letter *Aleph* associated with trump I, the Magician.[217] The second problem lay with the numbering of the Fool. In the Tarot de Marseille, the card was unnumbered but Lévi elected to place the trump between Judgment (XX) and the World (XXI). Frequently, he numbered it XXI and renumbered the World XXII.[218]

For Lévi, the kabbalah enabled the greatest synthesis of all of his rational, spiritual and mystical ideas, yet there is no evidence that he ever studied with Jewish kabbalists; the source of his information appears to be pseudo-kabbalistic commentaries such as Knorr von Rosenroth's *Kabbala Denudata.*[219] He also read works by Jakob Böhme, Emmanuel Swedenborg, Louis-Claude Saint-Martin and Fabre D'Olivet.[220] The most significant kabbalistic text that he was to use was *Oedipus Aegyptiacus* by Athanasius Kircher (1602–1680).[221] Kircher was a Jesuit priest who studiously searched for doctrines that anticipated Christian theology. Believing that Ham was the antecedent of the Egyptians, he stated that they had been the true custodians of kabbalah.[222] Kircher aligned the letters of the Hebrew alphabet and the Latin translations of the names of these letters, with the entire Renaissance cosmos of angels, zodiacal signs, planets and elements.[223] This alignment, rather than being a product of Jewish mystics, was conceived by Christians in the tradition of Pseudo-Dionysius and Saint Ambrose. Kircher's scheme was derived from that of Francesco Giorgio's *De Harmonia mundi* (*On the Harmony of the World*) printed in 1525.[224] It was significant that Lévi remained enamoured of Kircher's work, even though so much of it was discredited subsequent to the translation of hieroglyphics.[225]

Lévi associated each Hebrew letter and the relevant correspondences from Kircher's table with a tarot trump, so that *Aleph* corresponded with trump I (the Magician), *Beth* with trump II (the Priestess) and so on. Of the twenty-two letters, five also have 'final forms' when they occur at the end of words. Instead of associating a different trump with each form, Lévi linked two planets to trump XIII (Death) but failed to maintain consistency by only associating the Sun with Temperance.[226] Trump XV (the Devil) was associated with Mercury in this scheme and Lévi made this connection explicit by depicting the Devil with a caduceus, generally associated with Mercury.[227]

In fact, Lévi's depictions of the Chariot and the Devil were particularly interesting examples of eighteenth-century French tarot. Lévi became familiar with the doctrine of correspondences, which was popularised by Emmanuel Swedenborg, while he was serving an eleven-month jail term.[228] Swedenborg was highly influential on French society during the Enlightenment and especially so on Éliphas Lévi.[229] His influence was explicit on the card of the Chariot which bore the numeral seven as well as the Hebrew letter *Zain.* The French infatuation with all things Egyptian was evident in the transformation of the winged horses into Egyptian sphinxes. The Hindu symbol of the lingam decorated the front of the chariot, generally representative of the French fascination with India and Hinduism, coupled with the belief that India was also the repository of arcane knowledge.[230]

Sephiroth	Letters	Hononyms	Cosmic Ranks
1	*Aleph*	*doctrina*	Seraphim
2	*Beth*	*domus*	Cherubim
3	*Gimel*	*plenitudo*	Thrones
4	*Daleth*	*porta*	Dominations
5	*He*	*ecce*	Powers
6	*Vau*	*uncus*	Virtues
7	*Zain*	*arma*	Principalities
8	*Heth*	*vita*	Archangels
9	*Teth*	*Bonus*	Angels
10	*Yod*	*viri fortes*	Heroes
	Kaph	*manus*	First Motion
	Kaph final		Fixed Stars
	Lamed	*disciplina*	SATURN
	Mem	*ex ipsis*	JUPITER
	Mem final		MARS
	Nun	*sempiternum*	SUN
	Nun final		VENUS
	Samekh	*adiutorium*	MERCURY
	Ayin	*fons, oculus*	MOON
	Pe	*os*	soul
	Pe final		spirit
	Tzaddi	*iustitia*	matter
	Tzaddi final		the four elements
	Qoph	*vocatio*	mineral
	Resh	*caput*	vegetable
	Shin	*dentes*	animal
	Tau	*signum*	microcosm (human)

Table 5: A table of correspondences to Hebrew letters formulated by Athanasius Kircher. Planetary spheres were arranged according to their supposed distance above the earth, from Saturn to the Moon as the closest.[231]

Lévi's Devil was depicted as Baphomet, the demon allegedly worshipped by the Knights Templar. The exact nature or even the existence of a belief in Baphomet has never been conclusively demonstrated. The demon has been variously described as a cat, a skull or even a head with three faces.[232] On Lévi's trump, it takes a humanoid form with a goat's head and cloven hooves. Michael Ramsay and Christopher Love originated the idea that the Knights Templar possessed secret knowledge from the Temple that they had discovered in the Holy Land. This knowledge was said to have been

Figure 14: Lévi's Baphomet as the Devil in *Dogme et rituel de la haute magie.*

suppressed by both the Catholic Church, who had brought the Templars before the Inquisition, and the French Royal family, whose antecedent Philip the Fair had instigated the Inquisitorial process in an effort to clear his considerable debts to the military order.[233] On the Devil card, the presence of Baphomet suggested the idea of wisdom from the Holy Land. Baphomet pointed to the ground and the sky, recalling the wisdom legendarily inscribed on the Emerald Tablet, 'As above, so below' a direct reference to the idea of the microcosm echoing the macrocosm, an allusion to the doctrine of correspondences. As mentioned previously, the caduceus was a reference to Levi's assignation of correspondences derived from Kircher's, itself a reference to the *Corpus Hermeticum* and Hermes Trismegistus; the caduceus being associated with Mercury who was usually associated with Thoth. Lévi's reverence for Egyptian lore was further evidenced by his description of trump II (the High Priestess) as Isis, his Wheel (trump X) being surmounted by a sphinx and the promotion of the Juggler (trump I) to Magus, keeper of the doctrine of Hermeticism. As with the Devil, he pointed to the sky and to the ground: 'As above, so below.'[234]

In the minor arcana portion of the tarot deck, Lévi declined to explain the significance of the court cards.[235] Instead he provided a scant couplet:

KING, QUEEN, KNIGHT, ESQUIRE
The married pair, the youth, the child, the race;
Thy path by these to Unity retrace.[236]

There was no clue as to what function the cards would play or what they represented beyond the family unit. Lévi wrote that the four suits corresponded to the four cherubim which in turn were associated with the four parts of the Assyrian Sphinx.[237] Other correspondences were also attributed to the suits. The numeral cards Ace to ten were associated with the ten *sephiroth* of the Tree of Life: (1) Crown, (2) Wisdom, (3) Intelligence,

(4) Mercy, (5) Justice, (6) Beauty, (7) Conquest, (8) Triumph, (9) Foundation and (10) Kingdom.[238]

Suit-Signs	Cherub/Sphinx	Zodiac	Elements	Essences	Divine Name
Batons	lion	Leo	fire	sulphur	Yod
Cups	man	Aquarius	water	mercury	He
Swords	eagle	Scorpio	air	azoth	Vau
Coins	bull	Taurus	earth	salt	He

Table 6: Correspondences associated with tarot suit signs
according to Éliphas Lévi.[239]

In Lévi's book, *La Clef des grands mystères* (*The Key to the Great Mysteries*) published in 1861, he changed the astrological correspondences to those of the *Sefer Yeṣirah*, though he still maintained the trumps' association with the Hebrew letters. Éliphas Lévi, though he described the tarot trumps as he thought they should be, never produced a tarot deck yet his theories informed most subsequent interpretations of the deck.[240] In addition, he integrated tarot into the western magical tradition by associating the letters of the Hebrew alphabet with the tarot trumps. He died alone and in poverty on May 31 1875, an unfinished translation of the *Vision of Ezekiel* upon his desk.[241] The realisation of Lévi's dream of a rectified tarot had to wait until 1889, when a great admirer of Lévi's and founder of the Ordre Kabbalistique de la Rose-Croix, Stanislas de Guaïta, encouraged the Swiss occultist Oswald Wirth to restore the twenty-two arcana of the tarot to their hieroglyphic purity.[242]

Papus

The next tarotist of significance was Gérard-Anaclet-Vincent Encausse. Born in 1865 in the port city of La Coruña in Spain, Encausse and his family relocated to Paris in 1868. He studied medicine from 1885 but in tandem with his medical studies, developed an interest in the occult, reading the works of Éliphas Lévi in the Bibliothèque Nationale.[243] In 1887, he joined the Isis lodge of the Theosophical Society which had been established by Helena Blavatsky herself.[244] It was here that he first referred to himself as 'Papus': a term applied to one of the 'genii of the first hour' by Lévi and signifying 'physician'. From this time, Papus wrote prolifically on all aspects of the occult but also on medical and more mundane topics.[245] In his fifty-one years he was credited with having written some 260 titles.[246]

Figure 15: Lévi's Chariot as portrayed in
Dogme et rituel de la haute magie.

The Hermetic Brotherhood of Luxor was an international group that focused its attention on practical occultism and was to be the next organisation to attract Papus. By 1890, he had completely broken with the Theosophical Society at that time racked by serious internal dissent.[247] Papus had a passion for joining occult societies and this tendency was further evidenced by his election as Grand Master for life of the Martinist Order, established by Louis-Claude Saint-Martin and resurrected by Papus and his associates.[248] He was also a founding member of the Ordre Kabbalistique de la Rose-Croix created by Stanislas de Guaïta (1861–1897).[249] Papus established the Groupe Indépendant d'Études Ésotérique (Independent Group for Esoteric Studies) in December 1889 and it was from this group that he drew many candidates for his more secret Martinist and Rosicrucian orders.[250] The Hermetic Order of the Golden Dawn was an English Rosicrucian society which was established by Dr William Wynn Westcott, Samuel Liddell MacGregor Mathers and Dr William Robert Woodman in London in 1888.[251] By 1894, the Ahathoor Temple of the organisation was consecrated in Paris and Papus joined it the following year.[252] Papus was possessed of enormous energy and drive, writing prolifically and actively engaged in several occult societies; it was this that won him the respect of his fellow occultists.[253]

Papus released his premier work on tarot, *Le Tarot de Bohémiens*, in 1889; significant as it was the first systematic interpretation of tarot by a disciple of Lévi.[254] The book was illustrated by cards from the Tarot de Marseille deck but also with the trumps from Oswald Wirth's deck which was released in the same year.[255] Papus allowed for an Egyptian origin of the tarot deck, calling it the 'book of Thoth Hermes Trismegistus' but also the 'book of Adam, it is the book of the primitive Revelation of the ancient civilisations', eloquently demonstrating the Enlightenment predilection for syncretism.[256] He applied many spurious and inconsistent schemes to derive correspondences between both the major and minor arcana cards and the letters of the sacred name of God (*Yod-He-Vau-He*).[257] Papus drew much of his material from Lévi's *Clef des grands mystères*, which utilised the *Sefer Yeṣirah* instead of Kircher's *Oedipus Aegypticus* but again the correspondences between the planets and the tarot trumps were awkward and inconsistent.[258] He frequently cited Hindu doctrine and drew numerous correspondences between the Trinity of the Father, Son and the Holy Ghost, of the Trimurti of Brahma, Śiva and Viṣṇu and the triumvirate of Osiris, Isis and Horus.[259]

Papus applied three meanings to each trump: a Divine Meaning in the Divine World; a Magic Astral meaning in the Human World; and a Physical meaning in the Natural World. For example, the Juggler (Magician) represented God in the Divine World; Adam in the Human World; and the Active Universe in the Natural World.[260] The meanings of the cards were supposed to be derived from their correspondences yet they were often clearly derived from their pictorial symbolism as displayed on the Tarot de Marseille pack.[261]

As the nineteenth century drew to a close, there was an increasing trend away from the magical use of the tarot and a renewed emphasis on its divinatory aspects, and Papus was happy to capitalise on this new fashion.[262] He published *Le Tarot divinatoire: clef du tirage des cartes et des sorts* in 1909 which was entirely devoted to cartomancy, an occupation he primarily associated with women.[263] The book contained none of the complex calculations and correspondences that were evident in *Tarot des Bohémiens*, instead it was primarily a collection of other people's theories.[264] Appended to this new book were the designs for all seventy-eight of the tarot cards designed by Gabriel Goulinat.[265] The cards themselves had extremely wide margins to accommodate a variety of symbols. Each had an Arabic numeral at the top. The trumps were sequenced according to Lévi's scheme with the Fool bearing the number '0'.[266] In the left margin of the tarot trumps was a Roman letter(s) labelled 'Français'. Below that sat a Hebrew letter, then a Sanskrit letter and finally an Egyptian hieroglyph.[267] In the bottom margin of the card were written three meanings: spiritual, moral or alchemical, and physical though they did not correspond with those supplied in *Le Tarot de Bohémiens*.[268] The right-hand margin accommodated the name of a constellation of the zodiac or a planet, its symbol and the date on which the Sun entered it. The designs were altered to be more Egyptian yet generally they resembled Etteilla's original pack.[269] Papus died in 1916 from tuberculosis.[270] Perhaps his greatest service to the occult tarot was his systematic analysis of Lévi's work.[271] As with Lévi, his work was syncretistic; Hinduism, kabbalah, astrology and most prominently Egyptian motifs and lore, all found a place within his complex system of correspondences.

For over a hundred years from the last decades of the eighteenth century, the major tarotists were all French and completely oblivious to the original Italian tarocchi. They were also largely ignorant of the fact that the pattern of the Tarot de Marseille was just one among countless variations.[272] The most serious oversight, however, was their ignorance of the original ordering of the tarot sequence, remaining completely unaware that several variations existed. This was significant as the order of the trumps was crucial to their esoteric theories connected with kabbalah.[273]

Tarot has proven to be a clear lens through which to view the cultural currents of Enlightenment France from the end of the eighteenth century to the very beginning of the twentieth. Among its tarot trumps, the passion for finding commonalities between Christianity, Eastern religion (particularly Hinduism) and classical sources is evident. So is the desperate appeal of a lost Golden Age, so beguiling to a nation racked by strife, war and the fall of the Church. Emperor Napoleon fanned the flames of Egyptomania, already present in the occult community through the pages of the *Corpus Hermeticum*. This wisdom was given a new form in the cards of the tarot deck; its imagery resplendent with sphinxes, Nile queens and animal-headed deities. Various other esoteric streams such as kabbalism, Freemasonry and astrology, their popularity the result of the Counter-Enlightenment with its rejection of rationalist thought, similarly found their way into the complex and intriguing imagery of tarot. By the time the twentieth century dawned, tarot's transformation from a game into an esoteric device was complete, signalled by the permanent incorporation of the Fool into the grouping of tarot trumps. The next development in occult tarot took place across the channel, in Victorian England, where a largely unstable but always interesting, esoteric society called the Hermetic Order of the Golden Dawn was being established. The ramifications of this difficult birth are still being felt in occult and New Age circles the world over.

5

Across the Channel to England

It was during the French Occult Revival that tarot first became associated with esotericism, ritual magic and divination. Éliphas Lévi and Gérard Encausse incorporated the tarot trumps into a complex system of correspondences, linking them to the zodiacal signs, the Hebrew alphabet and all manner of esoteric schemes. Across the Channel in Victorian England, occultism was also gaining wide appeal but it would take some time before tarot became an integral component of this milieu. The development of esoteric tarot was intimately connected with a prominent Rosicrucian society, the Hermetic Order of the Golden Dawn. Embedded in its teachings were most of the currents that informed the occult worldview including Freemasonry, Egyptian magic, Hermeticism, the Celtic Revival and Christian mysticism. All of these traditions found expression in tarot symbolism.

Increased industrialisation, agricultural productivity and social welfare reforms meant that people were increasingly able to engage in more worldly pursuits such as the acquisition of wealth and to foster an interest in scientific advancement. In tandem with this fascination with materialism came a neglect of the spiritual aspects of existence. Eventually, there was a backlash against this cupidity and the intelligentsia embraced superstitious belief and occultism.[1] By the time Éliphas Lévi came to London in 1854, England was already beginning to show an enthusiasm for spiritualism.[2] Certainly by the 1880s, religious sects and spiritual groups were rife in the nation. The occult offered a new philosophy and a new faith.[3] Though it tended to attract a lunatic fringe, the core philosophies helped restore humankind to the centre of the universe. Many books about occultism became available and were in wide circulation including Lévi's *Mysteries of Magic* and Cornelius Agrippa's *Occult Philosophy*.[4]

The desire for a worldview that could comfortably accommodate science and metaphysics led to the creation of the Society for Psychical Research, an organisation which sought to empirically prove the existence of ghosts and other supernatural entities.[5] This study barely concealed the religious yearnings of its members; no longer able to accept the narrow constraints of

Christianity, yet needing to believe in something beyond the mundane. The Society was founded in 1882 by a group of Oxford dons centred around Henry Sidgwick and Frederic Myers.[6] In an address to the Synthetic Society, Sidgwick stated: 'Probably there never was a time when the amount of beliefs held by an average educated person, undemonstrated and unverified by himself, was greater than it is now.'[7] He was not talking about supernatural or religious beliefs; he was referring to science which he believed had an illicit authority in the minds of people. Though he did not discount the achievements and discoveries of science, he did dispute it as the sole intellectual authority worthy of consideration.[8]

Though some occultists sought to scientifically prove the stuff of religion, others used science to their own ends. Published in 1859, Charles Darwin's *On the Origin of the Species by Means of Natural Selection* immediately caused heated debate between the scientists who embraced the theory and those who believed in the literal truth of Genesis.[9] Carl Vogt, a scientist with an extreme view of materialism, vociferously stated that science had demolished religion, God and the realm of spirit.[10] In 1867, he released a book entitled *Microcephali* in which he described the skulls and behaviour of idiots as belonging to an earlier stage of humankind's evolution.[11] But as Vogt looked backward and saw humans as the descendants of apes, so the occultists looked forward and saw humankind evolving towards a more spiritual future. This modified and elaborated theory of spiritual evolution was also intertwined with that of reincarnation. For example, in Madame Blavatsky's *Anthrogenesis* from the *Secret Doctrine*, humankind was described as being descended from spiritual beings from another planet who took physical form and then attempted to evolve spiritually through a series of rebirths on different planets.[12]

The Nature of British Occultism

A British fascination with foreign cultures was facilitated by improved transport and communication, the ease of reproducing books and pamphlets, and the development of the disciplines of anthropology and archaeology. Topping this list of exotic cultures was that of Egypt. Even though the Rosetta Stone and hence hieroglyphics had been translated, Victorian society remained infatuated with all things Egyptian. One of the reasons was the extensive archaeological excavations that had taken place, exposing the grandeur and sophistication of Egyptian civilisation.[13] For occultists, Egyptian mythology held the double appeal of novelty and antiquity.[14] The British Museum, established by an Act of Parliament in 1756, possessed an impressive collection of Egyptian antiquities built upon a group of artefacts assembled by Dr Hans Sloane and the collection of travellers Colonel William Lethieullier and Pitt Lethieullier.[15] The collection was further bolstered by the surrender of the Rosetta Stone and other artefacts by the French after their defeat by the British in Egypt in 1801.[16] E. A. Wallis Budge, the Keeper of the Egyptian and Assyrian Antiquities in the British Museum from 1894 until 1924, obtained many artefacts for the British Museum including cuneiform tablets, papyri and other manuscripts.[17] His output of published works exceeded that of any other Egyptologist. His *Book of the Dead: The Hieroglyphic Transcript into English of the Papyrus of Ani* published in 1895 was to be enormously influential with British occultists. Another reason for Egypt's popularity was the Biblical narrative of the sojourn of the Israelites in Egypt and many still believed in the literal truth of the Bible. In addition, Egypt figured prominently in the works of classical historians and a person was not considered educated without some knowledge of the classics. This interest was fanned by the relative ease with which the Nile and the Egyptian monuments could be explored. Finally, the discoveries made in the relatively new discipline of Egyptology, including the ability to decipher hieroglyphics, aroused controversy and interest.[18]

It was not just cultures geographically remote that were appealing, cultures temporally remote were also fascinating, especially when they could be put to use to secure political advantage. The rediscovery or more correctly, the formulation of Britain's Celtic heritage came to be known as the 'Celtic Revival'. In addition to Ireland and Scotland, this movement embraced Brittany, Cornwall, and Wales and even the Isle of Man.[19] At first, the reform was centred on a concern for injustice and neglect, even so it was difficult for the political reformers to rally those they intended to help. The people of Ireland and Scotland did not have a sense of 'country' to unify them. They did not have the prophets to rally around and support them. Scottish and Irish Nationalists looked to the writers of the Celtic Revival to fill this role. The politicians and writers themselves looked to the work of folklorists who collected and analysed every scrap of information in a disinterested and supposedly rational way. Yet the scholars were trying to escape the immense pressures of the nineteenth century by escaping into a time perceived to be simpler and less rushed. Certainly, this was also true of the audience that enthusiastically consumed their work.[20]

Interestingly, the Celtic people came to be associated with witches, hobgoblins and other magical folk: many books were published on second sight and witchcraft. Andrew Lang, a psychical researcher and folklorist, insisted that the evidence of psychic research could be supplemented by collections of Celtic superstitions.[21] Folklorists became obsessed with tales of ghosts and supernatural occurrences and this gave a decidedly occultist bent to portrayals of Celtic society. Consequently, occultists incorporated Celtic deities and spirit beings into their rituals and doctrines, themselves playing a prominent role in the Celtic Revival.[22] Writer and occultist William Butler Yeats was one such person; his occult interests, political activism and literary output, overlapping to an extent that is largely unappreciated even today.

For many like Yeats, their first experience of occult philosophies was through the Theosophical Society. The Society was founded in 1875 in New York by Helena Petrovna Blavatsky, a mystically inclined Russian-born noblewoman and Colonel Henry Steel Olcott.[23] It endeavoured to unify Eastern and Western esoteric traditions into one world-embracing spiritual philosophy. It was also an attempt to reconcile the increasing dominance of the scientific paradigm with metaphysical belief.[24] The Society's focus on the east was to find a warm reception as Buddhism had come to exist in the Oriental libraries and institutes of the west. Western scholars knew what Buddhism should be and 'was'.[25] The objects of the Theosophical Society reflected the sometimes conflicting ideals of Modernism with its curiosity about other cultures, the increasing role of science, in this case applied to the investigation of occult phenomena, and the ambiguous role and nature of God. The objects of the Society were as follows:

1. The formation of a universal brotherhood without distinction of race, creed, sex, caste or colour.
2. The encouragement of studies in comparative religion, philosophy and science.
3. The investigation of unexplained laws of nature and the powers latent in man.[26]

In 1878, Olcott and Blavatsky set sail for India, supposedly at the behest of the hidden Masters: mysterious beings who Blavatsky claimed had tutored her in the esoteric arts on the astral plane.[27] They relocated the headquarters of the Theosophical Society to Adyar and it was here that Blavatsky met the editor of *Pioneer*, an influential Anglo-Indian newspaper.[28] His name was Alfred Percy Sinnett and he was to share Blavatsky's vision, popularising the synthesis of western occultism with eastern ideas.[29] In his scheme, Christ was demoted to just one of a number of great teachers that had appeared throughout history.[30] In a similar vein, Blavatsky wrote *Isis Unveiled* in 1877 and *The Secret Doctrine* in 1888.[31] The works expounded a revival of the idea of the *philosophia perennis*, the belief that all phenomena arose from an eternal, underlying principle which was fundamentally spiritual and was conspicuously manifested in individual enlightened souls.[32] Her verbose and largely plagiarised writings were strongly infused with eastern material and constituted an uneasy amalgam of Hindu *Vedānta*, Buddhism and Western esotericism underpinned by contemporary ideas of evolution.[33] In *The Secret Doctrine*, Blavatsky had claimed that modern tarot was a debased version of the original, found in the Babylonian cylinders ... antediluvian rhombs.'[34] This was an allusion to a variety of bullroarer or top called an *inyx*, which the Chaldeans used in ritual magic.[35] However, there was no evidence to suggest that there was anything Chaldean depicted in tarot symbolism.

Madame Blavatsky moved to London in 1887 and continued her work there with several young Theosophists; the London branch of the Society having being established there in 1883.[36] There tended to be a strong Eastern bias within the Society which began to cause dissatisfaction among the members. Some wished to study and practise Hermeticism, kabbalah, alchemy and an esoteric version of Christianity.[37] In 1883, some members of the London Lodge, among them the president of the Lodge, Dr Anna B. Kingsford, published a pamphlet entitled *A letter addressed to the fellows of the London Lodge of the Theosophical Society, by the president and a vice-president of the Lodge.* In this pamphlet they criticised Alfred Percy Sinnett's book, *Esoteric Buddhism*, which purported to be a summary of the teachings of Theosophy. Kingsford and Edward Maitland (the vice-president of the Lodge), proposed that two Sections be created; one to be formed by those who wanted to follow the teachings of the Tibetan Mahatmas under the leadership of Sinnett, and the other to extend research into other areas such as the study of Esoteric Christianity and Occidental Theosophy.[38] The tension between the 'western' and the 'eastern' factions within the London Lodge developed into a heated quarrel between Sinnett and Kingsford and their supporters. Blavatsky had to intervene, but in the end it became clear that the only solution was to follow Kingsford's and Maitland's proposal to found a Hermetic Lodge.[39]

Members wanted to be members of both lodges but this was prohibited by Olcott. Instead Anna Kingsford was induced to return her charter and very soon the Hermetic Lodge of the Theosophical Society became an independent organisation called the Hermetic Society.[40] One of Anna Kingsford's admirers was MacGregor Mathers, who dedicated his book *The Kabbalah Unveiled* to her and Edward Maitland.[41] Mathers met Anna Kingsford and through her Madame Blavatsky. He joined both the Hermetic Society and the Theosophical Society, and advised Blavatsky about some of the kabbalistic theories she discussed in the *Secret Doctrine.* He and William Wynn Westcott lectured for the Hermetic Society on various kabbalistic and Hermetic subjects.[42] When Kingsford died in the spring of 1888, Westcott had realised that the Hermetic Society was finished. He turned instead to the construction of a more practical and far more ambitious project—the creation of a body that combined occult teaching with a series of linked rituals based upon the stages of the kabbalistic Tree of Life.[43] Undoubtedly the Hermetic Order of the Golden Dawn, a society so intimately connected with the development of esoteric tarot, derived its subjects of study and its androgynous nature from the Hermetic Society.[44]

The structure and organisation of many occult societies, especially the Theosophical Society and the Golden Dawn, were modelled on those of esoteric Freemasonry. 'Fringe Rites' was the term given to those elements within Freemasonry which explored the esoteric constituents of the Western tradition. These rites blossomed from 1845, two years after the death of Augustus Frederick, the Duke of Sussex and Grand Master of the Grand Lodge of England since 1813.[45] The Rites that were recognised became known as additional or side Degrees because they were outside the Craft and not administered by the United Grand Lodge of England. These Degrees were tolerated so long as they did not claim to 'make or initiate Masons.'[46] Many Masonic occultists immersed themselves in these Fringe Rites though many, including acclaimed mystic Arthur Edward Waite, remained sceptical of their value. There was little doubt that the Fringe Rites impacted on the establishment of the Golden Dawn just as Freemasonry influenced its structure.[47]

A Freemasonic organisation of particular interest was the *Societas Rosicruciana in Anglia*. The history of this organisation was almost as mysterious as that of the Golden Dawn but appeared to have been derived from Scottish Freemasonry and allegedly from Éliphas Lévi via English occultist Kenneth Mackenzie.[48] It was founded in 1867 by Robert Wentworth Little apparently upon the basis of manuscripts found in Freemasons' Hall.[49] Only Master Masons could join the Society in spite of it being described as non-Masonic in its quarterly publication, *The Rosicrucian,* in 1871. Members had to be Masons as Rosicrucians and Masons shared certain secrets.[50] It is certain that the *Societas Rosicruciana in Anglia* exerted considerable influence upon the emerging Golden Dawn.[51] The three founders of the new order were also members of the *Societas Rosicruciana in Anglia* with both Dr Woodman and Dr Westcott achieving the office of Supreme Magus at different times.[52] Dr Woodman would be only a minor player in the history of the Golden Dawn, with Westcott and Mathers determining the direction of the Order's progress.

William Wynn Westcott

Dr William Wynn Westcott (1848–1925) led a double life as a respectable medical professional and clandestinely as a dedicated occultist. Upon graduation from medical school in 1871, he joined his Uncle's practice in Somerset, the same year he became a Freemason.[53] Though fully versed in the natural sciences, he was attracted to esoteric knowledge and in 1879 took a two year sabbatical to study the Hermetic sciences, kabbalah, alchemy and the lore of the Rosicrucians.[54] In 1880, he became Deputy Coroner for the Crown in North-East London and in due course became the Coroner for the district, holding office until 1918.[55] In 1886, he joined the Hermetic Society founded by Anna Kingsford.[56]

As already mentioned, Dr Westcott was a leading member of the *Societas Rosicruciana in Anglia* and was an associate of Madame Blavatsky.[57] He translated the *Sefer Yeṣirah* and the *Chaldean Oracles of Zoroaster* into English and combined a profound knowledge of magic, the early history of chess and the Enochian system of John Dee. Many years later, infamous magician Aleister Crowley stated that Westcott's interest in corpses was more than just a medical one, implying that Westcott dabbled in necromancy, though there was no evidence to support this assertion.[58]

In 1886, William Westcott sketched the tarot trumps. Though he did not include trump titles on his cards, he followed the Tarot de Marseille order and used recognisable subjects. He was clearly indebted to both Etteilla and the works of Éliphas Lévi. The margins of the trumps contained cursive inscriptions probably paralleling the kabbalistic realms of *Atziluth* (Emanation), *Briah* (Creation), *Yeṣirah* (Formation) and *Assiah* (Manifestation). In Westcott's theme, the equivalent terms were 'Divine World' (accommodated in the top margin), 'Celestial World' (in the bottom margin), 'Intellectual World' (in the right margin) and 'Terrestrial World (in the left margin).[59] These terms encapsulated the allegorical meanings that Lévi elaborated for the trump sequence. The captions in the right margins reduced to number symbolism relying on the numbers usual in the Tarot de Marseille. The inscriptions in the bottom margins were associated with the astrological correspondences as revealed by Lévi's reading of the *Sefer Yeṣirah*.[60] Following the kabbalistic theme, the bodies of the trumps contained the Hebrew letters as ascribed by Lévi, with *Aleph* corresponding to the first trump, *Shin* for the Fool and *Tau* for the World.[61]

The twenty-two chapters of Lévi's *Rituel de la haute magie* alluded to the corresponding twenty-two trump cards. In the final chapter, Lévi summarised the tarot symbolism for each trump and it was this that provided the inspiration for Westcott's trump imagery.[62] The symbolism was most different when Lévi's description was vague or inadequate and where Etteilla's deck lacked the standard trump. In such instances, Westcott failed to return to the common ancestral deck of the Tarot de Marseille.[63] He also wrote on tarot in his short treatise *Tabula Bembina, sive Mensa Isiaca* in 1887, which discussed the 'Isaic Table' otherwise known as the 'Bembine Tablet of Isis'.[64] Again, his theories were largely based on those of Lévi but with some significant differences.[65] He attributed Hebrew letters to the tarot trumps as he did in his tarot sketches. He also cited the *Sefer Yeṣirah* for his astrological correspondences. Unlike Lévi, however, he did not associate planets with double letters.[66] The suits were associated with various quaternaries including the letters of the Sacred Name, the four cherubim (Lion, Man, Eagle and Bull) and the letters of INRI, the inscription on the Holy Cross.[67] The numeral cards were associated with the ten *sephiroth* in the four kabbalistic worlds. Divination was made possible by the symbolic meaning ascribed to each card, again derived from those of Lévi.[68]

Éliphas Lévi's most influential works, *Dogme de la haute magie* and *Rituel de la haute magie*, were published as complete volumes in 1856 and obviously proved to be immensely important in Westcott's rendering of the tarot trumps, as they were to occultism in England generally.[69] Westcott, however, was already primed for Lévi's influence: he had a profound interest in kabbalah, evidenced by his translation of the *Sefer Yeṣirah*, and in all manner of esoteric systems.[70] What was most significant about Westcott's early rendering and interpretation of the trumps was how they differed from those subsequent to the formation of the Hermetic Order of the Golden Dawn. This theme will be picked up again later in this chapter.

Westcott immigrated to South Africa in 1919 to do some work for the Theosophical Society, dying there from Bright's disease in 1925.[71] It is certain that Westcott's esoteric knowledge was at least as deep as that of his co-occultist and Golden Dawn co-founder MacGregor Mathers. This fact was never in dispute at the time but has often been suggested in more recent years, to the detriment of Westcott, by protagonists of Mathers who himself never doubted that in this field Westcott was his equal.[72]

S. L. Mathers

In contrast to Westcott, MacGregor Mathers embraced the persona and trappings of an occultist. The son of a London clerk, he was educated at Bedford Grammar School, subsequently living in Bournemouth with his widowed mother.[73] While still very young, he immersed himself in occult studies, becoming a Freemason in 1877 and translating three of the most important books from the Latin of Knorr von Rosenroth's monumental *Kabbalah Denudata*. Shortly after this, he produced an English version of the *Key of Solomon*, probably the most widespread of all the medieval *grimoires*.[74] By 1882, he had joined the esoterically specialised *Societas Rosicruciana in Anglia*, taking the motto of the Clan MacGregor, *'S Rioghail Mo Dhream* ('Royal is my Race'). This he kept as one of his Golden Dawn mottoes, the other being *Deo Duce Comite Ferro* ('With God as my Leader and Sword as my Companion').[75]

In the true spirit of the Celtic Revival, Mathers aspired to a proud Celtic heritage, wearing full Highland dress and adopting the name 'Samuel Liddell MacGregor Mathers'.[76] It was under this moniker that he published his first work on tarot, *The Tarot: Its Occult Signification, Use in Fortune-Telling and Method of Play*, in 1888.[77] This was to be the first book on tarot occultism to be released in the United Kingdom and it was sold together with an imported tarot pack.[78] The work was largely derived from the writings of Antoine Court de Gébelin, Etteilla, Éliphas Lévi, Paul Christian and Jean-Alexandre Vaillant.[79] As with Westcott, Mather's ideas of tarot would undergo a significant evolution subsequent to the establishment of the Golden Dawn.

When she was just twenty-two, Mina Bergson met MacGregor Mathers while studying Egyptian antiquities or in the Reading Room at the British Museum.[80] Mina was the daughter of a Polish Jew and the Irish-Jewish daughter of a Yorkshire doctor. MacGregor and Mina were married on June 16 1890 by the Reverend William A. Ayton, a clergyman, alchemist and Golden Dawn initiate.[81] As soon as she married, Mina changed her first name to Moïna; a Celtic variant she felt was much more suited to her totally new life and ideas.[82] Moïna was also to play a prominent part in the history of the Golden Dawn.

The Hermetic Order of the Golden Dawn

The Hermetic Order of the Golden Dawn arose in England towards the end of the nineteenth century as a reaction against the strict scientific rationalism and the shortcomings of conventional religion of the period. Although it never had more than 300 members, its influence far exceeded that of many larger occult groups. The Order was the crowning glory of the occult revival, synthesising into a coherent whole a vast body of disparate material including Egyptian mythology, kabbalah, tarot, Enochian magic, alchemy, Rosicrucianism and astrology. Suddenly anything was possible and everything was knowable; every mundane action and reaction could be reinterpreted in esoteric terms. People from all walks of life were attracted to the promise of power and knowledge, among them the three who would become the founders of the Golden Dawn – Dr William Wynn Westcott, Samuel Liddell MacGregor Mathers and Dr William Robert Woodman. The Order came into being on 20 March 1888.[83]

The rituals and learning of the Hermetic Order of the Golden Dawn were drawn from a mysterious manuscript of indefinite origin. It contained fifty-seven pages written in a strange cipher alphabet that was created by Abbot Johann Trithemius and appeared in his book *Polgraphiae et Universelle Escriture Cabalistique* published in 1499.[84] Once deciphered, the manuscript contained brief outlines of five previously unknown rituals of a Rosicrucian nature in English. Wynn Westcott, in the official history of the Golden Dawn, wrote that he obtained the Cipher Manuscript from the Reverend

Adolphus Frederick Alexander Woodford.[85] This was almost certainly a fabrication.

There were several theories as to the origin of the Cipher Manuscript. A popular version had the manuscript originating with a Jewish Masonic lodge in Frankfurt called the *Zur aufgehenden Morgenröte* ('Toward the Rising Dawn'), related to a French lodge called *Aurore naissante* ('Rising Dawn') into which the novelist Lord Bulwer-Lytton was initiated in the mid-1800s.[86] There were other possible sources for either the Cipher Manuscript or the ideas upon which it was based. One was the eighteenth century organisation called *Chabrah Zereh aur bokher* ('Society of the Shining Light of Dawn'), headed from 1810 by the kabbalist Johann Friedrich Falk.[87] Virginia Moore stated that whether the Manuscript was found in Westcott's library or in a bookstall in Farringdon Road was a matter of controversy. According to a William Butler Yeats typescript of 1923 (unpublished), the Cipher Manuscript had been discovered by Woodford on an old bookstall in 1884.[88]

Though Arthur Edward Waite was the first to suggest Kenneth Mackenzie (1833–1886) as the author of the Cipher Manuscript, Freemasonic scholar Robert Gilbert was the first to offer any convincing evidence.[89] Kenneth Mackenzie was the editor of the *Royal Masonic Encyclopedia* (1877). He had met the magician Éliphas Lévi in Paris, had studied his writings and was well read in continental works of alchemy and magic. Mackenzie died in July 1886 and Westcott obtained many ritual documents from his wife.[90] In a lecture to the Society for Psychical Research in London, Gilbert stated that the drawings in the Cipher Manuscript stylistically resembled those in manuscripts which were undoubtedly copied by Mackenzie.[91] Gilbert suggested that the rituals outlined in the manuscript were formulated for the 'Society of Eight', a mystical Society dedicated to practical esoteric work that began its short life in 1883. It was the brainchild of Frederick Holland, a fellow-member of the *Societas Rosicruciana in Anglia*.[92] The most significant objection to Gilbert's hypothesis was that the Society of Eight, being a Masonic organisation, could not initiate women. It clearly stated in the Neophyte Opening ritual contained in the Cipher Manuscript: 'Fratres and Sorores of this temple of the Golden Dawn assist me at opening the Grade of Neophyte' – *Fratres and Sorores* – Brothers and *Sisters*.[93]

Subsequently, Gilbert offered another opinion regarding the provenance of the Cipher Manuscript; suggesting that the rituals were intended for the Royal Oriental Order of the Sat B'hai.[94] Westcott's involvement with that Order was confirmed in a letter to F. L. Gardner dated the 5th of April 1912, whereby Westcott requested that after his death his Sat B'hai papers (among others) be passed to Thomas Pattison and Bogdan Edwards.[95] The Sat B'hai was a quasi-Masonic order, supposedly imported from India in 1872, that under certain conditions admitted women to its lower three degrees. In 1886, it was controlled by John Yarker, who offered its members a detailed program of esoteric studies to supplement a set of rather uninspiring rituals.[96] The Order was the creation of Captain James Henry Lawrence Archer of the Indian Army, though Kenneth Mackenzie did most of the leg work, having joined in April 1875. As with the Golden Dawn, there were three chiefs, in this instance called Apexes, who answered to the One Supreme Apex, equivalent to a Secret Chief. By 9 November 1877, Mackenzie had written descriptions of several of its ceremonies.[97] It was possible that these outlines formed the basis of the mysterious manuscript. Kenneth Mackenzie had a passion for joining occult societies and possessed a special talent for writing rituals. He was well versed in esoteric lore and had met Éliphas Lévi in Paris in 1861.[98] Though it is difficult to conclusively determine for which rite the rituals of the Cipher Manuscript were intended, it seems probable that they were created by Kenneth Mackenzie.

Once the Cipher Manuscript was deciphered, William Westcott based the grade structure of the Golden Dawn on the grade structure published in the book *Der Rosenkreuzer in seiner Blöße* ('*The Rosicrucian in his Nakedness*') by Magister Pianco.[99] The grade structure of the *Societas Rosicruciana in Anglia* was also derived from the work.[100] It differed in that the Order accepted women who were addressed as '*Soror*'.[101] The Golden Dawn was actually only the first or Outer Order of three orders. The *Ordo Rosae Rubeae et Aureae Crucis* (R. R. et A. C.) was the Second or Inner Order, while the Third Order remained unnamed to the uninitiated.[102] This Third Order was the realm of the guiding forces of the Order, the 'Secret Chiefs' or spiritual Masters whose mundane existence was hidden from all who had not yet proved themselves worthy.[103] Interestingly, all of the temples of the Golden Dawn were dedicated to Egyptian gods.[104]

It was a rigidly hierarchical secret society that taught the practice as well as the theory of occultism. On admission, members took a Latin motto as the name by which they would be known within the Order.[105] Advancement depended on initiates displaying both a theoretical and practical aptitude for occult studies. Progress in the Order involved a symbolic ascent of the kabbalistic Tree of Life through a series of initiatory rituals that had been worked up from the outlines given in the original Cipher Manuscript.[106] The Outer contained five stages, the Neophyte Grade and four higher Grades, which corresponded to the first four of the ten stages into which the Tree of Life is divided. The symbolism appropriate to each grade was largely kabbalistic with the addition of astrology, alchemy, divination, the tarot and Egyptian mythology. In each case, the grade was represented by a numerical shorthand in addition to its title.[107] The sequence ran thus:

Neophyte $0° = 0°$
Zelator $1° = 10°$ corresponding to the *Sephira Malkuth*
Theoricus $2° = 9°$ corresponding to the *Sephira Yesod*
Practicus $3° = 8°$ corresponding to the *Sephira Hod*
Philosophus $4° = 7°$ corresponding to the *Sephira Netzach*[108]

There are six more *sephiroth* on the Tree of Life but the Grades appropriate to them lay in the Second Order, the *Roseae Rubis et Aureae Crucis* and in the Third Order that lay beyond it. Only about one third of members advanced to the Second Order. A knowledge of tarot was required to achieve the grade of Zelator $(1° = 10°)$.[109] First, the tarot trumps were mentioned and then the four suits and their correspondences. The correspondences listed followed the French tradition as expounded by Etteilla: Wands = Diamonds; Cups = Hearts; Swords = Spades; and Coins (or Pentacles) = Clubs.[110]

A separate tarot lecture was also supplied to Golden Dawn initiates of the Practicus grade; its original form being among the folios of the Cipher Manuscript.[111] The trumps were referred to as 'atus or mansions of Thoth' though elsewhere in the manuscript they were called 'keys'.[112] In the knowledge required to attain the level of Philosophus, a table headed 'synonyms in tarot divination' listed the Hebrew letters, the corresponding tarot trumps with their names and numbers, corresponding pathways between the *sephiroth* of the Tree of Life, elements, planets and zodiacal signs.[113] The tarot lecture began by stating that the ten numeral cards of each suit represented the ten *sephiroth*, the suit signs corresponded to the four kabbalistic worlds and the court cards – sixteen in all – stood for the fourfold Tetragrammaton. The remainder of the lecture explained the correspondences between the trumps and the pathways between the *sephiroth* of the Tree of Life and subsequently, to the twenty-letters of the Hebrew alphabet. The letters were classified as three mother letters associated with the elements, seven doubles which were associated with the planets and twelve singles corresponding to the signs of the zodiac. Though Éliphas Lévi was the first to specifically associate the tarot trumps with the letters of the Hebrew alphabet, the Golden Dawn was the first to align correspondences between the pathways of the Tree of Life and the trumps. These 'attributions' – as they were called by the Golden Dawn – enabled the trumps to be interpreted kabbalistically.[114]

This theory of tarot attributions was at odds with all kabbalistic theories of tarot that had preceded it. It agreed with that of Lévi only as far as it advocated arranging the tarot trumps in ascending numerical order.[115] Lévi originally placed the Fool below the Universe in the twenty-second or zero position; he placed Justice in the eighth position and Strength in the eleventh. The author of the Cipher Manuscript elevated the Fool to the first position, with each of the following major arcana cards being shuffled down a path. This put the Lovers on the Path of Zain-Gemini (XVII). It didn't, however, put Justice on the Path of Lamed-Libra, so the author made the appropriate substitution.[116] Justice and Strength were swapped to ensure a more appropriate astrological correspondence.[117]

Hebrew letter	Éliphas Lévi	Cipher Manuscript
Aleph	I	0
Beth	II	I
Gimel	III	II
Daleth	IV	III
He	V	IV
Vau	VI	V
Zain	VII	VI
Heth	VIII	VII
Teth	IX	XI
Yod	X	IX
Kaph	XI	X
Lamed	XII	VIII
Mem	XIII	XII
Nun	XIV	XIII
Samekh	XV	XIV
Ain	XVI	XV
Pe	XVII	XVI
Tzaddi	XVIII	XVII
Qoph	XIX	XVIII
Resh	XX	XIX
Shin	0	XX
Tau	XXI	XXI

Table 7: Table of correspondences between the tarot trumps and the Hebrew letters according to Éliphas Lévi and according to the Cipher Manuscript.[118]

The author of the Cipher Manuscript utilised the *Sefer Yeṣirah* as had Lévi and Papus but because the correspondences between the Hebrew letters and the trumps were different, so were the correspondences between the planets, elements, zodiacal signs and the tarot trumps.[119] The new correspondences are explained in the following table.

Sefer Yeṣirah	Papus	Cipher Manuscript
Aleph (**air**)	I	0 (Mat/Fool)
Beth (PLANET)	II MOON	I (Pagad/Juggler) MERCURY
Gimel (PLANET)	III VENUS	II (High Priestess) MOON
Daleth (PLANET)	IV JUPITER	III (Empress) VENUS
He (Aries)	V	IV (Emperor)
Vau (Taurus)	VI	V (Hierophant)
Zain (Gemini)	VII	VI (Lovers)
Heth (Cancer)	VIII	VII (Chariot)
Teth (Leo)	IX	VIII (Justice)
Yod (Virgo)	X	IX (Hermit)
Kaph (PLANET)	XI MARS	X (Wheel) JUPITER
Lamed (Libra)	XII	XI (Strength)
Mem (**water**)	XIII	XII (Man Hanged)
Nun (Scorpio)	XIV	XIII (Death)
Samekh (Sagittarius)	XV	XIV (Temperance)
Ain (Capricorn)	XVI	XV (Devil)
Pe (PLANET)	XVII MERCURY	XVI (Tower) MARS
Tzaddi (Aquarius)	XVIII	XVII (Star)
Qoph (Pisces)	XIX	XVIII (Moon)
Resh (PLANET)	XX SATURN	XIX (Sun) SUN
Shin (**fire**)	0	XX (Angels)
Tau (PLANET)	XXI SUN	XXI (Universe) SATURN

Table 8: Correspondences as given in the *Sefer Yeṣirah*, by Papus
and in the Cipher Manuscript.[120]

Just before the Golden Dawn was founded, Mathers published *The Tarot:
Its Occult Signification, Use in Fortune-Telling and Method of Play* (1888),
and Westcott published *Tabula Bembina, sive Mensa Isiaca* (*The Isaic
Tablet of Cardinal Bembo)* (1887). Both books gave Lévi's attributions as if
they were correct.[121] From 1888 onwards, they both became convinced that
the Cipher Manuscript attributions were right and that Lévi had got it wrong
(perhaps deliberately, the real attributions being kept secret). This certainly
made it unlikely that either Westcott or Mathers authored the Cipher
Manuscript.[122]

There were five tarot trump designs given in the Cipher Manuscript: two
were in the Practicus section and three in the Philosophus section. These
tarot keys were displayed on the altar during initiations.[123] In the Practicus
section were illustrations of the Sun (XIX) and Judgment (XX).[124] In the
Philosophus section were sketches of the Moon (XVIII), the Star (XVII) and
the Tower (XVI).[125] In the Theoricus section, there was not a sketch of the
Universe (XXI) but a description:[126] 'Circle round Queen Isis = Sandalphon.

Bears wands. Has crossed [l]eis (should read "legs"— the cipher symbols for "i" and "g" were mirror images of each other, but otherwise identical)'.[127] The sketches of those tarot trumps were fairly rough, but the symbolism was very similar to that of the Tarot de Marseille deck with the exception of the Star and the Tower which bore additional glyphs.

The Golden Dawn system of magic was initially largely based on the writings of Éliphas Lévi and consisted of Hermeticism blended with kabbalah and supplemented by the new teachings concerning esoteric tarot and its complicated array of correspondences.[128] In the Golden Dawn, this body of knowledge was augmented by completely new information, mostly written by MacGregor Mathers.[129] Tarot achieved a prominent place within this summa of esoteric lore both as a divinatory device and as a part of magical practice.[130] Hence, the Golden Dawn initiates believed that tarot could not only be used to foretell the future, it could also influence it. This was why members had to be suitably instructed in its use.[131] The basis of this knowledge was found in the Cipher Manuscript as part of the knowledge required to achieve the grade of

Figure 16: The Moon card as represented in the Cipher Manuscript.

Practicus. Members were required to keep the information secret; believing they alone could correctly interpret the tarot.[132] Of course, this information did not remain hidden and forms the basis for nearly all modern tarot interpretation.[133]

In this system, trump I became the Magician, trump II was the High Priestess, trump V the Hierophant and XXI became the Universe. These names became almost universal in subsequent cartomantic tarot decks. When Mathers designed a tarot pack to be copied by Golden Dawn members, he renumbered the cards of Strength and Justice, originally swapped to better align them to their corresponding Hebrew letters. This numbering became very common in tarot decks, further evidence of the influence of the Golden Dawn on cartomancy.[134] Though Mathers did not inscribe the Hebrew letters on the corresponding trump cards, he did use the pathways between the *sephiroth* to assign divinatory meanings to the cards.[135] He also based their meanings on their astrological associations.[136]

Once a Golden Dawn initiate was ready to enter the *Roseae Rubis et Aureae Crucis*, he or she had to acquire the knowledge contained within a document known as *Book T.*[137] The contents were largely concerned with the court cards and numeral cards of the four suits, and was not derived from the

Cipher Manuscript.[138] The suit of Batons was renamed 'Wands' and the suit of Coins was renamed 'Pentacles'. Swords and Cups sometimes became 'Daggers' and 'Chalices'. Among the court cards, the Knight was recast as the King and the King was demoted to a Prince and placed in a chariot.[139] The Knave became a Princess. As in Lévi's scheme, Mathers aligned the name of God – *Yod-He-Vau-He* – to the court cards. In the kabbalah, each letter was designated a quality which corresponded to a role in the patriarchal family of old and these correspondences were transferred to the court cards of each suit. He also aligned the roles to the elements and to the suit signs.[140]

Yod	Father	Active, emitting	Kings [Knights]	**fire**	Wands
He	Mother	Passive, receiving	Queens	**water**	Cups
Vau	Masculine	Balancing	Princes [Kings]	**air**	Swords
He	Feminine	Rejuvenating	Princesses [Knaves]	**earth**	Pentacles

Table 14: Court card correspondences as described by Mathers in *Book T.*[141]

Mathers made the correspondences yet more complicated. He associated each numerical value of the card with a *sephirah*. For example, the Aces were associated the *Sephirah Kether* and the tens were linked with *Malkuth.*[142] He also associated the number cards – with the exception of the Aces – to the thirty-six decans of Egyptian astrology (four suits with nine cards each). A planet and a divinatory meaning were associated with each card.[143] The symbolism depicted on the court cards in particular came from a diverse range of sources. Among the figures were Amazons,[144] characters from Scandinavian mythology,[145] astrological figures[146] and Greek deities.[147] The magical system of the Golden Dawn was essentially syncretistic and this was reflected in the wide range of imagery on the tarot. There was no longer any remembrance that tarot the deck had once been used to play a game. In the Golden Dawn, it was used exclusively for divination, ritual magic and meditation.

Originally members were required to make a copy of the tarot deck designed by Mathers and executed by his wife Moïna.[148] Initiates were to use the cards for both meditation and divination. The trump images were visualised as animate beings who could be encountered during trance.[149] Eventually the practice of copying cards was discontinued.[150] There are several modern interpretations of the Golden Dawn tarot deck. Chic and Sandra Tabatha Cisco produced a version following the descriptions given in *Book T.*

Aleister Crowley

Both the Inner and Outer Orders of the Golden Dawn continued to grow and work successfully. Those who joined the Outer Order and proved satisfactory progressed with little difficulty to the *Roseae Rubeae et Aureae Crucis*, with one notable exception. On 26 November 1898 a new member entered the Isis-Urania Temple, introduced to the Order by alchemist George Cecil Jones otherwise known as *Frater Volo Noscere* ('I want to know').[151] The newcomer adopted the motto *Perdurabo* ('I will endure') alongside his real name of Aleister Crowley.[152] Crowley developed a friendship with Mathers and together they developed the Celtic mysteries but these were quickly superseded by the Rites of Isis.[153]

Crowley had received his Neophyte initiation at Mark Mason's Hall and it was evident that he was a highly gifted magician. From Captain J. F. C.

Figure 17: The Hierophant from Crowley's Thoth Tarot (© Ordo Templi Orientis, 2009).

Fuller's account in the *Equinox,* it could be deduced that Crowley advanced through the grades of the Golden Dawn quickly.[154] Those grades not formally separated by automatic delays he took at the rate of one a month, and the succeeding ones at the prescribed intervals of three, seven and nine months. By the time he had taken his Portal grade, the members of the Isis-Urania Temple in London were rebelling against the autocratic leadership of Mathers.[155] Crowley's morals and conduct offended those who were conducting Temple work in London and the ruling Adepti refused to advance him further.[156] Soon after, Crowley was invited to Paris where he received the grade of Adeptus Minor from Mathers in the Ahathöor Temple. This act inflamed the differences which separated Mathers from his followers and increased the bitter hatred which the Order members bore towards Crowley.[157] But the conjunction of two headstrong and egotistical personalities rendered it probable that eventually Aleister Crowley and MacGregor Mathers would clash.[158]

In 1909, Crowley published his book *Liber 777* which contained the Golden Dawn's secret attribution of Hebrew letters to tarot trumps as well as extensive lists of other correspondences from many traditions.[159] In the same year, he also began to issue the *Equinox,* the official journal of the *Argentum*

Astrum which he founded after his break with Mathers.[160] His plan was to issue, every March and September, a large volume containing rituals and magical instructions.[161] In the various volumes of the *Equinox,* Crowley's garbled versions of the Golden Dawn teaching and ceremonials could be found.[162] Volume Three was scheduled to contain the Ceremony of the Grade of Adeptus Minor, the most important of the grade rituals employed by the Order.[163] No doubt Crowley wrote to Mathers to inform him of his plans. Had Mathers ignored the matter, few people would have learned anything of the Golden Dawn or of the *Equinox.* In an effort to prevent open dissemination of this secret information, Mathers instigated legal proceedings, an action which propagated a vast amount of adverse publicity for Crowley and the Order.[164] The court was sympathetic to the case of Mathers

Figure 18: Lust replaces Strength in Crowley's trump sequence (© Ordo Templi Orientis, 2009).

and an injunction was granted.[165] Crowley immediately lodged an appeal and the Court of Appeal set aside the injunction, permitting the immediate distribution of the periodical.[166] As a result, sensational articles appeared in most of the daily newspapers and both Mathers and Crowley were parodied in the press.[167] The rituals and teaching were badly mauled, rearranged beyond recognition and surrounded by yoga instructions, short stories, articles on sex magic, poetry and a host of miscellaneous odds and ends.[168] Some also reproduced a number of the diagrams used in the grade ceremonies; the material relating to tarot appearing in 1912.[169] Naturally this did nothing to enhance the reputation of the Golden Dawn.

Crowley's subsequent career was dogged by scandal and allegations of abuse. In 1913, he became the head of the British Branch of the *Ordo Templi Orientis* (O.T.O.), a German Society with links to the Martinists.[170] This office brought with it the grand title of 'Supreme and Holy King of Ireland, Iona, and all the Britains that are in the Sanctuary of the Gnosis'; Crowley referred to himself as 'Baphomet'.[171] In the same year, he published the *Liber Legis* (*The Book of the Law)* which contained material told to him some years earlier in Cairo by a spiritual visitor called Aiwaz.[172] Crowley believed Aiwaz was Horus who was also one of the Golden Dawn's Secret Chiefs but simultaneously his higher self and guardian angel.[173] The text predicted the 'Age of Horus' which heralded the foundation of a new religion which would supplant all others.[174] Crowley was urged to form a new movement of élite Thelemites. The term was popularised by French Renaissance writer François Rabelais, whose hero Gargantuan founded the Abbey of Theleme where all Christian values were inverted; this ribald author was a strange source indeed for an Egyptian deity![175] The tarot was mentioned within the *Liber Legis* with trump figures featuring in some of the numerological puzzles posed by Aiwaz.[176]

In 1920, Crowley moved to Sicily and established the Abbey of Thelema in an unsanitary villa at Céfalu.[177] In spite of his heroin addiction and poverty, he bestowed upon himself the grade of $10° = 1°$ Ipissimus.[178] Crowley wrote to Mathers informing him that the Secret Chiefs had appointed him the head of the Order and declared his new magical formula – Thelema. 'I did not expect or receive an answer,' said Crowley, 'and I declared war on Mathers accordingly.'[179] Various people were summoned to take part in this great experiment. Charles 'Raoul' Loveday, who was just twenty-three years old, fell victim to the lack of sanitation at the Abbey. He contracted fatal hepatitis and enteritis, the severity of the illness perhaps exacerbated by the ingestion of the blood from a cat ritually sacrificed by Crowley.[180] Loveday's widow returned to England and supplied the newspapers with graphic stories about life at the Abbey of Thelema.[181] Promiscuity, drug abuse, bestiality and the neglect of children from various unions were indelible features of daily life at the Abbey.[182] Mussolini's officials investigated allegations of Loveday's murder by magic; they found no evidence but expelled Crowley from the country.[183]

Though Crowley had always been interested in and worked with tarot, it was not until 1944 that he published the *Book of Thoth: A Short Essay on the Tarot of the Egyptians.* Limited editions of 200 copies were released simultaneously in London and New York.[184] Crowley adhered to the Golden Dawn system of symbolism and artist Lady Harris having urged Crowley to refine his tarot designs, subsequently painted them.[185] The paintings were unveiled on 1 July 1942 at the Berkeley Galleries in London.[186]

Aiwaz had approved the Golden Dawn system of aligning the trumps with the Hebrew letters except for the Star (trump XVII).[187] In *Liber Legis* he stated: 'All these old letters of my Book are aright; but צ [*Tzaddi*] is not the Star.'[188] The Golden Dawn Cipher Manuscript prescribed the exchange of trumps VIII and XI which resulted in better astrological correspondences such that Justice was associated with Libra and Strength with Leo.[189] The figure of Justice, on the corresponding trump card, held a set of scales which was also the symbol for Libra. On the Strength trump, a woman held open the jaws of a lion; the lion was also the symbol of Leo. Trumps VIII and XI could be viewed as having been rotated around the intervening sign of Virgo. Crowley set about changing the position of trump XVII in a symmetrical move, this time using Pisces as the pivot. Hence the Emperor (Aries) and the Star (Aquarius) swapped places. The letters on the cards were exchanged so that *Tzaddi* was no longer associated with the Star but with the Emperor, and this move had already been approved by Aiwaz. Crowley never attempted to explain this situation.[190]

Figure 19: The Magus from Crowley's Thoth Tarot (© Ordo Templi Orientis, 2009).

In the *Book of Thoth*, Crowley recast trump I (the Magician) as the 'Juggler'; trump XVI (the Tower) as the 'House of God', trump XX (Judgment) as 'Aeon' and trump XXI (the World) as the 'Universe'.[191] In addition, the Cardinal Virtues underwent a transformation: trump VIII (Justice) became 'Adjustment'; trump XI (Fortitude) became 'Lust' and trump XIV (Temperance) became 'Art'.[192] The suit signs corresponded to the four Elemental Weapons used in Golden Dawn rituals: Wands, Swords, Cups and Discs. The minor arcana court also underwent a transformation. The Knights were the highest court figures and were mounted.[193] The Queens were next in the hierarchy and were seated on a throne. The Princes driving chariots followed and as with the Golden Dawn system, they corresponded to the Kings of normal packs. The Princesses were standing, corresponding to the Jacks of other decks. The numeral cards took their meaning from the corresponding astrological decans as with the Golden Dawn. This relationship was made explicit by the inscription of the sigil of the planet and the appropriate sign for each decan upon the numeral cards.[194]

Lady Harris tried to capture the symbolism in abstract form so that the mood of the card corresponded to its meaning. Crowley also assigned the numeral cards to pairs of spirits, the seventy-two emanations from the Hebrew *Shem ha-MePhoresch* which were erroneously assigned to the thirty-six decans by the Golden Dawn adepts.[195] Crowley saw all sacred mysteries as expressing the same truth: the testing and transfiguration of the self.[196] This truth Crowley expressed in the complex symbolism of his tarot which was drawn from a variety of esoteric traditions including astrology, kabbalah, Greco-Roman-Egyptian mythologies, Arthurian and Celtic paganism, Rosicrucianism, Hermeticism and Gnosticism.[197] Gerd Ziegler estimated that there were some 1200 symbols depicted on Crowley's cards.[198] The deck was highly Egyptianised apparently due to the influence of Aiwaz.

Trump I in Crowley's deck bore the title of 'the Magus', in spite of the assignation of the name 'Juggler' in the *Book of Thoth*. The primary figure was that of Thoth-Hermes but Crowley also added a depiction of the Hindu monkey-god Hanuman, which he claimed was a degraded form of the symbol.[199] Symbols representing all four suits floated in the air about the central figure. Trump IV, the Emperor, was associated with the astrological sign of Aries; hence there was a lamb at the Emperor's foot and two rams stood behind him. In his left hand he held a staff topped by a ram's head.[200] The Hierophant, trump V, corresponded to the astrological sign of Taurus and to make this association explicit, he was seated on a bull and surrounded by elephants that allegedly have the nature of Taurus.[201] An Egyptian woman stood before the Hierophant representing Venus, the planetary ruler of the zodiacal sign.[202] Trump XI which would ordinarily have been 'Strength' or 'Fortitude' was recast by Crowley as 'Lust'. Instead of a woman gently prying open the jaws of a lion, a naked woman rode a composite beast which was still largely leonine.[203] The card was associated with the astrological sign of Leo.[204] In the background of the card were the ten *sephiroth*, not yet arranged, as a new Aeon required a new system of classification for the universe.[205] Trump XIII was still recognisable as Death with a skeleton holding a scythe being central to the symbolism of this card. Because this trump was associated with the sign of Scorpio and the letter Nun (meaning 'fish'), the whole scene was depicted as being underwater. The skeleton wore the two-horned headdress of Osiris.[206]

The Devil was depicted as a goat with long, spiral horns and a prominent third eye; the Hebrew letter, *Ayin*, associated with the trump in Crowley's scheme, means 'eye'.[207] The goat made overt the astrological association of this card with the sign of Capricorn and was said to represent the Greek deity Pan.[208] It stood in front of a giant phallus which penetrated a ring signifying potent creativity.[209] The angel on trump XX (Aeon) was replaced by the solar god Horus-Harpocrates, who stood beneath Nuit, the maternal sky.[210] According to myth, each day she gave birth to the sun. Crowley imagined Nuit as Ω (Omega), the last letter of the Greek alphabet and therefore she was symbolic of completion.[211] The trump sequence ended with trump XXI the Universe; a naked female figure danced in the middle of the card.

Interestingly, at the bottom was the skeleton of the periodic table 'showing the ninety-two known chemical elements, arranged according to their rank in the hierarchy.'[212]

The Thoth Tarot deck portrayed symbolism from a vast array of traditions and cultures; Crowley was obsessed by the search for commonalities between divergent systems and mythologies. This passion for syncretism was characteristic of Victorian England, which sought to learn more about its own fundamental nature by comparing itself to other cultures. It was a quest for the fundamental truths which all esoteric systems and religions were thought to contain. The deck was never published during the lifetimes of either Crowley or Harris.[213] It was not until 1969 that Major Grady L. McMurty, who had helped Crowley publish his *Book of Thoth*, were the paintings photographed and published.[214] Unfortunately, the reproductions were of a poor quality. In 1977, Gerald Yorke with the assistance of Stephan Skinner had the paintings photographed again. These photographs form the basis of contemporary editions of Crowley's Thoth Tarot.[215]

William Butler Yeats

Irish poet and writer William Butler Yeats joined the Hermetic Order of the Golden Dawn in 1890, adopting the motto '*Demon est Deus Inversus*' ('The Devil is the converse of God').[216] Crowley envied Yeats his genuine Irish background and talent for poetry and in turn Yeats described Crowley as 'an unspeakable mad person'.[217]

Yeats became immersed in Celtic folklore, as was evidenced by his literary output, and this engagement contributed to his belief that the imagination was central to the magical enterprise.[218] Much Irish literature, some from as early as the eight century CE, was being translated and becoming available to scholars for the first time.[219] The Celtic Archaeological Society and the Ossianic Society were formed solely for the purpose of making these texts accessible. Yeats wrote as a symbolist, describing the process as involving a series of concentric circles: beginning with his home, his village, his nation and finishing with the universe.[220] This was a literary equivalent to the theory of correspondences which played such a large part in occultist philosophy, particularly so with the Hermetic Order of the Golden Dawn. Yeats believed that the universe could not be approached without the clothing of familiar symbols and in this was heavily influenced by Emmanuel Swedenborg and his theory of correspondences.[221] While a member of the Theosophical Society, Yeats drew up his own table which he recorded in his journal.[222]

Spring	Summer	Autumn	Winter
Morning	Noon	Evening	Night
Youth	Adolescence	Manhood	Decay
Fire	Air	Water	Earth
East	South	West	North

Table 10: The table of correspondences drawn up by Yeats while he was still a member of the Theosophical Society.[223]

Yeats, in his *Stories of Red Hanrahan* (1905), remarked on the similarities between the four Treasures of the Tuatha de Danaan (the legendary inhabitants of Ireland) and the four aces of the tarot suits.[224] The treasures were the cauldron of the Dagda, the sword of Nuada, the stone of Fál and the spear of Lugh, and were viewed by some to be the prototypes of certain talismanic objects that appeared in the medieval tales of King Arthur and the Holy Grail.[225] Though the exact nature of the Holy Grail remains unknown, it was legendarily believed to be the chalice from which Jesus drank at the Last Supper and which was later used by Joseph of Arimathea to collect the blood of Christ as he died on the Cross. In the medieval tales, the procession of the Holy Grail featured maidens bearing three other ritualistic objects said to be a dish, a sword and the spear which the centurion Longinus thrust into Jesus' side to ensure his death. Proponents of this theory believed that these objects evolved from the four Celtic talismans.[226] Unfortunately, these four talismans did not consistently appear in the tales and even if they did, to forge a correspondence between the Celtic talismans and the four tarot suits becomes untenable in view of the proven derivation of playing cards from the Mamlūk Empire.

The tarot trumps, Yeats believed, formed a 'connected sentence' having to do with a moral thesis on the human will. Eleven of the major figures from the trump cards featured prominently in Yeats' work: the Wheel of Fortune, Death on horseback, the Sun, the Moon, the Tower, the Hermit, the Fool and the Magician.[227] Though Yeats did not create a deck of tarot cards that was publicly available, he was one of the first to link tarot with Celtic symbolism, an idea that is enormously popular today with at least ten different decks with the name *Celtic Tarot.*[228] Another Golden Dawn member, Arthur Edward Waite, was to develop this connection even further.

Arthur Edward Waite

Arthur Edward Waite was born in Brooklyn in 1857; the illegitimate son of an English mother and an American father who had been a sea captain.[229] After the death of Captain Waite at sea in 1858, Emma Lovell returned to England with her two children.[230] Waite was raised a Catholic and made a living from translating, writing and reviewing books on occult topics.[231] Early in 1891 at the age of thirty-four years, Arthur Edward Waite entered the Hermetic Order of the Golden Dawn as *Frater Sacramentum Regis Abscondere Bonum est* ('It is good to keep the Sacrament of the King').[232] He was the Order's ninety-ninth initiate but soon left, only to rejoin in 1896.[233] So innocuous did the Order seem that Waite encouraged his wife, Ada Lakeman, to join though *Soror Lumen Christi* ('The Light of Christ') attended no meetings after her initiation in 1891.[234] Waite was never on very good terms with either Westcott or Mathers.[235]

Together with fellow Golden Dawn members Palmer Thomas and Marcus Worsley Blackden, Waite hatched a conspiracy that would irreconcilably fracture the Golden Dawn. The trio formed the 'Secret Council of Rites' with the expressed aim to 'obtain and exercise jurisdiction over' a number of occult orders and fringe Masonic rites.[236] The 1903 Annual General Meeting of the Inner Order of the Golden Dawn dissolved in chaos and A. E. Waite proposed 'that those who regarded the Golden Dawn as capable of a mystical instead of a occult construction should and had indeed resolved to work independently, going their own way'. A substantial proportion of the Second Order Adepti followed him and the Outer Order of the Independent and Rectified Rite was born with its Inner Fellowship of the Rosy Cross.[237] It began its meetings at Mark Masons' Hall in November 1903.[238] With little justification, they retained the name of Isis-Urania. They appointed the Reverend William Alexander Ayton as their Third Chief, joining Waite and Blackden.[239] The new temple abandoned all magical work, abolished examinations within the Second Order and used heavily revised rituals designed to express a tortuous Christian mysticism.[240] Waite taught the members to pursue their spiritual quest not by rejecting reason but by retaining it.[241] These were adepts for whom magic had no appeal and who sought instead that mystical Union with God that was the final goal of man.[242] Waite concluded that the symbolism in each of the traditions of alchemy, kabbalah, Freemasonry and Rosicrucianism demonstrated a common route to a common end and a correct interpretation would lead to a revelation of concealed ways to spiritual illumination.[243] Later known as the Holy Order of the Golden Dawn, the Outer Order of the Independent and Rectified Rite survived a decade of intense rivalries and defections to groups such as

Rudolph Steiner's Anthroposophical Society, before Waite closed it down in 1914.[244]

In 1909, with Crowley's publication of the Secret Attributions of the Golden Dawn, Waite felt able to publish his own tarot deck without violating the secrecy of the Order.[245] Waite chose Pamela Colman Smith to bring his designs to fruition.[246] Though London-born, Colman Smith had American parents and studied art at the Pratt Institute in Brooklyn.[247] She received a flat sum for executing the tarot deck which was released at the end of 1909.[248] The pack was to become the first commercially available tarot deck in England and has remained the most popular.[249]

With the exception of the court cards and Aces, all of the cards bore Roman numerals at the top. The trump cards were numbered I to XXI with the Fool designated as 0. The Aces, court cards and trump cards also bore their names at the bottom of the card. As with the Golden Dawn decks, the suits signs of Swords, Wands, Cups and Pentacles were retained. However, the court was more traditional with the King and Queen enthroned, the Knight mounted on a horse and the Page standing. The Aces featured a large hand appearing from a cloud and holding one of the suit signs. The pip cards two through to ten were the most unusual feature of Waite's deck. As mentioned already, they bore their corresponding Roman numeral at the top of the card and featured the requisite number of suit emblems but these were incorporated into a scene in which people, buildings and landscapes were also accommodated. These scenes were designed to correspond to their divinatory meanings as ascribed by Waite.[250] These minor arcana cards, which originally corresponded to those of the ordinary playing card deck, were totally transformed to facilitate tarot's role in divination; a powerful illustration of tarot's evolution from a game to an esoteric device.

Figure 20: The Fool from the Rider Waite deck (Rider Tarot © U.S. Games Systems, 1971).

A fifteenth-century Ferrarese pack known as the 'Sola-Busca' deck also followed this scheme and it seems likely that Colman Smith and Waite drew their inspiration from this pack, photos of which were housed in the British Museum.[251] To publicise the deck, Waite wrote a short article for the *Occult*

Review, announcing that he had secured the services of 'a very skilful and original artist ... Miss Pamela Coleman Smith' though he misspelled her name. He also hinted at the involvement of another person.[252] This unnamed collaborator was thought to be William Butler Yeats.[253]

The names of the trumps basically followed those ascribed by Mathers; the exception being trump XXI which became the World rather than the Universe.[254] Waite maintained the positions of Strength as trump VIII and Justice as trump XI.[255] Mostly the designs of the trumps corresponded to those of the Tarot de Marseille; one exception being the Fool who in Waite's deck was resplendent in gorgeous clothes and held a wand in one hand and a rose in the other as he paused at the brink of a precipice. The Magician also differed markedly: above his head was the sign of infinity and on the table before him were spread the signs of the four suits.[256] The Priestess (trump II) had a lunar crescent at her feet and a solar cross on her breast. She held a scroll in her hands which was marked '*Tora*' and she was seated between white and black pillars inscribed 'J.' and 'B.' for Jachin and Boaz, the pillars of the mystic Temple.[257] This symbolism was

Figure 21: The High Priestess from the Rider Waite deck (Rider Tarot © U.S. Games Systems, 1971).

overtly Freemasonic and belied Waite's interest in this institution. Naked lovers each stood in front of a tree on trump VI. The woman stood in front of a fruit tree in which a snake curled around the trunk in an allusion to the Biblical Eve. A great winged figure was in the sky above them.[258] The Chariot (trump VII) was drawn by two sphinxes, one black and one white. The tunic of the warrior who rode it was covered in hieroglyphics.[259] Waite's Wheel of Fortune was a disc inscribed with Hebrew letters denoting the transliteration of 'TAROT' as 'ROTA' interspersed with the letters of the Tetragrammaton.[260] The corners of the card were occupied by the Living Creatures of Ezekiel. A strange figure in the middle of the wheel was said to represent 'the perpetual motion of a fluidic universe and for the flux of human life.'[261] A sphinx with a sword sat atop the wheel. A serpent slithered downwards to the left of it and the dog-headed god Anubis was on the bottom right of the wheel.[262] The Hanged Man was suspended by his right ankle from a living gallows in the shape of the letter 'T'. His arms were crossed behind his back and he had a halo around his head.[263] Death, as a skeleton in armour on a horse, carried a black flag, instead of a scythe. Around the feet of the horse were children and a bishop.[264] Many of the ideas for his symbolism were from Waite himself, the remainder derived from the works of Éliphas Lévi, Paul Christian and Papus.[265]

Figure 22: Death from the Rider Waite deck (Rider Tarot © U.S. Games Systems, 1971).

Waite spoke of the tarot symbolism as reflecting the mystic initiation, itself a metaphor for spiritual rebirth. Acknowledging the work of Mathers and Papus he wrote: 'We get, as it were, a spiritual history of man, or of the soul coming out from the Eternal, passing into the darkness of the material body, and returning to the height.'[266] The astrological and kabbalistic significance of the tarot trumps was made overt by Waite; the High Priestess rested her foot on a crescent moon.[267] The association of Venus with the Empress was made obvious by the heart-shaped shield bearing the sigil of Venus, which leant against her throne.[268] The arms of the throne of the Emperor were capped with rams' heads signifying the astrological sign of Aries.[269] These correspondences were identical to those set out in the teachings of the Golden Dawn. The trumps also bore the symbolism associated with Rosicrucianism; roses and crosses were found throughout the trump cards.[270] Prominently, the figure of Death carried a standard which displayed the Mystic Rose which signified life.[271] Likewise, the Fool held a white rose in his left hand.[272] Waite's homage to Freemasonry was seen in the black and white pillars of Jachin and Boaz on the Priestess card,[273] and in the presence of the sphinxes on the Chariot trump.[274] On the latter card, Waite also maintained Lévi's Hindu lingam, a modification of the corresponding Tarot de Marseille trump. Representations of light played a significant part in the symbolism as solar discs, wheels and arcs. These depictions of the Sun's path represented the journey of the soul. Gold also had a prominent place in the symbolism of this deck. Again, this was another metaphor for the ascent of spirit.[275] Above all, Waite was deeply immersed in Christian mysticism and so its symbolism was everywhere evident in the pack. The figure of Eve was seen on the Lovers.[276] The World card boasted the Four Living Creatures of Ezekiel.[277]

On the Ace of Cups, a dove bore a cross-marked host and 'descends to place the Wafer in the Cup.'[278] According to medieval legend, on Good Friday the Holy Spirit took the form of a dove and placed a host in the Holy Grail.

In later years, Waite became disillusioned with the Golden Dawn and its adherents.[279] In 1926, he wrote an article for the *Occult Review* entitled 'The Great Symbols of the Tarot'. In this he proclaimed that the tarot did not contain occult truths but rather mystical ones.[280] In addition, he stated elsewhere that he did not believe that there was a valid correspondence between the trump symbols and the Hebrew alphabet.[281] Instead, Waite came to see a different significance for the tarot suits. As with W. B. Yeats, he came to see the correspondences between the tarot suits and the Grail Hallows or Talismans of Celtic myth which he named as the Lance, the Dish, the Grail and the Sword.[282] He found an association between the suit of Wands and the spear or lance. He further associated the suit of Wands with the ordinary playing card suit of Diamonds, arguing that the tip of the spear was diamond-shaped.[283] He drew a connection between the tarot suit of Pentacles and the playing card suit of Clubs.[284] The club, he stated, resembled the shamrock which frequently was a decorative motive in the dish.[285] Waite named the dish as one of the Grail Hallows rather than the stone of Fál which Yeats had named.[286]

As with Alfred Nutt and Jessie Weston, he erroneously traced the legends of King Arthur and the Holy Grail back to earlier Celtic mythology.[287] He linked tarot with the Celtic mysteries by formulating a 'spread' or method of laying the cards out which he called 'an Ancient Celtic Method of Divination' though he did not specify what was especially Celtic about the process.[288] The spread became known as the 'Celtic Cross' and it remains one of the most popular used for tarot divination.[289]

Though I have concentrated on the development of tarot in England, there was also considerable interest in the deck as an esoteric device elsewhere in Europe. In Germany, Ernst Tristan Kurtzahn wrote on tarot in 1920 as well as about runes in the increasingly nationalistic, interwar milieu.[290] Woldemar von Uxkull's book on the subject was published in Munich two years later, entitled *Die Einweihung im alten Ägypten nach dem Buch Thoth* (*Initiation in Ancient Egypt in Accordance with the Book of Thoth*).[291] Perhaps the most renowned author on the deck at this time was August Frank Glahn. His book, *Das Deutsche Tarotbuch: Wahrsagung/Astrologie/ Weisheit, drei Stufen der Einweihung* (*The German Tarot-Book: Prediction/Astrology/Wisdom, Three Levels of Initiation*), published in 1924, became very popular; being reissued in 1930 and sold with a pack of tarot cards designed by Hans Schubert of Reinfeld.[292] All three authors depended largely on information derived from the French tradition of esoteric tarot in which legends of Egypt loomed large.

Tarot was also the subject of close study in the occultist circles of Russia at the beginning of the twentieth century. French occultism was very popular as was Madame Blavatsky's Theosophical Society.[293] Gregory O. Mebes (1869–1930) lectured extensively on tarot and in 1912, these lectures were published as a book, *Kurs entziklopedii okkultizma* (*Course on an 'Encyclopaedia of Occultism'*), the 'Encyclopaedia' being the tarot.[294] But it was Pyötr Demianovich Ouspensky (1878–1947) who was to emerge as the most influential of the Russian tarot authors, his books still widely available today. His *Symboly Taro* (*The Symbolism of the Tarot*) was published in 1912. Fifteen years later he revised his ideas and published them in *A New Model of the Universe* which also contained his thoughts on a range of other mystical systems.[295] Ouspensky was to join forces with the Greek-Armenian mystic Georges Ivanovich Gurdjieff (1872–1949) whose influence was widely disseminated through Ouspensky's writings, though their friendship was frequently troubled; it was through this connection that Ouspensky is primarily known today. Other significant Russian tarot scholars included Valentin Tomberg (1900–1973) and Mouni Sadhu (1888–1971) who was to resettle in Melbourne, Australia. It was here that he wrote *The Tarot: A Contemporary Course of the Quintessence of Hermetic Occultism* which was published 1962 and remains in print today.[296]

Similarly, the occult was a potent force in American culture. From the seventeenth century onwards, the populace was enamoured with Hermeticism, Rosicrucianism, astrology, water-witching, herbalism, alchemy and magic, brought to the New World by European migrants.[297] It was hardly surprising that an occult society, in some ways mirroring that of Europe yet more complex and diverse, should develop with its own societies, magical orders and American branches of European esoteric institutions; not forgetting that this was the original home of the Theosophical Society that would prove to be so influential the world over. Tarot was also an integral part of this occultic milieu with several significant volumes and decks being produced. Among those authors worthy of mention were Charles Stansfeld Jones (1886–1950), an early member of Aleister Crowley's *Argentum Astrum* who moved permanently to America from England;[298] another protégé of Crowley's, Israel Regardie (1907–1985), the man responsible for making public all of the Golden Dawn's ritual outlines and teachings;[299] and Paul Foster Case (1884–1954), the founder of the Builders of the Adytum (BOTA), a mystery school exploring topics such as esoteric psychology, meditation and astrology.[300] Even though these authors drew their material largely from the Hermetic Order of the Golden Dawn, their influence was not significant in comparison to that directly asserted by the British occultists.

It would be inaccurate to say that these German, Russian and American authors had no influence on the subsequent development of tarot but it was minor compared to that of the various members of the Hermetic Order of the Golden Dawn and its offshoots. These occultists were central to the development of esoteric and divinatory tarot in the nineteenth and early twentieth centuries. Their influence extends until the present day with the Rider-Waite (renamed the Colman-Waite) pack remaining the most popular divinatory deck created. Most modern methods of tarot interpretation were derived from the Golden Dawn system of correspondences, further developed by Waite and Crowley. The symbolism on these decks reflected the eclectic nature of the teachings of the Golden Dawn which included Rosicrucianism, Hermeticism, kabbalah, Freemasonry, the Greek mystery religions and Celtic mythology as expounded by the adherents of the Celtic Revival. The teachings of the Golden Dawn, in turn reflected the many streams that informed esoteric thought in Victorian England. Many of these esoteric traditions remain popular, their number and variety augmented by the many contemporary manifestations of esoteric and spiritual thought characteristic of the New Age. The influence of these characteristic manifestations of the New Age on tarot will be considered in detail in the next chapter.

6

Tarot and the New Age

The tarot decks created by Arthur Edward Waite and Aleister Crowley, both derived from the Golden Dawn tradition, have remained enormously popular. Even in the New Age, most modern decks utilise the symbolism, systems of correspondences and divinatory meanings originated by the members of the Golden Dawn and its offshoots. Waite's deck has been particularly influential; the illustration of minor arcana cards becoming standard in most contemporary decks. While retaining the central tenets of Golden Dawn divinatory meanings and symbolism, the sources of that imagery have changed considerably. Where once Egypt and classical mythology supplied the imagery, the pool of symbols has been augmented by a staggering array of other sources including eastern religions, indigenous cultures, science and other New Age modalities including crystals, angels and goddess worship.

The New Age is an intoxicating mix of East and West, where Buddhist Tantra bumps up against Native American shamanism, crystal healing and past-life regressions. Auras are examined, angels are consulted and groups gather to meditate for peace and environmental healing. Tarot is an integral part of this worldview, its symbolism confidently projecting each of these apparently divergent streams, to emerge as the New Age tool *par excellence*. Previously, occultists searched for the one true tarot; they 'rectified' or 'corrected' the deck in accordance with their beliefs. They judged that tarot had been deliberately altered to conceal its true purpose and meaning, or it had been carelessly copied resulting in an inadvertent loss of significance. With the advent of the New Age, tarot designers felt able to 're-imagine' the deck, no longer afraid to experiment, comfortable with creating links to other cultures or to create decks that fulfilled roles other than divination.[1] This chapter is concerned with how tarot symbolism has evolved within this heterogeneous context.

The broad spiritual philosophy of the New Age combines many systems of pre-existing movements and strands of thought that have their foundations in the occult-metaphysical community which gave rise to organisations such as the Theosophical Society.[2] Other significant influences include Spiritualism, New Thought, the Human Potential Movement, the Holistic Health Movement, Transpersonal Psychology, some Asian religions and the religions of indigenous peoples such as the Australian Aborigines and Native Americans.[3] Though it is thought to have directly emerged from the counterculture of the 1960s, it differs from it in several important ways. First, the New Age is not characterised by youth rebelling against their parents as with the '60s counterculture; people of all ages are attracted to the New Age.[4] Second, the New Age is not affiliated with any particular political faction. Whereas the counterculture called people to the streets for action, the New Age makes no such demands.[5] Significantly, psychedelic drug use is not encouraged by New Age advocates; instead consciousness is altered using meditative or even shamanistic techniques.[6]

William Blake originally coined the term 'New Age' in the preface to his poem *Milton* (1804),[7] but it was popularised by the Theosophist Alice Bailey.[8] The expression derives from the astrological notion of the 'Age of Aquarius' supplanting the 'Age of Pisces';[9] a time dominated by conservative Christian values and rationalism. 'Aquarian' values represent a re-enchantment and rediscovery of ancient wisdom.[10] Though the roots of the New Age have been readily traced, it remains difficult to establish the scope of the term. Paul Heelas, writing in 1996, describes it as the designation for 'those that maintain that inner spirituality – embedded within the self and the natural order as a whole – serves as *the* key to moving from all that is wrong with life to all that is right.'[11] Hence, the primary motivation of the New Age community is 'transformation' of the self, society and of humanity.[12] The movement adopts an enchanted worldview within a secular context; a kind of 'secularised esotericism', taking from Western Esotericism the pre-eminence of personal religious experience and reinterpreting it from a secular perspective; selectively using the methodology of science, comparative religion, evolutionism and psychology. Though there are many New Age groups with divergent views, what unites them is their opposition to the same things.[13]

Predominant Themes of New Age Thought

The trend towards the New Age corresponds with the move away from traditional religious institutions. Derived of the comfort and support of their religion, individuals construct a personal religiosity; picking and choosing what suits them.[14] Eclecticism and syncretism are integral to the movement.[15] There are several major streams that characterise New Age thought and religion. The first is an emphasis on channelling, though usually not of the recent dead as with Spiritualism.[16] Channelling refers to the belief that psychic mediums are able to serve as a channel for information from a source other than their normal selves.[17] These sources are frequently identified as entities living on 'higher levels of being' and may be described as ascended masters, spirit guides, angels, extraterrestrials, historical personalities, discarnate animals, nature spirits or the higher self. Generally, they are considered to have more insight, knowledge and wisdom than most humans.[18] The origins of channelling can be traced from Madame Blavatsky's Theosophical Society to Edgar Cayce and Helen Schucman and her *Course in Miracles*.[19] The term was first used by the UFO contact groups of the 1960s who sought to establish communication with extraterrestrials.[20] Channelling has also been used in the creation of tarot decks. For example, Herman Haindl claimed he sourced the symbolism for his *Haindl Tarot* via channelling; painting whatever symbols came to him without forethought or planning.[21]

Healing and personal growth are likewise important in the New Age literature.[22] The concept of mesmerism, as adopted by Phineas Pankhurst Quimby (1802–1866) in his New Thought Movement, had a significant impact on the New Age notion of health and sickness. An individual's health or lack thereof is viewed as being a product of that individual's imagination; an idea prevalent in the New Age.[23] Therapies advocated by New Age healers typically aim at healing the whole person rather than curing disease in isolation, tarot often being employed for this purpose. Many practitioners see the symbols of tarot as representing differing emotional or spiritual states. By learning the lessons of the symbols and incorporating that wisdom into their worldview, the querent may hope to divulge themselves of 'negativity' or 'emotional baggage'.[24] For example, Vicki Noble described a ritual using the *Motherpeace Round Tarot* which she claimed facilitated the healing of rape victims.[25] Christine Jette in her book, *Tarot for the Healing Heart*, described a number of 'layouts' for 'releasing the healer within.'[26] The *Aura Soma Tarot* (1997) combined tarot with the New Age healing and divination technique of Aura Soma, whereby bottles containing different coloured liquids were selected by the querent and 'read' by a practitioner in order to discern what lay behind a 'dis-ease' or other problem.[27] The *Aura Soma Tarot* deck did not retain the structure of traditional decks; instead it consisted of ninety-eight cards (numbered 0 to 97) – the additional twenty cards were repeats of twenty of the major arcane, displaying different imagery – but the backs of the cards were all different, each with a picture of a bottle and an image.[28] The cards were chosen and read in a similar manner to the aura-soma bottles used to diagnose and treat illness.

Science and the language of science have also been incorporated into New Age thought.[29] The search for a Grand Unified Theory can be considered a modern version of eighteenth-century *Naturphilosophie*.[30] The term here can be said to mean 'a both intuitive and rigorous approach focusing on the reality underlying phenomenal reality'.[31] This ardent search, while encompassing accepted scientific knowledge, should retain philosophical elegance, religious profundity and internal consistency.[32] The movies *What the Bleep* (2004) and the extended version *What the Bleep: Down the Rabbit Hole - Quantum Edition* (2006), which espoused a synthesis of quantum physics and spirituality, is evidence of this phenomenon. For admirers of the movies, there was a permanent website and a regular email newsletter, *The Bleeping Herald*, which examined related concepts.[33] A recent edition featured a discussion entitled *Quantum Thoughts on Tarot*.[34] Also making this link between the New Age and 'science' manifest was the *Voyager Tarot* of Ken Knutson and James Wanless.[35] Their deck embraced the symbolism of science, incorporating it alongside more traditional tarot symbolism. For example, trump XX, traditionally Judgment, became 'Time-Space'.[36]

The philosophy of deep ecology is an extension of this quasi-scientific worldview, aiming to integrate ethics, politics, biology and spirituality. It

Figure 23: The Kaiser replaces the Emperor in the Anti-Nuclear Wendländisches Tarot (1980).

moves away from the anthropocentric orientation of contemporary ethics, instead allowing each entity its own unique place and non-negotiable value.[37] The 'Gaia' hypothesis of ex-NASA scientist James Lovelock, which posits the Earth as a living being, is a further evolution of this idea.[38] In this scheme, humankind and the cosmos form a living whole or *unus mundus*, the unity of the world.[39] This ethic of deep ecology has found expression in tarot symbolism. The *Healing Earth Tarot* subtitled 'A Journey in Self-Discovery, Empowerment and Planetary Healing' (1994) and designed by David and Jyoti McKie, used images from a diverse range of cultures to signify the commonalities and common destiny of humanity intimately bound with the planet. The minor arcana court was made up the decidedly non-threatening Grandfather, Grandmother, Man and Woman within the suits of Wands, Rainbows, Pipes, Feathers, Shields and Crystals which have no obvious correlations to the four suits of traditional tarot.[40]

Deep ecology and the protest against wanton environmental destruction were also the predominant themes in the *Anti-Nuclear Wendländisches Tarot* (1980) designed and drawn by artist Waltraud Kremser.[41] The deck was published in response to a proposal to build a nuclear power station in the German region of Wendland.[42] The cards portrayed characters from the area though some illustrated themes with antinuclear sentiments. The *Kaiser* (Emperor), dressed in a business suit with a top hat with dollar bills stuffed into the band, nursed a large, phallic missile. The *Gerechtigkeit* (Justice) card showed a woman holding a set of scales. On one pan were a bird and flower weighing more than the other pan which held a nuclear power station, a statement of the worth of Nature as compared to the inadequacies and destruction of 'progress'.[43]

Just as the New Age has tried to align itself with the 'reputable' pursuit of science, it has frequently manipulated the jargon and principles of psychology to substantiate its claims. The psychotherapist most frequently used to this end is Carl Jung (1875–1961) with his theories of archetypes, the collective unconscious and synchronicity. Jung's work is frequently used to validate the correspondences between tarot symbolism and the symbolism within mythology, art and literature, as well as esoteric ideas and motifs from other cultures.[44] Sallie Nichols in her book *Jung and Tarot: An Archetypal Journey* urged us to connect with the 'archetypes' present in tarot symbolism to aid us on our journey towards wholeness, called by Jung 'individuation'.[45] Other tarotists saw the four suits of the minor arcana as corresponding to Jung's four functions of personality: Wands related to fiery 'intuition'; Cups related to watery 'feeling'; Swords to 'thinking' and Pentacles/Coins to 'sensation'.[46]

Sometime Jung's theories were more explicitly employed in the creation of tarot decks. In 1962, John Cooke and four others started experimenting with the ouija board, interrogating an entity referred to as the 'Nameless One' who progressively gave them instructions for rendering a modern interpretation of tarot.[47] In 1968, the images were released as posters – one for each of the twenty-two tarot trumps – and then as a limited edition of cards with a booklet called *The New Tarot: the Tarot for the Aquarian Age* written by Cooke and Rosalind Sharpe. The pack and booklet were reissued in 1969 and 1970 with two additional booklets entitled *G – the Royal Maze: Guide to the Game of Destiny* and *I – Instructions: a Synopsis of the Book of G.*[48] A complex system of correspondences was provided for both the four suits and the twenty-two trumps. The suit correspondences are listed below.

Suits	Elements	Functions	Senses	Direction	Quality	Races
Blades	Air	Thinking	Sight	North	Cold	White
Serpents	Fire	Feeling	Hearing	South	Hot	Black
Pears	Water	Intuition	Smell	East	Wet	Yellow
Stones	Earth	Sensation	Touch	West	Dry	Red

Table 11: A table of correspondences between the four tarot suits and other systems including Jung's four functions of personality used in the New Tarot.[49]

The functions were those described by Carl Jung and described the principle way in which individuals acquired knowledge. Jung's influence was also seen in Cooke and Sharpe's association of the tarot court with Jungian constructs.[50]

> **Queen** = the anima (the feminine self)
> **King** = consciousness
> **Page** = the eternal child (the future self)
> **Knight** = psychic breakthrough

Robert Wang's *Jungian Tarot* (1988, 2001) was specifically designed to facilitate the use of what Jung described as 'active imagination', the process in which the querent actively engaged with figures and symbols that appeared in dreams or fantasies.[51] For Wang, the Magician became the 'the Totality of the Self' with the potential to become either male or female.[52] The rest of the deck showed aspects of either gender. The idea was to meditate upon a card in order to reintegrate our 'own opposites'. For example, when meditating upon the Emperor, the querent would consider first his or her own father and then the Pure Father who is in all of us.[53] The cards are given supplementary titles such as 'Temperance: the Conciliatory Daughter', 'The World: the Daughter who Conceals Herself' and the 'King of Pentacles: the Responsible Father'.[54] Tarot became a psychotherapeutic device, considerably cheaper and more accessible than a therapist. Carl Sargent used the tarot to explain theories of personality including Freudian psychoanalysis, Jung's analytical psychology, the humanistic psychology of Carl Rogers and Abraham Maslow, and the personal construct psychology of George Kelly.[55] Sheldon Kopp also advocated the use of tarot in psychotherapy sessions and workshops with the incorporation of the imagery into personal mythology.[56]

Though tarot's role as a divinatory device was still paramount; the focus of the divination shifted. As was typical of the New Age, many of the divinatory practices were associated with self-development rather than with 'fortunetelling' *per se*. This could involve tarot scrying whereby the reader concentrated on a particular card, waiting for a vision which provided insight into an emotional or spiritual concern.[57] Tarot became a tool to facilitate inner transformation, the symbolism of the cards interpreted to discern inner psychological states and unconscious 'blockages' that could prevent an individual from reaching his or her potential.[58] Gail Fairfield described a system whereby tarot could be used not only to determine when a potential partner or friend might enter the querent's life but also the psychological problems that may inhibit the development of the relationship.[59] William C. Lammey advocated the use of tarot to discern the nature of our 'karmic contract' at birth: which issues we were 'meant' to deal with in this life and how we might resolve them so that we can roll over into the next life 'debt free'.[60] Similarly, the major arcana cards of the *Transition Tarot* were used to divine how a soul will fare before its judges after death and the minor arcana cards were used to form a protective 'amulet' to bring positive results.[61] Other New Age books detailed spells to bring about improvement in almost any aspect of life – love, finances, health, spirituality – but also to try and attain more specific goals.[62]

Already mentioned, the *Voyager Tarot* (1989) of Knutson and Wanless was created as a psychological tool for personal transformation.[63] Wanless claimed that we are the creators of our own reality through our beliefs and expectations and that by accessing visual symbols, we were able to reach these deep levels of belief and effect a transformation.[64] In contrast to the well-defined rubric of symbols used by esotericists to facilitate change, Wanless advocated using a larger, less conventional pool.[65] Consequently, the images on this deck ranged from animals, vegetables and elements to minerals, art and extraterrestrial worlds.[66] Wanless visualised the four suits of the minor arcana as being 'defined by DNA'. The suit of Crystals (mind) corresponded to Swords, Worlds (emotion) replaced the suit of Coins, Flowers (body) corresponded to the suit of Cups and Wands symbolised spirit.[67]

Combining Traditions and Methods

New Age practitioners will experiment with several techniques in sequence or at the same time.[68] Contemporary tarot echoed this eclectic approach, frequently combining the symbolism from two or more traditions within the same deck. In addition, multiple divinatory techniques may have been incorporated, creating unique decks utilising various systems. The *Astrological Tarot* (1982), designed by Italian astrologer and artist Stefania Trebucchi, was an example of a deck which also employed astrology. The first twelve trumps corresponded to the signs of the zodiac but the cards were not numbered according to tarot tradition. For example, card VIII was the

Sun rather than its usual placement in the trump sequence at XIV. Similarly, the cards did not carry the traditional tarot symbols. Instead the first dozen trumps featured various creatures supporting the wheel of the zodiac. The remaining trumps displayed an animal in the top part of the card with the wheel of the zodiac in the bottom portion along with the name of a planet and an illustration of an herb.[69] Another tarot deck utilising astro-

logical symbolism was the *Mandala Astrological Tarot* (1987), illustrated with abstract symbols of the planets and zodiacal signs rather than with the familiar figures of the tarot trumps.[70] There were some difficulties in many of the modern decks in maintaining the astrological correspondences outlined by the Golden Dawn. Since the time the original correspondences were formulated, three new planets have been discovered.[71] The cards of the *Astrotaro* (1985) of Carol Herzer Abrams illustrated the qualities associated with the planets and signs.[72] She also realigned the planets to different trumps to accommodate subsequent planetary discoveries, for example linking Mercury to Strength and Neptune to Temperance. A twenty-third trump 'Nemesis' had been added to signify karma.

Figure 24: Black Tortoises replace wands in the Feng Shui Tarot of Eileen and Peter Paul Connolly (© U.S. Games Systems, 2001).

Also in this spirit of eclecticism, *feng shui* has been incorporated into the schema of tarot in the *Feng Shui Tarot* (2001) created by the mother-and-son team of Eileen and Peter Paul Connolly.[73] The deck is illustrated with symbols derived from the Form School of *Feng Shui*. In spite of the name, it was not intended for *feng shui* analysis and the traditional meanings of the major arcana cards were retained though illustrated using symbols relevant to *feng shui*. The suits of the minor arcana cards were renamed White Tigers (Swords), Black Tortoises (Wands), Red Phoenix (Cups) and Green Dragons (Coins).[74]

The increasing tendency to combine tarot with other esoteric or mystical beliefs was also seen in the New Age tarot literature. Common combinations featured tarot with astrology, ritual magic, numerology or Wicca. For example, Diane Morgan's *Magical Tarot, Mystical Tao: Unlocking the Hidden Power of the Tarot Using the Ancient Secrets of the Tao Te Ching* combined the eastern tradition of Taoism with the western tradition of tarot.[75]

Morgan utilised the symbolism of the Rider-Waite tarot and combined it with ideas from the *Tao Te Ching*, for example:

Meditation 68: Five of Swords

The soldier in Tao in (sic) not violent.
The soldier in Tao is not angry.
He wins by not antagonising the enemy.

He leads by serving.
And is skilled with people,
Not weapons.
This is the path of Heaven.[76]

The Influence of Feminism

The most influential movement in the last thirty years seeking to undermine the modernist hierarchy, including that of organised religion, has been feminism. The combination and cross-fertilisation between spiritually-oriented feminism and neopaganism has resulted in the appearance of the Goddess movement.[77] Those engaged in spiritual feminism sought to resacralise the cosmos through the recognition and promotion of female deities, but also to transform human consciousness and the institutions of society. They rejected the Biblical traditions that depicted women as being inherently sinful and 'fallen'.[78] Most argued that it was necessary to incorporate women's stories into the cosmogony in order to precipitate the advent of the New Age.[79] Many of the modern feminist decks sought to facilitate this storytelling and gave voice and form to the resultant narratives.

One such deck was the *New Amazon Tarot* (1984) which was the result of collaboration between twenty-three artists including the instigators of the project: Billie Potts, River Lightwomoon and Susan S. Weed. There were often multiple versions of a card and a variety of artistic methodologies were employed including pen and ink drawing, photography, photomontage and woodcuts.[80] The court contained a Child, Amazon, Companion and Queen in each suit. The deck contained no images of men but did not demonise them either, instead creating positive images of women.[81] Another deck, the *Barbara Walker Tarot* (1985), sought to provide knowledge of goddess-centred religion.[82] Walker viewed the goddesses of antiquity as aspects of an original Goddess whose powers and authority have been systematically undermined by male writers and authorities.[83] In a similar manner, attention was directed towards female deities in the *Goddess Tarot* (1998) designed by Kris Waldherr. The deck displayed goddess imagery from many cultures including those of Egypt, Australia, China, Britain, Japan, Greece, Rome and Tibet.[84] Each suit was associated with a different goddess tradition; hence Pentacles was linked to the Hindu goddess of wisdom and fortune, Lakṣmī; the suit of Cups was linked to Venus, the Roman goddess of Love; Swords corresponded to the Egyptian goddess Isis; and Wands to the Norse goddess Freyja. Each major arcana card depicted a goddess from a different culture. 'Death' was recast as 'Transformation' and displayed the image of the Japanese goddess Ukemochi. Upon her death, her body was transformed into food and hence, life anew.[85]

The *Motherpeace Round Tarot* (1981) by Vicki Noble and Karen Vogel was specifically formulated to fulfil a feminist agenda.[86] The cards were round rather than the traditional rectangular shape, recalling the shape of the Moon, long associated with female energies and the roundness of the Mother Goddess.[87] The symbolism was drawn from many sources but particularly from Ancient Minoa, Greece and Africa with some Native American influences.[88] The major arcana cards for the most part retained their traditional titles though there have been some notable substitutions. The Hermit was replaced by a female counterpart, the 'Crone' and the Hanged Man was recast as the 'Hanged One'. The court consisted of the Shaman, Priestess, Daughter and Son. Though most of the figures were female, the Sun was depicted as a black male with five women. The Hierophant (Pope) was described in the accompanying text as a male dressed as a female, and the Hanged One was a female changed to a male.[89] Only the Devil and the Emperor were unambiguously male and these figures were negatively represented, symbolising patriarchal oppression. The Devil was seen seated at the top of a ziggurat, his domination made explicit by the chains that bound his slaves.[90]

It is not only women who have tried to redress the gender imbalance seen in traditional tarot. Hermann Haindl poured his life experiences into the creation of the *Haindl Tarot*, writing of a planet dominated by patriarchy, where all that was feminine was dishonoured.[91] Haindl was a teenager when the Nazis controlled much of Europe and was a prisoner of war in Russia before becoming an environmental activist with an interest in the spirituality of Native Americans and India.[92] In Haindl's deck, trump IV the Emperor is depicted as Odin who represented patriarchal religion. He stood away from the World Tree (*Yggdrasil*) which corresponded to the earth and to the mother. This theme was explored in the trump sequence until trump XII, where Odin, this time cast as the Hanged Man, was suspended by his leg from a symbol for Venus which rested in the tree, demonstrating his surrender to the feminine without violence.[93]

The *Haindl Tarot* also sought to transcend boundaries between the spiritual traditions of different cultures.[94] The card of the Hierophant

The Emperor

Figure 15: Odin plays the role of Emperor in the Haindl Tarot (© U.S. Games Systems, 1990).

symbolised reconciliation between Germans and Jews, a theme writ large by the assignation of both Hebrew letters and runes to the cards.[95] The court cards and Aces of each suit were associated with the mythology of particular cultures and also with a direction and an element. Hence, the suit of Wands was associated with Fire, the East and India.[96] The suit of Cups was linked to Water, the North and Europe. Swords were related to Air, the South and Egypt.[97] Finally, Stones (Coins) were associated with Earth, the West and the culture of America. In addition, the tarot court was reformulated as the Mother, Father, Daughter and Son.[98] The Mothers were archaic figures from mythology. The Fathers brought their force to consciousness; hence Odin brought the runes from the base of *Yggdrasil*. The Daughters and Sons presented a more personal view of their associated cultures.[99]

There have been several other decks espousing feminist principles including the *Shining Woman Tarot* (1992, reissued in 2001 as the *Shining Tribe Tarot)* designed by Rachel Pollack,[100] Ffiona Morgan's *Daughters of the Moon* deck (1983),[101] *A Poet's Tarot* (1986) from Jesse Cougar,[102] the *Transparent Tarot* (1985) of Susan Weed,[103] the *Goddesses of the Tarot* another by Susan Weed[104] and the *Tarot of the Crone* (2001) from Ellen Lorenzi-Prince.[105]

Neopaganism

Wouter Hanegraaff remains adamant that neopaganism is an integral part of the New Age Movement, though he is careful to exclude those revivals of pre-Christian culture that arose before the New Age.[106] Several scholars – and most neopagans – disagree; for example Aidan Kelly acknowledges that there are many similarities between neopaganism and some strands of New Age thought, but maintains that the differences are more significant.[107] In the context of this book, it is not crucial to determine whether or not neopaganism can be classified as legitimately belonging to the New Age. Though there are certain convergences, the New Age developed in the

United States during the 1970s and modern pagan witchcraft developed in
the United Kingdom from the 1950s making it clear that neopaganism is not
a direct product of the New Age.[108] Irrespective of this dispute, there are
many tarot decks and books that display symbolism which reflect neopagan
beliefs.

One such deck is the *Sacred Rose Tarot* (1982), designed by Johanna
Gargiulo-Sherman who took her inspiration from medieval stained-glass
windows, Byzantine icons and the 'pre-Christian religion of nature.'[109] The
deck was rendered in dark, rich colours with luxuriant foliage surrounding
the central figures.[110] The symbolism of the deck was drawn from Christian
and Hermetic traditions cast in a pagan context. Colour symbolism was also
employed with red being linked to passion, white to purity and so on.[111]
Feminine imagery related to spiritual and lunar qualities, with masculine
imagery linked to solar and physical qualities.[112] The image of the rose – as
the name of the deck would suggest – played a prominent role in the
symbolism; Gargiulo-Sherman likened it to the lotus in Eastern traditions.[113]
The minor arcana suits were associated with a different aspect and colour of
the rose. The Red Rose was associated with 'sacrifice' and the suit of Wands.
The White was linked to 'purity' and the suit of Cups. The suit of Swords
was related to the Blue Rose and the 'impossible'. Lastly, the White-Gold
Rose was linked to the tarot suit of Pentacles and to 'absolute achievement'.[114]

Arthurian themes have also proven popular with neopagans and tarotists
alike. The symbolism of the *Merlin Tarot* (1992, 2002), designed by Robert
Stewart and painted by Miranda Gray, was drawn from the works *Vita
Merlini* (*The Life of Merlin*) by Geoffrey of Monmouth and *Les Prophesies
de Merlin* (*The Prophesies of Merlin*).[115] The deck illustrated the esoteric
tradition of Celtic initiation. The sequence of the major arcana represented
the life of Merlin: the magician as a prophetic child was portrayed as the
'Fool', the 'Hermit' was Merlin as a wise man and the 'Hanged Man'
illustrated the result of one of Merlin's prophecies.[116] The suits were renamed
Fish (Cups), Beasts (Pentacles), Serpents (Wands) and Birds (Swords).[117]
Other decks exploiting this theme included Anne-Marie Ferguson's *Legend:
the Arthurian Tarot* (1995),[118] the *Arthurian Tarot* (1990, 1995) designed by
Caitlin and John Matthews,[119] the *King Arthur Tarot* (1984) of Maud
Reinertsen[120] and the *Avalon Tarot* (2000) of Joseph Viglioglia.[121]
Interestingly, Arthurian and overtly Celtic themes were commonly linked; a
mistaken coupling also made by Arthur Edward Waite following Alfred Nutt
and Jessie Weston.[122]

Exploring overtly Celtic traditions, the *Faery Wicca Tarot* (1999) from
Kisma K. Stepanich and Renée Christine Yates, also depicted Irish Wiccan
traditions.[123] Ogham characters were applied to each card and the horned
figure of Cerunnos replaced the Devil.[124] The deck was supplemented by

additional cards: the Tree of Life and the four gifts of the Crane Bag, the Apple Branch, the Hazel Wand and the Holy Stone.[125] Also exploring this tradition was the *Tarot of Wicca* (1983), designed by H. Kitagawa under the direction of A. Mokuseioh.[126] In this deck, the suit of Swords was recast as 'athames', a ritual dagger with the other suits more or less retaining the common suits signs of Wands, Chalices (Cups) and Pentacles.[127]

There are a number of tarot decks that drew from a wider range of Celtic sources. Among these decks were the *Celtic Tarot* (1990) designed by Courtney Davis,[128] another deck with the same name but a different design by Ti Birchrose (1988),[129] the *Sacred Circle Tarot* (1998) by Anna Franklin and Paul Mason,[130] the *Celtic Wisdom Tarot* (1999) designed by Caitlin Matthews and Olivia Rayner, the *Greenwood Tarot* (1996) of Chesca Potter and Mark Ryan,[131] the *Baum Tarot* (1984) of Frederick Hetmanns,[132] the *Celtic Dragon Tarot* created by D. J. Conway and Lisa Hunt (2001)[133] and the *Robin Wood Tarot* (1991) named for its creator.[134]

Just as many neopagan groups drew from the mythology of Scandinavia, so did numerous tarot decks. The *Norse Tarot* (1989) by Clive Barrett depicted a warrior race with several cards showing both male and female warriors, the latter finding representation on the cards of the Empress and Death.[135] The major arcana cards featured scenes from Norse mythology while the minor arcana cards illustrated the daily lives of medieval Vikings.[136] The figure of Odin appeared on many cards including the Magician and as the male figure in the Lovers. As with the *Haindl Tarot*, the Hanged Man of this deck represented Odin's self-sacrifice to gain the runes. Each trump card boasted a rune though the resultant order is not traceable back to the *Edda* or any other known source.[137] Sylvia Gainsford's *Tarot of the Northern Shadows* (1997) similarly explored the symbolism of Norse belief but combined it with that of the Celts. The suit of Swords portrayed figures from British and Continental Celtic legends. The suit of Rods featured the Norse pantheon of gods and goddesses; that of Cups showed the heroes from the Welsh saga the *Mabinogion* and the suit of Discs portrayed the Irish Celtic people.[138]

Published in England, *The White Goddess* (1948) and subsequently the *Greek Myths* (1955), written by Robert Graves, proved to be enormously influential among neopagans.[139] Consequently, many groups traced their spiritual heritage to the mythology of ancient Rome and Greece and this inclination was reflected in several contemporary tarot decks. Juliet Sharman-Burke and Liz Greene were the creators of the very popular *Mythic Tarot* (1986) which utilised the symbolism of Greek mythology, the creators believing that it lies at the very root of western civilisation.[140] The trump sequence depicted the deities of the Greek Pantheon and some of their exploits.[141] The Fool was represented by Dionysus and the Empress by

Demeter.[142] Strength showed Heracles killing the Nemean lion which was an interesting reference back to the fifteenth-century Visconti-Sforza deck. The card of the Lovers displayed the judgment of Paris which foreshadowed the Trojan War. The suits of the minor arcana were each associated with a particular myth. The suit of Cups elaborated the story of Eros and Psyche. The tale of Jason and the Golden Fleece was conveyed in the suit of Wands. The suit of Swords was associated with the story of Orestes and the cards of the suit of Pentacles depicted the story of Daedalus, the inventor.[143] The *Minotarot* (1982), designed by Eric Provoost, similarly drew its symbolism from classical mythology, specifically from the legend of Theseus, the labyrinth and the Minotaur.[144] Interestingly, Provoost added another character in the Minotoress.[145] This subjective reinterpretation and invention of myth and history is characteristic of New Age thought.[146]

Classical motifs were also featured in the *Olympus Tarot* (2002) of Manfredi Toraldo and Luca Raimondo. The suit signs were recast as Heroes (Swords), Creatures (Wands), Places (Cups) and Objects (Pentacles). Each major arcana card was linked to an Olympic deity; for example the Magician was associated with Zeus.[147] In an interesting turn, Japanese videogame developer and publisher Atlus developed the *Age of Mythology Tarot* (1990) from the *Megami Tensei* game series which were based on classical Greek and Roman mythology.[148]

The Hermetic Order of the Golden Dawn proved to be enormously influential on neopaganism through its approach to ritual magic and close association with the Celtic Revival.[149] And it is this organisation, through its linking of the trumps with the pathways of the kabbalistic Tree of Life, which has laid the foundation for all contemporary tarot divination. The *Golden Dawn Tarot* deck has already been discussed and remains popular to this day. Another deck with explicitly kabbalistic symbolism was the *Tree of Life Tarot* designed by Rufus Camphausen and drawn by Appalonia van Leeuwen. Each of the major arcana cards displayed the ten *sephiroth* of the Tree of Life but with the relevant pathway between them highlighted along with the corresponding Hebrew letter.[150] Each of the suits corresponded to a different colour and the number of the pip cards was matched by the number of highlighted *sephiroth*.[151] The purpose of the deck was to act as a psychospiritual 'map' for the exploration of the 'Self', the personality, the present situation and the potential of the querent.[152] The *Tarot of the Sephiroth* (2000), designed by Josephine Mori, Jill Stockwell and Dan Staroff was also based on the esoteric system of kabbalah.[153]

Godfrey Dowson released the *Hermetic Tarot* in 1979, a year after Robert Wang's *Golden Dawn Tarot*. Like Wang's deck, the *Hermetic Tarot* was based on that used by the Hermetic Order of the Golden Dawn. The cards had angelic names with astrological symbols worked into the pictures.[154] A

Hebrew letter was also displayed along with the number at the top of the trump cards.[155] Other decks embracing esoteric themes included the *Alchemical Tarot* (1995) designed by Rosemary Ellen Guiley and Robert M. Place,[156] the *Ceremonial Magic Tarot* (1992) of Marianne Peterson and Priscilla Schwei and the *Tarot of Ceremonial Magick* (1994) designed by Lon and Constance DuQuette and painted by David P. Wilson.[157]

A Fascination with other Religions and Cultures: Great and Small

As Matthew Fox wrote: 'mysticism is ... a common language, uttering a common experience. There is only one great underground river, though there are numerous wells into it – Buddhist wells and Taoist wells, Native American wells and Christian Wells, Islamic wells and Judaic wells.'[158] Though some New Agers rejected the traditional world religions as being repressive, unresponsive and out-of-touch, they generally acknowledged that they express some universal truths.[159]

The Age of Aquarius was viewed as a rejection of the dominant conservative Christian values, yet the essence of the teachings of Jesus as an affirmation of love and tolerance, persisted within the movement and was reflected in a number of tarot decks. Leslie Lewis created the *Christian Bible Tarot* (1995) to help those who used tarot come to terms with their Christian upbringing. Each card featured a title, divinatory meaning and a quote from the Old or New Testament. Major arcana cards also displayed a letter from the Hebrew alphabet.[160] Similarly, the *Bible Tarot* (1983) of Kathleen Binger illustrated scenes or parables from the Bible. Each card was numbered and featured a Hebrew letter along with its literal meaning. The Fool showed a blindfolded king being led by a blindfolded guide across a stone bier; the scene taken from Matthew 15: 13-14 which read: 'And if a blind man leads a blind man, both will fall into a pit.' The Magician card displayed the image of Moses before the Pharaoh. He had cast his rod down which had been transformed into a snake; this incident is related in Exodus 7: 8-10.[161] Interestingly, a similar connection was drawn by Corinne Heline in her book, *The Bible and the Tarot* (1969),[162] and by John Drane, Ross Clifford and Philip Johnson in *Beyond Prediction: the Tarot and Your Spirituality* (2001).[163]

Eastern traditions were readily embraced by the New Age movement. The influence of South Asian traditions was evidenced by the popularity of Hindu yoga and meditation techniques and the adoption of key Hindu notions such as 'cakras' and 'karma'.[164] Buddhism has also become important for authors of the New Age and some claim it is the fastest growing religion in Britain.[165] One tarot deck manifesting the influence of Buddhism is the *Kashmir Tarot* of Nicolaas van de Beek. In the original version of the deck, the cards were prohibitively expensive relief carvings made out of walnut by Abdul Salama.[166] Subsequently, a cardboard version was released. In this deck, Tibetan Buddhism was linked to the more traditional symbolism of tarot without an exegesis of Tibetan teachings. This was a deliberate statement; Van de Beek believing that tarot was fundamentally a western system though one still capable of showing the congruencies between east and west.[167] Hence, we had the Magician wearing a Tibetan headdress but with the usual emblems of the four suits. The High Priestess still held the Tora scroll in her lap (as with the Rider-Waite deck) but she sat before Tibetan mountains.[168]

The *Osho Zen Tarot* (1994) designed by Ma Deva Padma, loosely articulated Zen Buddhist principles as espoused by Osho (Bhagwan Shree Rajneesh).[169] Many of the major arcana cards were no longer recognisable yet others retained the essence of their former meaning. For example, 'Aloneness' replaced the 'Hermit' as trump IX. A small figure in the corner was dwarfed by the blankness of the rest of the card. The 'World' evolved into 'Completion' with a hand holding the last piece of a puzzle.[170] The *Buddhistic Fantasy Tarot* (1983), designed by Shigeki Gomi, boasted only the major arcana cards, representing phases in the life of the Buddha and different deities who corresponded to the traditional major arcana subjects. For example, trump VIII –usually Strength – was illustrated as Kongaorikishi (Deva King) who admonished those who were unwilling to commence the quest for truth and dispelled unjust intentions. An Asura played the part of the Devil (trump XV), who was an enemy of the gods in Hinduism but who was transformed into a protector in Buddhism.[171]

An intrinsic part of the New Age fascination with other cultures was the lure of indigenous spirituality. Though most saw this as a quest for inclusiveness that erased all differences, others viewed it as the reduction of indigenous practices to shallow therapeutic devices. Paradoxically, the appropriation of Australian Aboriginal culture was more popular in Europe and North America. In Australia, Native American culture was more interesting to consumers.[172] There are literally hundreds of tarot decks which used the symbolism of a diverse array of indigenous cultures.

Among those that explored the theme of Amerindian culture was the *Native American Tarot Deck* (1982) created by Magda Weck Gonzalez and J. A. Gonzalez, drawing its symbolism from a generalised pool of Native American imagery.[173] The imagery was intended to reflect the western cultural correspondences to that of indigenous America. For example, the Chariot transformed into the 'Sled' of the Inuit people, the Empress was recast as the 'Medicine Woman' and the Hierophant was reformed as the 'Shaman'.[174] The court became the Matriarch, Chief, Warrior and Maiden and the suit signs evolved into Blades (Swords), Pipes (Wands), Vessels (Cups) and Shields (Coins).[175] This pan-Indian approach was also exploited by Viola

Monreal's *Tarot of the Southwest Sacred Tribes: Tribes of Earth* (1996).[176] The designer primarily drew her symbolism from the Navajo, Apache and Pueblo Nations but also, to a much lesser extent, from some fifty-seven other sources. The suits of the minor arcana cards were associated with the four Nations of the Apache (Swords), Pueblo (Wands), Rio Grande Pueblo groups (Cups) and Navajo (Coins).[177]

Peter Balin designed the *Xultún Tarot* (1976), a deck recalling the symbolism of the Mayan Indians.[178] The sketches were made in Tikal, Guatemala and the major arcana cards were designed so that the images could form a single picture. Balin justified linking Mayan culture with tarot by concluding that both traditions drew meaning from the inherent structures of the cosmos and the human imagination.[179] A book, *The Flight of the Feathered Serpent* (1976), accompanied the deck, providing a detailed list of cor-respondences under the headings: De-scription, Interpretation, Significance, In-verted, Sexual Expression, Value, Color, Tone, Direction, Meaning and Astro-logical Symbol.[180] Balin drew heavily on the works of Carlos Castañeda casting doubt on the authenticity of the doctrine that he cites.[181] The major arcana cards, excluding the Fool and the Magician; were arranged into four rows of five cards and linked to the twenty days of the Mayan calendar. The four rows were fur-ther associated with the development of a sorcerer as described by Don Juan. The Sevens of each suit were labelled Lord of Valor (Staffs), Warrior of Futility (Swords), Lady of Debauch (Cups), Ser-vant of Failure (Jades) linking each suit to

MARIE LAVEAU

Figure 26: Marie Laveau replaces the Priestess in the New Orleans Voodoo Tarot
(© Sallie Ann Glassman, 1992).

a court card which were similarly named Lord, Lady, Warrior and Servant.[182]

The *Santa Fe Tarot* (1993) was another example in this category. It was crafted by artist Holly Huber and Tracy LeCocq, residents of New Mexico, who based the symbolism of their deck on Navajo Sand Paintings. The suits signs were recast as Lightning (Swords), Water (Cups), Rainbows (Wands) and Buffalos (Pentacles).[183] The cards were labelled to indicate their traditional identity and the corresponding Native American mythical character. For example, the 'Strength' card was recast as the 'Monster Slayer'

SIMBI D'L'EAU

Figure 27: Simbi d'l'eau adorns the equivalent of the 8 of Cups in the New Orleans Voodoo Tarot (© Sallie Ann Glassman, 1992).

and the 'Emergence Place' replaced the 'World' in the trump sequence.[184] The creation of the *Vision Quest Tarot* (1998) by Sante Fe artists Gaylan Sylvie Winter and Jo Dosé was also inspired by the lore of Native Americans.[185] Another deck that utilised this imagery was the *Medicine Woman Tarot* (1987) of Carol Bridges.[186]

Though not strictly speaking an indigenous religion, vodou has proved to be a popular source of material for New Age seekers. The *New Orleans Tarot* (1992) combined the mysterious religion with tarot which creators Louis Martinié and Sallie Ann Glassman justified by citing tarot's supposed origins in Egypt and linking it to vodou's African heritage.[187] In this deck, the trump cards were renamed 'Roads' and an additional 'wild card' was added bringing the number of trumps to twenty-three. The forty numbered pip cards were called 'Spirits' and the court cards were transformed into 'Temple Cards'. Each trump was associated with a letter of the Hebrew alphabet but also with a 'sacrifice'; a practice integral to vodou. The major arcana cards were renamed to be accommodated within the theme, for example trump II normally the Priestess or Popess, became the vodou queen Marie Laveau. The card was also associated with the sacrifice of salt and water.[188] The four suits were associated with the three vodou nations – and Santería – and roughly corresponded to the four elements in the west. Nations referred to a grouping of rites and spirits that walked together and were related by a common origin or theme.[189] The first of these was *Petro*, a form of worship common in Haiti, which corresponded to fire.[190] The second corresponded to the rites of the Congo Nation which were attributed to the element of water.[191] The *Rada* constituted the third nation and were associated with air. The fourth suit was associated with *Santería* and earth yet was treated as being independent of vodou in this deck.[192]

Several other decks combined the traditions of vodou, Santería and Condomblé with tarot. The *Legba Tarot of Voodoo* (1984) designed by Autumn Terzian, featured vodou gods on the trump cards and *loa* on the minor arcana cards.[193] Conceived by Zolrak and painted by Dürkön, the *Tarot of the Orishàs* (1994, 2000) depicted Brazilian Condomblé traditions.[194] Though many of the principal cards corresponded to major arcana cards, the deck was quite different from those used for traditional cartomancy. The first thirteen principal cards depicted the *Orishàs* with the remaining twelve showing other significant symbols such as 'Karma' and the 'Custodian Angel'.[195] The suits were named according to the four elements – Air, Fire, Water, Earth – with pip cards numbered from Ace to 10 with the addition of two cards: Element and Messenger.[196]

Similarly, many decks have explored the mythology and culture of Aboriginal Australia. While prospecting in Australia,

WILD CARD

LES BARONS

Figure 28: The Wild Card is a novel addition to the New Orleans Voodoo Tarot (© Sallie Ann Glassman, 1992).

Keith Courtenay-Peto claimed to have encountered an Aboriginal spiritual mentor who inspired him to create the *Australian Contemporary Dreamtime Tarot* (1991). Court cards displayed names derived from a number of Australian indigenous languages; for example, the Fool became '*Karadji*' and the Chariot transformed into the '*Whilpra*'. The suits were imagined as *muggils* (stone knives), *kundas* (digging sticks), *coolamons* (cups) and *wariats* (stones). The court was populated by the Tribal Elder, Earth Mother, Hunter and Maiden.[197] Other cultural tarots included the *Aztec Tarot* (1986) published by J. M. Simon of Paris and Piatnik and Söhne of Vienna,[198] and the *African Tarot* (1994) which embraced the symbolism of the Shangaan of South Africa.[199]

History Repeating

Though the broad history of tarot has been well established, New Age authors tenaciously cling to the erroneous histories promulgated by esotericists of the eighteenth and nineteenth centuries. Egypt is still frequently referred to as the 'home' of tarot, where the deck was crafted in order to conceal all manner of magical secrets.[200] Consequently, there are many tarot decks that utilised this theme, perpetuating the association of esoteric tarot with Egypt. The *Egipcios Kier Tarot* (1984) elaborated the beliefs, practices and social hierarchies of Egyptian culture.[201] The trump cards portrayed human figures rather than the gods and goddesses. For example, the card of the High Priestess showed the priestess of Isis rather than Isis herself.[202] The cards depicted various professions such as those of the Charioteer or Labourer, but also cards which served as a commentary on social conditions such as Magnificence which described how nobles set up their homes.[203] The major arcana cards were each marked with a hieroglyph, an alchemical sigil, a letter derived from a magical alphabet found in the seventeenth-century grimoire the *Key of Solomon the King*, a planetary symbol, an astrological sign and a Hebrew letter.[204] The minor arcana cards did not follow the traditional structure and instead were numbered 23 to 78, each card bearing an allegorical picture without a suit sign.[205]

The *Tarot of Transition* (1983) presented the major arcana as the gods and goddesses of Ancient Egypt.[206] The order of the trumps was rearranged to illustrate the mythological journey of the soul after death. Hence, the deck directed the querent to enact the soul's appearance before its judges after death rather than the traditional fortunetelling or psychological interpretations normally ascribed to tarot consultation.[207] The *Tarot of Transition* court was populated by the Pharaoh, the Queen, the Charioteer and Ushbati. Their task was to assist the querent in the Land of the Dead. Similarly, the four suits were redesigned to align with Egyptian symbolism; they became Ankhs (the key of life, Swords), the backbone of Osiris (Wands), Heset (the communion chalice, Cups) and Khepera (the Sun, Coins).[208]

Other examples of tarot dominated by 'Egyptian' imagery included the *Ibis Tarot* (1991) by Josef Machynka, the *Egyptian Tarot* (*I Tarocchi Egiziani*) (1996) designed by M. O. Wegener and Silvana Alasia,[209] Clive Barrett's *Ancient Egyptian Tarot* (1994),[210] the *Barath Egyptian Serigraphs* (1980) by Victorino del Pozo and the artist Suarez,[211] the *Book of Doors Tarot* by Athon Vegi,[212] the *Scarab Tarot* (1981) of Kathleen Binger,[213] and the *Egyptian Tarot 22* (1987) of Yoshio Karashima.[214]

Inexorably linked with the supposed Egyptian origins of tarot was the idea that gypsies brought the deck to Europe; when gypsies were still thought to be of Egyptian extraction. There were several decks which sought to make this connection explicit. The *Zigeuner Tarot* (1982) was painted by Walter Wegmuller, a self-professed Rom (Gypsy) who drew the imagery from Romany culture. For example, the Chariot was pulled by a goat and a chicken, animals commonly found in a Romany camp.[215] Another tarot designer that exploited this theme was Tchalaï Unger with her *Tarot Tzigane* (1984).[216] Not only was the Romany way of life expressed through the tarot symbolism but a discussion of the history was contained within the accompanying booklet. Interestingly, Unger also perpetuated the erroneous idea that tarot was derived from the Indian game of *chaturange*.[217] There were only thirty-eight cards in this deck with twenty-two of them loosely resembling the traditional major arcana cards, with the addition of sixteen pip cards comprised of a court of Father, Mother and Child and four Aces. The suit signs were linked to the four main Romany branches: the Kalderash of Central Europe, the Manush of Northern Italy, the Gypsies of Ireland and the Gitanos of Andalusia.[218] The suits were further linked to four tools which corresponded more or less to the traditional tarot suits: knives or scalpels (Kalderash, Swords); coins (Manush, Coins/Pentacles); pots, hoods or containers (Gypsies, Cups); and wooden sticks or musical instruments (Gitanos, wands).[219] The trump sequence detailed a version of the history of the Romany as formulated by the Rom. It began with their descent from the Rajput Princes who were displaced from their kingdom, forming different bands. It also encompassed the Rom belief that their people were from the stars and will ultimately return there. The penultimate trump, *O Geape Vimanaki*, showed a lingam and yoni figure representing the union of male and female elements. It also displayed the spaceship, *Vimana*, which will return the Romani to their stellar home.[220] The last trump, *Tataghi* (Heart of Fire), depicted the ultimate meaning of this journey, the return of the Rom to the place of their cosmic and divine origin.[221]

The *Buckland Romani Tarot* (2001) also explored the alleged link between tarot and gypsies.[222] Raymond Buckland was the son of a gypsy and in the book accompanying the *Romani Tarot*, he described his fascination with the deck his grandmother spent so much time poring over. Buckland directed artist Lissane Lake to paint the deck, thereby casting his ideas into material form. The symbolism of the deck closely resembled that of the Colman-Waite pack with some notable exceptions: the Magician was female supposedly because the majority of gypsy 'magicians' were female; likewise the Priestess of trump II became the *Puridai* or matriarch of the tribe. The figures on the cards were depicted as gypsies. On trump VIII – Strength, a beautiful woman opened the jaws of a performing bear rather than a lion.[223]

The persistence of this erroneous association of tarot with gypsies eloquently illustrates the New Age fascination with other cultures and particularly, the romance associated with this wandering race. In part, this fascination derived from the portrayal of gypsies in the media as mysteriously dark and beautiful, associated with divination, folklore and magical practice. To most people even now, the origins of gypsies are obscure, as they keep to themselves or are kept to themselves by discrimination and persecution within the wider community, enabling New Age seekers to form their own distorted notions of this race.

Most contemporary users of tarot are completely unaware of the deck's origins in the courts of northern Italy and are more likely to assign an Egyptian or gypsy provenance to it. The alteration of the structure of many New Age packs renders them completely unsuitable for their original purpose as a game. It has become the New Age tool *par excellence*, easily accommodated within the shifting patterns of use which has seen the focus of divination move from 'fortune-telling' to that facilitating self-development and healing. Indeed, many modern decks have been designed specifically to enable spiritual as well as physical healing which have become inexorably linked, the symbolism displayed on the cards reflecting this function. The diversity of tarot symbolism has also multiplied exponentially in response to the eclectic nature of New Age belief, where the rituals, mythology and religious practices of many cultures are considered to be equivalent and interchangeable. This syncretism sees the symbolism of Christianity, Buddhism and Hinduism sitting next to that of Australian Aborigines, Native Americans and other indigenous peoples. The jargon of science and psychology are often employed to justify and explain many New Age beliefs and practices and again, this tendency shows up in the symbolism of tarot and the justification of this symbolism in the New Age tarot literature.

Conclusion

Evolution is not a linear progression towards an ultimate result, but implies a tortuous path with many dead ends, parallel experiments and a blind fumbling towards adaptation. Consequently, it seems appropriate to apply this term to the process that has generated such a multiplicity of tarot decks. In this case, the adaptations were not triggered by the physical environment as with the long neck and lipped shell of the Galapagos tortoise, but by the cultural and social environment shaped by the reactions to war, religion, plague, enlightenment science, exposure to exotic cultures and other incendiary concerns. The result of this process of 'survival of the fittest' is an enhanced product, something more sophisticated than the original specimen, more specialised and better suited to its environment. The tarot decks that evolved with the vagaries of human notions about the world certainly fit this description. Tarot has evolved and been accommodated within the cultural currents of different times; its purpose altered to suit the prevailing attitudes and beliefs. The symbolism on the cards likewise reflects the fickle results of this human reflection.

Tarot itself evolved from the playing cards introduced into Europe form the Mamlūk Empire of the Middle East. Some fifty years after the deck's first Continental appearance, a young Duke Filippo Maria Visconti of the northern Italian city of Milan augmented it with the addition of a number of picture cards, 'sixteen celestial princes and barons'. Later, under the Duke's direction, the deck changed again though retained the basic structure of four suits with the addition of a number of picture cards. The Visconti di Modrone and Brambilla decks preceded the Visconti-Sforza deck which was to serve as the template for most subsequent tarots. A close investigation of its symbolism revealed that it reflected many of the concerns of the Italian Renaissance: the proximity of death, the fickle hand of fortune, the desirability of living a life of virtue, the importance of spirituality but also the contempt with which corporeal concerns were held, namely the corruption of the Church and the inefficacy of the Holy Roman Empire. More specifically, the tarot symbolism portrayed the lives and history of the Viscontis with their famous relative Sister Maifreda posing as the Popess and Francesco Sforza cast as Hercules killing the Nemean lion or Venice in another guise. The fickle hand of fortune was also reflected in tarot's function. It was created as a game; a potent allegory of Visconti life with its mixture of skill, cunning and chance, all souls being equal in the eyes of God.

In eighteenth-century France, tarot underwent its first major transformation, evolving into an esoteric device of divination. With tarot removed from its original environment, its symbolism lost its previous relevance and context, rendering its imagery mysterious. Hence, tarot's shift in function coincided with an altered view of the content of its symbolism, believed to be an expression of esoteric lore. Antoine Court de Gébelin reinterpreted the deck as the lost *Book of Thoth*. Its symbolism, he espoused, concealed the secrets of an ancient and wise Egyptian priesthood, forced to conceal their most precious secrets in a game to ensure their survival. Court de Gébelin's ideas found such a ready acceptance as the value of conventional religion was being questioned, and new heterogeneous forms of spirituality were emerging into the cultural milieu. The popularity of *Naturphilosophie* was reaching its peak and subtle links were sought between all things under the influence of Emmanuel Swedenborg. In this spirit, Éliphas Lévi forged connections between the tarot trumps and astrology, kabbalah and other such systems. Tarot symbolism was frequently Egyptianised, the hieroglyphics still fascinating in pre-Rosetta France, but there was also the addition of Indian motifs, Hebrew letters and astrological sigils. Tarot was assigned a role in ritual magic, its symbolism the microcosm that could affect change in the macrocosm but also as a divinatory device, the macrocosm reflected in its symbolism. The Fool was incorporated into the trump sequence, losing its status as a 'wildcard' and rendering the rectified packs unsuitable for use in game playing.

Across the Channel in England, the Occult Revival was already well underway. Initially, tarot played no part but it soon became central under the influence of the Hermetic Order of the Golden Dawn. Founded in 1888, with rituals outlined in the mysterious Cipher Manuscript, it was the crowning glory of the Occult Revival in England. It was the Golden Dawn's assignation of pathways of the Tree of Life to the tarot trumps that would form the basis of most modern forms of divinatory interpretation. Two Golden Dawn members were to make invaluable contributions to esoteric tarot. First, Aleister Crowley extended the association of tarot trumps with various esoteric schemes. Second, Arthur Edward Waite illustrated the minor arcana cards, those cards which began life as pip cards corresponding to the four suits of the Mamlūk deck, to facilitate their use in divination. In addition, Waite linked tarot to the Grail Mysteries and Christian mysticism, an association which persists to this day.

With the advent of the New Age, tarot was to evolve once more. It retained its divinatory role but the focus of that divination shifted. Where once it was used for fortunetelling, in the New Age it became associated with self-transformation and healing; it was used to fathom the nature of 'karmic contracts' and the spiritual causes of 'dis-ease'. Again, the symbolism on the deck, particularly of the major arcana cards, reflected the many streams of New Age thought and tarot became the New Age tool *par excellence*. The traditional symbolism of the trumps was augmented by that of many cultures, emerging healing modalities and the fascination with 'science', often used in combination, reflecting the eclectic and syncretistic tendencies of New Age thought. Hence, *feng shui* tarots, astrological tarots, tarots espousing Buddhist, feminist and environmental viewpoints emerged onto the scene. The structure of the deck has become fluid; subservient to its particular purpose or theme.

New Age tarotists and eighteenth-century esotericists sought a continuity in tarot's history from Ancient Egypt until the present day; discounting its use as a game to that of a clever device enlisted to protect esoteric wisdom. Though an Egyptian provenance for tarot has been proven beyond doubt to be fallacious, the belief is still perpetuated by a large number of New Age books and 'Egyptian' decks. Egypt is still viewed by many as the home of tarot but such views are nothing more than romantic flights of fancy, founded in a misinterpretation of symbolism too far removed from its original context to be readily comprehensible. There is no underlying esoteric scheme that forms the basis of a continuous tradition.

Such a finding begs the question: when we talk of tarot, what are we speaking about? Are there enough similarities between the fifteenth century deck painted by Michelino da Besozzo for Duke Visconti and the Aura Soma deck to call both 'tarot'? There is no continuity of purpose; one was used for game playing, the other for divination and healing. Neither is suited to the purpose of the other. There is no continuity of structure. The extant Visconti decks differed in structure from subsequent decks but also from each other. Modern tarot packs have a variable number of cards; some not even conforming to the basic pattern of major and minor arcana cards. Sometimes there are no pip cards at all or they are transformed, as in the Rider-Waite deck, as to be almost unrecognisable as such. There is no consistency of symbolism between those first decks and many subsequent ones. A certain trump sequence is common but certainly not universal. The deck of Michelino de Besozzo does not have trumps we recognise, let alone a familiar trump sequence. The Visconti decks consistently lacked the Tower and Devil cards which were added to tarot subsequently. The French and English esotericists altered the tarot symbolism to fit their altered purpose for the deck and their esoteric schemes. So in what way can we say that all of these decks are tarots?

Ludwig Wittgenstein proposed his theory of family resemblances to explain the development of the extension of concepts over time.[1] He espoused the idea that certain classes of referents could not be specified by a determinate property, but instead proposed that possession of a group of properties could indicate that something should probably belong in a certain class. He used the analogy of a family possessing certain characteristics of appearance as an indication of their relationship to one another.[2] This theory can be readily extrapolated to accommodate tarot. There are certain characteristics of many tarot decks that distinguish them from other packs. There is a characteristic seventy-eight-card structure which includes twenty-two trumps (or twenty-one trumps with a Fool card) and fifty-six pip cards distributed through four suits. Many packs exhibit a common trump sequence which begins with the Magician. There are certain symbols and names often associated with a particular tarot trump. Some tarot decks were used to play card games but others were used for divination. These characteristics are typically associated with tarot yet not all decks possess all of them. They may possess one or two and so it becomes possible for two decks to share no characteristics yet still fall into the common family of tarot. In this way there is a continuity between those early Italian decks and the kaleidoscopic variety of New Age tarots.

Having demonstrated a familial relationship between the decks discussed in this book, it becomes possible to track the cultural factors which precipitated tarot's evolution from a game to a divinatory and esoteric device, and subsequently as a tool for personal transformation. Tarot itself evolved from the ordinary playing card deck of the Mamlūk Empire; its subsequent development shaped by the prevailing cultural and social currents of the contexts in which it was found. The nature of these cultural imperatives is reflected in the symbolism of tarot particularly that of the trumps. Just as the changing physical environment of this planet brought about the demise of the dinosaurs, the changing cultural milieu proved unsuitable for the persistence of some earlier forms of tarot. Instead, new varieties better suited to the changing conditions evolved from those that went before. So, in sum, this is both a cultural history and a series of cultural histories, the former by virtue of those familial relationships that make tarot 'tarot', the latter because of the divergent functions, structures, multiplicity of symbolism and the vastly differing cultural milieus in which the tarot deck evolved.

Notes

NOTES TO INTRODUCTION

1   See Thomas Scoville and Hughes Hall, *The Metrosexual Tarot* [website] (Thomas Scoville, 2004 [cited 30 September 2005]); available from http://www.thomasscoville.com/metrosexual/. Thomas Scoville also created the Silicon Valley Tarot.

2   For example, see Amber Jayanti, *Tarot for Dummies*, ed. Joan L. Friedman, *For Dummies* (New York: Hungry Minds, 2001); Wilma Carroll, *The 2-Hour Tarot Tutor: The Fast, Revolutionary Method for Learning to Read Tarot Cards in Two Hour* (New York: Berkeley Books, 2004).

3   Frances Amelia Yates, *The Rosicrucian Enlightenment* (London: Routledge and Kegan Paul, 1972).

4   Frances Amelia Yates, *Giordano Bruno and the Hermetic Tradition*, *Routledge Classics* (London: Routledge, 1964).

5   Frances Amelia Yates, *The Occult Philosophy in the Elizabethan Age* (London: Ark Paperbacks, 1983).

6   For example see Antoine Faivre, "The Children of Hermes and the Science of Man," in *Hermeticism and the Renaissance: Intellectual History and the Occult in Early Modern Europe*, ed. Ingrid Merkel and Allen G. Debus, *Folger Institute Symposia* (Washington: Folger Books, 1988); Wouter J. Hanegraaff, "Empirical Method in the Study of Esotericism," *Methods and Theory in the Study of Religion* 7, no. 2 (1995).

7   See Detlef Hoffmann, *The Playing Card: An Illustrated History*, trans. C. S. V. Salt (Greenwich: New York Graphic Society Ltd, 1973).

8   See Michael Dummett with Sylvia Mann, *The Game of Tarot: From Ferrara to Salt Lake City* (London: Gerald Duckworth and Co. Ltd., 1980).

9   For example, see Dummett with Mann, *The Game of Tarot*, xxiv-xxv.

10   For example see Peter Burke, *Varieties of Cultural History* (Cambridge: Polity Press, 1997); Sally Ledger and Roger Luckhurst, eds., *The Fin De Siècle: A Reader in Cultural History C. 1880–1900* (Oxford: Oxford University Press, 2000).

NOTES TO CHAPTER ONE

1   The twenty-one trumps with the Fool are usually called the 'major arcana' by users of contemporary esoteric tarot.

2   These fifty-six cards are called the 'minor arcana' by users of contemporary esoteric tarot.

3   Stuart R. Kaplan, *The Encyclopedia of Tarot*, IV vols., Vol. I (New York: U. S. Games Systems, 1978; reprint, Second), 10.

4   Michael Dummett with Sylvia Mann, *The Game of Tarot: From Ferrara to Salt Lake City* (London: Gerald Duckworth and Co. Ltd., 1980), 6.

5   Ibid.

6   Franco Pratesi, "Italian Cards - New Discoveries: 9. Tarot in Bologna: Documents from the University Library," *The Playing Card* XXVII (1989): 136.

7   A portrait of Fibbia bears an inscription that credits him with the invention of *Tarocchino* and it is on this basis that Cicognara made his claim. Stuart R. Kaplan, *The Encyclopedia of Tarot*, IV vols., Vol. II (New York: U. S. Games Systems, 1986; reprint, Second), 3. This misinformation was repeated by many playing card scholars. See for example Mrs John King van Rensselaer, *Prophetical, Educational and Playing Cards* (London: Hurst and Blackett, Ltd, 1912), 312.

8   Freeman M. O'Donoghue, *Catalogue of the Collection of Playing Cards Bequeathed to the Trustees of the British Museum by the Late Lady Charlotte Schreiber* (London: Longmans and Co., 1901), 4.

9   See Edward A. Aviza, *Thinking Tarot* (New York: Simon and Schuster, 1997), 43; H. T. Morley, *Old and Curious Playing Cards: Their History and Types from Many Countries and Periods* (Secaucus: The Wellfleet Press, 1989), 17. Merlin appears to have been the first to posit this theory based on his misinterpretation of the word '*naibi*' which he thought meant 'tarot cards' instead of 'playing cards'. Ronald Decker, Thierry Depaulis, and Michael Dummett. *A Wicked Pack of Cards: The Origins of Occult Tarot* (London: Gerald Duckworth and Co. Ltd., 1996), 266.

10   For example see Judy Hall, *The Illustrated Guide to Divination* (New York: Godsfield Press, 2000), 28; Martin Hillman, "Telling Fortunes with Cards," *Fate & Fortune* 1974, 17.

11   Maurice Rickards, *The Encyclopedia of Ephemera: A Guide to the Fragmentary Documents of Everyday Life for the Collector, Curator, and Historian* (London: British Library, 2000), 239. Cultural analyst, Joyce Goggin of the University of Amsterdam, attributed the invention of the Joker to Emmaneul Juker of Utrecht in the mid-fourteenth century. I have found no other reference to this. See Joyce Goggin, "A History of Otherness: Tarot and Playing Cards from Early Modern Europe," *Journal for the Academic Study of Magic* 1, no. 1 (2003): 55.

12   Thierry Depaulis, *Tarot, Jeu Et Magie* (Paris: Bibliothèque Nationale, 1984), 33.

13   For example, 'The oldest reference in the West to playing cards is the mention of *naibi* in the manuscript dated Siena, 1299, entitled *Trattato del governo della familia* (Treatise on the Government of the Family) by Pipozzo di Sandro' in Alessandro Bellenghi, *Cartomancy*, trans. Julie Almond (London: Ebury Press, 1988), 16; 'Ambrose Firmin Didot (*Essai sur la typographie*) quotes a scrap of poetry from a French romance of 1328, which alludes to the folly of games of dice, checkers and cards' in Theodore Low de Vinne, *The Invention of Printing: A Collection of Facts and Opinions Descriptive of Early Prints and Playing Cards, the Block Books of the Fifteenth Century, the Legend of Lourens Janszoon Coaster, of Haarlem, and the Work of John Gutenberg and His Associates* (New York: Francis Hart & Co., 1876), 95. E. A. Bond stated that a Dominican friar, Johann Ingold, writing in 1482 asserted that playing cards entered Germany in 1300. This document cannot be said to be reliable. E. A. Bond, "History of Playing-Cards," *Athenæum*, no. 2621 (1878): 87.

14   This reference is to be found in the *Diccionari de rims* cited in Gherardo Ortalli, "The Prince and the Playing Cards: The Este Family and the Role of Courts at the Time of the Kartenspiel-Invasion," *Ludica: annali di storia e civilta del gioco* 2 (1996): 175.

15   Robert Steele, "A Notice of the Ludus Triumphorum and Some Early Italian Card Games; with Some Remarks on the Origin of the Game of Cards," *Archaeologia, or, Miscellaneous Tracts Relating to Antiquity* 57 (1900): 189, 202.

16   Bond, "History of Playing-Cards," 87–88.

17   Ortalli, "Prince and the Playing Cards," 176.

18   Jean de Coveluzzo in Catherine Perry Hargrave, *A History of Playing Cards and a Bibliography of Cards and Gaming* (New York: Dover Publications, Inc., 1966), 224; Also in Thomas Francis Carter, *The Invention of Printing in China and Its Spread Westward*, Revised ed. (New York: The Ronald Press Company, 1955), 185. Sayed Idries Shah ascribed the passage to Feliciano Busi as did Lady Harris. Marguerite Frieda Harris. "Exhibition of 78 Paintings of the Tarot Cards." In *Instructions for Aleister Crowley's Thoth Tarot Deck* edited by James Wasserman (Stamford: U. S. Games Systems, Inc., 1978): 35.

19   '1379. Fu recato in Viterbo il gioco delle carte da un saracino chiamato Hayl.' In another manuscript, there is the variant: 'il gioco delle carte, che in saracino parlare si chiama nayb.' Nicolo delle Tuccia in Detlef Hoffmann, *The Playing Card: An Illustrated History*. Translated by C. S. V. Salt (Greenwich: New York Graphic Society Ltd, 1973), 12.

20   '*Unum ludim de nayps qui sunt quadrazinte quatuor pecie*' cited in Kaplan, *Encyclopedia of Tarot II*, 1. The document can be viewed at the Archivo Historico de Protocolos Notariales, Barcelona.

21   de Vinne, *Invention of Printing*, 90–91; M. G. Kendall all cites a prohibition against card-playing in Paris, 1397. See M. G. Kendall. "Studies in the History of Probability and Statistics. V. A Note on Playing Cards." *Biometrika* 44, no. 1/2 (1957): 260.

22   Dummett with Mann, *The Game of Tarot*, 33–34.

23   Hargrave, *A History of Playing Cards*, 223.

24   Dummett with Mann, *The Game of Tarot*, 33–34.

25   Gerald Encausse (Papus) also drew a connection between Ganjifa and tarot. Gérard Encausse, *The Tarot of the Bohemians: Absolute Key to Occult Science; the Most Ancient Book in the World for the Use of Initiates*, trans. A. P. Morton, Third Edition, Revised ed. (Hollywood: Wilshire Book Company, 1971), 87.

26   Hargrave, *A History of Playing Cards*, 20.

27   R. Merlin, *Origine Des Cartes a Jouer, Recherches Nouvelles Sur Les Naïbis, Les Tarots Et Sur Les Autres Espèces De Cartes, Ouvrage Accompagnè D'un Album De Soixante-Quatorze Planches* (Paris: R. Merlin, 1869), 13.

28   F. Harold Smith, *Outline of Hinduism*, ed. Eric S. Waterhouse, *Great Religions of the East* (London: The Epworth Press, 1934), 89; Hargrave, *A History of Playing Cards*, 20–27.

29   Ibid.

30   Ibid.

31   Hargrave, *A History of Playing Cards*, 20–27.

32   Smith, *Outline of Hinduism*, 90.

33   Robert Charles Zaehner, *Hinduism*, ed. Christopher Butler, Robert Evans, and John Skorupski, Second ed., *Opus* (Oxford: Oxford University Press, 1966), 91.

34   Ibid. Stuart Kaplan believed this game was the direct ancestor of tarot. Stuart R. Kaplan, *Tarot Classic* (New York: U. S. Games Systems, 1972), 9–10.

35   Stanley Wolpert, *A New History of India*, Sixth ed. (New York: Oxford University Press, 2000), 135.

36   Hargrave, *A History of Playing Cards*, 20.

37   Dummett with Mann, *The Game of Tarot*, 59.

38   Roger Tilley, *A History of Playing Cards* (London: Studio Vista, 1973), 12.

39   Jean-Pierre Seguin, *Le Jeu De Carte* (Paris: Hermann, 1968), 25; Frederic C. Lane, *Venice: A Maritime Republic* (Baltimore: The Johns Hopkins University Press, 1973), 79, 129, 39.

40   Tilley, Roger. *A History of Playing Cards* (London: Studio Vista, 1973), 12.

41   Michael Dummett and Kamal Abu-Deeb. "Some Remarks on Mamluk Playing Cards."
     Journal of the Warburg and Courtauld Institutes 36 (1973): 107.
42   Dummett with Mann, *The Game of Tarot*, 34.
43   Carter, *The Invention of Printing in China*, 184.
44   Christina Olsen, "Carte Da Trionfi: The Development of Tarot in Fifteenth Century
     Italy" (Ph.D., University of Pennsylvania, 1994), 34–35.
45   Hoffmann, *The Playing Card*, 52.
46   Dummett with Mann, *The Game of Tarot*, 36.
47   Olsen, "Carte De Trionfi", 35.
48   Dummett with Mann, *The Game of Tarot*, 37–38.
49   Tilley, *History of Playing Cards*, 11. For an elaboration of this theory see Hargrave, *A
     History of Playing Cards*, 6.
50   Carter, *The Invention of Printing in China*, 192.
51   Dummett with Mann, *The Game of Tarot*, 38.
52   There was some northern Italian trade with China during the thirteenth and fourteenth
     centuries. See Frederic C. Lane. *Venice: A Maritime Republic* (Baltimore: The Johns
     Hopkins University Press, 1973), 79, 129.
53   Robert Irwin, *The Middle East in the Middle Ages: The Early Mamluk Sultanate
     1250–1382* (London: Croom Helm, 1986), 117, 130.
54   Ibid., 118.
55   Robert Klein, "Les Tarots Enluminé Du XVe Siècle," *L'Oeil*, no. 145 (1967): 12.
56   '*Jochs de Nayps plans, y alters jochs moreschs*' in Dummett and Abu-Deeb, "Some
     Remarks," 114.
57   Jean de Coveluzzo in Hargrave, *A History of Playing Cards*, 224.
58   Enno Littmann, *Die Erzählungen Aus Den Tausendundein Nächten : Vollständige
     Deutsche Ausgabe in Sechs Bänden. Zum Ersten Mal Nach Dem Arabischen Urtext
     Der Calcuttaer Ausgabe Vom Jahre 1839*, VI vols., Vol. III (Insel: Weisbaden, 1924),
     693; Dummett with Mann, *The Game of Tarot*, 42.
59   Dummett with Mann, *The Game of Tarot*, 42.
60   Goggin, "A History of Otherness," 49–50.
61   Hoffmann, *The Playing Card*, 18–19.
62   Olsen, "Carte De Trionfi", 37.
63   Dummett and Abu-Deeb, "Some Remarks," 106–07.
64   Dummett with Mann, *The Game of Tarot*, 39.
65   Olsen, "Carte De Trionfi", 40–41; Dummett with Mann, *The Game of Tarot*, 41.
66   Olsen, "Carte De Trionfi", 50.
67   Ibid., 49, 52.
68   Ibid., 54.
69   Hoffmann, *The Playing Card*, 19.
70   Olsen, "Carte De Trionfi", 37.
71   Dummett with Mann, *The Game of Tarot*, 40–41.
72   Various authors have erroneously stated that polo was unknown in Europe at this time.
     The Crusaders brought the game back to France in the twelfth century though it did not
     become popular until much later. See H. E. Chehabi and Allen Guttmann, "From Iran
     to All of Asia: The Origin and Diffusion of Polo," *The International Journal for the
     History of Polo* 19, no. 2–3 (2002): 390.
73   Kaplan, *Encyclopedia of Tarot I*, 7.
74   Sayed Idries Shah. *The Sufis* (New York: Anchor Books, 1971): 449–50. For an
     alternate theory of *Sūfī* provenance for the tarot see El-Moor, "The Occult Tradition of
     the Tarot." Jereer El-Moor, "The Occult Tradition of the Tarot in Tangency with Ibn
     'Arabi's Life and Teachings: Part Two," *The Journal of the Muhyiddin Ibn 'Arabi*

Society XXXII (2002). The idea of a *Ṣūfī* involvement with tarot had been elaborated by Sir Fairfax Leighton Cartwright in his three-volume novel *The Mystic Rose from the Garden of the King: a Fragment of the Vision of Sheikh Haji Ibrahim of Kerbela* (1899) and more recently by John D. Blakeley in *The Mystical Tower of the Tarot* (1974) and William C. Lammey in *Karmic Tarot* (1988). Ronald Decker and Michael Dummett. *A History of the Occult Tarot: 1870-1970.* (London: Gerald Duckworth & Co. Ltd., 2002): , 304-05.

75   Paul Huson, *Mystical Origins of the Tarot: From Ancient Roots to Modern Usage* (Rochester: Destiny Books, 2004), 21.

76   Ibid. For a history of the development of *Ṣūfism*, see J. Spencer Trimingham, *The Sufi Orders in Islam* (London: Oxford University Press, 1971), 1-30.

77   Huson, *Mystical Origins of the Tarot*, 21-22.

78   Omar Khayyám, *The Rubaiyat of Omar Khayyám*, trans. Edward Fitzgerald (London: George G. Harrap and Co. Ltd, c1930), L.

79   Huson, *Mystical Origins of the Tarot*, 22.

80   Ibid., 23-26.

81   Joseph H. Peterson is the producer of the popular Internet website *Twilit Grotto: Archives of Western Esoterica* found at http://www.esotericarchives.com. Huson, *Mystical Origins of the Tarot*, 25-26.

82   Ibid., 26.

83   Muhsin Fani, *Oriental Literature or the Dabistan*, trans. David Shea and Anthony Troyer (New York: Tudor Publishing Co., 1937), 21.

84   Fani, *The Dabistan*, 22.

85   Ibid., 22-23.

86   Huson, *Mystical Origins of the Tarot*, 26-27.

87   Ibid.

88   Ibid.

89   For example see Rosemund Tuve, "Notes on the Virtues and Vices: Part II," *Journal of the Warburg and Courtauld Institutes* 27 (1964): 11.

90   Huson, *Mystical Origins of the Tarot*, 28.

91   'Mameluke' in *Oxford English Dictionary* (Second) [Oxford English Dictionary Online] (Oxford University Press, 2005 [cited 18 August 2005]); available from http://dictionary.oed.com; Irwin, *Middle East in the Middle Ages*, 3.

92   Olsen, "Carte De Trionfi", 42.

93   Irwin, *Middle East in the Middle Ages*, 4.

94   Olsen, "Carte De Trionfi", 42.

95   Irwin, *Middle East in the Middle Ages*, 62-63.

96   Olsen, "Carte De Trionfi", 42.

97   Irwin, *Middle East in the Middle Ages*, 4.

98   Olsen, "Carte De Trionfi", 42.

99   Ibid.

100 Ibid., 46.

101 Chehabi and Guttmann, "From Iran to All of Asia," 390.

102 Olsen, "Carte De Trionfi", 51.

103 Ibid., 52-53.

104 Ibid., 55.

105 Dummett with Mann, *The Game of Tarot*, 68. This deck is sometimes known as the Yale pack or even the Cary-Yale pack.

106 H. T. Morley. *Old and Curious Playing Cards: Their History and Types from Many Countries and Periods.* (Secaucus: The Wellfleet Press, 1989), 22; Arthur Edward

Waite, *Shadows of Life and Thought: A Retrospective Review in the Form of Memoirs* (London: Selwyn and Blount, 1938), 186.

107   Ed S. Taylor, *The History of Playing Cards, with Anecdotes of Their Use in Conjuring, Fortune-Telling, and Card Sharping* (London: John Camden Hotten, 1865), 3.

108   Dummett with Mann, *The Game of Tarot*, 65–66.

109   Joseph Maxwell, *The Tarot*, trans. Ivor Powell (Saffron Walden: C. W. Daniel Company Limited, 1975), 16. This myth is still perpetuated even by respected scholars. For example, see Joseph Campbell, "Part I: Exoteric Tarot," in *Tarot Revelations*, ed. Richard Roberts (San Anselmo: Vernal Equinox Press, 1987), 4–5, 9. This is presented as fact even in fiction: 'But learned men ought to ascertain these little facts before they give out with such certitude that Tarok dates from the period of Charles the Sixth' in Gustav Meyrink, *The Golem*, trans. Madge Pemberton (London: Victor Gollancz Ltd, 1928), 113–14.

110   Charlene Elizabeth Gates. "The Tarot Trumps: Their Origin, Archetypal Imagery, and Use in Some Works of English Literature" (Ph. D., University of Oregon, 1982), 71–72.

111   Hoffmann, *The Playing Card*, 18.

112   Cynthia Giles. *The Tarot: History, Mystery and Lore* (New York: Paragon House, 1992), 12. William Andrew Chatto, *Facts and Speculations on the Origin and History of Playing Cards* (London: J. R. Smith, 1848).

113   M. L. D'Otrange, "Thirteen Tarot Cards from the Visconti-Sforza Set," *The Connoisseur* 133 (1954): 59.

114   For example see William C. Lammey, "What Is Karmic Tarot?," in *New Thoughts on Tarot: Transcripts from the First International Newcastle Tarot Symposium*, ed. Mary K. Greer and Rachel Pollack (North Hollywood: Newcastle Publishing Co., 1989), 110-11.

115   Gates, "The Tarot Trumps", 108. Interestingly enough, Patricia and Lionel Fanthorpe talk about symbolism consistent with that of the tarot trumps in a French church at Rennes-le-Château in their book about a priest who mysteriously came into a fortune. They proposed that he discovered an invaluable secret by breaking a secret tarot code. See Patricia Fanthorpe and Lionel Fanthorpe, *The Holy Grail Revealed: The Real Secret of Rennes-Le-Château* (San Bernadino: The Borgo Press, 1982), 123.

116   Gates, "The Tarot Trumps", 108.

117   For example see Beryl Smalley, *English Friars and Antiquity in the Early Fourteenth Century* (Oxford: Basil Blackwell, 1960).

118   Decker, Depaulis, and Dummett, *A Wicked Pack of Cards*, 52.

119   *The Book of Thoth* supposedly contains the secrets of alchemy. In some sources it is reported to have only two pages: one that described how to influence nature and the other described how to control the world of the dead. Other sources claimed that the *Book* was composed of forty-two volumes. See Peter Marshall, *The Philosopher's Stone: A Quest for the Secrets of Alchemy* (London: Macmillan, 2001), 182. Louis Claude de Saint-Martin founded the movement of Martinism (named for the thought of Martines de Pasqually) which advocated enlightened mysticism. For more information on Saint-Martin's Martinist philosophy see David Bates, "The Mystery of Truth: Louis-Claude De Saint-Martin's Enlightened Mysticism," *Journal of the History of Ideas* 61, no. 4 (2000).

120   Depaulis, *Jeu Et Magie*, 131.

121   Hargrave, *A History of Playing Cards*, 223.

122   Olsen, "Carte De Trionfi", 266.

123   Antoine Court de Gébelin, *Monde Primitif: Analysé Et Comparé Avec Le Monde Moderne, Considéré Dans L'histoire Naturelle De La Parole; Ou Grammaire*

Universelle Et Comparative, 9 vols., *Archives De La Linguistique Française; No.95* (Paris: 1774).

124 Arland Ussher, *The XXII Keys of the Tarot*, New ed. (Dublin: The Dolmen Press, 1969), 5-6.

125 Gates, "The Tarot Trumps", 99. For Herodotus' account of this invasion see Herodotus, *The Histories*, ed. E. V. Rieu, trans. Aubrey de Sélincourt, Revised ed., *Penguin Classics* (Harmondsworth: Penguin, 1972), 206-10.

126 Gates, "The Tarot Trumps", 99.

127 Arthur Edward Waite. *The Pictorial Key to the Tarot: Being Fragments of a Secret Tradition under the Veil of Divination.* Second ed. (London: Rider & Company, 1971. Reprint, Fifth), 52-54.

128 See Jean-Baptiste Pitois, *The History and Practice of Magic*, trans. James Kirkup and Julian Shaw, II vols., Vol. I (London: Forge Press, 1952); Pitois, *History and Practice Vol II.*

129 See Encausse, *The Tarot of the Bohemians.*

130 Carol Andrews, *The Rosetta Stone* (London: British Museum Publications Ltd, 1988; reprint, Seventh), 15-16; Rosalie David, *The Experience of Ancient Egypt* (London: Routledge, 2000), 72.

131 Though attributed to Nancy Fullwood, this book was allegedly channelled by Mrs Anna M. Fullwood. Gates, "The Tarot Trumps", 41. For an interesting review of this book see Claude Braydon, "The Song of Sano Tarot (Review)," *The Builder Magazine*, December 1929.

132 William Lindsay Gresham, *Nightmare Alley* (London: William Heineman Ltd, 1947), 59-60.

133 David Allen Harvey, "Beyond Enlightenment: Occultism, Politics, and Culture in France from the Old Regime to the Fin-De-Siècle," *The Historian* 65, no. 3 (2003): 676. Jean-Michel David posited a similar theory, instead proposing that the symbolism was derived from cylinder seals dating from the eighth century in Iraq. See Jean-Michel David, *Iraqi Archeological Remnants and Possible Influences on Tarot* (11) [Archived e-mail newsletter] (Association for Tarot Studies, 2003 [cited 23 June 2004]); available from http://www.association.tarotstudies.org.

134 Robert M. Place, *The Tarot: History, Symbolism, and Divination* (New York: Jeremy P. Tarcher/Penguin, 2005), 9.

135 Decker and Dummett, *History of the Occult Tarot*, 178.

136 O'Neill, *Tarot Symbolism*, 57.

137 David S. Katz, *The Occult Tradition: From the Renaissance to the Present Day* (London: Jonathan Cape, 2005), 23.

138 Wouter J. Hanegraaff, "The Study of Western Esotericism: New Approaches to Christian and Secular Culture." In *New Approaches to the Study of Religion: Regional, Critical, and Historical Approaches*, edited by Peter Antes, Armin W. Geertz and Randi R. Warne. (Berlin: Walter de Gruyter, 2004): 492-93.

139 Kocku von Stuckrad, *Western Esotericism: A Brief History of Secret Knowledge*, trans. Nicholas Goodrick-Clarke (London: Equinox Publishing Ltd, 2005), 56.

140 Clement Salaman, Dorine van Oyen, and William D. Wharton, *The Way of Hermes: The Corpus Hermeticum* (London: Duckworth, 1999): 82.

141 Brian P. Copenhaver, *Hermetica: The Greek Corpus Hermeticum and the Latin Asclepius in a New English Translation, with Notes and Introduction* (Cambridge: Cambridge University Press, 1992; reprint, First), l.

142 Giles, *The Tarot*, 24.

143 For example see Anne Hendren Coulter, "Pictures That Heal: Messages from the Tarot Current Research as a Guide to Medical Practice," *Alternative & Complementary Therapies* 10, no. 6 (2004): 339.

144 Walter Starkie, "Carmen and the Tarots," *American Record Guide* 31, no. 1 (1964): 5.

145 Milorad Pavic, *Last Love in Constantinople: A Tarot Novel for Divination*, trans. Christina Pribichevich-Zoric (London: Peter Owen, 1998), 5. The progression of the novel is determined by drawing tarot cards from a pack. Outlines of the cards are provided at the back of the book.

146 For example see Eden Gray, *The Complete Guide to the Tarot* (New York: Bantam, 1972), 6.

147 Ranking, "Tarot," 18–19.

148 Ibid.

149 Depaulis, *Jeu et Magie*, 131.

150 For example see Ussher, *The XXII Keys*, 5; D'Otrange, "Thirteen Tarot Cards," 59.

151 Dummett with Mann, *The Game of Tarot*, 136–37.

152 Ranking, "Tarot," 18–19; Gates, "The Tarot Trumps", 87.

153 Encausse, *The Tarot of the Bohemians*, 298.

154 O'Neill, *Tarot Symbolism*, 41–42.

155 See, P. D. Ouspensky, *The Symbolism of the Tarot: Philosophy of Occultism in Pictures and Numbers*, trans. A. L. Pogossky (New York: Dover Publications, Inc., 1976), 3–4.

156 See Éliphas Lévi, *Transcendental Magic: Its Doctrine and Ritual*, trans. Arthur Edward Waite, Revised ed. (London: Rider and Company, 1958).

157 Dummett with Mann, *The Game of Tarot*, 136. Presumably Merlin is referring to the book by Johann Gottlieb Immanuel Breitkopf, *Versuch den Ursprung der Spielkarten, die Einfuhrung des Leinenpapiers und den Anfang der Holzschneidekunst in Europa*, published in Leipzig 1784.

158 Pemberton in Meyrink, *Golem*, 100.

159 Ranking, "Tarot," 18–19.

160 Jessie L. Weston, *From Ritual to Romance* (Garden City: Doubleday Anchor Books, 1957), 79.

161 Chaman Lal, *Gipsies: Forgotten Children of India* (Deli: Government of India Press, 1962), 26.

162 Sergius Golowin, *The World of Tarot: The Gypsy Method of Reading the Tarot* (York Beach: Samuel Weiser, Inc., 1988), 7–10.

163 Ranking, "Tarot," 34.

164 For example, see Morley, *Old and Curious Playing Cards*, 17, 68; Boiteau d'Ambly, *Les Cartes À Jouer*, 3. Gerard Encausse (Papus) wrote a book entitled *Le Tarot des bohemians* the title of which was incorrectly translated into English as *The Tarot of the Bohemians* when in fact; the correct translation would have been *The Tarot of the Gypsies*. See Encausse, *The Tarot of the Bohemians*, 8, 239.

165 Peter Godwin, "Gypsies the Outsiders," *National Geographic* 199, no. 4 (2001): 72.

166 Ibid. Also see 'Gypsy' in *Oxford English Dictionary* (cited).

167 Johann Christian Christoph Rüdiger, *On the Indic Language and the Origin of the Gipsies* [website] (School of Languages, Linguistics and Culture, University of Manchester, Unknown 1782 [cited 17 October 2005]); available from http://ling.uni-graz.at/~romman/downloads/1/ruediger_translation.pdf.

168 Konrad Bercovici, *The Story of the Gypsies* (London: Jonathan Cape, 1929), 23. Many people erroneously believe that Grellmann was the first to connect gypsies to India.

169 Ibid.

170 Angus Fraser, *The Gypsies*, ed. James Campbell and Barry Cunliffe, Second ed., *The Peoples of Europe* (Oxford: Blackwell, 1995), 19.
171 P. Peeters, 'Histoire monastiques géorgiennes', *Analecta Bollandiana*, 36–37, 1917–19 in White, "Roma (Gypsies) in and around the Byzantine Empire." Martin Block's book *Gypsies: Their Life and their Customs* was to have a profound effect on Nazi ideology and informed the Nazis' decision to execute gypsies in concentration camps.
172 Fraser, *The Gypsies*, 49–50.
173 Ibid., 50.
174 Ibid, 52–53.
175 Fraser, *The Gypsies*, 52–53; Also, *Viaggio di Lionardo di Noccolo Frescobaldi in Egitto, e in Terra Santa 1383*, Rome 1818 in White, "Roma (Gypsies) in and around the Byzantine Empire."
176 Campbell, *Historical Linguistics*, 364.
177 For an example of the hypothesis discounting a gypsy involvement with tarot on the basis of their late arrival in Europe, see Gabriele Mandel, *Les Tarots Des Visconti* (Paris: Vilo, 1974).
178 For example, see Gillian Kemp, *The Romany Good Spell Book* (London: Vista, 1997), 17–18; Raymond Buckland, *Secrets of Gypsy Love Magic* (St Paul: Llewellyn Publications, 1990), 4.
179 See Dan Brown, *The Da Vinci Code: A Novel* (London: Bantam Press, 2003), 92.
180 For example, see Catherine Summers and Julian Vayne, *Personal Development with the Tarot* (London: Quantum, 2002), 10; Waite, *The Pictorial Key to the Tarot*, 8; Harold Bayley, *A New Light on the Renaissance Displayed in Contemporary Emblems* (New York: Benjamin Blom, 1909).
181 Steven Runciman, *The Medieval Manichee: A Study of the Christian Dualist Heresy* (Cambridge: Cambridge University Press, 1960), 179, 87.
182 Tilley, *History of Playing Cards*, 25–26.
183 Euan Cameron, *Waldenses: Rejections of the Holy Church in Medieval Europe* (Malden: Blackwell Publishers Ltd, 2000), 2.
184 Ibid.
185 Walter L. Wakefield, *Heresy, Crusade and Inquisition in Southern France: 1100–1250* (London: George Allen & Unwin Ltd, 1974), 16.
186 Cameron, *Waldenses*, 158.
187 Tilley, *History of Playing Cards*, 26.
188 Cameron, *Waldenses*, 216.
189 For a full description of the game of *pachisi* see R. C. Bell, *Board and Table Games from Many Civilisations*, 2 vols., Vol. 1 (London: Oxford University Press, 1960), 9–12.
190 Stephen E. Franklin, *Origins of the Tarot Deck: A Study of the Astronomical Substructure of Game and Divining Boards* (Jefferson: McFarland & Company, Inc., 1988), 21–22.
191 For example, see Stuart R. Kaplan, *The Classical Tarot: Its Origins, Meanings and Divinatory Use* (Wellingborough: The Aquarian Press Limited, 1980), 8–9. Interestingly, Gerard Encausse (Papus) thought that *chaturange* (*Tchaturanga*) was derived from tarot rather than the other way around. See Encausse, *The Tarot of the Bohemians*, 86–87.
192 Dummett with Mann, *The Game of Tarot*, 43.
193 Hoffmann, *The Playing Card*, 20.
194 Dummett with Mann, *The Game of Tarot*, 43.
195 Bellenghi, *Cartomancy*, 14.
196 Steele, "Notice of the Ludus Triumphorum," 188. The Tarot de Mantegna was once erroneously attributed to Mantegna of Padua, hence the name of the deck. It does not

resemble a conventional tarot deck. Instead, it consists of fifty cards representing the different states of life, the muses, the virtues, the planets, the liberal arts, and the sciences. For a complete description of this deck see John Park, "A Cosmological Tarot Hypothesis - Virtue Triumphant: The Seven Virtues V. The Seven Mortal Sins," *The Playing Card* 31, no. 3 (2002): 127.

197   O'Donoghue, *Catalogue of the Collection*, 2.

198   Seguin, *Le Jeu De Carte*, 25.

199   Kaplan, *Tarot Classic*, 13–14.

200   Douglas, *The Tarot*, 18.

201   Dobkin, "Fortune's Malice," 134.

202   Bellenghi, *Cartomancy*, 11.

203   Jean de Coveluzzo in Hargrave, *A History of Playing Cards*, 224.

204   Dummett with Mann, *The Game of Tarot*, 43. Simon Wintle suggested that the Italians probably found it easier to say 'Naib' then 'kanjifah' which was the Arabic name for cards. Simon Wintle. *A 'Moorish' Sheet of Playing Cards* [website]. World of Playing Cards, 1987 [cited 22 August 2006]. Available from http://www.wopc.co.uk/spain/moorish2.jpg.

205   Dummett with Mann, *The Game of Tarot*, 65.

206   Hoffmann, *The Playing Card*, 17.

207   A *tarocco bolognese* pack in the British Museum features the Fibbia arms on the Queen of Batons and the Queen of Coins boasts the arms of the Bentivoglio family. The pack was made somewhere between 1725 and 1750 and is therefore of too late a date to be considered as evidence in support of the hypothesis that Prince Fibbia was the originator of *tarocchino* and hence, tarot. Dummett with Mann, *The Game of Tarot*, 67.

208   Dummett with Mann, *The Game of Tarot*, 66–67.

209   Ibid.

210   Michael Dummett and John McLeod, *A History of Games Played with the Tarot Pack: The Game of Triumphs*, 2 vols., Vol. 1 (Lewiston: Edwin Mellen Press, 2004), 17–18.

211   Depaulis, *Jeu Et Magie*, 34.

212   Little, *Hermitage* (cited) - *The Birth of the Tarot* (http://www.tarothermit.com/birth.htm).

213   Dummett and McLeod, *A History of Games*, 17–18. Records from the *Registro di Guardaroba* of the court of Ferrara, dated 1516 and 1517, mention the purchase of two or four '*para de tarocchi*'. See Olsen, "Carte De Trionfi", 23.

214   Decker, Depaulis, and Dummett, *A Wicked Pack of Cards*, 41.

215   Kaplan, *Encyclopedia of Tarot II*, 5.

216   Bellenghi, *Cartomancy*, 11.

217   Alfred Douglas. *The Tarot: The Origins, Meaning and Uses of the Cards.* (Harmondsworth: Penguin Books Ltd, 1974), 21.

218   Hyacinthe Chobaut, *Les Maîtres Cartiers d'Avignon du XVème siècle à la Révolution* (Vaison-la-Romaine, 1955), 25 cited in Dummett and McLeod, *A History of Games*, 17.

219   Thierry Depaulis, "Des 'Cartes Communément Appelées Taraux' 2ème Partie," *The Playing Card* 32, no. 5 (2004): 244.

220   Ibid., 244–49.

221   Gates, "The Tarot Trumps", 11.

222   Giles, *The Tarot*, 3, 5.

223   Ibid.

224   Beverly Moon, ed., *An Encyclopedia of Archetypal Symbolism* (Boston: Shambhala, 1991), 151.

225   Gates, "The Tarot Trumps", 11.
226   'Le nom de ce Jeu est pur Egyptien: il est compose du mot Tar, qui signifie voie, chemin, & du mot RO, ROS, ROG, qui signifie Roi, Royal. C'est, mot-a-mot, le chemin Royal de la vie.' de Gébelin, *Monde Primitif.*
227   Encausse, *The Tarot of the Bohemians*, 11.
228   Ibid.
229   Giles, *The Tarot*, 4.
230   For example, see Bellenghi, *Cartomancy*, 11.
231   Decker and Dummett, *History of the Occult Tarot*, 58.
232   van Rensselaer, *Prophetical, Educational and Playing Cards*, 34.
233   Gates, "The Tarot Trumps", 11-12.
234   Giles, *The Tarot*, 4.
235   "'My good friend, how loud do you want life to shout her answers in your ear aloud? There is no need for you to know, of course, that the word "Tarok," or "Tarot," bears the same significance as the Jewish "Tora," that is to say, "*The Law*," or the old Egyptian "Tarut," "*One who is asked*," derived from the old Zend word "Tarisk," meaning "*I require an answer.*"' Meyrink, *Golem*, 113-14.
236   Bellenghi, *Cartomancy*, 11.
237   Aleister Crowley, *The Book of Thoth: A Short Essay on the Tarot of the Egyptians* (York Beach: Samuel Weiser, Inc., 1991), 4. A 'notariquon' or 'notarikon' is a system of exegetical abbreviation used by Jews. Either each letter in a word is thought to stand for a whole word, or a word is divided into shorter components with separate meanings.
238   Bellenghi, *Cartomancy*, 11.
239   Ibid.
240   Shah, *Sufis*, 449.
241   Bellenghi, *Cartomancy*, 11.

NOTES TO CHAPTER TWO

1   Werner L. Gundersheimer, *Ferrara: The Style of a Renaissance Despotism* (Princeton: Princeton University Press, 1973), 14-15.
2   The Guelfs and Ghibellines were political factions that supported the Papacy and the Holy Roman Empire respectively in central and northern Italy from the 11th until the 13th century. John Larner, *Italy in the Age of Dante and Petrarch 1216-1380*, ed. Denys Hay, 7 vols., Vol. 2, *A Longman History of Italy* (London: Longman, 1980), 32.
3   Ella Noyes, *The Story of Ferrara, Mediaeval Towns* (Nendeln: Kraus Reprint, 1970), 33.
4   Jacob Burckhardt, *The Civilization of the Renaissance in Italy*, trans. S. G. C. Middlemore, *Penguin Classics* (London: Penguin Books, 1990), 48.
5   Will Durant, *The Renaissance: A History of Civilization in Italy from 1304-1576 AD*, ed. Will Durant and Ariel Durant, X vols., Vol. V, *The Story of Civilization* (New York: Simon and Schuster, 1953; reprint, Thirteenth), 261.
6   Noyes, *Ferrara*, 32.
7   Durant, *The Renaissance*, 262.
8   Burckhardt, *The Civilization of the Renaissance*, 48.
9   Michael Dummett, "Sulle Origini Dei Tarocchi Popolari," in *I Tarocchi : Le Carte Di Corte: Bioco E Magia Alla Corte Degli Estensi*, ed. Giordano Berti and Andrea Vitali (Bologna: Nuova Alfa, 1987), 78. There was a possible reference in court documents of the previous year. Maestro Jacopo de Sagramoro was commissioned to paint some cards to be sent as a gift to Lady Bianca Maria Visconti of Milan. The cards referred to

are not explicitly tarot cards. This document was only uncovered in March 2003. See 'Document B' at Ross Gregory Caldwell, *Trionfi.Com* [website] (Caldwell, Ross Gregory, December 2005 [cited 7 February 2006]); available from http://www.trionfi.com.

10   Giuliana Algeri, "Un Gioco Per Le Corti: I Tarocchi Miniati," in *I Tarocchi : Le Carte Di Corte: Bioco E Magia Alla Corte Degli Estensi*, ed. Giordano Berti and Andrea Vitali (Bologna: Nuova Alfa, 1987), 21–24.

11   Giulio Bertoni, *Poesie Leggende Costumanze Del Medio Evo*, Second ed. (Bologna: Arnaldo Forni, 1976), 218.

12   Michael Dummett with Sylvia Mann. *The Game of Tarot: From Ferrara to Salt Lake City* (London: Gerald Duckworth and Co. Ltd., 1980), 67.

13   Gherardo Ortalli, "The Prince and the Playing Cards: The Este Family and the Role of Courts at the Time of the Kartenspiel-Invasion," *Ludica: annali di storia e civilta del gioco* 2 (1996): 184.

14   Bertoni, *Poesie Leggende Costumanze Del Medio Evo*, 218.

15   Ortalli, "Prince and the Playing Cards," 185.

16   Christina Olsen, "Carte Da Trionfi: The Development of Tarot in Fifteenth Century Italy" (Ph. D., University of Pennsylvania, 1994), 80.

17   Lionel Cust, "The Frescoes in the Casa Borromeo at Milan," *The Burlington Magazine for Connoisseurs* 33, no. 184 (1918): 8. The Borromeo family was important in banking and commerce in Milan in the fifteenth century. Dummett with Mann, *The Game of Tarot*, 67–68.

18   See Raimond van Marle, *The Development of the Italian Schools of Painting*, XIX vols., Vol. VII (New York: Hacker Art Books, 1970), 145.

19   Dummett with Mann, *The Game of Tarot*, 68.

20   Ibid.

21   Olsen, "Carte De Trionfi", 132. Michael Dummett reported that the rules governing games played with the tarot deck were not recorded until the sixteenth century, therefore it is impossible for us to guess if the game being played in the fresco at the Casa Borromeo utilised a tarot deck or not. See Michael Dummett and John McLeod, *A History of Games Played with the Tarot Pack: The Game of Triumphs*, 2 vols., Vol. 1 (Lewiston: Edwin Mellen Press, 2004), 13.

22   Michelino da Besozzo (d. 1450) worked in Milan from 1394 until 1442. John Larner, *Culture and Society in Italy 1290–1420* (London: B. T. Batsford Ltd, 1971), 235.

23   Franceschino Zavattari was one of a family of painters active in Milan. He is thought to have worked from 1414 and died sometime between 1453 and 1457. Janice Shell, *Zavattari* [Online reference source] (Grove Art Online, Oxford University Press, 2006 [cited 16 February 2006]); available from http://www.groveart.com/.

24   Pisanello's work was complementary to the rising humanism of the time, boasting sumptuous detail with a sense of luxury. Stefano Zuffi, *The Renaissance* (London: Collins, 2002), 104.

25   Pietro Toesca, *La Pittura E La Miniatura Nella Lombardia Dai Più Antichi Monumenti Alla Metà Del Quattrocento* (Milano: Istituto editoriale Cisalpino-La Goliardica, 1982), 510–13.

26   Dummett does not believe this pack can be described as 'tarot'. See Dummett with Mann, *The Game of Tarot*, 82.

27   Olsen, "Carte De Trionfi", 1.

28   The letter by Jacopo Antonio Marcello and the treatise by Marziano da Tortona are preserved in the *Bibliothèque Nationale* in Paris, codex Lat. 8745. Olsen, "Carte De Trionfi", 23.

29   Ibid., 1–2.

30 The Visconti library was catalogued in 1426, 1459 and 1469. Astrological treatises featured prominently in the collection and would have been available to Marziano. See Elisabeth Pellegrin, *La Bibliothèque Des Visconti Et Des Sforza Ducs De Milan, Au XVe Siecle, Publications De L'institut De Recherche Et D'histoire Des Textes* (Paris: Service des Publications du C. N. R. S., 1955).

31 Olsen, "Carte De Trionfi", 106–07, 39. There is one confusing aspect to this scenario. Though the treatise was supposedly commissioned by Duke Filippo Maria Visconti, it was written in Latin. The Duke was not adept at Latin and frequently requested theologians to address him in Italian, rather than in Latin. Dorothy Muir, *A History of Milan under the Visconti* (London: Methuen & Co. Ltd., 1924), 170-71.

32 Olsen, "Carte De Trionfi", 139.

33 Franco Pratesi, "Italian Cards - New Discoveries: 10. The Earliest Tarot Pack Known," *The Playing Card* XVIII, no. 2 (1989): 33.

34 L. Collison-Morley, *The Story of the Sforzas* (London: George Routledge and Sons, 1933), 31-32.

35 Gertrude Moakley, *The Tarot Cards Painted by Bonifacio Bembo for the Visconti-Sforza Family: An Iconographic and Historical Study* (New York: The New York Public Library, 1966), 52.

36 P. C. Decembrio, "Playing Cards for the Duke of Milan," in *Italian Art 1400-1500: Sources and Documents*, ed. Creighton E. Gilbert, *The History of Art Series* (Englewood Cliffs: Prentice-Hall, Inc., 1980), 210-11. This passage is seen as problematic as it implied that Marziano actually painted the images yet there is no record of him having ever being a painter. Decembrio probably intended to assert that Marziano was the 'intellectual' creator of the deck. See Robert Klein, "Les Tarots Enluminé Du XVe Siècle," *L'Oeil*, no. 145 (1967): 51. Though Decembrio does mention the word '*ludus*' (game) in connection with the pack, he does not specifically refer to '*trionfi*' or '*triomphi*' which would confirm the deck was the same as that mentioned in Marcello's letter and Marziano's treatise. See Dummett with Mann, *The Game of Tarot*, 82.

37 Pratesi, "New Discoveries 10," 33.

38 Ibid., 34.

39 Olsen, "Carte De Trionfi", 142.

40 Dummett with Mann, *The Game of Tarot*, 25. 'Turtles' possibly refer to 'Turtledoves'.

41 '*Harum vero Avium ordo est quia nulla earum species in alteram vis habet*' Marziano in Pratesi, "New Discoveries 10," 34.

42 '*Aquilarum et turturarum multae paucis praesunt ... foenicum una et columbarum pluribus paucores imperant*'. Marziano in Pratesi, "New Discoveries 10," 34.

43 Olsen, "Carte De Trionfi", 142.

44 Pratesi, "New Discoveries 10," 36–37.

45 Olsen, "Carte De Trionfi", 143.

46 Ibid., 143–44.

47 Olsen, "Carte De Trionfi", 143–44.

48 Dummett with Mann, *The Game of Tarot*, 82.

49 Olsen, "Carte De Trionfi", 2.

50 Bonifacio Bembo was employed by Francesco and Bianca Sforza, and later by their son Galeazzo Maria Sforza, to create frescoes, restore artworks and undertake other projects including painting tarot cards. Flavio Boggi, *Bonifacio Bembo* [Online reference source] (Grove Art Online, Oxford University Press, 2006 [cited 23 February 2006]); available from http://www.groveart.com/.

51 The Visconti di Modrone pack is held at the Beinecke Library at Yale University. Michael Dummett, *The Visconti-Sforza Tarot Cards* (New York: George Braziller,

Inc., 1986), 5. Some estimates suggest these cards were painted as early as 1420 though a later date is more likely.

52   Dummett, *Visconti-Sforza Tarot*, 13.

53   Dummett with Mann, *The Game of Tarot*, 77. The four Cardinal Virtues are *Fortitudo* (Fortitude); *Prudentia* (Prudence); *Temperantia* (Temperance) and *Justitia* (Justice). Jennifer O'Reilly, *Studies in the Iconography of the Virtues and Vices in the Middle Ages* (New York: Garland Publishing, Inc., 1988), 44–45.

54   Dummett with Mann, *The Game of Tarot*, 77.

55   Dummett, *Visconti-Sforza Tarot*, 13.

56   The Brambilla deck is now housed in the Pinacoteca di Brera in Milan. Dummett, "Tarocchi Popolari," 78.

57   Cynthia Giles. *The Tarot: History, Mystery and Lore* (New York: Paragon House, 1992), 13.

58   Dummett, "Tarocchi Popolari," 78. The Visconti-Sforza deck is split between the Pierpont Morgan Library in New York, the Academia Carrara in Bergamo and the Colleoni family also in Bergamo. Toesca, *Istituto Editoriale Cisalpino-La Goliardica*, 527. The deck is believed to have been painted sometime between 1440 and 1470.

59   The six cards are thought to have been painted about twenty years later by an unknown artist of the Ferrarese school. Thierry Depaulis, *Tarot, Jeu Et Magie* (Paris: Bibliothèque Nationale, 1984), 38.

60   Dummett with Mann, *The Game of Tarot*, 69.

61   Dummett, *Visconti-Sforza Tarot*, 13.

62   Raimond van Marle and Robert Klein maintained that Zavattari was responsible for painting the deck. See van Marle, *Italian Schools of Painting*, 174. This theory has more recently been endorsed by Giuliana Algeri. See Depaulis, *Jeu Et Magie*, 37.

63   Michael Dummett concurred. 'Milan was one of the original centres of Tarot; probably it was at the court of Filippo Maria Visconti, Duke of Milan, that the pack and the game were invented.' Dummett and McLeod, *A History of Games*, 111. This was a reversal of an earlier position stated thus: 'My choice would be Ferrara, because the atmosphere of the d'Este court there—irreverent, pleasure-loving, steeped in romance, devoted to play of every kind—was conducive to such an invention ...' Dummett, *Visconti-Sforza Tarot*, 6. This view is reiterated in Ronald Decker and Michael Dummett, *A History of the Occult Tarot: 1870–1970* (London: Gerald Duckworth & Co. Ltd., 2002), ix.

64   Dummett and McLeod, *A History of Games*, 111.

65   It should be noted that no Devil or Tower cards have been found in fifteenth-century tarot decks. It is difficult to determine whether or not they were there and were subsequently lost or if they were not part of the deck at that time. Robert O'Neill believed the latter, saying that they would have offended delicate female sensibilities. Robert V. O'Neill, *Tarot Symbolism* (Lima: Fairway Press, 1986), 81.

66   As the title suggests, the works of Leonardo da Vinci feature prominently in this work. See Dan Brown, *The Da Vinci Code: A Novel* (London: Bantam Press, 2003).

67   The Teenage Mutant Ninja Turtles are named after the Renaissance painters Raffaello Santi (Raphael), Michelangelo, Leonardo Da Vinci and Donato di Betto Bardi (Donatello). The characters were created by Peter A. Laird and Kevin B. Eastman. Peter Laird, *The Official Teenage Mutant Ninja Turtles Website!* [website] (Mirage Publishing, Inc., 22 February 2006 [cited 2 March 2006]); available from http://www.ninjaturtles.com/.

68   Brian Pullan, *A History of Early Renaissance Italy from the Mid-Thirteenth to the Mid-Fifteenth Century* (London: Allen Lane, 1973), 226. It should be noted that this view of the Renaissance economy remains controversial. For example, Georges Duby argued that the plague left fewer people to enjoy the same amount of wealth and hence

standards of living generally rose. Georges Duby, *Art and Society in the Middle Ages*, trans. Jean Birrell (Cambridge: Polity Press, 2000), 65–66.

69   Judith C. Brown, "Prosperity or Hard Times in Renaissance Italy," *Renaissance Quarterly* 42, no. 4 (1989): 761.

70   Ibid.

71   Pullan, *History of Early Renaissance Italy*, 226.

72   Johan Huizinga, *The Autumn of the Middle Ages*, trans. Rodney J. Payton and Ulrich Mammitzsch (Chicago: University of Chicago Press, 1996), 156.

73   Dom Jean Leclercq, Dom François Vandenbroucke, and Louis Bouyer. *The Spirituality of the Middle Ages*. Translated by The Benedictines of Holme Eden Abbey. 2 vols. Vol. 2. (New York: Seabury Press, 1986), 481.

74   Denys Hay, *The Church in Italy in the Fifteenth Century: The Birbeck Lectures, 1971* (Cambridge: Cambridge University Press, 1977), 27.

75   Norbert Elias, *The Society of Individuals*, trans. Edmund Jephcott (Oxford: Basil Blackwell, 1991), 197.

76   Evelyn Welch, *Art and Society in Italy 1350-1500*, Oxford History of Art (Oxford: Oxford University Press, 1997), 9.

77   John Stephens, *The Italian Renaissance: The Origins of Intellectual and Artistic Change before the Reformation* (London: Longman, 1990), xvii.

78   Harry Elmer Barnes, *An Intellectual and Cultural History of the Western World*, Third Revised ed., 3 vols., Vol. 2 (New York: Dover Publications, Inc., 1965), 555.

79   Roberto Weiss, "Italian Humanism in Western Europe," in *Italian Renaissance Studies*, ed. E. F. Jacob (London: Faber and Faber, 1960), 69.

80   Paul Oskar Kristeller, *The Classics and Renaissance Thought*, Martin Classical Lectures (Cambridge: Harvard University Press, 1955), 9–10.

81   Gianozzo Manetti (1396-1459) prepared a Latin translation of the Greek New Testament for Pope Nicholas V. The fullest expression of his ideals can be found in the work *De dignitate et excellentia hominis*. Gordon Campbell, *Gianozzo Manetti* [Oxford Reference Online] (The Oxford Dictionary of the Renaissance, Oxford University Press, 2003 [cited 2 March 2006]); available from http://www.oxfordreference.com/.

82   Francesco Petrarca (1304-1374), one of the foremost humanist writers of the fourteenth century, composed most of his works in Latin. He came into the service of the Visconti in 1353. Paula Findlen, "Understanding the Italian Renaissance," in *The Italian Renaissance: The Essential Readings*, ed. Paula Findlen, *Blackwell Essential Readings in History* (Malden: Blackwell Publishing, 2002), 4–5.

83   Larner, *Italy 1290-1420*, 228.

84   Chamberlin, *The Count of Virtue*, 15–16.

85   Durant, *The Renaissance*, 180.

86   Chamberlin, *The Count of Virtue*, 32.

87   Durant, *The Renaissance*, 180.

88   Mary Hollingsworth, *Patronage in Renaissance Italy: From 1400 to the Early Sixteenth Century* (Baltimore: The Johns Hopkins University Press, 1994), 163.

89   Apparently Gian Galeazzo had prayed to the Virgin Mary for a son and had been so grateful for the success of his prayer, that all his children bore her name. Durant, *The Renaissance*, 181.

90   David Nicholas, *The Transformation of Europe 1300-1600*, The Arnold History of Europe (London: Arnold, 1999), 26.

91   Durant, *The Renaissance*, 181.

92   Ibid.

93   Collison-Morley, *Sforzas*, 31–32.

94   Christopher Hibbert, *The Rise and Fall of the House of Medici* (Harmondsworth: Penguin Books, 1979; reprint, Third), 79.
95   Muir, *History of Milan*, 5.
96   Paul Strathern, *The Medici: Godfathers of the Renaissance* (London: Random House, 2003), 116.
97   Burckhardt, *The Civilisation of the Renaissance*, 63.
98   Muir, *History of Milan*, 133–35.
99   Collison-Morley, *Sforzas*, 31–32.
100 Burckhardt, *The Civilisation of the Renaissance*, 63.
101 Durant, *The Renaissance*, 181–82.
102 The Visconti library housed several treatises on chess. Pearl Kibre, "The Intellectual Interests Reflected in the Libraries of the Fourteenth and Fifteenth Centuries," *Journal of the History of Ideas* 7, no. 3 (1946): 293.
103 Durant, *The Renaissance*, 182. The Visconti library contained many books about astrology. See Kibre, "Intellectual Interests," 287. For an account of the popularity of astrology in the European courts see Thomas M. Greene, "Magic and Festivity at the Renaissance Court: The 1987 Josephine Waters Bennett Lecture," *Renaissance Quarterly* 40, no. 4 (1987): 637–38.
104 Muir, *History of Milan*, 170–71. The Visconti library contained many books about various forms of divination and the occult arts.
105 Muir, *History of Milan*, 170–71.
106 Hibbert, *House of Medici*, 80.
107 Strathern, *Medici*, 116–17.
108 Muir, *History of Milan*, 170–71.
109 Strathern, *Medici*, 116–17.
110 Muir, *History of Milan*, 170–71.
111 Hibbert, *House of Medici*, 80.
112 Gary Ianziti, *Humanistic Historiography under the Sforzas: Politics and Propaganda in Fifteenth-Century Milan* (Oxford: Clarendon Press, 1988), 20.
113 Burckhardt, *The Civilisation of the Renaissance*, 63–64.
114 Strathern, *Medici*, 117.
115 Ianziti, *Humanistic Historiography*, 20.
116 Collison-Morley, *Sforzas*, 45–46.
117 Ianziti, *Humanistic Historiography*, 20.
118 Hans Baron, "A Struggle for Liberty in the Renaissance: Florence, Venice, and Milan in the Early Quattrocento, Part 2," *The American Historical Review* 58, no. 3 (1953): 564.
119 Durant, *The Renaissance*, 183.
120 Ronald Decker, Thierry Depaulis, and Michael Dummett, *A Wicked Pack of Cards: The Origins of Occult Tarot* (London: Gerald Duckworth and Co. Ltd., 1996), 32.
121 This was the pseudonym of Teofilo Folengo, 1491-1544. Dummett and McLeod, *A History of Games*, 1.
122 Pietro Marsilli, "I Tarocchi Nella Vita Di Società, La Vita Di Società Nei Tarocchi," in *I Tarocchi : Le Carte Di Corte : Bioco E Magia Alla Corte Degli Estensi*, ed. Giordano Berti and Andrea Vitali (Bologna: Nuova Alfa, 1987), 99.
123 Richard Kieckhefer, *Magic in the Middle Ages*, Cambridge Medieval Textbooks (Cambridge: Cambridge University Press, 1989), 90.
124 See Melanchthon, "Initia Doctrinae Physicae," in *The Occult in Early Modern Europe: A Documentary History*, ed. P. G. Maxwell-Stuart, *Documents in History Series* (Houndmills: Macmillan, 1999), 6. For an account of the popularity of reading bodily signs see William Armand Lessa, "Somatomancy: Precursor of the Science of Human Constitution," in *Reader in Comparative Religion: An Anthropological Approach*, ed.

William Armand Lessa and Evon Z. Vogt (Evanston: Row, Peterson and Company, 1958), 314–26.

125 William Monter, *Ritual, Myth and Magic in Early Modern Europe* (Athens: Ohio University Press, 1984), 32–33; D. P. Walker, *Spiritual and Demonic Magic from Ficino to Campanella*, ed. G. Bing, *Studies of the Warburg Institute* (London: Warburg Institute, 1958), 43.

126 *Ars memoria* referred to the practice of developing memory by dividing the material to be remembered into small units and to key these into a rigid, readily reconstructable order. See Mary J. Carruthers, *The Book of Memory: A Study of Memory in Medieval Culture*, ed. Alastair Minnis, *Cambridge Studies in Medieval Literature* (Cambridge: Cambridge University Press, 1990), 7. *Ars memorativa* involved looking at pictures which acted as a visual stimulus to memory. Particular aspects of the picture were linked to a specific piece of information to be remembered. Paul Huson and David V. Barrett are among those who believed that tarot was used as an aid to memory. See Paul Huson, *The Devil's Picturebook: The Compleat Guide to Tarot Cards: Their Origins and Their Usage* (London: Sphere Books Ltd, 1972), 62–63; David V. Barrett, *Secret Societies: From the Ancient and Arcane to the Modern and Clandestine* (London: Blandford, 1997), 148.

127 Frances AmeliaYates. *The Art of Memory* (Harmondsworth: Penguin Books Ltd, 1966), 93.

128 Certainly there were works in the Visconti library that described the art of memory. See Pellegrin, *La Bibliothèque Des Visconti Et Des Sforza*, 100.

129 R. Chambers, ed., *The Book of Days: A Miscellany of Popular Antiquities in Connection with the Calendar Including Anecdote, Biography, & History, Curiosities of Literature and Oddities of Human Life and Character*, 2 vols., Vol. 2 (London: W. & R. Chambers, 1883), 780.

130 Hoffmann, *The Playing Card*, 38.

131 For a description on the characteristics of images that render them easily remembered, see Keith A. Wollen and Matthew G. Margres, "Bizarreness and the Imagery Multiprocess Model," in *Imagery and Related Mnemonic Processes: Theories, Individual Differences, and Applications*, ed. Mark A. McDaniel and Michael Pressley (New York: Springer-Verlag, 1987), 104.

132 For an example of how trump order varied between regions see Depaulis, *Jeu Et Magie*, 18.

133 Christina Olsen believed that the trump cards were not numbered so as to make the game more difficult and to enhance the faculty of memory. See Olsen, "Carte De Trionfi", 166.

134 Dummett and McLeod, *A History of Games*, 1.

135 Kate T. Steinitz, "The Tarot Cards Painted by Bonifacio Bembo: An Iconographic and Historical Study [Review]," *Art Bulletin* 51, no. 2 (1969): 188–89.

136 Peter Burke, *Popular Culture in Early Modern Europe* (London: Temple Smith, 1978), 188–89.

137 Burckhardt, *The Civilisation of the Renaissance*, 300. For a full account of the depiction of triumphs see Werner Weisbach, *Trionfi* (Berlin: G. Grote, 1919).

138 Charlene Elizabeth Gates, "The Tarot Trumps: Their Origin, Archetypal Imagery, and Use in Some Works of English Literature" (Ph. D., University of Oregon, 1982), 75.

139 Renee Neu Watkins, "Petrarch and the Black Death: From Fear to Monuments," *Studies in the Renaissance* 19 (1972): 219.

140 Ernest Hatch Wilkins, "Preface," in *The Triumphs of Petrarch* (Chicago: The University of Chicago Press, 1962), v.

141 Pellegrin, *La Bibliothèque Des Visconti Et Des Sforza*, 109, 19, 60-62, 212-13, 58–59.

142   Dummett with Mann, *The Game of Tarot*, 87.
143   Moakley, *Tarot Cards Painted by Bonifacio Bembo*, 13–16.
144   Collison-Morley, *Sforzas*, 31–32.
145   Muir, *History of Milan*, 133–35, 70–71.
146   Olsen, "Carte De Trionfi", 28.
147   Christina Olsen proposed that the symbolism of tarot trumps may have been inspired by the elaborate processions that accompanied prominent marriages in Milan. See Olsen, "Carte De Trionfi", 28.
148   O'Neill, *Tarot Symbolism*, 81.
149   Giles, *The Tarot*, 16–17.
150   Wilkins, "Triumphs of Petrarch," v.
151   James Hall, *Dictionary of Subjects and Symbols in Art* (London: John Murray, 1974), 310.
152   See Dummett, *Visconti-Sforza Tarot*, 112–13.
153   Hall, *Subjects and Symbols*, 310.
154   See Dummett, *Visconti-Sforza Tarot*, 116–17.
155   Hall, *Subjects and Symbols*, 310.
156   See Dummett, *Visconti-Sforza Tarot*, 126–27.
157   Hall, *Subjects and Symbols*, 310.
158   See 'Moakley 101: Part 2' in Little, *Hermitage* (cited).
159   See Robert V. O'Neill, *Iconology of the Star Cards* [website] (Visionary Networks, 2006 [cited 7 March 2006]); available from http://www.tarot.com.
160   Hall, *Subjects and Symbols*, 310.
161   See Dummett, *Visconti-Sforza Tarot*, 122–23.
162   Hall, *Subjects and Symbols*, 310.
163   Robert V. O'Neill, *Iconology of the World Cards* [website] (Visionary Networks, 2006 [cited 7 March 2006]); available from http://www.tarot.com.
164   See Dummett, *Visconti-Sforza Tarot*, 138–39.
165   Huson, *Mystical Origins of the Tarot*, 39.
166   Glynne Wickham, *The Medieval Theatre*, Third ed. (Cambridge: Cambridge University Press, 1987), 21–22.
167   Keith D. Lilley, "Cities of God? Medieval Urban Forms and Their Christian Symbolism," *Transactions of the Institute of British Geographers* 29, no. 3 (2004): 305.
168   Wickham, *Medieval Theatre*, 106.
169   Huson, *Mystical Origins of the Tarot*, 35, 37.
170   John Wesley Harris, *Medieval Theatre in Context* (New York: Routledge, 1992), 155.
171   O'Reilly, *Iconography of the Virtues and Vices*, 1.
172   Huson, *Mystical Origins of the Tarot*, 36.
173   James C. Clark, "Introduction," in *The Dance of Death*, Hans Holbein (London: Phaidon Press Ltd, 1947), 7; Ad de Vries, *Dictionary of Symbols and Imagery* (Amsterdam: North-Holland Publishing Company, 1974), 131.
174   See Hans Holbein, *The Dance of Death* (London: Phaidon Press Ltd, 1947).
175   The Magician, the Popess, the Empress, the Emperor, the Pope, Love, the Chariot, Justice, the Old Man, the Wheel of Fortune, Strength, the Hanged Man and Death. Huson, *Mystical Origins of the Tarot*, 37.
176   Ibid., 38. The Four Last Things are Death, Judgment, Heaven and Hell. See C. A. Patrides, "Renaissance and Modern Thought on the Last Things: A Study in Changing Conceptions," *Harvard Theological Review* 51, no. 3 (1958).
177   Wickham, *Medieval Theatre*, 99.
178   Muir, *History of Milan*, 133–35, 70–71.

179   William Marston Seabury, *The Tarot Cards and Dante's Divine Comedy* (New York: Privately printed, 1951).
180   Seabury, *Tarot and Dante*, 1.
181   Elmer Davis in Ibid.
182   Joseph Campbell, "Part I: Exoteric Tarot," in *Tarot Revelations*, ed. Richard Roberts (San Anselmo: Vernal Equinox Press, 1987), 4–5.

NOTES TO CHAPTER THREE

1   This theme is also explored by Tom Tadfor Little, *The Hermitage: Tarot History* [website] (2001 [cited 5 April 2004]); available from http://www.tarothermit.com/ - *Marziano da Tortona: Inventor of the Tarot* (http://www.tarothermit.com/ marziano.htm).

2   Robert Burns in Elizabeth Knowles, ed., *The Oxford Dictionary of Quotations*, Sixth ed. (Oxford: Oxford University Press, 2004), 76.

3   Michael Dummett and John McLeod, *A History of Games Played with the Tarot Pack: The Game of Triumphs*, 2 vols., Vol. 1 (Lewiston: Edwin Mellen Press, 2004), 13.

4   Franco Pratesi, "Italian Cards - New Discoveries: 10. The Earliest Tarot Pack Known," *The Playing Card* XVIII, no. 2 (1989): 34.

5   Cynthia Giles, *The Tarot: History, Mystery and Lore* (New York: Paragon House, 1992), 8–9; Michael Dummett, *The Visconti-Sforza Tarot Cards* (New York: George Braziller, Inc., 1986), 7–8.

6   Dorothy Muir, *A History of Milan under the Visconti* (London: Methuen & Co. Ltd., 1924), 5.

7   Ibid., 133.

8   Stuart R. Kaplan, *The Encyclopedia of Tarot*, IV vols., Vol. II (New York: U. S. Games Systems, 1986; reprint, Second), 188. The trump order elaborated in the poem by Susio is believed to have been the one followed in Milan. Dummett, *Visconti-Sforza Tarot*, 9.

9   Variants of this name included *il Bagatto, il Bagattino, il Begato* and *il Bagotti*. See Dummett, *Visconti-Sforza Tarot*, 102.

10   The English word 'baggage' is also derived from this root. 'Bagatelle' in *Oxford English Dictionary* (Second) [website] (Oxford University Press, 2005 [cited 18 August 2005]); available from http://dictionary.oed.com.

11   Dummett, *Visconti-Sforza Tarot*, 102.

12   Christina Olsen. "Carte Da Trionfi: The Development of Tarot in Fifteenth Century Italy" (Ph.D., University of Pennsylvania, 1994), 120–21.

13   Claudia Cieri-Via, "L'iconografia Degli Arcani Maggiori," in *I Tarocchi: Le Carte Di Corte: Bioco E Magia Alla Corte Degli Estensi*, ed. Giordano Berti and Andrea Vitali (Bologna: Nuova Alfa, 1987), 162.

14   Olsen, "Carte De Trionfi", 120–21.

15   For more information about this treatise see Lynn Thorndike, "Robertus Anglicus and the Introduction of Demons and Magic into Commentaries Upon the Sphere of Sacrobosco," *Speculum* 21, no. 2 (1946). Christina Olsen referred to a copy of the treatise owned by the Este in Ferrara but this copy was not printed until 1472 and so must be dismissed as a direct source of the symbolism used on the trump card of *il Bagatella*.

16   Olsen, "Carte De Trionfi", 166.

17   Ruth Mellinkoff, *Outcasts: Signs of Otherness in Northern European Art of the Late Middle Ages*, ed. Walter Horn, Two vols., Vol. One: Text, *California Studies in the History of Art* (Berkeley: University of California Press, 1993), 39–40.

18   Ibid., 54.

19   Ronald Decker, Thierry Depaulis, and Michael Dummett. *A Wicked Pack of Cards: The Origins of Occult Tarot* (London: Gerald Duckworth and Co. Ltd., 1996), 44.

20   E. W. Brooks, "Die Entstehung Des Kirchenstaates Und Der Curiale Begriff 'Res Publica Romanorum:' Ein Beitrag Zum Frankischen Kirchen-Und Staatsrecht [Review]," *English Historical Review* 16, no. 61 (1901): 131.

21   E. R. Chamberlin, *The Count of Virtue: Giangaleazzo Visconti Duke of Milan* (London: Eyre & Spottiswoode, 1965), 54–55.

22   John Larner, *Italy in the Age of Dante and Petrarch 1216–1380*, ed. Denys Hay, 7 vols., Vol. 2, *A Longman History of Italy* (London: Longman, 1980), 32.

23   Brian Pullan, *A History of Early Renaissance Italy from the Mid-Thirteenth to the Mid-Fifteenth Century* (London: Allen Lane, 1973), 55.

24   Barbara Newman, "The Heretic Saint: Gugliema of Bohemia, Milan, and Brunate," *Church History* 74, no. 1 (2005): 18.

25   Chamberlin, *The Count of Virtue*, 54–55.

26   Pullan, *History of Early Renaissance Italy*, 234–35.

27   Hans Baron, "A Struggle for Liberty in the Renaissance: Florence, Venice, and Milan in the Early Quattrocento, Part 1," *The American Historical Review* 58, no. 2 (1953): 277–78.

28   David Nicholas, *The Transformation of Europe 1300–1600*, *The Arnold History of Europe* (London: Arnold, 1999), 25–26.

29   Pullan, *History of Early Renaissance Italy*, 51.

30   Chamberlin, *The Count of Virtue*, 53.

31   Denys Hay, *The Church in Italy in the Fifteenth Century: The Birbeck Lectures, 1971* (Cambridge: Cambridge University Press, 1977), 27.

32   Nicholas, *Europe 1300–1600*, 26.

33   Strathern, Paul. *The Medici: Godfathers of the Renaissance* (London: Random House, 2003), 35.

34   Chamberlin, *The Count of Virtue*, 15–16.

35   Pullan, *History of Early Renaissance Italy*, 235.

36   F. R Webber, *Church Symbolism: An Explanation of the More Important Symbols of the Old and New Testament, the Primitive, the Mediaeval and the Modern Church*, Second, revised ed. (Detroit: Gale Research Company, 1971), 63.

37   Cieri-Via, "Arcani Maggiori," 165. This is the same eagle that Wenceslas permitted Gian Galeazzo to use after conferring upon him the hereditary dukedom of Milan. See Mary Hollingsworth, *Patronage in Renaissance Italy: From 1400 to the Early Sixteenth Century* (Baltimore: The Johns Hopkins University Press, 1994), 163.

38   Cieri-Via, "Arcani Maggiori," 165.

39   Count Emiliano di Parravicino, "Three Packs of Italian Tarocco Cards," *The Burlington Magazine for Connoisseurs* 3, no. 9 (1903): 241.

40   L. Collison-Morley, *The Story of the Sforzas* (London: George Routledge and Sons, 1933), 31–32; Muir, *History of Milan*, 133–35.

41   See Dummett, *Visconti-Sforza Tarot*, 111.

42   George Ferguson, *Signs and Symbols in Christian Art* (New York: Oxford University Press, 1959), 97.

43   Huson, *Mystical Origins of the Tarot*, 92–93.

44   Muir, *History of Milan*, 138.

45 O'Neill, *Tarot Symbolism*, 58. Most modern authors discount the existence of such a sect. Ronald Hutton, *The Triumph of the Moon: A History of Modern Pagan Witchcraft* (Oxford: Oxford University Press, 1999), 144-49. For the original account of this sect see Charles Godfrey Leland, *Aradia: The Gospel of the Witches* (London: C. W. Daniel Company, 1974).

46 For example see Arthur Edward Waite, *Shadows of Life and Thought: A Retrospective Review in the Form of Memoirs* (London: Selwyn and Blount, 1938), 188.

47 Rosemary Pardoe and Darroll Pardoe, *The Female Pope: The Mystery of Pope Joan* (Wellingborough: Crucible, 1998), 29-30.

48 Martin Polonus, *Chron. Pont. Et Imp; Monumenta Germaniae Historica: Scriptores*, XXII, 428 cited in Pardoe and Pardoe, *Female Pope*, 11.

49 Newman, "Heretic Saint," 28.

50 Martin Polonus, *Chron. Pont. Et Imp; Monumenta Germaniae Historica: Scriptores*, XXII, 428 cited in Pardoe and Pardoe, *Female Pope*, 11; Olsen, "Carte De Trionfi", 240.

51 Jean de Mailly, *Chron. Univ. Mett; Monumenta Germaniae Historica: Scriptores*, XXIV, p. 514 cited in Pardoe and Pardoe, *Female Pope*, 16.

52 For example, see J. N. D. Kelly. *Pope Joan* [Oxford Reference Online]. Oxford Dictionary of Popes: Oxford University Press, 1991 [cited 21 March 2006]. Available from http://www.oxfordreference.com/.

53 Newman, "Heretic Saint," 28.

54 For example, Bill Butler wrote of a tale from the *Arabian Knights* called 'The Fisherman's Wife', which he believed was brought back to Europe by the Crusaders. In this tale, a magical flounder grants the fisherman's wife three wishes, one of which is to be Pope. See Bill Butler. *Dictionary of the Tarot* (New York: Schocken Books, 1975), 117.

55 Newman, "Heretic Saint," 28.

56 Henry Charles Lea, *A History of the Inquisition of the Middle Ages*, The Harbor Scholars' Classics Edition ed., IV vols., Vol. III (New York: S A Russell Publishers, 1955; reprint, Second), 90-91.

57 Newman, "Heretic Saint," 4.

58 Lea, *Inquisition Vol. III*, 90-91.

59 Newman, "Heretic Saint," 4; Lea, *Inquisition Vol. III*, 90-91.

60 Stephen Wessley, "The Thirteenth-Century Gugliemites: Salvation through Women," in *Medieval Women Dedicated and Presented to Professor Rosalind M. T. Hill on the Occasion of Her Seventieth Birthday*, ed. Derek Baker, *Studies in Church History: Subsidia* (Oxford: Basil Blackwell, 1978), 294.

61 Newman, "Heretic Saint," 4.

62 Lea, *Inquisition Vol. III*, 95-96.

63 Wessley, "Thirteenth-Century Gugliemites," 294.

64 Lea, *Inquisition Vol. III*, 95-96.

65 Wessley, "Thirteenth-Century Gugliemites," 298.

66 Newman, "Heretic Saint," 4, 17.

67 Lea, *Inquisition Vol. III*, 91.

68 Newman, "Heretic Saint," 19.

69 Lea, *Inquisition Vol. III*, 95-96.

70 Newman, "Heretic Saint," 19.

71 Muir, *History of Milan*, 15-24.

72 The details of these charges are elucidated in Newman, "Heretic Saint," 19-20.

73 Ibid.: 21-23.

74 Muir, *History of Milan*, 11.

75   Newman, "Heretic Saint," 26–27.
76   Ibid.: 27, 30.
77   Ibid.: 32.
78   Ibid.: 3, 5–6.
79   See Mellinkoff, Ruth. *Outcasts: Signs of Otherness in Northern European Art of the Late Middle Ages*. Edited by Walter Horn. 2 vols. Vol. 1: Text, *California Studies in the History of Art* (Berkeley: University of California Press, 1993), 17
80   The papal triple tiara was not introduced until 1315 and so was absent from this painting. Ferguson, *Christian Art*, 97.
81   Samuel Weller Singer, *Researches into the History of Playing Cards; with Illustrations of the Origin of Printing and Engraving on Wood* (London: R. Triphook, 1816), 29. He quoted from the poem of *Bertuldo con Bertuldino* that was printed in Bologna in 1736: '... trovarvisi dentro semi di buon fine, e di scelta erudizione, e *il Ginerbelti* ne scrisse la storia, ed origine, facendo vedere, che I Tarrocchini non sono altro, se non la` tragica facenda de *Geremei Guelfi, e Lambertazzi Ghibellini*, così il *Valdemusi da Prusilio* ne distese la varia fortuna.'
82   Olsen, "Carte De Trionfi", 234.
83   See Dummett, *Visconti-Sforza Tarot*, 112–13.
84   Robert Steele, "A Notice of the Ludus Triumphorum and Some Early Italian Card Games; with Some Remarks on the Origin of the Game of Cards," *Archaeologia, or, Miscellaneous Tracts Relating to Antiquity* 57 (1900): 190.
85   Strathern, *Medici*, 116–17.
86   Giuliana Algeri, "Un Gioco Per Le Corti: I Tarocchi Miniati," in *I Tarocchi : Le Carte Di Corte : Bioco E Magia Alla Corte Degli Estensi*, ed. Giordano Berti and Andrea Vitali (Bologna: Nuova Alfa, 1987), 28.
87   Dummett, *Visconti-Sforza Tarot*, 13–14.
88   di Parravicino, "Italian Tarocco Cards," 242.
89   C. D. Gilbert, "Blind Cupid," *Journal of the Warburg and Courtauld Institutes* 33 (1970): 304.
90   Erwin Panofsky, *Studies in Iconology: Humanistic Themes in the Art of the Renaissance* (New York: Harper & Row, 1972), 112–13.
91   Gilbert, "Blind Cupid," 305.
92   Panofsky, *Studies in Iconology*, 104, 09.
93   Gilbert, "Blind Cupid," 305.
94   Panofsky, *Studies in Iconology*, 97.
95   Chamberlin, *The Count of Virtue*, 31–33, 40.
96   Muir, *History of Milan*, 62.
97   D. W. Robertson, Jr, "The Concept of Courtly Love as an Impediment to the Understanding of Medieval Texts," in *The Meaning of Courtly Love: Papers of the First Annual Conference of the Center for Medieval and Renaissance Studies State University of New York at Binghamton March 17–18, 1967*, ed. F. X. Newman (Albany: State University of New York Press, 1968), 1.
98   Johan Huizinga, *The Autumn of the Middle Ages*, trans. Rodney J. Payton and Ulrich Mammitzsch (Chicago: University of Chicago Press, 1996), 126.
99   Antonio Viscardi, "Arthurian Influences on Italian Literature from 1200 to 1500," in *Arthurian Literature in the Middle Ages: A Collaboartive History*, ed. Roger Sherman Loomis (Oxford: Clarendon Press, 1959), 428. The Visconti library contained many books relating to these themes. See Pearl Kibre, "The Intellectual Interests Reflected in the Libraries of the Fourteenth and Fifteenth Centuries," *Journal of the History of Ideas* 7, no. 3 (1946): 269.
100   Muir, *History of Milan*, 170–71.

101 Cieri-Via, "Arcani Maggiori," 169.
102 Jacob Burckhardt, *The Civilisation of the Renaissance in Italy*, trans. S. G. C. Middlemore (New York: Times Mirror, 1960), 63; Hollingsworth, *Patronage in Renaissance Italy*, 166.
103 Dummett, *Visconti-Sforza Tarot*, 116.
104 Will Durant, *The Renaissance: A History of Civilization in Italy from 1304–1576 Ad*, ed. Will Durant and Ariel Durant, X vols., Vol. V, *The Story of Civilization* (New York: Simon and Schuster, 1953; reprint, Thirteenth), 183.
105 Peter Burke, *Popular Culture in Early Modern Europe* (London: Temple Smith, 1978), 188–89.
106 Little, *Hermitage* (cited) – *The History of the Chariot Card* (http://www.tarothermit.com/chariot.htm); di Parravicino, "Italian Tarocco Cards," 242.
107 A similar theme is posited by Tom Tadfor Little though he stated that this Trump could have represented Chastity, a theory that was also explored by Robert V. O'Neill. See Little, *Hermitage* (cited) – *The History of the Chariot Card* (http://www.tarothermit.com/chariot.htm); Robert V. O'Neill, *Iconology of the Chariot Cards* [website] (Visionary Networks, 2006 [cited 7 March 2006]); available from http://www.tarot.com.
108 Huizinga, *Autumn*, 126.
109 J. C. Cooper, *An Illustrated Encyclopaedia of Traditional Symbols* (London: Thames and Hudson, 1978), 33; J. E. Cirlot, *A Dictionary of Symbols*, trans. Jack Sage, Second ed. (New York: Philosophical Library, 1971; reprint, Fifth), 374.
110 Cooper, *Illustrated Encyclopaedia*, 33.
111 Dante Alighieri, *The Divine Comedy*, trans. Allen Mandelbaum, *Everyman's Library* (London: Everyman Publishers, 1995), 354.
112 Cooper, *Illustrated Encyclopaedia*, 33.
113 See William Langland, *Piers Plowman*, Revised ed., 3 vols., Vol. 1 (London: Athlone Press, 1997).
114 Cooper, *Illustrated Encyclopaedia*, 33.
115 Webber, *Church Symbolism*, 63.
116 For example, see Erwin Panofsky and Fritz Saxl, "A Late Antique Religious Symbol in Works by Holbein and Titian," *Burlington Magazine for Connoisseurs* 49, no. 283 (1926): 180.
117 Muir, *History of Milan*, 170–71.
118 Jacob Burckhardt, *The Civilization of the Renaissance in Italy*, trans. S. G. C. Middlemore, *Penguin Classics* (London: Penguin Books, 1990), 26.
119 Burckhardt, *The Civilization of the Renaissance*, 121. Obviously, the term 'Renaissance' came to signify more than a classical revival. It came to incorporate the ideas of humanism, secularism, nationalism and commercial entrepreneurialism. See Welch, *Art and Society*, 9.
120 Burckhardt, *The Civilization of the Renaissance*, 129–30.
121 Joscelyn Godwin, "Introduction," in *Hypnerotomachia Polophili: The Strife of Love in a Dream*, ed. Francesco Colonna (London: Thames & Hudson, 1999), vii.
122 Erwin Panofsky, *Renaissance and Renascences in Western Art* (New York: Harper Row, 1972), 173.
123 Adolf Katzenellenbogen, *Allegories of the Virtues and Vices in Medieval Art from Early Christian Times to the Thirteenth Century* (New York: W. W. Norton and Company Inc., 1964), vii.
124 Huizinga, *Autumn*, 243.
125 Edgar Wind. *Pagan Mysteries in the Renaissance*. Revised ed. (Harmondsworth: Penguin Books, 1967), 27.

126   Roger Sherman Loomis, "The Allegorical Siege in the Art of the Middle Ages," *American Journal of Archaeology* 23, no. 3 (1919): 255.

127   Thomas F. O'Meara, "Virtues in the Theology of Thomas Aquinas," *Theological Studies* 58, no. 2 (1997): 254.

128   Jennifer O'Reilly, *Studies in the Iconography of the Virtues and Vices in the Middle Ages* (New York: Garland Publishing, Inc., 1988), 74.

129   For example, E. H. Gombrich, *Symbolic Images: Studies in the Art of the Renaissance II*, Third ed., vol. II (Oxford: Phaidon, 1985), 87.

130   Glynne Wickham. *The Medieval Theatre.* Third ed. (Cambridge: Cambridge University Press, 1987), 26–27.

131   di Parravicino, "Italian Tarocco Cards," 242.

132   James Hall, *Dictionary of Subjects and Symbols in Art* (London: John Murray, 1974), 127. Modern tarot creator Brian Williams erroneously reported that this representation of Fortitude was rarely seen outside of tarot. The Fortitude card from his recent *Minchiate Tarot* shows a woman holding a column. Fortitude was also represented in a similar manner in later Renaissance decks. Emily E. Auger, *Tarot and Other Meditation Decks: History, Theory, Aesthetics, Typology* (Jefferson: McFarland & Company Inc., 2004), 20.

133   Raimond van Marle, *Iconographie De L'art Profane Au Moyen-Age Et À La Renaissance Et La Décoration Des Demeures*, II vols., Vol. II (New York: Hacker Art Books, 1971), 16.

134   Thomas Aquinas in Archer Woodford, "Mediaeval Iconography of the Virtues; a Poetic Portraiture," *Speculum* 28, no. 3 (1953): 523.

135   See David Carr, "The Cardinal Virtues and Plato's Moral Psychology," *The Philosophical Quarterly* 38, no. 151 (1988): 192–93.

136   Dummett, *Visconti-Sforza Tarot*, 118.

137   Hall, *Subjects and Symbols*, 148.

138   Percy Preston, *A Dictionary of Pictorial Subjects from Classical Literature: A Guide to Their Identification in Works of Art* (New York: Charles Scribner's Sons, 1983), 166.

139   Michael Evans, "Allegorical Women and Practical Men: The Iconography of the *Artes* Reconsidered," in *Medieval Women Dedicated and Presented to Professor Rosalind M. T. Hill on the Occasion of Her Seventieth Birthday*, ed. Derek Baker, *Studies in Church History: Subsidia* (Oxford: Basil Blackwell, 1978), 305.

140   Robert O'Neill. *Tarot Symbolism* (Lima: Fairway Press, 1986), 20.

141   Satia Bernen and Robert Bernen, *Myth and Religion in European Painting 1270–1700: The Stories as the Artists Knew Them* (New York: George Braziller, 1973), 236.

142   Ibid., 238.

143   Strathern, *Medici*, 78–79.

144   Muir, *History of Milan*, 147.

145   Durant, *The Renaissance*, 183.

146   Lynn Thorndike, *The History of Medieval Europe*, Third ed. (Cambridge: Houghton Mifflin Company, 1945), 590.

147   Gary Ianziti, *Humanistic Historiography under the Sforzas: Politics and Propaganda in Fifteenth-Century Milan* (Oxford: Clarendon Press, 1988), 20.

148   Durant, *The Renaissance*, 183.

149   Mark Phillips, "A Newly Discovered Chronicle by Marco Parenti," *Renaissance Quarterly* 31, no. 2 (1978): 159.

150   Hans Baron, "A Struggle for Liberty in the Renaissance: Florence, Venice, and Milan in the Early Quattrocento, Part 2." *The American Historical Review* 58, no. 3 (1953): 566.

151   Thorndike, *Medieval Europe*, 590.

152   Durant, *The Renaissance*, 183.

153 Baron, "A Struggle for Liberty," 566–67.
154 Charles M. Rosenberg, "Piety and Patronage in Renaissance Venice: Bellini, Titian, and the Franciscans," *Italica* 65, no. 3 (1988): 274.
155 Machael A. Jacobsen, "A Sforza Miniature by Cristoforo Da Preda," *Burlington Magazine* 116, no. 851 (1974): 95.
156 For example, see Ronald W. Vince, "Virtues and Vices," in *A Companion to the Medieval Theatre*, ed. Ronald W. Vince (New York: Greenwood Press, 1989), 373.
157 Panofsky, *Studies in Iconology*, 13.
158 See Plato, *The Republic*, ed. Betty Radice, trans. Desmond Lee, Second ed., *Penguin Classics* (London: London, 2003), 131–56.
159 Hall, *Subjects and Symbols*, 183.
160 Cooper, *Illustrated Encyclopaedia*, 33.
161 John Brian Campbell, "Trajan," in *The Oxford Companion to Classical Civilization*, ed. Simon Hornblower and Antony Spawforth (Oxford: Oxford Univerity Press, 1998).
162 For example, see the impressive painting of Eugene Delacroix, *La justice de Trajan.*
163 For example, this figure is also seen on the tomb of Clarence II at Bamberg Cathedral. See van Marle, *Iconographie De L'art Profane*, 15.
164 Hall, *Subjects and Symbols*, 297.
165 M. L. D'Otrange, "Thirteen Tarot Cards from the Visconti-Sforza Set," *The Connoisseur* 133 (1954): 58.
166 Aquinas, T. (1947–1948). Summa Theologica. London, Burns & Oates.
167 Detlef Hoffmann, *The Playing Card: An Illustrated History*, trans. C. S. V. Salt (Greenwich: New York Graphic Society Ltd, 1973), 19.
168 Woodford, "Mediaeval Iconography of the Virtues," 524.
169 Vince, "Virtues and Vices," 373.
170 Ibid.
171 Vince, "Virtues and Vices," 373.
172 Ferguson, *Christian Art*, 104. This symbolic meaning rests on the Epistle to the Hebrews 6:19, which referred to the everlasting virtue of God's counsel in these words, 'Which hope we have as an anchor of the soul, both sure and steadfast ...' I did consider the possibility that the symbol was actually a fish hook and was some reference to Jesus: the Greek word for fish, *icthus*, being an acronym for Jesus Christ Son of God Saviour. However, there was no precedence for such an interpretation in Renaissance art.
173 Vince, "Virtues and Vices," 373.
174 Andrea Vitali, "Arcani Svelati," in *I Tarocchi: Le Carte Di Corte : Bioco E Magia Alla Corte Degli Estensi*, ed. Giordano Berti and Andrea Vitali (Bologna: Nuova Alfa, 1987), 151.
175 di Parravicino, "Italian Tarocco Cards," 242–45.
176 Vince, "Virtues and Vices," 373.
177 Stuart R. Kaplan. *The Encyclopedia of Tarot.* IV vols. Vol. I (New York: U. S. Games Systems, 1978), 91.
178 John Stephens, *The Italian Renaissance: The Origins of Intellectual and Artistic Change before the Reformation* (London: Longman, 1990), xvii.
179 Pullan, *History of Early Renaissance Italy*, 171–72.
180 Jean Seznec, *The Survival of the Pagan Gods: The Mythological Tradition and Its Place in Renaissance Humanism and Art*, ed. Bollingen Foundation, trans. Barbara F. Sessions, *Bollingen Series* (Princeton: Princeton University Press, 1972), 28.
181 The virtues were also considered to be very necessary in the life of a prince. From the the time of St Augustine's *City of God* (*Civitas Dei*) numerous treatises were written about the necessary qualities of a prince, and as such, the virtues were considered to be

particularly important. Interestingly, Duke Filippo Maria Visconti showed himself to be unsuitable as the 'perfect prince' by showing a lack of respect for the Church hierarchy and by being a tyrant. For a fuller description of the attributes of the 'perfect prince' see Born, L. K. (1928). "The Perfect Prince: A Study in Thirteenth- and Fourteenth-Century Ideals." Speculum **3** (4): 470–504.

182 Decker, Depaulis, and Dummett, *A Wicked Pack of Cards*, 45.

183 Panofsky, *Studies in Iconology*, 79.

184 Cooper, *Illustrated Encyclopaedia*, 86.

185 It is interesting to note that Time is sometimes called πολιός (grey-headed) in Greek poetry. Panofsky, *Studies in Iconology*, 71–72.

186 Cieri-Via, "Arcani Maggiori," 171.

187 Muir, *History of Milan*, 133–35.

188 From the end of the fifteenth century, Time and Death were frequently linked. Panofsky, *Studies in Iconology*, 83.

189 Niccolò Machiavelli. *The Prince*. Translated by George Bull. Edited by E. V. Rieu, *Penguin Classics* (Harmondsworth: Penguin Books, 1961), 40.

190 David M. Robinson, "The Wheel of Fortune," *Classical Philology* 41, no. 4 (1946): 207.

191 Jean Delumeau, *Sin and Fear: The Emergence of a Western Guilt Culture 13th-18th Centuries*, trans. Eric Nicholson (New York: St Martin's Press, 1990), 153–54.

192 Hall, *Subjects and Symbols*, 127–28. Many erroneously cite Boëthius as the first to employ the allegory of the wheel of fortune. For example, see Huson, *Mystical Origins of the Tarot*, 38.

193 'rotam volubili orbe versamus infima summis, summa infimis, mutare gaudemus.' Boëthius in Robinson, "Wheel," 214.

194 Bayard Ranking, "The History of Probability and the Changing Concept of the Individual," *Journal of the History of Ideas* 27, no. 4 (1966): 484.

195 Delumeau, *Sin and Fear*, 153–54.

196 Machiavelli, *The Prince*, 130.

197 Malory's *Le Morte d'Arthur* was written in the fifteenth century. The actual sources for the work remain controversial. See Robert H. Wilson, "Malory's 'French Book' Again," *Comparative Literature* 2, no. 2 (1950).

198 Delumeau, *Sin and Fear*, 155.

199 Ibid., 156.

200 Decker, Depaulis, and Dummett, *A Wicked Pack of Cards*, 45.

201 See Panofsky, *Studies in Iconology*, 110, 12.

202 Hall, *Subjects and Symbols*, 127–28.

203 Preston, *Dictionary of Pictorial Subjects*, 97.

204 Hall, *Subjects and Symbols*, 127–28.

205 Cieri-Via, "Arcani Maggiori," 172.

206 Gilbert, "Blind Cupid," 305.

207 Panofsky, *Studies in Iconology*, 112–13.

208 Baron, "A Struggle for Liberty," 564.

209 Christopher Hibbert. *The Rise and Fall of the House of Medici*. Harmondsworth: Penguin Books, 1979 81.

210 Giles, *The Tarot*, 15–16. Thierry Depaulis also reported that the card was sometimes called *l'Impiccato* , *l'Appicato* or il Penduto. Depaulis, *Jeu Et Magie*, 19.

211 Samuel Y. Jr Edgerton, *Pictures and Punishment: Art and Criminal Prosecution During the Florentine Renaissance* (Ithaca: Cornell University Press, 1985), 15, 50.

212 Samuel Y. Jr Edgerton, "Icons of Justice," *Past and Present*, no. 89 (1980): 30–31.

213 Burke, *Culture and Society*, 136–37.

214 Keith Christiansen. "A Hanged Man by Filippino." *Burlington Magazine* 136, no. 1099 (1994): 705.

215 Werner L. Gundersheimer, "Renaissance Concepts of Shame and Pocaterra's Dialoghi Della Vergogna," *Renaissance Quarterly* 47, no. 1 (1994): 34.

216 Huson, *Mystical Origins of the Tarot*, 114-15.

217 See Matthew 26, 69-75; Luke 22, 54-62; John 18, 15-17 and 25-27.

218 Mitchell B. Merback, *The Thief, the Cross and the Wheel: Pain and the Spectacle of Punishment in Medieval and Renaissance Europe*, ed. Peter Burke, et al., *Picturing History* (London: Reaktion Books, 1999), 187-88.

219 Rossell Hope Robbins, *The Encyclopedia of Witchcraft and Demonology* (London: Peter Nevill Limited, 1959), 267.

220 Dummett, *Visconti-Sforza Tarot*, 124.

221 Edgerton, *Pictures and Punishment*, 88-89.

222 Citing the *Statua civitatis Mediolani* (Milan 1480), fol. 90 r. 'Giorgio Giulini, ed., *Memorie della Città di Milano* (Milan, 1770), pt. II, p. 510: 'Cum in parietibus Pallati Novi Communis Mediolani sint picte certe ymagines; quedam presentantes falsitatem Testium, quedam vilium Notariorum, quedam Campsorum, & Mercatorum, que quamvis videantur esse facte ad confuxionem, & infamiam Falsariorum, tamen non solum actoribus ipsarum falsitatum pro huiusmodi picturis ipsis Falsariis reditur scandalum, & infamia, ymo totaliter Civitati, in conspectus maxime Forasteriorum ipsas figures plerumque spectantium, quicunque vident ymaginantur, & quasi firmiter credunt, quod major pars Civium parvam fidem agnoschant, &magnis falsitatibus involuti sint. Ea propter statuiter, quod omnes ipse picture amoveantur, & in futurum nullus pingatur, sed acriter, & fortius puniatur, aliquot in contrarium non obstante.' In David Freedberg, *The Power of Images: Studies in the History and Theory of Response* (Chicago: The University of Chicago Press, 1989), 251-53.

223 Edgerton, *Pictures and Punishment*, 92.

224 Giles, *The Tarot*, 15-16.

225 Edgerton, *Pictures and Punishment*, 92; Baron, "A Struggle for Liberty," 566.

226 Decker, Depaulis, and Dummett, *A Wicked Pack of Cards*, 60-61.

227 Christiansen, "A Hanged Man," 705.

228 Jacques Levron, *Le Diable Dans L'art* (Paris: Éditions Auguste Picard, 1935), 65.

229 Stuart Clark, *Thinking with Demons: The Idea of Witchcraft in Early Modern Europe* (Oxford: Oxford University Press, 1997), 341. The term 'Black Death' was first used retrospectively in the seventeenth century. At the time, it was simply referred to as '*la peste*' ('the plague'). Harry Hearder, *Italy: A Short History* (Cambridge: Cambridge University Press, 1990), 97.

230 Ann G. Carmichael, "Contagion Theory and Contagion Practice in Fifteenth-Century Milan," *Renaissance Quarterly* 44, no. 2 (1991): 215.

231 Pullan, *History of Early Renaissance Italy*, 206-07.

232 Margaret Aston, *The Fifteenth Century: The Prospect of Europe* (London: Thames and Hudson, 1968), 19-20.

233 Carmichael, "Contagion Theory," 213.

234 Aston, *The Fifteenth Century*, 19-20.

235 George Huppert, *After the Black Death: A Social History of Early Modern Europe*, ed. Harvey J. Graff, *Interdisciplinary Studies in History* (Bloomington: Indiana University Press, 1986), 11.

236 Carmichael, "Contagion Theory," 214.

237 Ibid.: 215-21.

238 Kibre, "Intellectual Interests," 292.

239 Carmichael, "Contagion Theory," 226.

240   Pullan, *History of Early Renaissance Italy*, 207.
241   Evelyn Welch. *Art and Society in Italy 1350-1500, Oxford History of Art*. Oxford: Oxford University Press, 1997., 23-25.
242   Aston, *The Fifteenth Century*, 18.
243   Carmichael, "Contagion Theory," 215-21.
244   Delumeau, *Sin and Fear*, 96.
245   F. Edward Hulme, *The History, Principles and Practice of Symbolism in Christian Art* (London: Swan Sonnenschein & Co., 1908), 96-97.
246   Delumeau, *Sin and Fear*, 35-36.
247   Levron, *Le Diable*, 67.
248   Ibid.
249   Durant, *The Renaissance*, 28-34. See Charles S. Singleton, "On Meaning in the Decameron," *Italica* 21, no. 3 (1944).
250   Gertrude Grace Sill, *A Handbook of Symbols in Christian Art* (New York: Touchstone, 1996), 34.
251   Sill, *Handbook of Symbols*, 34.
252   Ibid. For a description of *memento mori* in fifteenth-century Italian art see Horst W. Janson, "A 'Memento Mori' among Early Italian Prints," *Journal of the Warburg and Courtauld Institutes* 3, no. 3/4 (1940): 243.
253   Liana DeGirolami Cheney, "Dutch Vanitas Paintings: The Skull," in *The Symbolism of Vanitas in the Arts, Literature, and Music*, ed. Liana DeGirolami Cheney (Lewiston: Edwin Mellen Press, 1992), 116.
254   Huizinga, *Autumn*, 156.
255   This legend is sometimes known as the *Three Quick and the Three Dead*.
256   Levron, *Le Diable*, 66.
257   James C. Clark, "Introduction," in *The Dance of Death*, Hans Holbein (London: Phaidon Press Ltd, 1947), 7.
258   Alma Espinosa, "Music and the *Danse Macabre*: A Survey," in *The Symbolism of Vanitas in the Arts, Literature and Music: Comparative and Historical Studies*, ed. Liana DeGirolami Cheney (Lewiston: Edwin Mellen Press, 1992), 15, 25.
259   Ad de Vries, *Dictionary of Symbols and Imagery* (Amsterdam: North-Holland Publishing Company, 1974), 131.
260   Russell, *Witchcraft in the Middle Ages*, 136-37.
261   Delumeau, *Sin and Fear*, 99.
262   William Monter, *Ritual, Myth and Magic in Early Modern Europe* (Athens: Ohio University Press, 1984), 13-14.
263   Sill, *Handbook of Symbols*, 34.
264   See Hans Holbein, *The Dance of Death* (London: Phaidon Press Ltd, 1947).
265   Hulme, *Symbolism in Christian Art*, 95. Michael Dummett erroneously assumed that these representations of death stemmed from the artist's poor knowledge of anatomy. See Dummett, *Visconti-Sforza Tarot*, 126.
266   Cirlot, *A Dictionary of Symbols*, 31.
267   Ferguson, *Christian Art*, 28.
268   Mellinkoff, *Outcasts*, 39-40.
269   Butler, *Dictionary of the Tarot*, 159.
270   Christopher McIntosh, *The Astrologers and Their Creed: An Historical Outline* (London: Arrow Books, 1971), 100.
271   Anthony Grafton, "Starry Messengers: Recent Work in the History of Western Astrology," *Perspectives on Science* 8, no. 1 (2000): 75.
272   Ibid.
273   McIntosh, *Astrologers and Their Creed*, 102.

274 Ibid., 103.

275 Larner, *Italy in the Age of Dante and Petrarch*, 17.

276 Seznec, *Survival of the Pagan Gods*, 59.

277 Collison-Morley, *Sforzas*, 31-32.

278 Muir, *History of Milan*, 133-35.

279 L. Beltrami, *Il Castello Di Milano:(Castrum, Portae, Jovis) Sotto Il Dominio Dei Visconti E Degli Sforza, 1368-1535* (Milan: U. Hoepli, 1894), 101-02.

280 Jacobsen, "Sforza Miniature," 91.

281 Grafton, "Starry Messengers," 76.

282 See Christina Olsen. *The Art of Tarot, A Tiny Folio* (New York: Abbeville Press, 1995), 82.

283 Giles, *The Tarot*, 15.

284 See Olsen, *Art of Tarot*, 91.

285 See Dummett, *Visconti-Sforza Tarot*, 131.

286 Ferguson, *Christian Art*, 24.

287 Hans Biedermann, *Dictionary of Symbolism*, trans. James Hulbert (New York: Facts on File, 1992), 224. For an example of this association see Millard Meiss, "The Madonna of Humility," *Art Bulletin* 18, no. 4 (1936): 435.

288 Panofsky, *Studies in Iconology*, 110.

289 Michael Dummett specifically stated that the *putto* is without wings, yet the illustration on the page facing that statement shows a *putto* with small dark wings. See Dummett, *Visconti-Sforza Tarot*, 134-35. The *putto* is identical to those painted on the card of the World, also in the Visconti-Sforza deck. See Dummett, *Visconti-Sforza Tarot*, 139.

290 See Dummett, *Visconti-Sforza Tarot*, 135.

291 Alva William Steffler, *Symbols of the Christian Faith* (Grand Rapids: William B. Eerdmans Publishing Company, 2002), 16; Panofsky, *Studies in Iconology*, 110.

292 Steffler, *Symbols of the Christian Faith*, 16.

293 Pullan, *History of Early Renaissance Italy*, 171-72.

294 McIntosh, *Astrologers and Their Creed*, 100.

295 Hall, *Subjects and Symbols*, 186.

296 John Wesley Harris. *Medieval Theatre in Context* (New York: Routledge, 1992), 91.

297 Delumeau, *Sin and Fear*, 52.

298 Thorndike, *Medieval Europe*, 481.

299 Ibid.

300 di Parravicino, "Italian Tarocco Cards," 245.

301 Mary Rasmussen, "Kulturgeschichte Des Horns (a Pictorial History of the Horn)," *Notes* 35, no. 2 (1978): 321.

302 Francis Edwards, *Ritual and Drama: The Medieval Theatre* (Guildford: Lutterworth Press, 1976), 97.

303 di Parravicino, "Italian Tarocco Cards," 245.

304 Dummett, *Visconti-Sforza Tarot*, 138.

305 Muir, *History of Milan*, 173.

306 See Marianna Jenkins. "The Iconography of the Hall of the Consistory in the Palazzo Pubblico, Siena." *Art Bulletin* 54, no. 4 (1972): 436.

307 Keith D. Lilley, "Cities of God? Medieval Urban Forms and Their Christian Symbolism," *Transactions of the Institute of British Geographers* 29, no. 3 (2004): 300.

308 Ibid.: 302.

309 Wickham, *Medieval Theatre*, 25-26.

310 Ibid.

311 Garry Wills, *Saint Augustine* (London: Phœnix, 1999), 41-48.

312   Chamberlin, *The Count of Virtue*, 11. Muir also described the city as being red. Muir, *History of Milan*, 173.

313   H. P. Gerhard, *The World of Icons*, trans. Irene R. Gibbons (London: John Murray, 1971), 185.

314   Leonid A. Ouspensky and Vladimir Lossky, *The Meaning of Icons*, trans. G. E. H. Palmer and E. K. Kadloubovsky, Revised ed. (Crestwood: St Vladimir's Seminary Press, 1982; reprint, Third), 132.

315   Joanna Woods-Marsden, "Images of Castles in the Renaissance: Symbols of 'Signoria'/Symbols of Tyranny," *Art Journal* 48, no. 2 (1989): 130–31.

316   Ibid.: 134.

317   Machiavelli, *The Prince*, 118.

318   Woods-Marsden, "Images of Castles in the Renaissance," 130–31, 134.

319   Lilley, "Cities of God?" 307.

320   For example, see Stuart R. Kaplan, *Fortune-Telling with Tarot Cards: An Illustrated Guide to Spreading and Interpreting the 1JJ Tarot, Fortune-Telling With ...* (London: Diamond Books, 1995), 9.

321   Michael Dummett and Kamal Abu-Deeb, "Some Remarks on Mamluk Playing Cards," *Journal of the Warburg and Courtauld Institutes* 36 (1973): 110.

322   Maurice Rickards, *The Encyclopedia of Ephemera: A Guide to the Fragmentary Documents of Everyday Life for the Collector, Curator, and Historian* (London: British Library, 2000), 239. Félix Fournier placed the invention of the Joker at the beginning of the twentieth century though the earlier date is more likely. See Félix Alfaro Fournier, *Playing Cards: General History from Their Creation to the Present Day* (Vitoria: Heraclio Fournier, 1982), 211.

323   Dummett and Abu-Deeb, "Some Remarks," 110.

324   Joyce Goggin, "A History of Otherness: Tarot and Playing Cards from Early Modern Europe," *Journal for the Academic Study of Magic* 1, no. 1 (2003): 55.

325   Dummett and McLeod, *A History of Games*, 5.

326   Decker, Depaulis, and Dummett, *A Wicked Pack of Cards*, 43–44.

327   Dummett, *Visconti-Sforza Tarot*, 100.

328   Olsen, "Carte De Trionfi", 237.

329   Mellinkoff, *Outcasts*, 29.

330   Luther Link, *The Devil: A Mask without a Face*, ed. Peter Burke, et al., *Picturing History* (London: Reaktion Books, 1995), 59.

331   Mellinkoff, *Outcasts*, 204.

332   Ibid., 115.

333   Olsen, "Carte De Trionfi", 235–36.

334   Dummett, *Visconti-Sforza Tarot*, 100.

335   Paolo Vitti et al., "Iodine Deficiency Disorders in Europe," *Public Health Nutrition* 4, no. 2b (2001): 529.

336   Strabismus is a condition where both eyes cannot focus on the one point. In the vernacular this is frequently referred to as being 'cross-eyed'. Basil S. Hetzel, "Iodine and Neuropsychological Development," *Journal of Nutrition* 130, no. 2S (2000): 493.

337   C. Als et al., "Through the Artist's Eye: Visible Signs of Illness from the 14th to the 20th Century: Systematic Review of Portraits," *British Medical Journal* 325, no. 7378 (2002): 1499.

338   Mellinkoff, *Outcasts*, 17, 115.

339   Olsen, "Carte De Trionfi", 237.

340   Gertrude Moakley, *The Tarot Cards Painted by Bonifacio Bembo for the Visconti-Sforza Family: An Iconographic and Historical Study* (New York: The New York Public Library, 1966), 113–14.

341 For example, see the Chariot, the Cardinal Virtues, the Sun, etc.

342 Moakley, *Tarot Cards Painted by Bonifacio Bembo*, 113–14.

343 Maria José Palla, "Carnaval, Parvo Et "Monde À L'envers" Chez Gil Vincente," in *Carnival and the Carnivalesque: The Fool, the Reformer, the Wildman, and Others in Early Modern Theatre*, ed. Konrad Eisenbichler and Wim Hüsken, *Ludus: Medieval and Early Renaissance Theatre and Drama* (Amsterdam: Rodopi, 1999), 170–71.

344 Alexander Orloff. *Carnival: Myth and Cult* (Wörgl: Perlinger Verlag, 1980), 15.

345 Mellinkoff, *Outcasts*, 136.

346 Dummett with Mann, *The Game of Tarot*, 169.

347 Dummett, *Visconti-Sforza Tarot*, 128.

348 Vitali, "I Tarocchi," 145.

349 Decker, Depaulis, and Dummett, *A Wicked Pack of Cards*, 28.

350 Depaulis, *Jeu Et Magie*, 19.

351 Decker, Depaulis, and Dummett, *A Wicked Pack of Cards*, 46.

352 Dummett, *Visconti-Sforza Tarot*, 128. Le maison Dieu usually referred to a building where the sick poor were cared for. Butler, *Dictionary of the Tarot*, 169.

353 Little, *Hermitage* (cited) – *The History of the Tower (Fire) Card* (http://www.tarothermit.com/tower.htm); O'Neill, *Tarot Symbolism*, 81.

354 Whitaker, *King Arthur in Art*, 2; Michael J. Curley, *Geoffrey of Monmouth*, *Twayne's English Authors Series* (New York: Twayne Publishers, 1994), 40.

355 Welch, *Art and Society*, 30. The Visconti library contained many books relating to these themes. See Pearl Kibre. "The Intellectual Interests Reflected in the Libraries of the Fourteenth and Fifteenth Centuries." *Journal of the History of Ideas* 7, no. 3 (1946): 269.

356 This is described in Genesis 11. See Vitali, "I Tarocchi," 147.

357 Sill, *Handbook of Symbols*, 145.

358 Biedermann, *Dictionary of Symbolism*, 26.

359 Bernen and Bernen, *Myth and Religion*, 257. For example, see Pieter Brueghel's rendition of the Tower of Babel.

360 It is interesting to note that the story of Sodom and Gomorrah was also posited as a possible source of the symbolism on the Tower card. Vitali, "I Tarocchi," 145.

361 Little, *Hermitage* (cited) – *The History of the Tower (Fire) Card* (http://www.tarothermit.com/tower.htm).

362 Muir, *History of Milan*, 8.

363 'Della Torre' literally means 'From the Tower'. *Signoria* is a particular form of governing body popular in the Italian city states taking the form of a personal or family despotism. Pullan, *History of Early Renaissance Italy*, 156–57.

364 Pullan, *History of Early Renaissance Italy*, 156–57.

365 Ibid. The *podestà* was responsible for law and order. Usually an outsider was employed in order to maintain neutrality. K. D. Vernon, "Ueber Die Anfänge Der Signorie in Oberitalien: Ein Beitrag Zur Italienischen Verfassungsgeschichte [Review]," *English Historical Review* 16, no. 61 (1901): 135.

366 Pullan, *History of Early Renaissance Italy*, 157.

367 Wessley, "Thirteenth-Century Gugliemites," 297

368 Pullan, *History of Early Renaissance Italy*, 157.

369 Muir, *History of Milan*, 8–9; Vernon, "Ueber Die Anfänge Der Signorie in Oberitalien," 136.

370 Pullan, *History of Early Renaissance Italy*, 156–57.

371 Muir, *History of Milan*, 9.

372 Wessley, "Thirteenth-Century Gugliemites," 297.

373 Newman, "Heretic Saint," 7.

374   Pullan, *History of Early Renaissance Italy*, 157.
375   Muir, *History of Milan*, 9.
376   Pullan, *History of Early Renaissance Italy*, 158.
377   Muir, *History of Milan*, 9.
378   Pullan, *History of Early Renaissance Italy*, 158.
379   Muir, *History of Milan*, 9-10.
380   Hearder, *Italy*, 79-80.
381   Muir, *History of Milan*, 10.
382   Pullan, *History of Early Renaissance Italy*, 158-59.
383   Muir, *History of Milan*, 11.
384   Pullan, *History of Early Renaissance Italy*, 158-59.
385   Newman, "Heretic Saint," 24.
386   Muir, *History of Milan*, 11.
387   Pullan, *History of Early Renaissance Italy*, 158-59.
388   Muir, *History of Milan*, 12.
389   Pullan, *History of Early Renaissance Italy*, 158-59.
390   Ibid., 159.
391   Newman, "Heretic Saint," 18.
392   Hearder, *Italy*, 79-80.
393   Pullan, *History of Early Renaissance Italy*, 159.
394   Ibid., 159-60.
395   Hearder, *Italy*, 80.
396   For example, see Eddie Geoghegan, *Coats of Arms from Ireland and around the World* [Website] (Eddie Geoghegen, 14 February 1990 [cited 9 May 2006]); available from http://www.heraldry.ws/.
397   Dummett with Mann, *The Game of Tarot*, 71.
398   Kaplan, *Encyclopedia of Tarot II*, 11.
399   Little, *Hermitage* (cited) - *The History of the Tower (Fire) Card* (http://www.tarothermit.com/tower.htm); O'Neill, *Tarot Symbolism*, 81.
400   Luther Link, *The Devil: The Archfiend in Art from the Sixth to the Sixteenth Century* (New York: Harry N. Abrams, Inc., 1996), 72.
401   Levron, *Le Diable*, 62.
402   Link, *The Archfiend in Art*, 72.
403   Link, *Mask without a Face*, 15-16.
404   Link, *The Archfiend in Art*, 74.
405   Link, *Mask without a Face*, 44.
406   Link, *The Archfiend in Art*, 72.
407   Levron, *Le Diable*, 63.
408   Link, *The Archfiend in Art*, 146.
409   Ibid., 183.
410   Norman Cohn, *Europe's Inner Demons: An Enquiry Inspired by the Great Witch-Hunt*, ed. Norman Cohn, *The Columbus Centre Series: Studies in the Dynamics of Persecution and Extermination* (Bungay: Sussex University Press, 1975), 60.
411   Link, *The Archfiend in Art*, 146.
412   Levron, *Le Diable*, 62.
413   Hutton, *Triumph of the Moon*, 46.
414   Link, *Mask without a Face*, 51-52.
415   Samuel Kinser, "Why Is Carnival So Wild?," in *Carnival and the Carnivalesque: The Fool, the Reformer, the Wildman, and Others in Early Modern Theatre*, ed. Konrad Eisenbichler and Wim Hüsken, *Ludus: Medieval and Early Renaissance Theatre and Drama* (Amsterdam: Rodopi, 1999), 55.

416 Link, *Mask without a Face*, 59.
417 Robert Hughes. *Heaven and Hell in Western Art* (London: Weidenfeld and Nicolson, 1968), 176–77.
418 Link, *Mask without a Face*, 67–68.
419 Levron, *Le Diable*, 89.
420 Darren Olderidge, "Protestant Conceptions of the Devil in Early Stuart England," *History* 85, no. 278 (2000): 233.
421 Robert Muchembled, *A History of the Devil from the Middle Ages to the Present*, trans. Jean Birrell (Cambridge: Polity Press, 2003), 1.
422 Link, *Mask without a Face*, 188.
423 Link, *The Archfiend in Art*, 74.
424 Muchembled, *A History of the Devil*, 54–55.
425 Link, *Mask without a Face*, 189.
426 Jeffrey Burton Russell. *Witchcraft in the Middle Ages* (Ithaca: Cornell University Press, 1972), 113.
427 Olderidge, "Conceptions of the Devil," 232–33.
428 Julio Caro Baroja, "Witchcraft and Catholic Theology," in *Early Modern European Witchcraft: Centres and Peripheries*, ed. Bengt Ankarloo and Gustav Henningsen (Oxford: Clarendon Press, 1990), 38.
429 Olderidge, "Conceptions of the Devil," 233.
430 Muchembled, *A History of the Devil*, 52–53.
431 Zakiya Hanafi, *The Monster in the Machine: Magic, Medicine, and the Marvellous in the Time of the Scientific Revolution* (Durham: Duke University Press, 2000), 47.
432 Ottavia Niccoli, *Prophecy and People in Renaissance Italy*, trans. Lydia G. Cochrane (Princeton: Princeton University Press, 1990), xiv, 31.
433 Katherine Park and Lorraine J. Daston, "Unnatural Conceptions: The Study of Monsters in Sixteenth- and Seventeenth-Century France and England," *Past and Present*, no. 92 (1981): 23.
434 Durant, *The Renaissance*, 526.
435 Hughes, *Heaven and Hell*, 215.
436 Niccoli, *Prophecy and People*, 32–33.
437 C. J. S. Thompson, *The Mystery and Lore of Monsters with Accounts of Some Giants, Dwarfs and Prodigies* (New York: University Books, 1968), 49.
438 Muchembled, *A History of the Devil*, 80.
439 Hanafi, *The Monster in the Machine*, 51.
440 Wayne Shumaker, *The Occult Sciences in the Renaissance: A Study in Intellectual Patterns* (Berkeley: University of California Press, 1972), 95.
441 Muchembled, *A History of the Devil*, 82.
442 Shumaker, *Occult Sciences in the Renaissance*, 95.
443 Hanafi, *The Monster in the Machine*, 36.
444 Thompson, *Mystery and Lore of Monsters*, 37.
445 Delumeau, *Sin and Fear*, 136.
446 Ibid., 136–37.
447 Ibid., 137.
448 Juliette Wood, "The Celtic Tarot and the Secret Traditions: A Study in Modern Legend Making," *Folklore* 109 (1998): 16.
449 Thompson, *Mystery and Lore of Monsters*, 49.
450 Pierre Boaistuau. "Histoires Prodigieuses." In *The Occult in Early Modern Europe: A Documentary History*, edited by P. G. Maxwell-Stuart (Houndmills: Macmillan, 1999), 12.

451 See several different representations of the Monster of Ravenna in Niccoli, *Prophecy and People*, 35–52.

NOTES TO CHAPTER FOUR

1 Michael Dummett and John McLeod, *A History of Games Played with the Tarot Pack: The Game of Triumphs*, 2 vols., Vol. 1 (Lewiston: Edwin Mellen Press, 2004), 13–15.
2 Michael Dummett, "Préface," in *Tarot, Jeu Et Magie*, ed. Thierry Depaulis (Paris: Bibliothèque Nationale, 1984), 10.
3 Christina Olsen, "Carte Da Trionfi: The Development of Tarot in Fifteenth Century Italy" (Ph. D., University of Pennsylvania, 1994), 266.
4 Cynthia Giles, *The Tarot: History, Mystery and Lore* (New York: Paragon House, 1992), 14–15.
5 Detlef Hoffmann, *The Playing Card: An Illustrated History*, trans. C. S. V. Salt (Greenwich: New York Graphic Society Ltd, 1973), 17.
6 Dummett and McLeod, *A History of Games*, 15–16.
7 Ronald Decker, Thierry Depaulis, and Michael Dummett. *A Wicked Pack of Cards: The Origins of Occult Tarot* (London: Gerald Duckworth and Co. Ltd., 1996), 36.
8 Michael Dummett with Sylvia Mann. *The Game of Tarot: From Ferrara to Salt Lake City* (London: Gerald Duckworth and Co. Ltd., 1980), 135.
9 Decker, Depaulis, and Dummett, *A Wicked Pack of Cards*, 45.
10 Dummett with Mann, *The Game of Tarot*, 135.
11 Decker, Depaulis, and Dummett, *A Wicked Pack of Cards*, 46.
12 In some ways this card resembled the World from the hand-painted Visconti-Sforza deck where two naked figures (*putti*) with scarves, held up a globe containing a walled city. The two male figures on the Tarot de Marseille Sun card held up their arms as if holding up the sun. They were similarly naked except for a scarf each.
13 Heather Child and Dorothy Colles, *Christian Symbols Ancient and Modern: A Handbook for Students* (New York: Charles Scribner's Sons, 1971), 173.
14 Stuart R. Kaplan, *The Encyclopedia of Tarot*. IV vols. Vol. II (New York: U. S. Games Systems, 1986), 184–85.
15 Decker, Depaulis, and Dummett, *A Wicked Pack of Cards*, 48.
16 See Franco Pratesi, "Italian Cards - New Discoveries: 9. Tarot in Bologna: Documents from the University Library," *The Playing Card* XXVII (1989).
17 Decker, Depaulis, and Dummett, *A Wicked Pack of Cards*, 50.
18 Ibid., 50–51, 74.
19 Norbert Elias, *State Formation and Civilization*, trans. Edmund Jephcott, 2 vols., Vol. 2, *The Civilizing Process* (Oxford: Basil Blackwell, 1982), 291.
20 Harry Elmer Barnes, *An Intellectual and Cultural History of the Western World*, Third Revised ed., 3 vols., Vol. 2 (New York: Dover Publications, Inc., 1965), 844.
21 Egon Friedell, *A Cultural History of the Modern Age: The Crisis of the European Soul from the Black Death to the World War*, trans. Charles Francis Atkinson, III vols., Vol. III (New York: Alfred A. Knopf, 1954; reprint, Third), 178–79.
22 David Allen Harvey, "Beyond Enlightenment: Occultism, Politics, and Culture in France from the Old Regime to the Fin-De-Siècle," *The Historian* 65, no. 3 (2003): 665.
23 Robert Sobel, *The French Revolution: A Concise History and Interpretation* (Gloucester: Peter Smith, 1967), 112.

24 David Martin, *A General Theory of Secularization*, ed. Philip Rieff and Bryan R. Wilson, *Explorations in Interpretative Sociology* (Oxford: Basil Blackwell, 1978), 102.

25 Lesslie Newbigin, *Honest Religion for Secular Man* (London: SCM Press Ltd, 1966), 69.

26 Harvey, "Beyond Enlightenment," 666.

27 Wouter J. Hanegraaff, "The Study of Western Esotericism: New Approaches to Christian and Secular Culture," in *New Approaches to the Study of Religion: Regional, Critical, and Historical Approaches*, ed. Peter Antes, Armin W. Geertz, and Randi R. Warne, *Religion and Reason* (Berlin: Walter de Gruyter, 2004), 496.

28 Barnes, *Intellectual and Cultural History*, 844-45.

29 David S. Katz, *The Occult Tradition: From the Renaissance to the Present Day* (London: Jonathan Cape, 2005), 115.

30 Kocku von Stuckrad, *Western Esotericism: A Brief History of Secret Knowledge*, trans. Nicholas Goodrick-Clarke (London: Equinox Publishing Ltd, 2005), 109.

31 Katz, *The Occult Tradition*, 115.

32 Tanya M. Luhrmann, *Persuasions of the Witch's Craft: Ritual Magic in Contemporary England* (Cambridge: Harvard University Press, 1989), 39-40.

33 Katz, *The Occult Tradition*, 115-16.

34 Harvey, "Beyond Enlightenment," 665.

35 James Webb, *The Occult Underground* (La Salle: Open Court Publishing Company, 1974), 296.

36 Harvey, "Beyond Enlightenment," 666.

37 Antoine Faivre, *Access to Western Esotericism*, ed. David Appelbaum, *SUNY Series in Western Esoteric Traditions* (Albany: State University of New York Press, 1994), 72.

38 Bruce F. Campbell, *Ancient Wisdom Revived: A History of the Theosophical Movement* (Berkeley: University of California Press, 1980), 14.

39 Allen G. Debus, "Alchemy in an Age of Reason: The Chemical Philosophers in Early Eighteenth-Century France," in *Hermeticism and the Renaissance: Intellectual History and the Occult in Early Modern Europe*, ed. Ingrid Merkel and Allen G. Debus, *Folger Institute Symposia* (Washington: Folger Books, 1988), 232-33.

40 Harvey, "Beyond Enlightenment," 667-68.

41 Katz, *The Occult Tradition*, 171.

42 Harvey, "Beyond Enlightenment," 669.

43 For a description of Martinism in France, see David Bates, "The Mystery of Truth: Louis-Claude De Saint-Martin's Enlightened Mysticism," *Journal of the History of Ideas* 61, no. 4 (2000).

44 John David Wortham, *British Egyptology: 1549-1906* (Newton Abbot: David & Charles, 1971), 49.

45 James Stevens Curl, *Egyptomania: The Egyptian Revival: A Recurring Theme in the History of Taste* (Manchester: Manchester University Press, 1994), 225.

46 Liselotte Dieckmann, *Hieroglyphics: The History of a Literary Symbol* (St Louis: Washington University Press, 1970), 228.

47 Ibid, 26-27.

48 Rosalie David, *The Experience of Ancient Egypt* (London: Routledge, 2000), 72.

49 Wortham, *British Egyptology*, 47.

50 J. J. Clarke, *Oriental Enlightenment: The Encounter between Asian and Western Thought* (London: Routledge, 1997), 16.

51 Philip C. Almond, *The British Discovery of Buddhism* (Cambridge: Cambridge University Press, 1988), 62.

52 Clarke, *Oriental Enlightenment*, 20, 55.

53 Katz, *The Occult Tradition*, 157.

54   Ibid.
55   Gershom Scholem. *Origins of the Kabbalah*. Translated by Allan Arkush (Philadelphia: Jewish Publication Society, 1987), 26–27.
56   Scholem, *Kabbalah*, 25.
57   Faivre, *Western Esotericism*, 55.
58   von Stuckrad, *Western Esotericism*, 34.
59   Scholem, *Kabbalah*, 5.
60   von Stuckrad, *Western Esotericism*, 38.
61   Faivre, *Western Esotericism*, 59.
62   von Stuckrad, *Western Esotericism*, 41.
63   Faivre, *Western Esotericism*, 60.
64   Denis Saurat, *Literature and Occult Tradition: Studies in Philosophical Poetry*, trans. Dorothy Bolton (Port Washington: Kennikat Press, Inc., 1966), 74.
65   Faivre, *Western Esotericism*, 59.
66   Ibid.
67   Arthur McCalla, "The Structure of French Romantic Histories of Religions," *Numen* 45, no. 3 (1998): 265.
68   Harvey, "Beyond Enlightenment," 681.
69   Katz, *The Occult Tradition*, 68.
70   For a full account of the origins of Freemasonry see David Stevenson, *The Origins of Freemasonry: Scotland's Century, 1590–1710* (Cambridge: Cambridge University Press, 1988).
71   Margaret C. Jacob. *The Radical Enlightenment: Pantheists, Freemasons and Republicans*. Edited by J. H. Shennan, *Early Modern Europe Today* (London: George Allen & Unwin, 1981), 109.
72   Katz, *The Occult Tradition*, 68.
73   Dena Goodman, *The Republic of Letters: A Cultural History of the French Enlightenment* (Ithaca: Cornell University Press, 1994), 253.
74   Ibid., 254–58.
75   Decker, Depaulis, and Dummett, *A Wicked Pack of Cards*, 19, 168.
76   Katz, *The Occult Tradition*, 75.
77   Decker, Depaulis, and Dummett, *A Wicked Pack of Cards*, 19.
78   Ibid.
79   Katz, *The Occult Tradition*, 76.
80   Robert A. Gilbert, *Freemasonry and Esoteric Movements* [webpage] (Canonbury Masonic Research Centre, 2000 [cited 21 July 2002]); available from http://www.canonbury.ac.uk/library/lectures/freemasonry_and_esoteric_movement.htm.
81   Decker, Depaulis, and Dummett, *A Wicked Pack of Cards*, 20.
82   Margaret C. Jacob. *The Origins of Freemasonry: Facts & Fictions* (Philadelphia: University of Pennsylvania Press, 2006), 12.
83   Faivre, *Western Esotericism*, 80.
84   Katz, *The Occult Tradition*, 81.
85   Dummett and McLeod, *A History of Games*, 39.
86   Decker, Depaulis, and Dummett, *A Wicked Pack of Cards*, xi.
87   Emily E. Auger, *Tarot and Other Meditation Decks: History, Theory, Aesthetics, Typology* (Jefferson: McFarland & Company Inc., 2004), 102.
88   Christopher McIntosh, *Eliphas Lévi and the French Occult Revival* (London: Rider and Company, 1972), 50. Antoine Court de Gébelin was passionately interested in the uses and history of allegory. See Antoine De Baecque, "The Allegorical Image of France, 1750–1800: A Political Crisis of Representation," *Representations* 47, no. Special Issue: National Cultures before Nationalism (1994): 118–20.

89   Giordano Berti, "Il Libro Di Thot, Ovvero, L'interpretazione Esoterica Del Tarocco,"
      in *I Tarocchi : Le Carte Di Corte : Bioco E Magia Alla Corte Degli Estensi*, ed.
      Giordano Berti and Andrea Vitali (Bologna: Nuova Alfa, 1987), 186.
90   Michael R. Lynn, "Enlightenment in the Public Sphere: The Musée De Monsieur and
      Scientific Culture in Late Eighteenth-Century Paris," *Eighteenth-Century Studies* 32, no.
      4 (1999): 466.
91   Harvey, "Beyond Enlightenment," 666.
92   Faivre, *Western Esotericism*, 74. Interestingly, similar views were voiced by Jean-
      Jacques Rousseau in his *Discours sur les origines de l'inégalité*. Peter Gay, *The Party of
      Humanity: Essays in the French Enlightenment* (New York: W. W. Norton and
      Company Inc., 1971), 259.
93   Harvey, "Beyond Enlightenment," 674.
94   Antoine Court de Gébelin, *Monde Primitif: Analysé Et Comparé Avec Le Monde
      Moderne, Considéré Dans L'histoire Naturelle De La Parole; Ou Grammaire
      Universelle Et Comparative*, 9 vols., *Archives De La Linguistique Française; No.95*
      (Paris: 1774), II, 165, 60-61.
95   Harvey, "Beyond Enlightenment," 673-74.
96   Thierry Depaulis. *Tarot, Jeu Et Magie* (Paris: Bibliothèque Nationale, 1984), 131.
97   Berti, Giordano. "Il Libro Di Thot, Ovvero, L'interpretazione Esoterica Del Tarocco."
      In *I Tarocchi : Le Carte Di Corte : Bioco E Magia Alla Corte Degli Estensi*, edited by
      Giordano Berti and Andrea Vitali (Bologna: Nuova Alfa, 1987), 186.
98   Olsen, "Carte De Trionfi", 266.
99   Dummett with Mann, *The Game of Tarot*, 104.
100   Olsen, "Carte De Trionfi", 267.
101   Dummett with Mann, *The Game of Tarot*, 104.
102   Decker, Depaulis, and Dummett, *A Wicked Pack of Cards*, 60.
103   Samuel Liddell MacGregor Mathers, "On the Tarot Trumps," in *The Complete
      Golden Dawn Cipher Manuscript*, ed. Darcy Küntz, *Golden Dawn Studies Series*
      (Edmonds: Holmes Publishing Group, 1996), 175.
104   Catherine Perry Hargrave. *A History of Playing Cards and a Bibliography of Cards and
      Gaming* (New York: Dover Publications, Inc., 1966), 223.
105   Decker, Depaulis, and Dummett, *A Wicked Pack of Cards*, 61.
106   Dummett with Mann, *The Game of Tarot*, 104.
107   Richard Cavendish. *The Tarot* (London: Chancellor Press, 1986), 125.
108   Dummett with Mann, *The Game of Tarot*, 104.
109   Decker, Depaulis, and Dummett, *A Wicked Pack of Cards*, 61.
110   Dummett with Mann, *The Game of Tarot*, 104.
111   Ibid
112   Decker, Depaulis, and Dummett, *A Wicked Pack of Cards*, 62.
113   A reproduction of Court de Gébelin's trump subjects can be found in Kaplan,
      Encyclopedia of Tarot I, 139.
114   Katz, *The Occult Tradition*, 23.
115   Wouter Hanegraaff. "The Study of Western Esotericism: New Approaches to Christian
      and Secular Culture." In *New Approaches to the Study of Religion: Regional, Critical,
      and Historical Approaches*, edited by Peter Antes, Armin W. Geertz and Randi R.
      Warne (Berlin: Walter de Gruyter, 2004: 492-93).
116   Clement Salaman, Dorine van Oyen, and William D. Wharton, *The Way of Hermes:
      The Corpus Hermeticum* (London: Duckworth, 1999), 82.
117   Brian P. Copenhaver. *Hermetica: The Greek Corpus Hermeticum and the Latin
      Asclepius in a New English Translation, with Notes and Introduction* (Cambridge:
      Cambridge University Press, 1992), 1.

118 Decker, Depaulis, and Dummett, *A Wicked Pack of Cards*, 66.
119 Olsen, "Carte De Trionfi", 267.
120 Decker, Depaulis, and Dummett, *A Wicked Pack of Cards*, 68.
121 Dummett with Mann, *The Game of Tarot*, 105.
122 Decker, Depaulis, and Dummett, *A Wicked Pack of Cards*, 69.
123 Dummett with Mann, *The Game of Tarot*, 105.
124 Decker, Depaulis, and Dummett, *A Wicked Pack of Cards*, 69.
125 Ibid.
126 Ibid.
127 Decker, Depaulis, and Dummett, *A Wicked Pack of Cards*, 69.
128 Ibid.
129 Ibid.
130 Dummett with Mann, *The Game of Tarot*, 105.
131 The Tarot de Besançon pack was similar to the Tarot de Marseille with some minor
     variations including the replacement of the Pope and Popess with Jupiter and Juno
     respectively. It is not thought to originate from Besançon. See Kaplan, *Encyclopedia of
     Tarot II*, 163.
132 Decker, Depaulis, and Dummett, *A Wicked Pack of Cards*, 70.
133 Court de Gébelin, *Monde Primitif*, VIII, 399.
134 Robert Charles Zaehner, *Hinduism*, ed. Christopher Butler, Robert Evans, and John
     Skorupski, Second ed., *Opus* (Oxford: Oxford University Press, 1966), 62.
135 Decker, Depaulis, and Dummett, *A Wicked Pack of Cards*, 70-71.
136 Dummett with Mann, *The Game of Tarot*, 105.
137 Decker, Depaulis, and Dummett, *A Wicked Pack of Cards*, 71.
138 Ibid.
139 Court de Gébelin, *Monde Primitif*, 72.
140 Dummett with Mann, *The Game of Tarot*, 105.
141 Hargrave, *A History of Playing Cards*, 77-79.
142 Decker, Depaulis, and Dummett, *A Wicked Pack of Cards*, 76.
143 Ibid. Éliphas Lévi referred to him as a hairdresser (*perruqier*) and Papus (Gerard
     Encausse) called him an apprentice hairdresser (*garçon coiffeur*). Dummett with Mann,
     The Game of Tarot, 106, 71. Several more modern tarot authors repeat this error. For
     example Roger Tilley, *A History of Playing Cards* (London: Studio Vista, 1973), 100-
     01.
144 Dummett with Mann, *The Game of Tarot*, 106.
145 Decker and Dummett, *History of the Occult Tarot*, x.
146 Decker, Depaulis, and Dummett, *A Wicked Pack of Cards*, 74-75.
147 Dummett with Mann, *The Game of Tarot*, 106.
148 Decker, Depaulis, and Dummett, *A Wicked Pack of Cards*, 80-81.
149 Ibid., 82.
150 Christopher McIntosh. *Éliphas Lévi and the French Occult Revival* (London: Rider
     and Company, 1972), 50.
151 This is also reported erroneously as fact in several more recent tarot books. See Stuart
     R. Kaplan, *Tarot Classic* (New York: U. S. Games Systems, 1972), 42.
152 Decker, Depaulis, and Dummett, *A Wicked Pack of Cards*, 83.
153 Tilley, *History of Playing Cards*, 100-01.
154 McIntosh, *Éliphas Lévi*, 51.
155 Charlene Elizabeth Gates, "The Tarot Trumps: Their Origin, Archetypal Imagery, and
     Use in Some Works of English Literature" (Ph. D., University of Oregon, 1982), 40.
156 Dummett with Mann, *The Game of Tarot*, 108.
157 Decker, Depaulis, and Dummett, *A Wicked Pack of Cards*, 84.

158 Dummett with Mann, *The Game of Tarot*, 108.
159 Ibid.
160 Ibid.
161 Stuart R. Kaplan, *The Encyclopedia of Tarot*. IV vols. Vol. I (New York: U. S. Games Systems, 1978), 140.
162 Decker, Depaulis, and Dummett, *A Wicked Pack of Cards*, 86.
163 Frequently spelt '*Pymander*' or even '*Poemandres*'. Katz, *The Occult Tradition*, 25.
164 Gates, "The Tarot Trumps", 40.
165 Dummett with Mann, *The Game of Tarot*, 108.
166 Decker, Depaulis, and Dummett, *A Wicked Pack of Cards*, 86–87.
167 Dummett with Mann, *The Game of Tarot*, 108.
168 Decker, Depaulis, and Dummett, *A Wicked Pack of Cards*, 87.
169 Kaplan, *Tarot Classic*, 44.
170 Decker, Depaulis, and Dummett, *A Wicked Pack of Cards*, 89–90.
171 McIntosh, *Eliphas Lévi*, 52.
172 Kaplan, *Encyclopedia of Tarot II*, 398.
173 Decker, Depaulis, and Dummett, *A Wicked Pack of Cards*, 90–91.
174 Giles, *The Tarot*, 26.
175 Ibid.
176 'Jéjalel' was Hugand's kabbalistic name.
177 Decker, Depaulis, and Dummett, *A Wicked Pack of Cards*, 147.
178 Dummett with Mann, *The Game of Tarot*, 112.
179 Decker, Depaulis, and Dummett, *A Wicked Pack of Cards*, 144–145.
180 Ibid.
181 Ibid, 147.
182 Ibid., 148.
183 Dummett with Mann, *The Game of Tarot*, 112.
184 Decker, Depaulis, and Dummett, *A Wicked Pack of Cards*, 149.
185 Ibid.
186 Dummett with Mann, *The Game of Tarot*, 112.
187 McIntosh, *Eliphas Lévi*, 74.
188 Thomas A. Williams, *Eliphas Lévi: Master of Occultism* (Birmingham: University of Alabama Press, 1975), 6–7.
189 Williams, *Master of Occultism*, 10–12.
190 Ibid., 13.
191 McIntosh, *Eliphas Lévi*, 81.
192 Decker, Depaulis, and Dummett, *A Wicked Pack of Cards*, 167.
193 Williams, *Master of Occultism*, 16–19.
194 Decker, Depaulis, and Dummett, *A Wicked Pack of Cards*, 180.
195 Williams, *Master of Occultism*, 62–63.
196 Faivre, *Western Esotericism*, 88.
197 Ronald Hutton. *The Triumph of the Moon: A History of Modern Pagan Witchcraft* (Oxford: Oxford University Press, 1999), 70.
198 Faivre, *Western Esotericism*, 88.
199 Arthur Edward Waite, *The Holy Kabbalah: A Study of the Secret Tradition in Israel as Unfolded by Sons of the Doctrine for the Benefit and Consolation of the Elect Dispersed through the Lands and Ages of the Greater Exile* (New Hyde Park: University Books, 1970; reprint, Sixth), 555.
200 Richard Cavendish defines 'High Magic' as the 'attempt to gain so consummate an understanding and mastery of oneself and the environment as to transcend all human

limitations and become superhuman or divine.' Richard Cavendish, *A History of Magic* (London: Arkana, 1990), 12.

201   von Stuckrad, *Western Esotericism*, 103.
202   Faivre, *Western Esotericism*, 88.
203   Dummett with Mann, *The Game of Tarot*, 115.
204   Decker, Depaulis, and Dummett, *A Wicked Pack of Cards*, 169.
205   Ibid., 170.
206   For example, read his denouncement of Etteilla's writings 'Their most remarkable points are the obstinate perseverance and incontestable good faith of the author, who all his life perceived the grandeur of the occult sciences, but was destined to die at the gate of the sanctuary without ever penetrating behind the veil.' Éliphas Lévi, *Transcendental Magic: Its Doctrine and Ritual*, trans. Arthur Edward Waite, Revised ed. (London: Rider and Company, 1958), 177–78.
207   Lévi, *Transcendental Magic*, 177–78.
208   Decker and Dummett, *History of the Occult Tarot*, 30.
209   Decker, Depaulis, and Dummett, *A Wicked Pack of Cards*, 171.
210   Williams, *Master of Occultism*, 35.
211   McIntosh, *Eliphas Lévi*, 148.
212   'The universal key of magical works is that of all ancient religious dogmas – the key of the Kabalah and the Bible, the Little Key of Solomon. Now, this Clavicle, regarded as lost for centuries, has been recovered by us, and we have been able to open the sepulchres of the ancient world, to make the dead speak, to behold the monuments of the past in all their splendour, to understand the enigmas of every sphinx and to penetrate all sanctuaries.' Lévi, *Transcendental Magic*, 378.
213   Decker, Depaulis, and Dummett, *A Wicked Pack of Cards*, 172, 89–90.
214   Ibid., 172.
215   Decker, Depaulis, and Dummett, *A Wicked Pack of Cards*, 172.
216   Dummett with Mann, *The Game of Tarot*, 118.
217   Decker, Depaulis, and Dummett, *A Wicked Pack of Cards*, 173.
218   Ibid.
219   Williams, *Master of Occultism*, 70-87.
220   McIntosh, *Eliphas Lévi*, 96.
221   The *Oedipus Aegyptiacus* was a study of Egyptian-Coptic culture and language, which was published between 1636 and 1676. Kircher believed that all languages had a common origin and that all religions worshipped the one God, an idea that was to become popular in eighteenth-century France. Fred Brauen, "Athanasius Kircher (1602-1680)," *Journal of the History of Ideas* 43, no. 1 (1982): 129-30.
222   Ibid.
223   Decker and Dummett, *History of the Occult Tarot*, 17.
224   Decker, Depaulis, and Dummett, *A Wicked Pack of Cards*, 15.
225   David, *Ancient Egypt*, 71.
226   Decker, Depaulis, and Dummett, *A Wicked Pack of Cards*, 187.
227   Ibid.
228   Faivre, *Western Esotericism*, 72.
229   Williams, *Master of Occultism*, 20, 35.
230   Dummett with Mann, *The Game of Tarot*, 118.
231   From Depaulis, and Dummett, *A Wicked Pack of Cards*, 16.
232   Piers Paul Read, *The Templars: The Dramatic History of the Knights Templar, the Most Powerful Military Order of the Crusades* (London: Phoenix Press, 1999), 266.
233   Ibid.
234   Decker, Depaulis, and Dummett, *A Wicked Pack of Cards*, 188.

235 Ibid., 185.
236 Lévi, *Transcendental Magic*, 99.
237 Ibid.
238 Dummett with Mann, *The Game of Tarot*, 117.
239 Decker, Depaulis, and Dummett, *A Wicked Pack of Cards*, 186.
240 Dummett with Mann, *The Game of Tarot*, 118.
241 Williams, *Master of Occultism*, 159.
242 Decker, Depaulis, and Dummett, *A Wicked Pack of Cards*, 238.
243 Danny L. Jorgensen. *The Esoteric Scene, Cultic Milieu, and Occult Tarot*. Edited by J. Gordon Melton, *Cults and Nonconventional Religious Groups: A Collection of Outstanding Dissertations and Monographs* (New York: Garland Publishing, Inc., 1992), 147.
244 Alex Owen. *The Place of Enchantment: British Occultism and the Culture of the Modern* (Chicago: University of Chicago Press, 2004), 44.
245 Dummett with Mann, *The Game of Tarot*, 128.
246 Decker, Depaulis, and Dummett, *A Wicked Pack of Cards*, 235-36.
247 Ibid.
248 Ibid., 237.
249 Owen, *Place of Enchantment*, 44-45.
250 Decker, Depaulis, and Dummett, *A Wicked Pack of Cards*, 238.
251 Darcy Küntz, "Introduction: From the Ashes of the Cipher Manuscript to the Creation of the Golden Dawn," in *The Golden Dawn Source Book*, ed. Darcy Küntz, *Golden Dawn Studies Series* (Edmonds: Holmes Publishing Group, 1996), 15.
252 Decker, Depaulis, and Dummett, *A Wicked Pack of Cards*, 242.
253 Ibid., 237.
254 Though *'Le Tarot des Bohémiens'* literally translates as 'Tarot of the Gypsies' it usually appeared in English as *The Tarot of the Bohemians*. Dummett with Mann, *The Game of Tarot*, 152.
255 Cavendish, *The Tarot*, 31.
256 Encausse, *The Tarot of the Bohemians*, 7.
257 Arthur Edward Waite "Preface to the English Translation." In *The Tarot of the Bohemians: Absolute Key to Occult Science; the Most Ancient Book in the World for the Use of Initiates*, by Gerard Encausse (Hollywood: Wilshire Book Company, 1971), xiv.
258 Ibid., xvi.
259 See for example Encausse, *The Tarot of the Bohemians*, 103-04.
260 Dummett with Mann, *The Game of Tarot*, 131.
261 Decker, Depaulis, and Dummett, *A Wicked Pack of Cards*, 249.
262 Ibid., 255-56.
263 Cavendish, *The Tarot*, 31.
264 Decker, Depaulis, and Dummett, *A Wicked Pack of Cards*, 256.
265 Dummett with Mann, *The Game of Tarot*, 134.
266 Decker, Depaulis, and Dummett, *A Wicked Pack of Cards*, 256.
267 Dummett with Mann, *The Game of Tarot*, 134.
268 Decker, Depaulis, and Dummett, *A Wicked Pack of Cards*, 257.
269 Ibid.
270 Katz, *The Occult Tradition*, 173.
271 Decker, Depaulis, and Dummett, *A Wicked Pack of Cards*, 261.
272 Giles, *The Tarot*, 25.
273 Decker, Depaulis, and Dummett, *A Wicked Pack of Cards*, 37.

NOTES TO CHAPTER FIVE

1   James Webb, *The Occult Underground* (La Salle: Open Court Publishing Company, 1974), 7–8.

2   Thomas A. Williams, *Eliphas Lévi: Master of Occultism* (Birmingham: University of Alabama Press, 1975), 89.

3   Leon Surette, *The Birth of Modernism: Ezra Pound, T.S. Eliot, W.B. Yeats and the Occult* (Montreal: McGill-Queen's University Press, 1994), 256.

4   R. F. Foster, *W. B. Yeats: A Life*, II vols., Vol. I: The Apprentice Mage (Oxford: Oxford University Press, 1997), 50.

5   Peter Washington, *Madame Blavatsky's Baboon: A History of the Mystics, Mediums, and Misfits Who Brought Spiritualism to America* (New York: Schocken Books, 1995), 13.

6   Ibid., 80.

7   Henry Sidgwick in 'Authority: Scientific and Theological' in *Sidgwick, A Memoir* quoted in Frank Miller Turner, *Between Science and Religion: The Reaction to Scientific Naturalism in Late Victorian England* (New Haven: Yale University Press, 1974), 60.

8   Ibid., 61.

9   Gregory P. Elder, *Chronic Vigour: Darwin, Anglicans, Catholics, and the Development of a Doctrine of Providential Evolution* (Lanham: University Press of America, Inc., 1996), 30.

10   Owen Chadwick, *The Secularization of the European Mind in the Nineteenth Century* (Cambridge: Cambridge University Press, 1975), 167.

11   J. MacGregor Allan, "Carl Vogt's Lectures on Man," *Anthropological Review* 7, no. 25 (1869): 179.

12   David S. Katz, *The Occult Tradition: From the Renaissance to the Present Day* (London: Jonathan Cape, 2005), 168.

13   Tanya M. Luhrmann, *Persuasions of the Witch's Craft: Ritual Magic in Contemporary England* (Cambridge: Harvard University Press, 1989), 40.

14   Kathleen Raine, *Yeats, the Tarot and the Golden Dawn*, ed. Liam Miller, *New Yeats Papers II* (Dublin: Dolmen Press, 1972), 7.

15   John David Wortham, *British Egyptology: 1549–1906* (Newton Abbot: David & Charles, 1971), 38.

16   Rosalie David. *The Experience of Ancient Egypt* (London: Routledge, 2000), 73.

17   Warren Royal Dawson and Eric P. Uphill, *Who Was Who in Egyptology*, Third Revised by M. L. Bierbrier ed. (London: The Egypt Exploration Society, 1995), 71.

18   Wortham, *British Egyptology*, 92–93.

19   Webb, *Occult Underground*, 318–19.

20   Ibid.

21   Ibid., 320–21.

22   Ibid.

23   J. J. Clarke. *Oriental Enlightenment: The Encounter between Asian and Western Thought* (London: Routledge, 1997), 89.

24   Luhrmann, *Persuasions of the Witch's Craft*, 39.

25   Philip C. Almond, *The British Discovery of Buddhism* (Cambridge: Cambridge University Press, 1988), 13.

26   Washington, *Madame Blavatsky's Baboon*, 69.

27   Bruce F. Campbell. *Ancient Wisdom Revived: A History of the Theosophical Movement* (Berkeley: University of California Press, 1980), 78.

28 Washington, *Madame Blavatsky's Baboon*, 61.
29 Katz, *The Occult Tradition*, 165.
30 Virginia Moore. *The Unicorn: William Butler Yeats' Search for Reality*. New York: Octagon Books, 1973., 19.
31 Clarke, *Oriental Enlightenment*, 89.
32 Campbell, *Ancient Wisdom Revived*, 36.
33 Clarke, *Oriental Enlightenment*, 89.
34 Blavatsky in Decker and Dummett, *History of the Occult Tarot*, 34.
35 Ibid., 306.
36 Washington, *Madame Blavatsky's Baboon*, 90.
37 Daniel van Egmond, "Western Esoteric Schools in the Late Nineteenth and Early Twentieth Centuries," in *Gnosis and Hermeticism from Antiquity to Modern Times*, ed. Roelof van den Broek and Wouter J. Hanegraaff, (New York: State University of New York Press, 1998), 322.
38 Alan Pert. *Red Cactus: The Life of Anna Kingsford* (Watson's Bay: Books & Writers, 2006), 116-17.
39 Washington, *Madame Blavatsky's Baboon*, 76.
40 Diana Burfield. "Theosophy and Feminism: Some Explorations in Nineteenth Century Biography." In *Women's Religious Experience*, edited by Pat Holden (London: Croom Helm, 1983), 39.
41 van Egmond, "Western Esoteric Schools," 322-23.
42 Robert A. Gilbert. *The Golden Dawn and the Esoteric Section* (London: Theosophical History Centre, 1987), 3.
43 Foster, *W. B. Yeats: A Life*, 77.
44 Gilbert, *Esoteric Section*, 3-4.
45 Darcy Küntz, "Introduction: From the Ashes of the Cipher Manuscript to the Creation of the Golden Dawn," in *The Golden Dawn Source Book*, ed. Darcy Küntz, *Golden Dawn Studies Series* (Edmonds: Holmes Publishing Group, 1996), 15.
46 Ibid.
47 Ronald Hutton, *The Triumph of the Moon: A History of Modern Pagan Witchcraft* (Oxford: Oxford University Press, 1999), 52.
48 John Senior, *The Way Down and Out: The Occult in Symbolist Literature* (New York: Greenwood Press, 1968), 154.
49 Christopher McIntosh, *The Rosicrucians: The History, Mythology, and Rituals of an Esoteric Order*, Third Revised ed. (York Beach: Samuel Weiser, Inc., 1997), 98.
50 Moore, *Unicorn*, 128-29.
51 Ithell Colquhoun, *Sword of Wisdom: Macgregor Mathers and 'the Golden Dawn'* (London: Neville Spearman, 1975), 131.
52 McIntosh, *Rosicrucians*, 99.
53 Carroll 'Poke' Runyon. "The History of the Cypher Manuscript." In *Secrets of the Golden Dawn Cypher Manuscript*, edited by Carroll 'Poke' Runyon (Silverado: C. H. S., Inc., 2000), 11.
54 Robert A. Gilbert, *The Golden Dawn Scrapbook: The Rise and Fall of a Magical Order* (York Beach: Samuel Weiser, Inc., 1997), 79.
55 Alex Owen, *The Place of Enchantment: British Occultism and the Culture of the Modern* (Chicago: University of Chicago Press, 2004), 55.
56 Ronald Decker and Michael Dummett. *A History of the Occult Tarot: 1870-1970* (London: Gerald Duckworth & Co. Ltd., 2002), 53.
57 Owen, *Place of Enchantment*, 55.
58 Francis King, *Ritual Magic in England: 1887 to the Present Day* (London: Neville Spearman, 1970), 47-48.

59 Decker and Dummett, *History of the Occult Tarot*, 53.
60 Ibid.
61 Ibid.
62 Ibid., 54.
63 Ibid., 55.
64 Gareth Medway, "Aurora Mysteriorum," in *The Golden Dawn Source Book*, ed. Darcy Küntz, *Golden Dawn Studies Series* (Edmonds: Holmes Publishing Group, 1996), 162.
65 Decker and Dummett, *History of the Occult Tarot*, 55.
66 Ibid., 55.
67 Ibid., 56.
68 Ibid.
69 Antoine Faivre, *Access to Western Esotericism*, ed. David Appelbaum, *SUNY Series in Western Esoteric Traditions* (Albany: State University of New York Press, 1994), 88.
70 Ibid.
71 Colquhoun, *Sword of Wisdom*, 171.
72 Robert A. Gilbert, "From Cipher to Enigma: The Role of William Wynn Westcott in the Creation of the Hermetic Order of the Golden Dawn," in *Secrets of the Golden Dawn Cypher Manuscript*, ed. Carroll 'Poke' Runyon (Silverado: C.H.S., Inc., 2000), 211.
73 McIntosh, *Rosicrucians*, 99.
74 King, *Ritual Magic in England*, 48–49.
75 Ibid., 51.
76 Hutton, *Triumph of the Moon*, 76.
77 Gareth Medway. "Aurora Mysteriorum." In *The Golden Dawn Source Book*, edited by Darcy Küntz (Edmonds: Holmes Publishing Group, 1996), 162.
78 Decker with Dummett, *History of the Occult Tarot*, 57.
79 Dummett with Mann, *The Game of Tarot*, 151.
80 Mary Katherine Greer. *Women of the Golden Dawn: Rebels and Priestesses* (Rochester: Park Street Press, 1995), 45.
81 Gilbert, *The Golden Dawn Scrapbook*, 115.
82 Owen, *Place of Enchantment*, 63.
83 Francis King, "The Origins of the Golden Dawn," in *The Golden Dawn Source Book*, ed. Darcy Küntz, *Golden Dawn Studies Series* (Edmonds: Holmes Publishing Group, 1996), 123–24.
84 Carroll 'Poke' Runyon, "An Analysis of the Cypher Manuscript," in *Secrets of the Golden Dawn Cypher Manuscript*, ed. Carroll 'Poke' Runyon (Silverado: C. H. S., Inc., 2000; reprint, Second), 38.
85 William Wynn Westcott, "The Historical Lecture," in *The Golden Dawn Source Book*, ed. Darcy Küntz, *Golden Dawn Studies Series* (Edmonds: Holmes Publishing Group, 1996), 48.
86 Greer, *Women of the Golden Dawn*, 419–20.
87 Ibid.
88 Moore, *Unicorn*, 131.
89 Arthur Edward Waite, *The Brotherhood of the Rosy Cross: Being Records of the House of the Holy Spirit in Its Inward and Outward History* (New York: University Books, 1961), 584.
90 Robert A. Gilbert, "Provenance Unknown: A Tentative Solution to the Riddle of the Cipher Manuscript of the Golden Dawn," in *The Complete Golden Dawn Cipher Manuscript*, ed. Darcy Küntz, *The Golden Dawn Study Series* (Edmonds: Holmes Publishing Group, 1996), 19–21.
91 Medway, "Aurora Mysteriorum," 165.

92   Robert A. Gilbert, "Supplement to 'Provenance Unknown': The Origins of the Golden Dawn," in *The Golden Dawn Source Book*, ed. Darcy Küntz, *Golden Dawn Studies Series* (Edmonds: Holmes Publishing, 1996), 11.

93   See Carroll 'Poke' Runyon, *Secrets of the Golden Dawn Cypher Manuscript* (Silverado: C. H. S., Inc, 2000; reprint, Second), 67.

94   Gilbert, *The Golden Dawn Scrapbook*, 5-6.

95   William Wynn Westcott, "Letter to F. L. Gardner," in *The Golden Dawn Companion: A Guide to the History, Structure, and Workings of the Hermetic Order of the Golden Dawn*, ed. Robert A. Gilbert (Wellingborough: Aquarian Press, 1986), 80.

96   Gilbert, *The Golden Dawn Scrapbook*, 5-6.

97   Ellic Howe. "Fringe Masonry in England, 1870-85." *Ars Quatuor Coronatorum* 85 (1972): 267.

98   Francis King, *Astral Projection, Ritual Magic, and Alchemy: Golden Dawn Material by S.L. Macgregor Mathers and Others* (Rochester: Destiny Books, 1987), 32.

99   Richard Cavendish. *A History of Magic* (London: Arkana, 1990), 139.

100   Küntz, "Ashes of the Cipher Manuscript," 16-17.

101   Ellic Howe, *The Magicians of the Golden Dawn: A Documentary History of a Magical Order 1887-1923* (London: Routledge and Kegan Paul, 1972), 11.

102   Raine, *Tarot and the Golden Dawn*, 9.

103   Greer, *Women of the Golden Dawn*, 64.

104   Dummett with Mann, *The Game of Tarot*, 150.

105   Robert A. Gilbert, "'Two Circles to Gain and Two Squares to Lose': The Golden Dawn in Popular Fiction," in *Secret Texts: The Literature of Secret Societies*, ed. Marie Mulvey and Ormsby-Lennin Roberts, Hugh, *AMS Studies in Cultural History* (New York: AMS Press, 1995), 304.

106   Moore, *Unicorn*, 133-34.

107   Gilbert, "Two Circles to Gain," 304.

108   Owen, *Place of Enchantment*, 57.

109   See Küntz, ed., *Cipher Manuscript*, 74-77.

110   Decker and Dummett, *History of the Occult Tarot*, 77.

111   See Küntz, ed., *Cipher Manuscript*, 119-31.

112   Decker and Dummett, *History of the Occult Tarot*, 81.

113   Cynthia Giles, *The Tarot: History, Mystery and Lore* (New York: Paragon House, 1992), 42. See Küntz, ed., *Cipher Manuscript*, 116-17.

114   Decker and Dummett, *History of the Occult Tarot*, 81-82.

115   Ibid.

116   Runyon, "An Analysis," 53.

117   Stuart R. Kaplan, *The Encyclopedia of Tarot*, IV vols., Vol. II (New York: U. S. Games Systems, 1986; reprint, Second), 183.

118   From Decker and Dummett, *History of the Occult Tarot*, 82-83.

119   Ibid., 83.

120   From Ibid.

121   Medway, "Aurora Mysteriorum," 162.

122   Ibid.

123   Runyon, "An Analysis," 54.

124   Runyon, *Secrets of the Golden Dawn*, 119.

125   Ibid., 147, 49, 53.

126   Runyon, "An Analysis," 54.

127   Runyon, *Secrets of the Golden Dawn*, 101.

128   McIntosh, *Rosicrucians*, 100; Raine, *Tarot and the Golden Dawn*, 15.

129   Robert Wang, *An Introduction to the Golden Dawn Tarot Including the Original Documents on Tarot from the Order of the Golden Dawn with Explanatory Notes* (York Beach: Samuel Weiser, Inc., 1978), 14.
130   Decker and Dummett, *History of the Occult Tarot*, 96.
131   Robert V. O'Neill, *Tarot Symbolism* (Lima: Fairway Press, 1986), 46.
132   Decker and Dummett, *History of the Occult Tarot*, 96.
133   Wang, *Introduction to the Golden Dawn Tarot*, 14.
134   Ibid.
135   Raine, *Tarot and the Golden Dawn*, 16.
136   Decker and Dummett, *History of the Occult Tarot*, 97.
137   *Book T* was reproduced in *The Equinox* as 'A Description of the Cards of the Tarot' by Aleister Crowley. See Samuel Liddell MacGregor Mathers, "A Description of the Cards of the Tarot," *Equinox* 1, no. 8 (1912).
138   Decker and Dummett, *History of the Occult Tarot*, 97.
139   Ibid.
140   Ibid., 98.
141   From Decker and Dummett, *History of the Occult Tarot*, 98.
142   Mathers, "Cards of the Tarot," 153.
143   For a table of meanings and correspondences of the suit cards see Mathers, "Cards of the Tarot," 148-52.
144   For example, the Princess of the Shining Flame (The Knave of Wands) See Mathers, "Cards of the Tarot," 161.
145   For example, the Lord of the Flame and the Lightning (Knight of Wands) and the Princess of the Waters (Knave of Cups) See Ibid.: 159, 65.
146   For example, Castor and Pollux on the Lord of the Wings and the Breezes (Knight of Swords). See Ibid.: 165-66.
147   For example, a figure resembling Diana and Minerva on the Princess of the Rushing Winds (Knave of Swords). See Ibid.: 168.
148   Emily E. Auger, *Tarot and Other Meditation Decks: History, Theory, Aesthetics, Typology* (Jefferson: McFarland & Company Inc., 2004), 6.
149   King, ed., *Astral Projection*, 51.
150   For the original illustrations see Darcy Küntz, ed., *The Golden Dawn Court Cards as Drawn by William Wynn Westcott & Moïna Mathers*, Golden Dawn Studies Series (Edmonds: Holmes Publishing Group, 1996).
151   Israel Regardie, *My Rosicrucian Adventure: A Contribution to a Recent Phase of the History of Magic, and a Study in the Technique of Theurgy* (Chicago: The Aries Press, 1936), 22-23. Crowley gave the date as 18 November 1898. Aleister Crowley, *The Confessions of Aleister Crowley: An Autohagiography* (London: Arkana, 1979), 176.
152   Robert A. Gilbert, ed., *The Golden Dawn Companion: A Guide to the History, Structure, and Workings of the Hermetic Order of the Golden Dawn* (Wellingborough: Aquarian Press, 1986), 3.
153   Howe, *Magicians of the Golden Dawn*, 200-02.
154   Moore, *Unicorn*, 159.
155   Regardie, *My Rosicrucian Adventure*, 22-23.
156   John Symonds. *The Great Beast: The Life of Aleister Crowley* (London: Rider and Company, 1951. Reprint, Fifth), 32.
157   King, *Modern Ritual Magic*, 70.
158   Regardie, *My Rosicrucian Adventure*, 23-24.
159   Gilbert, "From Cipher to Enigma," 104.
160   Gilbert, *The Golden Dawn Scrapbook*, 82-83.
161   Regardie, *My Rosicrucian Adventure*, 27-28.

162 Gilbert, *The Golden Dawn Scrapbook*, 82–83.
163 Regardie, *My Rosicrucian Adventure*, 27–28.
164 Gilbert, *The Golden Dawn Scrapbook*, 83.
165 Symonds, *The Great Beast*, 108–09.
166 King, *Modern Ritual Magic.*
167 Howe, *Magicians of the Golden Dawn*, 43.
168 Regardie, *My Rosicrucian Adventure*, 24–25.
169 Dummett with Mann, *The Game of Tarot*, 158.
170 Symonds, *The Great Beast*, 121.
171 Owen, *Place of Enchantment*, 218.
172 The full title of the work is *Liber L vel Legis sub figura CCXX, as delivered by LXXVIII unto DCLXVI.* See Aleister Crowley, "Liber L Vel Legis Sub Figura CCXX, as Delivered by LXXVIII Unto DCLXVI," *The Equinox* I, no. X (1913).
173 John Symonds, "Introduction," in *The Confessions of Aleister Crowley: An Autohagiography*, ed. John Symonds and Kenneth Grant (London: Arkana, 1979), 19–20.
174 Crowley, *Confessions*, 399.
175 Symonds, *The Great Beast*, 62.
176 Decker and Dummett, *History of the Occult Tarot*, 148.
177 Owen, *Place of Enchantment*, 218.
178 Symonds, *The Great Beast*, 172.
179 Crowley, *Confessions*, 403.
180 Symonds, *The Great Beast*, 207–09.
181 Owen, *Place of Enchantment*, 219.
182 Symonds, *The Great Beast*, 155.
183 Ibid., 214–15.
184 Cavendish, *The Tarot*, 38.
185 Wang, *Introduction to the Golden Dawn Tarot*, 22.
186 Colquhoun, *Sword of Wisdom*, 251.
187 Decker and Dummett, *History of the Occult Tarot*, 153.
188 Crowley, *The Book of Thoth*, 9, 39.
189 Dummett with Mann, *The Game of Tarot*, 158.
190 Decker and Dummett, *History of the Occult Tarot*, 154.
191 Ibid.
192 Dummett with Mann, *The Game of Tarot*, 159.
193 Decker and Dummett, *History of the Occult Tarot*, 154.
194 Ibid.
195 The names are the spirits are derived by taking three verses of Exodus (14, 19, 20 and 21) which contain seventy-two letters. They are placed under one another and seventy-two names are derived with the addition of the suffixes -al or -ah depending on whether they are male or female. Aleister Crowley. *The Book of Thoth: A Short Essay on the Tarot of the Egyptians* (York Beach: Samuel Weiser, Inc., 1991), 43.
196 Decker and Dummett, *History of the Occult Tarot*, 154.
197 Jorgensen, *Esoteric Scene*, 154.
198 Gerd Ziegler. *Tarot: Mirror of the Soul: Handbook for the Aleister Crowley Tarot* (York Beach: Samuel Weiser, Inc., 1986), 3.
199 Crowley, *The Book of Thoth*, 69–72.
200 Ziegler, *Tarot: Mirror of the Soul*, 22.
201 Ibid., 2.
202 Crowley, *The Book of Thoth*, 79.
203 Ziegler, *Tarot: Mirror of the Soul*, 38.

204   Crowley, *The Book of Thoth*, 92.
205   Ibid., 95.
206   Crowley, *The Book of Thoth*, 100.
207   Ibid., 105.
208   Ziegler, *Tarot: Mirror of the Soul*, 45.
209   Ibid.
210   Decker and Dummett, *History of the Occult Tarot*, 154.
211   Ibid.
212   Crowley claimed this table was the work of science writer J. W. N. Sullivan but in reality it was constructed by Danish physicist Julius Thomsen. Decker and Dummett, *History of the Occult Tarot*, 339.
213   James Wasserman. *Instructions for Aleister Crowley's Thoth Tarot Deck* (Stamford: U. S. Games Systems, Inc., 1978), 5.
214   Auger, *Tarot and Other Meditation Decks*, 6.
215   Ibid.
216   Moore, *Unicorn*, 135.
217   Symonds, *The Great Beast*, 33. For Crowley's opinion of W. B. Yeats see Crowley, *Confessions*, 166.
218   Foster, *W. B. Yeats: A Life*, 98–101.
219   Richard Ellmann, *The Identity of Yeats* (London: Faber and Faber, 1954), 16.
220   Moore, *Unicorn*, 33.
221   Washington, *Madame Blavatsky's Baboon*, 15.
222   Ellmann, *Identity of Yeats*, 26.
223   Ibid.
224   Malcolm Godwin, *The Holy Grail: Its Origins, Secrets, and Meaning Revealed* (London: Bloomsbury, 1994), 46.
225   See Paul Huson, *Mystical Origins of the Tarot: From Ancient Roots to Modern Usage* (Rochester: Destiny Books, 2004), 19.
226   Ibid.
227   Moore, *Unicorn*, 59–60.
228   For example see Auger, *Tarot and Other Meditation Decks*, 127.
229   Juliette Wood, *Secret Traditions in the Modern Tarot: Folklore and the Occult Revival* [website] (2001 [cited 7 September 2003]); available from http://www.juliette.wood.btinternet.co.uk/tarot.htm.
230   Decker and Dummett, *History of the Occult Tarot*, 120.
231   Wood, *Secret Traditions in the Modern Tarot* (cited).
232   Darcy Küntz. "Cross-Index of Golden Dawn Members and Mottoes." In *The Golden Dawn Source Book*, edited by Darcy Küntz (Edmonds: Holmes Publishing Company, 1996), 219.
233   Robert A. Gilbert, ed., *Hermetic Papers of A. E. Waite: The Unknown Writings of a Modern Mystic, Roots of the Golden Dawn Series* (Wellingborough: The Aquarian Press, 1987), 7.
234   Gilbert, ed., *Papers of A. E. Waite*, 7.
235   Howe, *Magicians of the Golden Dawn*, 71.
236   Decker and Dummett, *History of the Occult Tarot*, 121.
237   Greer, *Women of the Golden Dawn*, 277.
238   Thomas Willard, "Acts of the Companions: A.E. Waite's Fellowship and the Novels of Charles Williams," in *Secret Texts: The Literature of Secret Societies*, ed. Marie Mulvey and Ormsby-Lennin Roberts, Hugh, *Ams Studies in Cultural History* (New York: AMS Press, 1995), 271.
239   King, *Modern Ritual Magic*, 95.

240 Ibid., 96.
241 Gilbert, ed., *Papers of A. E. Waite*, 11.
242 Ibid., 9.
243 Kaplan, *Encyclopedia of Tarot II*, 154.
244 Willard, "Acts of the Companions," 271.
245 Decker and Dummett, *History of the Occult Tarot*, 129.
246 Waite, *Shadows of Life and Thought*, 185.
247 Auger, *Tarot and Other Meditation Decks*, 1.
248 Decker and Dummett, *History of the Occult Tarot*, 131.
249 Auger, *Tarot and Other Meditation Decks*, 6. Subsequently, many editions of this deck
     have been released. Some decks bear imagery that has been recoloured. Many others
     have slightly altered symbolism or are renamed in another language. For some
     examples of these different decks see, Stuart R. Kaplan and Jean Huets. *The
     Encyclopedia of Tarot*. IV vols. Vol. IV (Stamford: U. S. Games Systems, Inc., 2005),
     484–92.
250 See Arthur Edward Waite, *The Pictorial Key to the Tarot: Being Fragments of a Secret
     Tradition under the Veil of Divination*. Second ed. (London: Rider & Company, 1971.
     Reprint, Fifth), 70.
251 Dummett with Mann, *The Game of Tarot*, 154.
252 Arthur Edward Waite, "The Tarot: A Wheel of Fortune," *The Occult Review* X, no. 12
     (1909): 310.
253 Roger Parisious made this assertion in his lecture, 'Figures in a Dance: W. B. Yeats and
     the Waite-Rider Tarot' at the Golden Dawn conference held in London in April 1987.
     See Decker and Dummett, *History of the Occult Tarot*, 135, 336.
254 Ibid., 132
255 Kaplan erroneously wrote that Waite was the first to use this arrangement. See Kaplan,
     Tarot Classic, 62.
256 Waite, *The Pictorial Key to the Tarot*, 72–75.
257 Ibid., 76–79.
258 Waite, *The Pictorial Key to the Tarot*, 92–95.
259 Ibid., 96–99.
260 Ibid., 108–09.
261 Ibid.
262 Ibid.
263 Ibid., 116–17.
264 Ibid., 120–21.
265 Decker and Dummett, *History of the Occult Tarot*, 133.
266 Waite in Ibid., 139.
267 Waite, *The Pictorial Key to the Tarot*, 76–77.
268 Ibid., 80–81.
269 Ibid., 84–85.
270 Decker and Dummett, *History of the Occult Tarot*, 140.
271 Waite, *The Pictorial Key to the Tarot*, 120–21.
272 Ibid., 152–53.
273 Ibid., 76–77.
274 Decker and Dummett, *History of the Occult Tarot*, 140.
275 Ibid.
276 Waite, *The Pictorial Key to the Tarot*, 92–93.
277 Ibid., 156–57.
278 Ibid., 224–25.
279 Decker and Dummett, *History of the Occult Tarot*, 157.

280   Arthur Edward Waite, "The Great Symbols of the Tarot," *Occult Review* 43 (1926): 19.
281   Decker and Dummett, *History of the Occult Tarot*, 157.
282   Richard Barber, *The Holy Grail: Imagination and Belief* (Cambridge: Harvard University Press, 2004), 296; Wood, *Secret Traditions in the Modern Tarot* (cited).
283   See Arthur Edward Waite, *The Hidden Church of the Holy Graal: Its Legends and Symbolism Considered in Their Affinity with Certain Mysteries of Initiation and Other Traces of a Secret Tradition in Christian Times* (London: Rebman Limited, 1909), 603.
284   Waite, *The Hidden Church of the Holy Graal*, 603.
285   Waite, *The Holy Grail*, 574.
286   For modern proponents of this theory see Hilary Anderson, "Bringing Swords out of Depression and Darkness," in *New Thoughts on Tarot: Transcripts from the First International Tarot Symposium*, ed. Mary K. Greer and Rachel Pollack (North Hollywood: Newcastle Publishing Co., 1989), 11.
287   Wood, *Secret Traditions in the Modern Tarot* (cited).
288   Waite, *The Pictorial Key to the Tarot*, 299.
289   For example see Corrine Kenner, *Tarot Journaling: Using the Celtic Cross to Unveil Your Hidden Story* (Woodbury: Llewellyn Publications, 2006).
290   Decker and Dummett, *History of the Occult Tarot*, 188–89.
291   Ibid., 191.
292   Ibid., 195.
293   Ibid., 199.
294   Ibid., 200.
295   Jorgensen, *Esoteric Scene*, 156.
296   See Mouni Sadhu, *The Tarot: A Contemporary Course of the Quintessence of Hermetic Occultism* (Hollywood: Melvin Powers Wilshire Book Company, 1962; reprint, Second).
297   Arthur Versluis, *The Esoteric Origins of the American Renaissance* (Oxford: Oxford University Press, 2001), 4.
298   Decker and Dummett, *History of the Occult Tarot*, 160–61.
299   See Israel Regardie, *The Golden Dawn: A Complete Course in Practical Ceremonial Magic: The Original Account of the Teachings, Rites, and Ceremonies of the Hermetic Order of the Golden Dawn (Stella Matutina) as Revealed by Israel Regardie*, Sixth, revised and enlarged ed., *Llewellyn's Golden Dawn Series* (St Paul: Llewellyn Publications, 1989; reprint, Tenth).
300   Wang, *Introduction to the Golden Dawn Tarot*, 9.

NOTES TO CHAPTER SIX

1   Some authors also encourage 'seekers' to create their own decks. See Antero Alli, "The Neuro-Tarot: Designing Your Own Deck of Cards," *Whole Earth Review*, no. 72 (1991).
2   Kay Alexander, "Roots of the New Age," in *Perspectives on the New Age*, ed. James R. Lewis and J. Gordon Melton, *SUNY Series in Religious Studies* (Albany: State University of New York Press, 1992), 30.
3   Wouter J. Hanegraaff. *New Age Religion and Western Culture: Esotericism in the Mirror of Secular Thought*. Edited by David Appelbaum, *SUNY Series, Western Esoteric Traditions* (New York: State University of New York Press, 1998), 53–55.
4   Ibid., 10–11.
5   Ibid.

6   Ibid.

7   David S. Katz, *The Occult Tradition: From the Renaissance to the Present Day* (London: Jonathan Cape, 2005), 195.

8   Kocku von Stuckrad. *Western Esotericism: A Brief History of Secret Knowledge.* Translated by Nicholas Goodrick-Clarke (London: Equinox Publishing Ltd, 2005), 140.

9   Adam Possamai, *Religion and Popular Culture: A Hyper-Real Testament*, ed. Gabriel Fragnière, Vol. 7, *Gods, Humans and Religions* (Brussells: P.I.E. - Peter Lang, 2005).

10   Hanegraaff, *New Age Religion and Western Culture*, 302.

11   Paul Heelas, *The New Age Movement: The Celebration of the Self and the Sacralization of Modernity* (Oxford: Blackwell Publishers, 1996), 16.

12   Melton, J. Gordon. "New Thought and the New Age." In *Perspectives on the New Age*, edited by James R. Lewis and J. Gordon Melton (Albany: State University of New York Press, 1992) 19.

13   Katz, *The Occult Tradition*, 196.

14   Rodney Stark and William Sims Bainbridge, *The Future of Religion: Secularization, Revival and Cult Formation* (Berkeley: University of California Press, 1985), 447.

15   James R. Lewis, "Approaches to the Study of the New Age Movement," in *Perspectives on the New Age*, ed. James R. Lewis and J. Gordon Melton, *SUNY Series in Religious Studies* (Albany: State University of New York Press, 1992), 7.

16   Katz, *The Occult Tradition*, 196.

17   For a detailed account of channelling in the New Age see Suzanne Riordan, "Chaneling: A New Revelation?," in *Perspectives on the New Age*, ed. James R. Lewis and J. Gordon Melton, *SUNY Series in Religious Studies* (Albany: State University of New York Press, 1992).

18   Hanegraaff, *New Age Religion and Western Culture*, 23–24.

19   Melton, "New Thought," 22. Spiritualism predated Blavatsky but communications were not usually with the 'spiritually evolved' who lived on another 'plane'. Messages were restricted to rapping, aports, passive writing and direct (disembodied) voice. See Alex Owen, *The Darkened Room: Women, Power and Spiritualism in Late Victorian England* (London: Virago Press, 1989).

20   Melton, "New Thought," 21.

21   Rachel Pollack, An Overview of the Variety of New Tarot Decks: Emphasis on European Decks." In *New Thoughts on Tarot: Transcripts from the First International Tarot Symposium*, edited by Mary K. Greer and Rachel Pollack (North Hollywood: Newcastle Publishing, 1989), 138.

22   Catherine L. Albanese, "The Magical Staff: Quantum Healing in the New Age," in *Perspectives on the New Age*, ed. James R. Lewis and J. Gordon Melton, *SUNY Series in Religious Studies* (Albany: State University of New York Press, 1992), 75.

23   For example, Richard Bach's reluctant messiah in the New Age novel, *Illusions*, speaks to his followers: 'Within each of us lies the power of our consent to health and to sickness, to riches and to poverty, to freedom and to slavery. It is we who control these, and not another.' Richard Bach, *Illusions: The Adventures of a Reluctant Messiah* (London: Heinemann, 1977), 13.

24   For example see Mary K. Greer, "Healing Emotional Pain with the Tarot," in *New Thoughts on Tarot: Transcripts from the First International Newcastle Tarot Symposium*, ed. Mary K. Greer and Rachel Pollack (North Hollywood: Newcastle Publishing Co., 1989).

25   Rachel Pollack, *The New Tarot* (Wellingborough: The Aquarian Press, 1989), 113.

26   Christine Jette, *Tarot for the Healing Heart: Using Inner Wisdom to Heal Body and Mind* (St Paul: Llewellyn Publications, 2001), 5.

27   For a full description of aura-soma see Mike Booth and Carol McKnight, *The Aura-Soma Sourcebook: Color Therapy for the Soul* (Rochester: Healing Arts Press, 2006). The *Aura Soma Tarot* was created by Phyllis Mahon, Rory Baxter and Andy Quick. Stuart R. Kaplan and Jean Huets, *The Encyclopedia of Tarot*, IV vols., Vol. IV (Stamford: U. S. Games Systems, Inc., 2005), 229.

28   Kaplan and Huets, *Encyclopedia of Tarot IV*, 229.

29   Hanegraaff, *New Age Religion and Western Culture*, 62.

30   Katz, *The Occult Tradition*, 197.

31   Antoine Faivre, "Nature: Religious and Philosophical Speculations," in *The Encyclopedia of Religion*, ed. Mircea Eliade (New York: Macmillan, 1987), 336.

32   Hanegraaff, *New Age Religion and Western Culture*, 63–64.

33   See Lord of the Wind Films, *What the Bleep* [website] (Lord of the Wind Films, 18 May 2004 [cited 18 July 2006]); available from http://www.whatthebleep.com.

34   Bill Vincent, "Quantum Thoughts on Tarot," *The Bleeping Herald*, no. 15 (2006).

35   Pollack, *New Tarot*, 126.

36   Ibid.

37   von Stuckrad, *Western Esotericism*, 143.

38   See Jim E. Lovelock, *Gaia: A New Look at Life on Earth* (Oxford: Oxford University Press, 2000).

39   von Stuckrad, *Western Esotericism*, 144.

40   Emily E. Auger, *Tarot and Other Meditation Decks: History, Theory, Aesthetics, Typology* (Jefferson: McFarland & Company Inc., 2004), 116.

41   Stuart R. Kaplan, *The Encyclopedia of Tarot*, IV vols, Vol. III (Stamford: U.S. Games Systems, Inc., 2002), 61, 68.

42   Ibid., 61.

43   Ibid. 68–69.

44   Auger, *Tarot and Other Meditation Decks*, 7; John Drane, Ross Clifford, and Philip Johnson, *Beyond Prediction: The Tarot and Your Spirituality* (Oxford: Lion Publishing, 2001), 25–26. In addition, a number of books have been written which specifically explore the theme of Jungian archetypes and tarot. For example, Sallie Nichols, *Jung and Tarot: An Archetypal Journey* (New York: Samuel Weiser, 1980) and Karen Hamaker-Zondag, *Tarot as a Way of Life: A Jungian Approach to the Tarot* (York Beach: Samuel Weiser, 1997).

45   Sallie Nichols. *Jung and Tarot: An Archetypal Journey* (New York: Samuel Weiser, 1980), 7–10.

46   Hilary Anderson, "Bringing Swords out of Depression and Darkness," in *New Thoughts on Tarot: Transcripts from the First International Tarot Symposium*, ed. Mary K. Greer and Rachel Pollack (North Hollywood: Newcastle Publishing Co., 1989), 12.

47   Ronald Decker and Michael Dummett, *A History of the Occult Tarot: 1870-1970* (London: Gerald Duckworth & Co. Ltd., 2002), 312.

48   Ibid., 312–13.

49   Ibid.

50   Ibid., 313.

51   Kaplan and Huets, *Encyclopedia of Tarot IV*, 386.

52   Ibid.

53   Ibid.

54   Ibid., 390–91.

55   Carl Sargent, *Personality, Divination and the Tarot* (London: Rider, 1988), 9.

56   Sheldon Kopp, *The Hanged Man: Psychotherapy and the Forces of Darkness* (Palo Alto: Science and Behavior Books, 1974), 6.

57   For example, see Perdita Carnivean, "Scrying the Tarot," *Witchcraft*, March-April 2004, 53; Lady Lorelei, *Tarot Life Planner: Change Your Destiny and Enrich Your Life* (London: Hamlyn, 2004), 166–67.

58   See Catherine Summers and Julian Vayne, *Personal Development with the Tarot* (London: Quantum, 2002), 30; Amber K and Azrael Arynn K, *Heart of Tarot: An Intuitive Approach* (St Paul: Llewellyn Publications, 2002), 9.

59   See Gail Fairfield, "Creating, Maintaining and Enhancing Relationships," in *New Thoughts on Tarot: Transcripts from the First International Newcastle Tarot Symposium*, ed. Mary K. Greer and Rachel Pollack (North Hollywood: Newcastle Publishing Co., 1989).

60   See William C. Lammey, "What Is Karmic Tarot?" in *New Thoughts on Tarot: Transcripts from the First International Newcastle Tarot Symposium*, ed. Mary K. Greer and Rachel Pollack (North Hollywood: Newcastle Publishing Co., 1989).

61   Pollack, *New Tarot*, 106.

62   See Terry Donaldson, *The Tarot Spellcaster: Over 40 Spells to Enhance Your Life with the Power of Tarot Magic* (London: New Burlington Books, 2001), 6–7.

63   Pollack, *New Tarot*, 126.

64   Ibid.

65   Ibid; K and K, *Heart of Tarot*, 106.

66   Pollack, *New Tarot*, 126.

67   Stuart R. Kaplan, *The Encyclopedia of Tarot*. IV vols. Vol. III. (Stamford: U.S. Games Systems, Inc., 2002), 646.

68   William Sims Bainbridge, *The Sociology of Religious Movements* (New York: Routledge, 1997), 362.

69   Kaplan, *Encyclopedia of Tarot III*, 80–81.

70   Pollack, "Overview of the Variety," 131.

71   The demotion of Pluto to a dwarf planet is a very recent event and has therefore not had a significant impact on astrological correspondences in tarot at this time.

72   Pollack, "Overview of the Variety," 131; Pollack, *New Tarot*, 155.

73   See U.S. Games Systems, Inc., *Catalog #61*, 14.

74   Kaplan and Huets, *Encyclopedia of Tarot IV*, 335, 37.

75   See Diane Morgan, *Magical Tarot, Mystical Tao: Unlocking the Hidden Power of the Tarot Using the Ancient Secrets of the Tao Te Ching* (New York: St Martin's Griffin, 2003).

76   Ibid., 202

77   Hanegraaff, *New Age Religion and Western Culture*, 86. For an exposition of the overlap between feminist spirituality and the New Age see Mary Farrell Bednarowski, "The New Age Movement and Feminist Spirituality: Overlapping Conversations at the End of the Century," in *Perspectives on the New Age*, ed. James R. Lewis and J. Gordon Melton, *SUNY Series in Religious Studies* (Albany: State University of New York Press, 1992).

78   Bednarowski, "Feminist Spirituality," 168–169.

79   Ibid., 174.

80   Pollack, *New Tarot*, 116.

81   Ibid., 118.

82   Kaplan, *Encyclopedia of Tarot III*, xv, 646.

83   Auger, *Tarot and Other Meditation Decks*, 41.

84   Ibid., 43–4.

85   Auger, *Tarot and Other Meditation Decks*, 44.

86   Kaplan, *Encyclopedia of Tarot III*, xv, 609, 10–12.

87   Pollack, *New Tarot*, 110.

88 Auger, *Tarot and Other Meditation Decks*, 45.

89 See Vicki Noble, *Motherpeace: A Way to the Goddess through Myth, Art, and Tarot* (San Francisco: Harper, 1994).

90 Auger, *Tarot and Other Meditation Decks*, 45-6, 184.

91 Pollack, "Overview of the Variety," 138.

92 Pollack, *New Tarot*, 28.

93 Ibid., 29.

94 Ibid.

95 Auger, *Tarot and Other Meditation Decks*, 19. Runes are from the Germanic alphabet called Futhark. They were originally used for literary and magical purposes in Scandinavia, Iceland and Britain between the third and seventh centuries CE. Interestingly, Hermann Haindl has also created the *Haindl Rune Oracle* (1999). Arland Ussher was the first tarotist to determine correspondences between the tarot trumps and runes. Decker and Dummett, *History of the Occult Tarot*, 303-04.

96 Sandra A.Thomson. *Pictures from the Heart: A Tarot Dictionary* (New York: St Martin's Griffin, 2003), 29.

97 Kaplan and Huets, *Encyclopedia of Tarot IV*, 374.

98 Pollack, *New Tarot*, 31.

99 Kaplan and Huets, *Encyclopedia of Tarot IV*, 374.

100 Auger, *Tarot and Other Meditation Decks*, 46-47.

101 Kaplan, *Encyclopedia of Tarot III*, 166.

102 Pollack, *New Tarot*, 121-22.

103 Kaplan, *Encyclopedia of Tarot III*, 515-16.

104 Pollack, *New Tarot*, 123-24.

105 Kaplan and Huets, *Encyclopedia of Tarot IV*, 295, 97.

106 Hanegraaff, *New Age Religion and Western Culture*, 78.

107 Aidan A. Kelly, "An Update on Neopagan Witchcraft in America," in *Perspectives on the New Age*, ed. James R. Lewis and J. Gordon Melton, *SUNY Series in Religious Studies* (Albany: State University of New York Press, 1992), 136.

108 Hutton, Ronald. *The Triumph of the Moon: A History of Modern Pagan Witchcraft* (Oxford: Oxford University Press, 1999), 411. For a fuller exposition of this debate see D. Riches. (2003). "Counter-Cultural Egalitarianism: A Comparative Analysis of New Age and Other 'Alternative Communities'." Culture and Religion 4(1): 119-139.

109 Pollack, *New Tarot*, 58.

110 Ibid., 58-59.

111 Kaplan, *Encyclopedia of Tarot III*, 629.

112 Pollack, *New Tarot*, 59.

113 Kaplan, *Encyclopedia of Tarot III*, 629.

114 Pollack, *New Tarot*, 59.

115 Auger, *Tarot and Other Meditation Decks*, 22, 124.

116 Pollack, "Overview of the Variety," 127-28.

117 Auger, *Tarot and Other Meditation Decks*, 124.

118 Kaplan and Huets, *Encyclopedia of Tarot IV*, 393, 97.

119 Auger, *Tarot and Other Meditation Decks*, 124.

120 Kaplan, *Encyclopedia of Tarot III*, 308-09.

121 Kaplan and Huets, *Encyclopedia of Tarot IV*, 232, 34-35.

122 Juliette Wood, *Secret Traditions in the Modern Tarot: Folklore and the Occult Revival* [website] (2001 [cited 7 September 2003]); available from http://www.juliette.wood.btinternet.co.uk/tarot.htm.

123 Kaplan and Huets, *Encyclopedia of Tarot IV*, 330-31.

124 Auger, *Tarot and Other Meditation Decks*, 128.

125   Ibid.
126   Kaplan, *Encyclopedia of Tarot III*, 537.
127   Ibid., 537, 39.
128   Auger, *Tarot and Other Meditation Decks*, 127.
129   Pollack, *New Tarot*, 91-92. Upon further investigation I discovered another six decks
      with the name *Celtic Tarot* including one, created by Benito Jacovitti, which depicts the
      Celts in a particularly amusing way. See Kaplan and Huets, *Encyclopedia of Tarot IV*,
      259, 67.
130   Auger, *Tarot and Other Meditation Decks*, 127.
131   Ibid.
132   Kaplan, *Encyclopedia of Tarot III*, 92, 95.
133   Kaplan and Huets, *Encyclopedia of Tarot IV*, 267, 73.
134   Ibid., 597, 600.
135   Pollack, *New Tarot*, 90.
136   Kaplan and Huets, *Encyclopedia of Tarot IV*, 442.
137   Pollack, *New Tarot*, 90, 91.
138   Kaplan and Huets, *Encyclopedia of Tarot IV*, 442.
139   Hutton, *Triumph of the Moon*, 272.
140   Kaplan, *Encyclopedia of Tarot III*, 609.
141   Pollack, *New Tarot*, 70.
142   Kaplan, *Encyclopedia of Tarot III*, 612.
143   Pollack, *New Tarot*, 71.
144   Kaplan, *Encyclopedia of Tarot III*, xv, 347.
145   Pollack, *New Tarot*, 73.
146   Possamai, *Religion and Popular Culture*, 55.
147   Kaplan and Huets, *Encyclopedia of Tarot IV*, 444, 47.
148   Ibid., 610.
149   It should be noted that the influence of this organization extended beyond this context
      to occult and New Age circles generally.
150   Auger, *Tarot and Other Meditation Decks*, 19.
151   Pollack, "Overview of the Variety," 130.
152   Auger, *Tarot and Other Meditation Decks*, 66.
153   Kaplan and Huets, *Encyclopedia of Tarot IV*, 513.
154   Pollack, *New Tarot*, 141.
155   Ibid., 142.
156   Kaplan and Huets, *Encyclopedia of Tarot IV*, 207, 10-11.
157   See U.S. Games Systems, Inc. *Tarot Catalog #61* (Stamford: U. S. Games Systems,
      Inc., 2004), 27.
158   Matthew Fox, *The Coming of the Cosmic Christ: The Healing of Mother Earth and the
      Birth of a Global Renaissance* (San Francisco: Harper, 1988), 230.
159   Hanegraaff, *New Age Religion and Western Culture*, 328.
160   Kaplan and Huets, *Encyclopedia of Tarot IV*, 279, 81.
161   Kaplan, *Encyclopedia of Tarot III*, 99-100.
162   Corinne Heline, *The Bible and the Tarot* (Marina del Rey: De Vorss & Co., 1969;
      reprint, Sixth).
163   Drane, Clifford, and Johnson, *Beyond Prediction*.
164   Andrea Grace Diem and James R. Lewis. "Imagining India: The Influence of Hinduism
      on the New Age Movement." In *Perspectives on the New Age*, edited by James R.
      Lewis and J. Gordon Melton (Albany: State University of New York Press, 1992), 48.
165   Heelas, *The New Age Movement*, 55. A quick look on the internet shows that Islam
      and Paganism are also strong contenders for the title.

166   Kaplan, *Encyclopedia of Tarot III*, xvi, 302, 304-05.

167   Pollack, *New Tarot*, 101.

168   Kaplan, *Encyclopedia of Tarot III*, 304-05.

169   Kaplan and Huets, *Encyclopedia of Tarot IV*, 450. See Ma Deva Padma and Osho, *Osho Zen Tarot: The Transcendental Game of Zen*, Second ed. (New York: St Martin's Press, 1994).

170   Auger, *Tarot and Other Meditation Decks*, 114.

171   Ibid. 121-123.

172   Possamai, *Religion and Popular Culture*, 53, 4.

173   Auger, *Tarot and Other Meditation Decks*, 134.

174   Kaplan, *Encyclopedia of Tarot III*, 615.

175   Pollack, *New Tarot*, 86-87.

176   Kaplan and Huets, *Encyclopedia of Tarot IV*, 528, 31.

177   Auger, *Tarot and Other Meditation Decks*, 134-35.

178   Danny L. Jorgensen, *The Esoteric Scene, Cultic Milieu, and Occult Tarot*, ed. J. Gordon Melton, *Cults and Nonconventional Religious Groups: A Collection of Outstanding Dissertations and Monographs* (New York: Garland Publishing, Inc., 1992), 157.

179   Pollack, *New Tarot*, 82.

180   Auger, *Tarot and Other Meditation Decks*, 133.

181   Castañeda wrote a series of books about a Yacqui shaman named Don Juan Matus who he claims to have met. The authenticity of these works is a matter of some controversy.

182   Pollack, *New Tarot*, 83-85.

183   Kaplan and Huets, *Encyclopedia of Tarot IV*, 507.

184. Auger, *Tarot and Other Meditation Decks*, 133.

185   Kaplan and Huets, *Encyclopedia of Tarot IV*, 585.

186   Pollack, *New Tarot*, 88-89.

187   Louis Martinié and Sallie Ann Glassman, *The New Orleans Voodoo Tarot* (Rochester: Destiny Books, 1992), 1.

188   Ibid., 11-13.

189   Ibid., 26.

190   Kaplan and Huets, *Encyclopedia of Tarot IV*, 435.

191   Martinié and Glassman, *Voodoo Tarot*, 27.

192   Kaplan and Huets, *Encyclopedia of Tarot IV*, 435.

193   Kaplan, *Encyclopedia of Tarot III*, 313, 16.

194   Kaplan and Huets, *Encyclopedia of Tarot IV*, 450, 52.

195   Zolrak and Dürkön, *The Tarot of the Orishàs*, Second ed. (St Paul: Llewellyn Publications, 2000; reprint, Fifth), 6-7.

196   Zolrak and Dürkön, *Orishàs*, 3-7.

197   Kaplan and Huets, *Encyclopedia of Tarot IV*, 232-233.

198   Kaplan, *Encyclopedia of Tarot III*, 85, 89.

199   Kaplan and Huets, *Encyclopedia of Tarot IV*, 207.

200   Stuart Kaplan takes a detailed look at the place of Egypt in tarot lore. See 'The Ancient Egyptian Temple' in Kaplan and Huets, *Encyclopedia of Tarot IV*, 699-720.

201   Auger, *Tarot and Other Meditation Decks*, 104.

202   Pollack, *New Tarot*, 107.

203   Ibid., 106.

204   Pollack, *New Tarot*, 108.

205   Kaplan, *Encyclopedia of Tarot III*, 578.

206   Pollack, "Overview of the Variety," 135.

207   Pollack, *New Tarot*, 105.

208   Ibid., 106
209   Auger, *Tarot and Other Meditation Decks*, 104.
210   Ibid., 106. This deck is interesting because it links Egyptian and Arthurian mythological traditions.
211   Kaplan, *Encyclopedia of Tarot III*, 92–93.
212   Ibid., 111, 15.
213   Ibid., 470, 72–73.
214   Kaplan and Huets, *Encyclopedia of Tarot IV*, 631.
215   Pollack, *New Tarot*, 94.
216   Kaplan, *Encyclopedia of Tarot III*, 641.
217   Pollack, *New Tarot*, 95.
218   Kaplan, *Encyclopedia of Tarot III*, 641.
219   Pollack, *New Tarot*, 97.
220   Ibid., 96–97.
221   Interestingly through this deck, Unger shows an awareness that gypsies came from India even if their ultimate origin apparently did lie in the stars.
222   Kaplan and Huets, *Encyclopedia of Tarot IV*, 250.
223   Ibid., 252–53.

NOTES TO CONCLUSION

1   For a full exposition of this theory see Ludwig Wittgenstein, *Philosophical Investigations*, trans. G. E. M. Anscombe, Second ed. (Oxford: Basil Blackwell, 1968).
2   Daren Kemp, *New Age: A Guide – Alternative Spiritualities from Aquarian Conspiracy to Next Age* (Edinburgh: Edinburgh University Press, 2004), 7.

Bibliography

Albanese, Catherine L. "The Magical Staff: Quantum Healing in the New Age." In *Perspectives on the New Age*, edited by James R. Lewis and J. Gordon Melton, 68-84. Albany: State University of New York Press, 1992.

Alexander, Kay. "Roots of the New Age." In *Perspectives on the New Age*, edited by James R. Lewis and J. Gordon Melton, 30-47. Albany: State University of New York Press, 1992.

Algeri, Giuliana. "Un Gioco Per Le Corti: I Tarocchi Miniati." In *I Tarocchi : Le Carte Di Corte : Bioco E Magia Alla Corte Degli Estensi*, edited by Giordano Berti and Andrea Vitali, 21-43. Bologna: Nuova Alfa, 1987.

Alighieri, Dante. *The Divine Comedy*. Translated by Allen Mandelbaum, *Everyman's Library*. London: Everyman Publishers, 1995.

Allan, J. MacGregor. "Carl Vogt's Lectures on Man." *Anthropological Review* 7, no. 25 (1869): 177-84.

Alli, Antero. "The Neuro-Tarot: Designing Your Own Deck of Cards." *Whole Earth Review*, no. 72 (1991): 28-33.

Allin, Michael. *Zarafa*. London: Review, 1998.

Almond, Philip C. *The British Discovery of Buddhism*. Cambridge: Cambridge University Press, 1988.

Als, C., Y. Stüssi, U. Boschung, U. Tröhler, and J. H. Wäber. "Through the Artist's Eye: Visible Signs of Illness from the 14th to the 20th Century: Systematic Review of Portraits." *British Medical Journal* 325, no. 7378 (2002): 1499-502.

Anderson, Hilary. "Bringing Swords out of Depression and Darkness." In *New Thoughts on Tarot: Transcripts from the First International Tarot Symposium*, edited by Mary K. Greer and Rachel Pollack, 9-22. North Hollywood: Newcastle Publishing Co., 1989.

Andrews, Carol. *The Rosetta Stone*. London: British Museum Publications Ltd, 1988. Reprint, Seventh.

Ankarloo, Bengt, and Gustav Henningsen, eds. *Early Modern European Witchcraft: Centres and Periphery*. Oxford: Clarendon Press, 1990.

Anonymous. *The Mabinogion*. Translated by Gwyn Jones and C. E. Tuttle. New Revised ed, *Everyman's Library*. London: J. M. Dent, 1993.

Antes, Peter, Armin W. Geertz, and Randi R. Warne, eds. *New Approaches to the Study of Religion: Regional, Critical, and Historical Approaches*. Edited by Jacques Waaredenburg. Vol. 1, *Religion and Reason*. Berlin: Walter de Gruyter, 2004.

Aquinas, T. (1947-1948). *Summa Theologica*. London, Burns & Oates.

Aston, Margaret. *The Fifteenth Century: The Prospect of Europe*. London: Thames and Hudson, 1968.

Auger, Emily E. *Tarot and Other Meditation Decks: History, Theory, Aesthetics, Typology.* Jefferson: McFarland & Company Inc., 2004.

Aviza, Edward A. *Thinking Tarot.* New York: Simon and Schuster, 1997.

Bach, Richard. *Illusions: The Adventures of a Reluctant Messiah.* London: Heinemann, 1977.

Bainbridge, William Sims. *The Sociology of Religious Movements.* New York: Routledge, 1997.

Baker, Derek, ed. *Medieval Women Dedicated and Presented to Professor Rosalind M. T. Hill on the Occasion of Her Seventieth Birthday, Studies in Church History: Subsidia.* Oxford: Basil Blackwell, 1978.

Barber, Richard. *The Holy Grail: Imagination and Belief.* Cambridge: Harvard University Press, 2004.

Barmann, Lawrence. "Confronting Secularization: Origins of the London Society for the Study of Religion." *Church History* 62, no. 1 (1993): 22-40.

Barnes, Harry Elmer. *An Intellectual and Cultural History of the Western World.* Third Revised ed. 3 vols. Vol. 2. New York: Dover Publications, Inc., 1965.

Baroja, Julio Caro. "Witchcraft and Catholic Theology." In *Early Modern European Witchcraft: Centres and Peripheries*, edited by Bengt Ankarloo and Gustav Henningsen, 19-44. Oxford: Clarendon Press, 1990.

Baron, Hans. "A Struggle for Liberty in the Renaissance: Florence, Venice, and Milan in the Early Quattrocento, Part 1." *The American Historical Review* 58, no. 2 (1953): 265-89.

——. "A Struggle for Liberty in the Renaissance: Florence, Venice, and Milan in the Early Quattrocento, Part 2." *The American Historical Review* 58, no. 3 (1953): 544-70.

Barrett, David V. *Secret Societies: From the Ancient and Arcane to the Modern and Clandestine.* London: Blandford, 1997.

Bates, David. "The Mystery of Truth: Louis-Claude De Saint-Martin's Enlightened Mysticism." *Journal of the History of Ideas* 61, no. 4 (2000): 635-55.

Bayley, Harold. *A New Light on the Renaissance Displayed in Contemporary Emblems.* New York: Benjamin Blom, 1909.

Bednarowski, Mary Farrell. "The New Age Movement and Feminist Spirituality: Overlapping Conversations at the End of the Century." In *Perspectives on the New Age*, edited by James R. Lewis and J. Gordon Melton, 167-78. Albany: State University of New York Press, 1992.

Bell, R. C. *Board and Table Games from Many Civilisations.* 2 vols. Vol. 1. London: Oxford University Press, 1960.

Bellenghi, Alessandro. *Cartomancy.* Translated by Julie Almond. London: Ebury Press, 1988.

Beltrami, L. *Il Castello Di Milano:(Castrum, Portae, Jovis) Sotto Il Dominio Dei Visconti E Degli Sforza, 1368-1535.* Milan: U. Hoepli, 1894.

Benham, W. Gurney. *Playing Cards: History of the Pack and Explanations of its Many Secrets.* London: Ward, Lock and Co., Ltd, 1931.

Bercovici, Konrad. *The Story of the Gypsies.* London: Jonathan Cape, 1929.

Bernen, Satia, and Robert Bernen. *Myth and Religion in European Painting 1270-1700: The Stories as the Artists Knew Them.* New York: George Braziller, 1973.

Berti, Giordano. "Il Libro Di Thot, Ovvero, L'interpretazione Esoterica Del Tarocco." In *I Tarocchi : Le Carte Di Corte : Bioco E Magia Alla Corte Degli Estensi,* edited by Giordano Berti and Andrea Vitali. Bologna: Nuova Alfa, 1987.

Berti, Giordano, and Andrea Vitali, eds. *I Tarocchi: Le Carte Di Corte : Bioco E Magia Alla Corte Degli Estensi.* Bologna: Nuova Alfa, 1987.

Bertoni, Giulio. *Poesie Leggende Costumanze Del Medio Evo.* Second ed. Bologna: Arnaldo Forni, 1976.

Biedermann, Hans. *Dictionary of Symbolism.* Translated by James Hulbert. New York: Facts on File, 1992.

Blavatsky, Helena Petrovna. *The Secret Doctrine.* Third Revised ed. 4 vols. Vol. 2 Anthropogenesis. London: Theosophical Publishing House, 1893-1897.

Boaistuau, Pierre. "Histoires Prodigieuses." In *The Occult in Early Modern Europe: A Documentary History,* edited by P. G. Maxwell-Stuart. Houndmills: Macmillan, 1999.

Boccaccio, Giovanni. *The Decameron.* Translated by Mark Musa and Peter E. Bondanella. New York: Norton, 1982.

Boggi, Flavio. *Bonifacio Bembo* [online reference source]. Grove Art Online, Oxford University Press, 2006 [cited 23 February 2006]. Available from http://www.groveart.com/.

Boiteau d'Ambly, Paul. *Les Cartes À Jouer Et La Cartomancie.* Paris: L. Hachette et cie, 1854.

Bond, E. A. "History of Playing-Cards." *Athenæum,* no. 2621 (1878): 87-88.

Booth, Mike, and Carol McKnight. *The Aura-Soma Sourcebook: Color Therapy for the Soul.* Rochester: Healing Arts Press, 2006.

Born, L. K. (1928). "The Perfect Prince: A Study in Thirteenth- and Fourteenth-Century Ideals." Speculum 3(4): 470-504.

Brauen, Fred. "Athanasius Kircher (1602-1680)." *Journal of the History of Ideas* 43, no. 1 (1982): 129-34.

Braydon, Claude. "The Song of Sano Tarot (Review)," *The Builder Magazine,* December (1929).

Brooks, E. W. "Die Entstehung Des Kirchenstaates Und Der Curiale Begriff 'Res Publica Romanorum:' Ein Beitrag Zum Frankischen Kirchen-Und Staatsrecht [Review]." *English Historical Review* 16, no. 61 (1901): 130-32.

Brown, Dan. *The Da Vinci Code: A Novel.* London: Bantam Press, 2003.

Brown, Judith C. "Prosperity or Hard Times in Renaissance Italy." *Renaissance Quarterly* 42, no. 4 (1989): 761-80.

Buckland, Raymond. *Secrets of Gypsy Love Magic.* St Paul: Llewellyn Publications, 1990.

Budge, E. A. Wallis, ed. *The Book of the Dead: The Hieroglyphic Transcript into English of the Papyrus of Ani.* New York: Gramercy Books, 1995.

Burckhardt, Jacob. *The Civilization of the Renaissance in Italy.* Translated by S. G. C. Middlemore, *Penguin Classics.* London: Penguin Books, 1990.

Burdel, Claude. "Tarot of Marseille." Torino: Lo Scarabeo, 2000.

Burfield, Diana. "Theosophy and Feminism: Some Explorations in Nineteenth Century Biography." In *Women's Religious Experience*, edited by Pat Holden, 27–56. London: Croom Helm, 1983.

Burke, Peter. *The Italian Renaissance: Culture and Society in Italy.* Revised ed. Cambridge: Polity Press, 1986.

——. *Popular Culture in Early Modern Europe.* London: Temple Smith, 1978.

——. *Varieties of Cultural History.* Cambridge: Polity Press, 1997.

Butler, Bill. *Dictionary of the Tarot.* New York: Schocken Books, 1975.

Caldwell, Ross Gregory. *Trionfi.Com* [website]. Caldwell, Ross Gregory, December 2005 [cited 7 February 2006]. Available from http://www.trionfi.com.

Cameron, Euan. *Waldenses: Rejections of the Holy Church in Medieval Europe.* Malden: Blackwell Publishers Ltd, 2000.

Campbell, Bruce F. *Ancient Wisdom Revived: A History of the Theosophical Movement.* Berkeley: University of California Press, 1980.

Campbell, Gordon. *Gianozzo Manetti* [Oxford Reference Online]. The Oxford Dictionary of the Renaissance, Oxford University Press, 2003 [cited 2 March 2006]. Available from http://www.oxfordreference.com/.

Campbell, John Brian. *Trajan* [Oxford Reference Online]. The Oxford Companion to Classical Civilization, Oxford University Press, 1998 [cited 8 August 2006]. Available from http://www.oxfordreference.com/.

Campbell, Joseph. "Part I: Exoteric Tarot." In *Tarot Revelations*, edited by Richard Roberts, 2–37. San Anselmo: Vernal Equinox Press, 1987.

Campbell, Lyle. *Historical Linguistics: An Introduction.* Edinburgh: Edinburgh University Press, 1998.

Carmichael, Ann G. "Contagion Theory and Contagion Practice in Fifteenth-Century Milan." *Renaissance Quarterly* 44, no. 2 (1991): 213–56.

Carr, David. "The Cardinal Virtues and Plato's Moral Psychology." *The Philosophical Quarterly* 38, no. 151 (1988): 186–200.

Carroll, Wilma. *The 2-Hour Tarot Tutor: The Fast, Revolutionary Method for Learning to Read Tarot Cards in Two Hours ...* New York: Berkeley Books, 2004.

Carruthers, Mary J. *The Book of Memory: A Study of Memory in Medieval Culture.* Edited by Alastair Minnis, *Cambridge Studies in Medieval Literature.* Cambridge: Cambridge University Press, 1990.

Carter, Thomas Francis. *The Invention of Printing in China and Its Spread Westward.* Revised ed. New York: The Ronald Press Company, 1955.

Case, Paul Foster. *The Tarot: A Key to the Wisdom of the Ages.* First Paperback ed. New York: Jeremy P. Tarcher/Penguin, 2006.

Cavendish, Richard. *Encyclopedia of the Unexplained: Magic, Occultism and Parapsychology.* London: Routledge and Kegan Paul, 1974.

——. *A History of Magic.* London: Arkana, 1990.

——. *The Tarot.* London: Chancellor Press, 1986. Reprint, Third.

Chadwick, Owen. *The Secularization of the European Mind in the Nineteenth Century.* Cambridge: Cambridge University Press, 1975.

Chamberlin, E. R. *The Count of Virtue: Giangaleazzo Visconti Duke of Milan.* London: Eyre & Spottiswoode, 1965.

Chambers, R., ed. *The Book of Days: A Miscellany of Popular Antiquities in Connection with the Calendar Including Anecdote, Biography, & History, Curiosities of Literature and Oddities of Human Life and Character.* 2 vols. London: W. & R. Chambers, 1883.

Chatto, William Andrew. *Facts and Speculations on the Origin and History of Playing Cards.* London: J. R. Smith, 1848.

Chehabi, H. E., and Allen Guttmann. "From Iran to All of Asia: The Origin and Diffusion of Polo." *The International Journal for the History of Polo* 19, no. 2–3 (2002): 384–200.

Cheney, Liana DeGirolami. "Dutch Vanitas Paintings: The Skull." In *The Symbolism of Vanitas in the Arts, Literature, and Music*, edited by Liana DeGirolami Cheney, 113–76. Lewiston: Edwin Mellen Press, 1992.

———, ed. *The Symbolism of Vanitas in the Arts, Literature, and Music: Comparative and Historical Studies.* Lewiston: Edwin Mellen Press, 1992.

Child, Heather, and Dorothy Colles. *Christian Symbols Ancient and Modern: A Handbook for Students.* New York: Charles Scribner's Sons, 1971.

Christiansen, Keith. "A Hanged Man by Filippino." *Burlington Magazine* 136, no. 1099 (1994): 705.

Cieri-Via, Claudia. "L'iconografia Degli Arcani Maggiori." In *I Tarocchi : Le Carte Di Corte: Bioco E Magia Alla Corte Degli Estensi*, edited by Giordano Berti and Andrea Vitali, 158–83. Bologna: Nuova Alfa, 1987.

Clark, James C. "Introduction." In *The Dance of Death*, Hans Holbein. London: Phaidon Press Ltd, 1947.

Clark, Stuart. *Thinking with Demons: The Idea of Witchcraft in Early Modern Europe.* Oxford: Oxford University Press, 1997.

Clarke, J. J. *Oriental Enlightenment: The Encounter between Asian and Western Thought.* London: Routledge, 1997.

Cohn, Norman. *Europe's Inner Demons: An Enquiry Inspired by the Great Witch-Hunt.* Edited by Norman Cohn, *The Columbus Centre Series: Studies in the Dynamics of Persecution and Extermination.* Bungay: Sussex University Press, 1975.

Collison-Morley, L. *The Story of the Sforzas.* London: George Routledge and Sons, 1933.

Colonna, Francesco. *Hypnerotomachia Poliphili: The Strife of Love in a Dream.* Translated by Joscelyn Godwin. London: Thames & Hudson, 1999.

Colquhoun, Ithell. *Sword of Wisdom: Macgregor Mathers and 'the Golden Dawn'.* London: Neville Spearman, 1975.

Cooper, J. C. *An Illustrated Encyclopaedia of Traditional Symbols.* London: Thames and Hudson, 1978.

Copenhaver, Brian P. *Hermetica: The Greek Corpus Hermeticum and the Latin Asclepius in a New English Translation, with Notes and Introduction.* Cambridge: Cambridge University Press, 1992. Reprint, First.

Coulter, Anne Hendren. "Pictures That Heal: Messages from the Tarot Current Research as a Guide to Medical Practice." *Alternative & Complementary Therapies* 10, no. 6 (2004): 339–42.

Court de Gébelin, Antoine. *Monde Primitif: Analysé Et Comparé Avec Le Monde Moderne, Considéré Dans L'histoire Naturelle De La Parole; Ou*

Grammaire Universelle Et Comparative. 9 vols, *Archives De La Linguistique Française; No.95.* Paris, 1774.

Crowley, Aleister. *The Book of Thoth: A Short Essay on the Tarot of the Egyptians.* York Beach: Samuel Weiser, Inc., 1991.

——. *The Confessions of Aleister Crowley: An Autohagiography.* London: Arkana, 1979.

——. *Liber 777:* The Hermetic Library, 1909.

——. "Liber L Vel Legis Sub Figura Ccxx, as Delivered by LXXVIII unto DCLXVI." *The Equinox* I, no. X (1913): 9–33.

Crowley, Aleister, and Marguerite Frieda Harris. *Aleister Crowley Thoth Tarot Deck.* Stamford: U. S. Games Systems, Inc., 1983.

Curl, James Stevens. *Egyptomania: The Egyptian Revival: A Recurring Theme in the History of Taste.* Manchester: Manchester University Press, 1994.

Curley, Michael J. *Geoffrey of Monmouth, Twayne's English Authors Series.* New York: Twayne Publishers, 1994.

Cust, Lionel. "The Frescoes in the Casa Borromeo at Milan." *The Burlington Magazine for Connoisseurs* 33, no. 184 (1918): 8–14.

David, Jean-Michel. *Iraqi Archeological Remnants and Possible Influences on Tarot* (11) [Archived e-mail newsletter]. Association for Tarot Studies, 2003 [cited 23 June 2004]. Available from http://www.association.tarotstudies.org.

David, Rosalie. *The Experience of Ancient Egypt.* London: Routledge, 2000.

Dawson, Warren Royal, and Eric P. Uphill. *Who was Who in Egyptology.* Third ed. revised by M. L. Bierbrier. London: The Egypt Exploration Society, 1995.

De Baecque, Antoine. "The Allegorical Image of France, 1750–1800: A Political Crisis of Representation." *Representations* 47, Special Issue: National Cultures before Nationalism (1994): 111–43.

de Vinne, Theodore Low *The Invention of Printing: A Collection of Facts and Opinions Descriptive of Early Prints and Playing Cards, the Block Books of the Fifteenth Century, the Legend of Lourens Janszoon Coaster, of Haarlem, and the Work of John Gutenberg and His Associates.* New York: Francis Hart & Co., 1876.

de Vries, Ad. *Dictionary of Symbols and Imagery.* Amsterdam: North-Holland Publishing Company, 1974.

Debus, Allen G. "Alchemy in an Age of Reason: The Chemical Philosophers in Early Eighteenth-Century France." In *Hermeticism and the Renaissance: Intellectual History and the Occult in Early Modern Europe*, edited by Ingrid Merkel and Allen G. Debus, 231–50. Washington: Folger Books, 1988.

Decembrio, P. C. "Playing Cards for the Duke of Milan." In *Italian Art 1400–1500: Sources and Documents*, edited by Creighton E. Gilbert, 210–11. Englewood Cliffs: Prentice-Hall, Inc., 1980.

Decker, Ronald, Thierry Depaulis, and Michael Dummett. *A Wicked Pack of Cards: The Origins of Occult Tarot.* London: Gerald Duckworth and Co. Ltd., 1996.

Decker, Ronald, and Michael Dummett. *A History of the Occult Tarot: 1870–1970.* London: Gerald Duckworth & Co. Ltd., 2002.

Delumeau, Jean. *Sin and Fear: The Emergence of a Western Guilt Culture 13th-18th Centuries.* Translated by Eric Nicholson. New York: St Martin's Press, 1990.

Depaulis, Thierry. "Des 'Cartes Communément Appelées Taraux' 2ème Partie." *The Playing Card* 32, no. 5 (2004): 244–49.

———. *Tarot, Jeu Et Magie.* Paris: Bibliothèque Nationale, 1984.

di Parravicino, Count Emiliano. "Three Packs of Italian Tarocco Cards." *The Burlington Magazine for Connoisseurs* 3, no. 9 (1903): 237–51.

Dieckmann, Liselotte. *Hieroglyphics: The History of a Literary Symbol.* St Louis: Washington University Press, 1970.

Diem, Andrea Grace, and James R. Lewis. "Imagining India: The Influence of Hinduism on the New Age Movement." In *Perspectives on the New Age*, edited by James R. Lewis and J. Gordon Melton, 48–67. Albany: State University of New York Press, 1992.

Dobkin, Marlene. "Fortune's Malice: Divination, Psychotherapy, and Folk Medicine in Peru." *The Journal of American Folklore* 82, no. 324 (1969): 132–41.

Donaldson, Terry. *The Tarot Spellcaster: Over 40 Spells to Enhance Your Life with the Power of Tarot Magic.* London: New Burlington Books, 2001.

D'Otrange, M. L. "Thirteen Tarot Cards from the Visconti-Sforza Set." *The Connoisseur* 133 (1954): 54–60.

Douglas, Alfred. *The Tarot: The Origins, Meaning and Uses of the Cards.* Harmondsworth: Penguin Books Ltd, 1974.

Drane, John, Ross Clifford, and Philip Johnson. *Beyond Prediction: The Tarot and Your Spirituality.* Oxford: Lion Publishing, 2001.

Duby, Georges. *Art and Society in the Middle Ages.* Translated by Jean Birrell. Cambridge: Polity Press, 2000.

Dummett, Michael. "Préface." In *Tarot, Jeu Et Magie*, edited by Thierry Depaulis. Paris: Bibliothèque Nationale, 1984.

———. "Sulle Origini Dei Tarocchi Popolari." In *I Tarocchi : Le Carte Di Corte : Bioco E Magia Alla Corte Degli Estensi*, edited by Giordano Berti and Andrea Vitali, 78–85. Bologna: Nuova Alfa, 1987.

———. *The Visconti-Sforza Tarot Cards.* New York: George Braziller, Inc., 1986.

Dummett, Michael, and Kamal Abu-Deeb. "Some Remarks on Mamluk Playing Cards." *Journal of the Warburg and Courtauld Institutes* 36 (1973): 106–28.

Dummett, Michael, Giuliana Algeri, and Giordano Berti. "Tarocchi Popolari E Tarocchi Fantastici." In *I Tarocchi : Le Carte Di Corte : Bioco E Magia Alla Corte Degli Estensi*, edited by Giordano Berti and Andrea Vitali, 86–94. Bologna: Nuova Alfa, 1987.

Dummett, Michael, with Sylvia Mann. *The Game of Tarot: From Ferrara to Salt Lake City.* London: Gerald Duckworth and Co. Ltd., 1980.

Dummett, Michael, and John McLeod. *A History of Games Played with the Tarot Pack: The Game of Triumphs.* 2 vols. Vol. 1. Lewiston: Edwin Mellen Press, 2004.

———. *A History of Games Played with the Tarot Pack: The Game of Triumphs.* 2 vols. Vol. 2. Lewiston: Edwin Mellen Press, 2004.

Durant, Will. *The Renaissance: A History of Civilization in Italy from 1304-1576 Ad.* Edited by Will Durant and Ariel Durant. X vols. Vol. V, *The Story of Civilization.* New York: Simon and Schuster, 1953. Reprint, Thirteenth.

Edgerton, Samuel Y. Jr. "Icons of Justice." *Past and Present*, no. 89 (1980): 23-38.

———. *Pictures and Punishment: Art and Criminal Prosecution During the Florentine Renaissance.* Ithaca: Cornell University Press, 1985.

Edwards, Francis. *Ritual and Drama: The Medieval Theatre.* Guildford: Lutterworth Press, 1976.

Eisenbichler, Konrad, and Wim Hüsken, eds. *Carnival and the Carnivalesque: The Fool, the Reformer, the Wildman, and Others in Early Modern Theatre.* Edited by Wim Hüsken, *Ludus: Medieval and Early Renaissance Theatre and Drama.* Amsterdam: Rodopi, 1999.

Elder, Gregory P. *Chronic Vigour: Darwin, Anglicans, Catholics, and the Development of a Doctrine of Providential Evolution.* Lanham: University Press of America, Inc., 1996.

Eliade, Mircea, ed. *The Encyclopedia of Religion.* New York: Macmillan, 1987.

Elias, Norbert. *The Society of Individuals.* Translated by Edmund Jephcott. Oxford: Basil Blackwell, 1991.

———. *State Formation and Civilization.* Translated by Edmund Jephcott. 2 vols. Vol. 2, *The Civilizing Process.* Oxford: Basil Blackwell, 1982.

Ellmann, Richard. *The Identity of Yeats.* London: Faber and Faber, 1954.

El-Moor, Jereer. "The Occult Tradition of the Tarot in Tangency with Ibn 'Arabi's Life and Teachings: Part Two." *The Journal of the Muhyiddin Ibn 'Arabi Society* XXXII (2002).

Encausse, Gérard. *The Tarot of the Bohemians: Absolute Key to Occult Science; the Most Ancient Book in the World for the Use of Initiates.* Translated by A. P. Morton. Third Edition, Revised ed. Hollywood: Wilshire Book Company, 1971.

Espinosa, Alma. "Music and the *Danse Macabre*: A Survey." In *The Symbolism of Vanitas in the Arts, Literature and Music: Comparative and Historical Studies*, edited by Liana DeGirolami Cheney, 15-31. Lewiston: Edwin Mellen Press, 1992.

Evans, Michael. "Allegorical Women and Practical Men: The Iconography of the *Artes* Reconsidered." In *Medieval Women Dedicated and Presented to Professor Rosalind M. T. Hill on the Occasion of Her Seventieth Birthday*, edited by Derek Baker, 305-29. Oxford: Basil Blackwell, 1978.

Fairfield, Gail. "Creating, Maintaining and Enhancing Relationships." In *New Thoughts on Tarot: Transcripts from the First International Newcastle Tarot Symposium*, edited by Mary K. Greer and Rachel Pollack, 57-72. North Hollywood: Newcastle Publishing Co., 1989.

Faivre, Antoine. *Access to Western Esotericism.* Edited by David Appelbaum, *SUNY Series in Western Esoteric Traditions.* Albany: State University of New York Press, 1994.

———. "The Children of Hermes and the Science of Man." In *Hermeticism and the Renaissance: Intellectual History and the Occult in Early Modern Europe*, edited by Ingrid Merkel and Allen G. Debus, 424-35. Washington: Folger Books, 1988.

———. "Nature: Religious and Philosophical Speculations." In *The Encyclopedia of Religion*, edited by Mircea Eliade, 328–37. New York: Macmillan, 1987.

Faivre, Antoine, and Wouter J. Hanegraaff, eds. *Western Esotericism and the Science of Religion: Selected Papers Presented at the 17th Congress of the International Association for the History of Religions, Mexico City 1995.* Edited by Gary Trompf, Wouter Hanegraaff and John Cooper, *Gnostica.* Bondgenotenlaan: Peeters, 1998.

Fani, Muhsin. *Oriental Literature or the Dabistan.* Translated by David Shea and Anthony Troyer. New York: Tudor Publishing Co., 1937.

Fanthorpe, Patricia, and Lionel Fanthorpe. *The Holy Grail Revealed: The Real Secret of Rennes-Le-Château.* San Bernadino: The Borgo Press, 1982.

Faxon, Alicia. "Some Perspectives on the Transformation of the Dance of Death in Art." In *The Symbolism of Vanitas in the Arts, Literature, and Music: Comparative and Historical Studies*, edited by Liana DeGirolami Cheney, 33–66. Lewiston: Edwin Mellen Press, 1992.

Ferguson, George. *Signs and Symbols in Christian Art.* New York: Oxford University Press, 1959.

Findlen, Paula. "Understanding the Italian Renaissance." In *The Italian Renaissance: The Essential Readings*, edited by Paula Findlen, 4–40. Malden: Blackwell Publishing, 2002.

———, ed. *The Italian Renaissance: The Essential Readings, Blackwell Essential Readings in History.* Malden: Blackwell Publishing, 2002.

Foster, R. F. *W. B. Yeats: A Life.* II vols. Vol. I: The Apprentice Mage. Oxford: Oxford University Press, 1997.

Fournier, Félix Alfaro. *Playing Cards: General History from their Creation to the Present Day.* Vitoria: Heraclio Fournier, 1982.

Fox, Matthew. *The Coming of the Cosmic Christ: The Healing of Mother Earth and the Birth of a Global Renaissance.* San Francisco: Harper, 1988.

Franklin, Stephen E. *Origins of the Tarot Deck: A Study of the Astronomical Substructure of Game and Divining Boards.* Jefferson: McFarland & Company, Inc., 1988.

Fraser, Angus. *The Gypsies.* Edited by James Campbell and Barry Cunliffe. Second ed, *The Peoples of Europe.* Oxford: Blackwell, 1995.

Freedberg, David. *The Power of Images: Studies in the History and Theory of Response.* Chicago: The University of Chicago Press, 1989.

Friedell, Egon. *A Cultural History of the Modern Age: The Crisis of the European Soul from the Black Death to the World War.* Translated by Charles Francis Atkinson. III vols. Vol. III. New York: Alfred A. Knopf, 1954. Reprint, Third.

Gardner, Richard. *The Tarot Speaks.* London: Tandem, 1976.

Gates, Charlene Elizabeth. "The Tarot Trumps: Their Origin, Archetypal Imagery, and Use in Some Works of English Literature." Ph. D., University of Oregon, 1982.

Gay, Peter. *The Party of Humanity: Essays in the French Enlightenment.* New York: W. W. Norton and Company Inc., 1971.

Geoghegan, Eddie. *Coats of Arms from Ireland and around the World* [Website]. Eddie Geoghegen, 14 February 1990 [cited 9 May 2006]. Available from http://www.heraldry.ws/.

Gerhard, H. P. *The World of Icons*. Translated by Irene R. Gibbons. London: John Murray, 1971.

Gilbert, C. D. "Blind Cupid." *Journal of the Warburg and Courtauld Institutes* 33 (1970): 304–05.

Gilbert, Creighton E., ed. *Italian Art 1400–1500: Sources and Documents*. Edited by H. W. Janson, *The History of Art Series*. Englewood Cliffs: Prentice-Hall, Inc., 1980.

Gilbert, Robert A. *Freemasonry and Esoteric Movements* [webpage]. Canonbury Masonic Research Centre, 2000 [cited 21 July 2002]. Available from http://www.canonbury.ac.uk/library/lectures/freemasonry_and_esoteric_mo vemen.htm.

——. "From Cipher to Enigma: The Role of William Wynn Westcott in the Creation of the Hermetic Order of the Golden Dawn." In *Secrets of the Golden Dawn Cypher Manuscript*, edited by Carroll 'Poke' Runyon. Silverado: C.H.S., Inc., 2000.

——. *The Golden Dawn and the Esoteric Section*. London: Theosophical History Centre, 1987.

——. *The Golden Dawn Scrapbook: The Rise and Fall of a Magical Order*. York Beach: Samuel Weiser, Inc., 1997.

——. "Provenance Unknown: A Tentative Solution to the Riddle of the Cipher Manuscript of the Golden Dawn." In *The Complete Golden Dawn Cipher Manuscript*, edited by Darcy Küntz, 17–26. Edmonds: Holmes Publishing Group, 1996.

——. "Supplement to 'Provenance Unknown': The Origins of the Golden Dawn," in *The Golden Dawn Source Book*, ed. Darcy Küntz, *Golden Dawn Studies Series*. Edmonds: Holmes Publishing, 1996.

——. "'Two Circles to Gain and Two Squares to Lose': The Golden Dawn in Popular Fiction." In *Secret Texts: The Literature of Secret Societies*, edited by Marie Mulvey and Ormsby-Lennin Roberts, Hugh. New York: AMS Press, 1995.

——, ed. *Hermetic Papers of A. E. Waite: The Unknown Writings of a Modern Mystic, Roots of the Golden Dawn Series*. Wellingborough: The Aquarian Press, 1987.

Giles, Cynthia. *The Tarot: History, Mystery and Lore*. New York: Paragon House, 1992.

Godwin, Joscelyn. "Introduction." In *Hypnerotomachia Polophili: The Strife of Love in a Dream*, edited by Francesco Colonna, vii–xvii. London: Thames & Hudson, 1999.

Godwin, Malcolm. *The Holy Grail: Its Origins, Secrets, and Meaning Revealed*. London: Bloomsbury, 1994.

Godwin, Peter. "Gypsies the Outsiders." *National Geographic* 199, no. 4 (2001): 72–79.

Goggin, Joyce. "A History of Otherness: Tarot and Playing Cards from Early Modern Europe." *Journal for the Academic Study of Magic* 1, no. 1 (2003): 45-74.

Golowin, Sergius. *The World of Tarot: The Gypsy Method of Reading the Tarot.* York Beach: Samuel Weiser, Inc., 1988.

Gombrich, E. H. *Symbolic Images: Studies in the Art of the Renaissance II.* Third ed. Vol. II. Oxford: Phaidon, 1985.

Goodman, Dena. *The Republic of Letters: A Cultural History of the French Enlightenment.* Ithaca: Cornell University Press, 1994.

Grafton, Anthony. "Starry Messengers: Recent Work in the History of Western Astrology." *Perspectives on Science* 8, no. 1 (2000): 70-83.

Gray, Eden. *The Complete Guide to the Tarot.* New York: Bantam, 1972.

Greene, Thomas M. "Magic and Festivity at the Renaissance Court: The 1987 Josephine Waters Bennett Lecture." *Renaissance Quarterly* 40, no. 4 (1987): 636-59.

Greer, Mary Katherine "Healing Emotional Pain with the Tarot." In *New Thoughts on Tarot: Transcripts from the First International Newcastle Tarot Symposium,* edited by Mary K. Greer and Rachel Pollack, 73-91. North Hollywood: Newcastle Publishing Co., 1989.

———. *Women of the Golden Dawn: Rebels and Priestesses.* Rochester: Park Street Press, 1995.

Greer, Mary Katherine, and Rachel Pollack, eds. *New Thoughts on Tarot: Transcripts from the First International Newcastle Tarot Symposium.* North Hollywood: Newcastle Publishing Co., Inc., 1989.

Gresham, William Lindsay. *Nightmare Alley.* London: William Heineman Ltd, 1947.

Gundersheimer, Werner L. *Ferrara: The Style of a Renaissance Despotism.* Princeton: Princeton University Press, 1973.

———. "Renaissance Concepts of Shame and Pocaterra's Dialoghi Della Vergogna." *Renaissance Quarterly* 47, no. 1 (1994): 34-56.

Haindl, Hermann. *Haindl Tarot Deck.* New York: U. S. Games Systems, 1990.

Hall, James. *Dictionary of Subjects and Symbols in Art.* London: John Murray, 1974.

Hall, Judy. *The Illustrated Guide to Divination.* New York: Godsfield Press, 2000.

Hamaker-Zondag, Karen. *Tarot as a Way of Life: A Jungian Approach to the Tarot.* York Beack: Samuel Weiser, 1997.

Hanafi, Zakiya. *The Monster in the Machine: Magic, Medicine, and the Marvellous in the Time of the Scientific Revolution.* Durham: Duke University Press, 2000.

Hanegraaff, Wouter J. "Empirical Method in the Study of Esotericism." *Methods and Theory in the Study of Religion* 7, no. 2 (1995): 99-129.

———. "Introduction: The Birth of a Discipline." In *Western Esotericism and the Science of Religion,* edited by Antoine Faivre and Wouter J. Hanegraaff. Bondgenotenlaan: Peeters, 1998.

———. *New Age Religion and Western Culture: Esotericism in the Mirror of Secular Thought.* Edited by David Appelbaum, *SUNY Series, Western Esoteric Traditions.* New York: State University of New York Press, 1998.

——. "Some Remarks on the Study of Western Esotericism." *Esoterica* 1 (1999): 3-19.

——. "The Study of Western Esotericism: New Approaches to Christian and Secular Culture." In *New Approaches to the Study of Religion: Regional, Critical, and Historical Approaches*, edited by Peter Antes, Armin W. Geertz and Randi R. Warne, 489-519. Berlin: Walter de Gruyter, 2004.

Hargrave, Catherine Perry. *A History of Playing Cards and a Bibliography of Cards and Gaming.* New York: Dover Publications, Inc., 1966.

Harper, George Mills, ed. *Yeats and the Occult.* Edited by Robert O'Driscoll and Lorna Reynolds, *Yeats Studies Series.* London: The Macmillan Press Ltd, 1976.

Harris, John Wesley. *Medieval Theatre in Context.* New York: Routledge, 1992.

Harris, Marguerite Frieda. "Exhibition of 78 Paintings of the Tarot Cards." In *Instructions for Aleister Crowley's Thoth Tarot Deck*, edited by James Wasserman, 34-49. Stamford: U. S. Games Systems, Inc., 1978.

——. "Exhibition of Playing Cards: The Tarot (Book of Thoth)." In *Instructions for Aleister Crowley's Thoth Tarot Deck*, edited by James Wasserman, 19-33. Stamford, 1978.

Harvey, David Allen. "Beyond Enlightenment: Occultism, Politics, and Culture in France from the Old Regime to the Fin-De-Siècle." *The Historian* 65, no. 3 (2003): 665-94.

Hay, Denys. *The Church in Italy in the Fifteenth Century: The Birbeck Lectures, 1971.* Cambridge: Cambridge University Press, 1977.

——. *Italy in the Age of Dante and Petrarch 1216-1380*, ed. Denys Hay, 7 vols., Vol. 2, *A Longman History of Italy* (London: Longman, 1980), 32.

Hay, Denys, and John Law. *Italy in the Age of the Renaissance 1380-1530.* Edited by Denys Hay, *Longman History of Italy.* London: Longman, 1989.

Hearder, Harry. *Italy: A Short History.* Cambridge: Cambridge University Press, 1990.

Heelas, Paul. *The New Age Movement: The Celebration of the Self and the Sacralization of Modernity.* Oxford: Blackwell Publishers, 1996.

Heline, Corinne. *The Bible and the Tarot.* Marina del Rey: De Vorss & Co., 1969. Reprint, Sixth.

Herodotus. *The Histories.* Translated by Aubrey de Sélincourt. Edited by E. V. Rieu. Revised ed, *Penguin Classics.* Harmondsworth: Penguin, 1972.

Hetzel, Basil S. "Iodine and Neuropsychological Development." *Journal of Nutrition* 130, no. 2S (2000): 493-95.

Hibbert, Christopher. *The Rise and Fall of the House of Medici.* Harmondsworth: Penguin Books, 1979. Reprint, Third.

Hillman, Martin. "Telling Fortunes with Cards." *Fate & Fortune* 1974, 16-22.

Hoffmann, Detlef. "Introduction." In *Tarot, Jeu Et Magie*, edited by Thierry Depaulis. Paris: Bibliothèque Nationale, 1984.

——. *The Playing Card: An Illustrated History.* Translated by C. S. V. Salt. Greenwich: New York Graphic Society Ltd, 1973.

Holbein, Hans. *The Dance of Death.* London: Phaidon Press Ltd, 1947.

Hollingsworth, Mary. *Patronage in Renaissance Italy: From 1400 to the Early Sixteenth Century.* Baltimore: The Johns Hopkins University Press, 1994.

Hornung, Erik. *The Secret Lore of Egypt: Its Impact on the West*. Translated by David Lorton. Ithaca: Cornell University Press, 2001.

Howe, Ellic. "Fringe Masonry in England, 1870-85." *Ars Quatuor Coronatorum* 85 (1972): 242-95.

——. *The Magicians of the Golden Dawn: A Documentary History of a Magical Order 1887-1923*. London: Routledge and Kegan Paul, 1972.

Hughes, Robert. *Heaven and Hell in Western Art*. London: Weidenfeld and Nicolson, 1968.

Huizinga, Johan. *The Autumn of the Middle Ages*. Translated by Rodney J. Payton and Ulrich Mammitzsch. Chicago: University of Chicago Press, 1996.

Hulme, F. Edward. *The History, Principles and Practice of Symbolism in Christian Art*. London: Swan Sonnenschein & Co., 1908.

Huppert, George. *After the Black Death: A Social History of Early Modern Europe*. Edited by Harvey J. Graff, *Interdisciplinary Studies in History*. Bloomington: Indiana University Press, 1986.

Huson, Paul. *The Devil's Picturebook: The Compleat Guide to Tarot Cards: Their Origins and Their Usage*. London: Sphere Books Ltd, 1972.

——. *Mystical Origins of the Tarot: From Ancient Roots to Modern Usage*. Rochester: Destiny Books, 2004.

Hutton, Ronald. *The Triumph of the Moon: A History of Modern Pagan Witchcraft*. Oxford: Oxford University Press, 1999.

Ianziti, Gary. *Humanistic Historiography under the Sforzas: Politics and Propaganda in Fifteenth-Century Milan*. Oxford: Clarendon Press, 1988.

Irwin, Robert. *The Middle East in the Middle Ages: The Early Mamluk Sultanate 1250-1382*. London: Croom Helm, 1986.

Jacob, Margaret C. *The Origins of Freemasonry: Facts & Fictions*. Philadelphia: University of Pennsylvania Press, 2006.

——. *The Radical Enlightenment: Pantheists, Freemasons and Republicans*. Edited by J. H. Shennan, *Early Modern Europe Today*. London: George Allen & Unwin, 1981.

Jacobsen, Machael A. "A Sforza Miniature by Cristoforo Da Preda." *Burlington Magazine* 116, no. 851 (1974): 91-96.

Janson, Horst W. "A 'Memento Mori' among Early Italian Prints." *Journal of the Warburg and Courtauld Institutes* 3, no. 3/4 (1940): 243-48.

Jayanti, Amber. *Tarot for Dummies*. Edited by Joan L. Friedman, *For Dummies*. New York: Hungry Minds, 2001.

Jenkins, Marianna. "The Iconography of the Hall of the Consistory in the Palazzo Pubblico, Siena." *Art Bulletin* 54, no. 4 (1972): 430-51.

Jette, Christine. *Tarot for the Healing Heart: Using Inner Wisdom to Heal Body and Mind*. St Paul: Llewellyn Publications, 2001.

Jorgensen, Danny L. *The Esoteric Scene, Cultic Milieu, and Occult Tarot*. Edited by J. Gordon Melton, *Cults and Nonconventional Religious Groups: A Collection of Outstanding Dissertations and Monographs*. New York: Garland Publishing, Inc., 1992.

K, Amber, and Azrael Arynn K. *Heart of Tarot: An Intuitive Approach*. St Paul: Llewellyn Publications, 2002.

Kaplan, Stuart R. *The Classical Tarot: Its Origins, Meanings and Divinatory Use.* Wellingborough: The Aquarian Press Limited, 1980.

———. *The Encyclopedia of Tarot.* IV vols. Vol. I. New York: U. S. Games Systems, 1978. Reprint, Second.

———. *The Encyclopedia of Tarot.* IV vols. Vol. II. New York: U. S. Games Systems, 1986. Reprint, Second.

———. *The Encyclopedia of Tarot.* IV vols. Vol. III. Stamford: U.S. Games Systems, Inc., 2002.

———. *Fortune-Telling with Tarot Cards: An Illustrated Guide to Spreading and Interpreting the 1JJ Tarot, Fortune-Telling With ...* London: Diamond Books, 1995.

———. *Tarot Classic.* New York: U. S. Games Systems, 1972.

Kaplan, Stuart R., and Jean Huets. *The Encyclopedia of Tarot.* IV vols. Vol. IV. Stamford: U. S. Games Systems, Inc., 2005.

Katz, David S. *The Occult Tradition: From the Renaissance to the Present Day.* London: Jonathan Cape, 2005.

Katzenellenbogen, Adolf. *Allegories of the Virtues and Vices in Medieval Art from Early Christian Times to the Thirteenth Century.* New York: W. W. Norton and Company Inc., 1964.

Kelly, Aidan A. "An Update on Neopagan Witchcraft in America." In *Perspectives on the New Age*, edited by James R. Lewis and J. Gordon Melton, 136–51. Albany: State University of New York Press, 1992.

Kelly, J. N. D. *Pope Joan* [Oxford Reference Online]. Oxford Dictionary of Popes: Oxford University Press, 1991 [cited 21 March 2006]. Available from http://www.oxfordreference.com/.

Kemp, Daren. *New Age: A Guide - Alternative Spiritualities from Aquarian Conspiracy to Next Age.* Edinburgh: Edinburgh University Press, 2004.

Kemp, Gillian. *The Fortune-Telling Book.* London: Orion, 2001.

———. *The Romany Good Spell Book.* London: Vista, 1997.

Kendall, M. G. "Studies in the History of Probability and Statistics. V. A Note on Playing Cards." *Biometrika* 44, no. 1/2 (1957): 260–62.

Khayyám, Omar. *The Rubaiyat of Omar Khayyám.* Translated by Edward Fitzgerald. London: George G. Harrap and Co. Ltd, c1930.

Kibre, Pearl. "The Intellectual Interests Reflected in the Libraries of the Fourteenth and Fifteenth Centuries." *Journal of the History of Ideas* 7, no. 3 (1946): 257–97.

Kieckhefer, Richard. *Magic in the Middle Ages, Cambridge Medieval Textbooks.* Cambridge: Cambridge University Press, 1989.

King, Francis. "Introduction." In *Astral Projection, Ritual Magic, and Alchemy: Golden Dawn Material by S.L. Macgregor Mathers and Others*, edited by Francis King. Rochester: Destiny Books, 1987.

———. *Modern Ritual Magic: The Rise of Western Occultism.* Bridport: Prism Press, 1989.

———. "The Origins of the Golden Dawn." In *The Golden Dawn Source Book*, edited by Darcy Küntz, 123–24. Edmonds: Holmes Publishing Group, 1996.

——. *Ritual Magic in England: 1887 to the Present Day*. London: Neville Spearman, 1970.

——, ed. *Astral Projection, Ritual Magic, and Alchemy: Golden Dawn Material by S.L. Macgregor Mathers and Others*. Rochester: Destiny Books, 1987.

Kingsford, Anna Bonus, and Edward Maitland. *The Perfect Way, or, the Finding of Christ*. Fifth ed. London: J. M. Watkins, 1923.

Kinser, Samuel. "Why Is Carnival So Wild?" In *Carnival and the Carnivalesque: The Fool, the Reformer, the Wildman, and Others in Early Modern Theatre*, edited by Konrad Eisenbichler and Wim Hüsken, 43-88. Amsterdam: Rodopi, 1999.

Klein, Robert. "Les Tarots Enluminé Du XVᵉ Siècle." *L'Oeil*, no. 145 (1967): 10-17, 51-52.

Knowles, Elizabeth, ed. *The Oxford Dictionary of Quotations*. Sixth ed. Oxford: Oxford University Press, 2004.

Kopp, Sheldon. *The Hanged Man: Psychotherapy and the Forces of Darkness*. Palo Alto: Science and Behavior Books, 1974.

Kristeller, Paul Oskar. *The Classics and Renaissance Thought, Martin Classical Lectures*. Cambridge: Harvard University Press, 1955.

Kulke, Hermann, and Dietmar Rothermund. *A History of India*. Third ed. Routledge: London, 1998.

Küntz, Darcy. "Cross-Index of Golden Dawn Members and Mottoes." In *The Golden Dawn Source Book*, edited by Darcy Küntz, 177-221. Edmonds: Holmes Publishing Company, 1996.

——, ed. *The Complete Golden Dawn Cipher Manuscript*. Edited by Darcy Kuntz, *Golden Dawn Studies Series*. Edmonds: Holmes Publishing Group, 1996.

——, ed. *The Golden Dawn Court Cards as Drawn by William Wynn Westcott & Moïna Mathers*. Edited by Darcy Küntz, *Golden Dawn Studies Series*. Edmonds: Holmes Publishing Group, 1996.

——, ed. *The Golden Dawn Source Book*. Edited by Darcy Küntz, *Golden Dawn Studies Series*. Edmonds: Holmes Publishing Group, 1996.

Laird, Peter. *The Official Teenage Mutant Ninja Turtles Website!* [website]. Mirage Publishing, Inc., 22 February 2006 [cited 2 March 2006]. Available from http://www.ninjaturtles.com/.

Lal, Chaman. *Gipsies: Forgotten Children of India*. Deli: Government of India Press, 1962.

Lammey, William C. "What Is Karmic Tarot?" In *New Thoughts on Tarot: Transcripts from the First International Newcastle Tarot Symposium*, edited by Mary K. Greer and Rachel Pollack, 109-22. North Hollywood: Newcastle Publishing Co., 1989.

Lane, Frederic C. *Venice: A Maritime Republic*. Baltimore: The Johns Hopkins University Press, 1973.

Langland, William. *Piers Plowman*. Revised ed. 3 vols. Vol. 1. London: Athlone Press, 1997.

Larner, John. *Culture and Society in Italy 1290-1420*. London: B. T. Batsford Ltd, 1971.

——. *Italy in the Age of Dante and Petrarch 1216-1380*. Edited by Denys Hay. 7 vols. Vol. 2, *A Longman History of Italy*. London: Longman, 1980.

Lea, Henry Charles. *A History of the Inquisition of the Middle Ages*. The Harbor Scholars' Classics Edition ed. IV vols. Vol. I. New York: S A Russell Publishers, 1955. Reprint, Second.

———. *A History of the Inquisition of the Middle Ages*. The Harbor Scholars' Classics Edition ed. IV vols. Vol. III. New York: S A Russell Publishers, 1955. Reprint, Second.

Leclercq, Dom Jean, Dom François Vandenbroucke, and Louis Bouyer. *The Spirituality of the Middle Ages*. Translated by The Benedictines of Holme Eden Abbey. 2 vols. Vol. 2. New York: Seabury Press, 1986.

Ledger, Sally, and Roger Luckhurst, eds. *The Fin De Siècle: A Reader in Cultural History C. 1880-1900*. Oxford: Oxford University Press, 2000.

Leland, Charles Godfrey. *Aradia: The Gospel of the Witches*. London: C. W. Daniel Company, 1974.

Lessa, William Armand. "Somatomancy: Precursor of the Science of Human Constitution." In *Reader in Comparative Religion: An Anthropological Approach*, edited by William Armand Lessa and Evon Z. Vogt, 314-26. Evanston: Row, Peterson and Company, 1958.

Lessa, William Armand, and Evon Z. Vogt, eds. *Reader in Comparative Religion: An Anthropological Approach*. Evanston: Row, Peterson and Company, 1958.

Lévi, Éliphas. *Transcendental Magic: Its Doctrine and Ritual*. Translated by Arthur Edward Waite. Revised ed. London: Rider and Company, 1958.

Levron, Jacques. *Le Diable Dans L'art*. Paris: Éditions Auguste Picard, 1935.

Lewis, James R. "Approaches to the Study of the New Age Movement." In *Perspectives on the New Age*, edited by James R. Lewis and J. Gordon Melton, 1-14. Albany: State University of New York Press, 1992.

Lewis, James R., and J. Gordon Melton. "Introduction." In *Perspectives on the New Age*, edited by James R. Lewis and J. Gordon Melton, ix-xii. Albany: State University of New York Press, 1992.

———, eds. *Perspectives on the New Age*. Edited by Harold Coward, *SUNY Series in Religious Studies*. Albany: State University of New York Press, 1992.

Lilley, Keith D. "Cities of God? Medieval Urban Forms and Their Christian Symbolism." *Transactions of the Institute of British Geographers* 29, no. 3 (2004): 296-313.

Link, Luther. *The Devil: A Mask without a Face*. Edited by Peter Burke, Sander L. Gilman, Roy Porter and Bob Scribner, *Picturing History*. London: Reaktion Books, 1995.

———. *The Devil: The Archfiend in Art from the Sixth to the Sixteenth Century*. New York: Harry N. Abrams, Inc., 1996.

Little, Tom Tadfor. *The Hermitage: Tarot History* [website]. 2001 [cited 5 April 2004]. Available from http://www.tarothermit.com/.

Littmann, Enno. *Die Erzählungen Aus Den Tausendundein Nächten: Vollständige Deutsche Ausgabe in Sechs Bänden. Zum Ersten Mal Nach Dem Arabischen Urtext Der Calcuttaer Ausgabe Vom Jahre 1839*. VI vols. Vol. III. Insel: Weisbaden, 1924.

Lo Scarabeo. *Tarot of Marseille*. Torino: Lo Scarabeo, 2000.

Loomis, Roger Sherman. "The Allegorical Siege in the Art of the Middle Ages." *American Journal of Archaeology* 23, no. 3 (1919): 255-69.

——, ed. *Arthurian Literature in the Middle Ages: A Collaborative History.* Oxford: Clarendon Press, 1959.

Lord of the Wind Films. *What the Bleep* [website]. Lord of the Wind Films, 18 May 2004 [cited 18 July 2006]. Available from http://www. whatthebleep.com.

Lorelei, Lady. *Tarot Life Planner: Change Your Destiny and Enrich Your Life.* London: Hamlyn, 2004.

Lovelock, Jim E. *Gaia: A New Look at Life on Earth.* Oxford: Oxford University Press, 2000.

Luhrmann, Tanya M. *Persuasions of the Witch's Craft: Ritual Magic in Contemporary England.* Cambridge: Harvard University Press, 1989.

Lynn, Michael R. "Enlightenment in the Public Sphere: The Musée De Monsieur and Scientific Culture in Late Eighteenth-Century Paris." *Eighteenth-Century Studies* 32, no. 4 (1999): 463-76.

Machiavelli, Niccolò. *The Prince.* Translated by George Bull. Edited by E. V. Rieu, *Penguin Classics.* Harmondsworth: Penguin Books, 1961. Reprint, twenty-second.

Mandel, Gabriele. *Les Tarots Des Visconti.* Paris: Vilo, 1974.

Mann, A. T. *The Secrets of the Tarot: A Guide to Inner Wisdom.* London: Thorsons, 2002.

Mann, Sylvia. *Collecting Playing Cards.* New ed. London: Howard Baker Press, 1973.

Marshall, Peter. *The Philosopher's Stone: A Quest for the Secrets of Alchemy.* London: Macmillan, 2001.

Marsilli, Pietro. "I Tarocchi Nella Vita Di Società, La Vita Di Società Nei Tarocchi." In *I Tarocchi : Le Carte Di Corte : Bioco E Magia Alla Corte Degli Estensi,* edited by Giordano Berti and Andrea Vitali, 95-110. Bologna: Nuova Alfa, 1987.

Marteau, Paul. *Le Tarot De Marseille.* Paris: Arts et Métiers Graphiques, 1949.

Martin, David. *A General Theory of Secularization.* Edited by Philip Rieff and Bryan R. Wilson, *Explorations in Interpretative Sociology.* Oxford: Basil Blackwell, 1978.

Martinié, Louis, and Sallie Ann Glassman. *The New Orleans Voodoo Tarot.* Rochester: Destiny Books, 1992.

Mathers, Samuel Liddell MacGregor. "A Description of the Cards of the Tarot." *Equinox* 1, no. 8 (1912): 144-214.

——. "On the Tarot Trumps." In *The Complete Golden Dawn Cipher Manuscript,* edited by Darcy Küntz, 175-78. Edmonds: Holmes Publishing Group, 1996.

——. *The Tarot: Its Occult Signification, Use in Fortune-Telling, and Method of Play, Etc.* New York: S. Weiser, 1969.

Maxwell, Joseph. *The Tarot.* Translated by Ivor Powell. Saffron Walden: C. W. Daniel Company Limited, 1975.

Maxwell-Stuart, P. G., ed. *The Occult in Early Modern Europe: A Documentary History.* Edited by Jeremy Black, *Documents in History Series.* Houndmills: Macmillan Press Ltd, 1999.

McCalla, Arthur. "The Structure of French Romantic Histories of Religions." *Numen* 45, no. 3 (1998): 258–86.

McDaniel, Mark A., and Michael Pressley, eds. *Imagery and Related Mnemonic Processes: Theories, Individual Differences, and Applications.* New York: Springer-Verlag, 1987.

McIntosh, Christopher. *The Astrologers and Their Creed: An Historical Outline.* London: Arrow Books, 1971.

——. *Éliphas Lévi and the French Occult Revival.* London: Rider and Company, 1972.

——. *The Rosicrucians: The History, Mythology, and Rituals of an Esoteric Order.* Third Revised ed. York Beach: Samuel Weiser, Inc., 1997.

Medway, Gareth. "Aurora Mysteriorum." In *The Golden Dawn Source Book*, edited by Darcy Küntz, 161–67. Edmonds: Holmes Publishing Group, 1996.

Meiss, Millard. "The Madonna of Humility." *Art Bulletin* 18, no. 4 (1936): 435–65.

Melanchthon. "Initia Doctrinae Physicae." In *The Occult in Early Modern Europe: A Documentary History*, edited by P. G. Maxwell-Stuart. Houndmills: Macmillan, 1999.

Mellinkoff, Ruth. *Outcasts: Signs of Otherness in Northern European Art of the Late Middle Ages.* Edited by Walter Horn. 2 vols. Vol. 1: Text, *California Studies in the History of Art.* Berkeley: University of California Press, 1993.

——. *Outcasts: Signs of Otherness in Northern European Art of the Late Middle Ages.* Edited by Walter Horn. 2 vols. Vol. 1: Illustrations, *California Studies in the History of Art.* Berkeley: University of California Press, 1993.

Melton, J. Gordon. "New Thought and the New Age." In *Perspectives on the New Age*, edited by James R. Lewis and J. Gordon Melton, 15–29. Albany: State University of New York Press, 1992.

Merback, Mitchell B. *The Thief, the Cross and the Wheel: Pain and the Spectacle of Punishment in Medieval and Renaissance Europe.* Edited by Peter Burke, Sander L. Gilman, Roy Porter and Bob Scribner, *Picturing History.* London: Reaktion Books, 1999.

Merkel, Ingrid, and Allen G. Debus, eds. *Hermeticism and the Renaissance: Intellectual History and the Occult in Early Modern Europe.* Edited by Barbara A. Mowat, *Folger Institute Symposia.* Washington: Folger Shakespeare Library, 1988.

Merlin, R. *Origine Des Cartes a Jouer, Recherches Nouvelles Sur Les Naïbis, Les Tarots Et Sur Les Autres Espèces De Cartes, Ouvrage Accompagnè D'un Album De Soixante-Quatorze Planches.* Paris: R. Merlin, 1869.

Meyrink, Gustav. *The Golem.* Translated by Madge Pemberton. London: Victor Gollancz Ltd, 1928.

Moakley, Gertrude. *The Tarot Cards Painted by Bonifacio Bembo for the Visconti-Sforza Family: An Iconographic and Historical Study.* New York: The New York Public Library, 1966.

Monter, William. *Ritual, Myth and Magic in Early Modern Europe*. Athens: Ohio University Press, 1984.

Moon, Beverly, ed. *An Encyclopedia of Archetypal Symbolism*. Boston: Shambhala, 1991.

Moore, Virginia. *The Unicorn: William Butler Yeats' Search for Reality*. New York: Octagon Books, 1973.

Morgan, Diane. *Magical Tarot, Mystical Tao: Unlocking the Hidden Power of the Tarot Using the Ancient Secrets of the Tao Te Ching*. New York: St Martin's Griffin, 2003.

Morgan, Ffiona. *Daughters of the Moon Tarot*. Boulder: Daughters of the Moon, 1984.

Morley, H. T. *Old and Curious Playing Cards: Their History and Types from Many Countries and Periods*. Secaucus: The Wellfleet Press, 1989.

Muchembled, Robert. *A History of the Devil from the Middle Ages to the Present*. Translated by Jean Birrell. Cambridge: Polity Press, 2003.

Muir, Dorothy. *A History of Milan under the Visconti*. London: Methuen & Co. Ltd., 1924.

Murray, H. J. R. *A History of Board Games Other Than Chess*. Oxford: Clarendon Press, 1952.

Newbigin, Lesslie. *Honest Religion for Secular Man*. London: SCM Press Ltd, 1966.

Newman, Barbara. "The Heretic Saint: Gugliema of Bohemia, Milan, and Brunate." *Church History* 74, no. 1 (2005): 1-38.

Niccoli, Ottavia. *Prophecy and People in Renaissance Italy*. Translated by Lydia G. Cochrane. Princeton: Princeton University Press, 1990.

Nicholas, David. *The Transformation of Europe 1300-1600, The Arnold History of Europe*. London: Arnold, 1999.

Nichols, Sallie. *Jung and Tarot: An Archetypal Journey*. New York: Samuel Weiser, 1980.

Noble, Vicki. *Motherpeace: A Way to the Goddess through Myth, Art, and Tarot*. San Francisco: Harper, 1994.

Noyes, Ella. *The Story of Ferrara, Mediaeval Towns*. Nendeln: Kraus Reprint, 1970.

Nutt, Alfred. *Studies on the Legend of the Holy Grail with Especial Reference to the Hypothesis of Its Celtic Origin*. New York: Cooper Square Publishers, Inc., 1965.

O'Donoghue, Freeman M. *Catalogue of the Collection of Playing Cards Bequeathed to the Trustees of the British Museum by the Late Lady Charlotte Schreiber*. London: Longmans and Co., 1901.

Olderidge, Darren. "Protestant Conceptions of the Devil in Early Stuart England." *History* 85, no. 278 (2000): 232-46.

Olsen, Christina. *The Art of Tarot, A Tiny Folio*. New York: Abbeville Press, 1995.

——. "Carte Da Trionfi: The Development of Tarot in Fifteenth Century Italy." Ph.D., University of Pennsylvania, 1994.

O'Meara, Thomas F. "Virtues in the Theology of Thomas Aquinas." *Theological Studies* 58, no. 2 (1997): 254-85.

O'Neill, Robert V. *Iconology of the Star Cards* [website]. Visionary Networks, 2006 [cited 7 March 2006]. Available from http://www.tarot.com.

——. *Iconology of the World Cards* [website]. Visionary Networks, 2006 [cited 7 March 2006]. Available from http://www.tarot.com.

——. *Tarot Symbolism*. Lima: Fairway Press, 1986.

O'Reilly, Jennifer. *Studies in the Iconography of the Virtues and Vices in the Middle Ages*. New York: Garland Publishing, Inc., 1988.

Orloff, Alexander. *Carnival: Myth and Cult*. Wörgl: Perlinger Verlag, 1980.

Ortalli, Gherardo. "The Prince and the Playing Cards: The Este Family and the Role of Courts at the Time of the Kartenspiel-Invasion." *Ludica: annali di storia e civilta del gioco* 2 (1996): 175–205.

Ouspensky, Leonid A., and Vladimir Lossky. *The Meaning of Icons*. Translated by G. E. H. Palmer and E. K. Kadloubovsky. Revised ed. Crestwood: St Vladimir's Seminary Press, 1982. Reprint, Third.

Ouspensky, P. D. *The Symbolism of the Tarot: Philosophy of Occultism in Pictures and Numbers*. Translated by A. L. Pogossky. New York: Dover Publications, Inc., 1976.

Owen, Alex. *The Darkened Room: Women, Power and Spiritualism in Late Victorian England*. London: Virago Press, 1989.

——. *The Place of Enchantment: British Occultism and the Culture of the Modern*. Chicago: University of Chicago Press, 2004.

Oxford English Dictionary (Second) [website]. Oxford University Press, 2005 [cited 18 August 2005]. Available from http://dictionary.oed.com.

Padma, Ma Deva, and Osho. *Osho Zen Tarot: The Transcendental Game of Zen*. Second ed. New York: St Martin's Press, 1994.

Palla, Maria José. "Carnaval, Parvo Et "Monde À L'envers" Chez Gil Vincente." In *Carnival and the Carnivalesque: The Fool, the Reformer, the Wildman, and Others in Early Modern Theatre*, edited by Konrad Eisenbichler and Wim Hüsken, 165–82. Amsterdam: Rodopi, 1999.

Panofsky, Erwin. *Renaissance and Renascences in Western Art*. New York: Harper Row, 1972.

——. *Studies in Iconology: Humanistic Themes in the Art of the Renaissance*. New York: Harper & Row, 1972.

Panofsky, Erwin, and Fritz Saxl. "A Late Antique Religious Symbol in Works by Holbein and Titian." *Burlington Magazine for Connoisseurs* 49, no. 283 (1926): 177–81.

Pardoe, Rosemary, and Darroll Pardoe. *The Female Pope: The Mystery of Pope Joan*. Wellingborough: Crucible, 1998.

Park, John. "A Cosmological Tarot Hypothesis - Virtue Triumphant: The Seven Virtues V. The Seven Mortal Sins." *The Playing Card* 31, no. 3 (2002): 127–33.

Park, Katherine, and Lorraine J. Daston. "Unnatural Conceptions: The Study of Monsters in Sixteenth- and Seventeenth-Century France and England." *Past and Present*, no. 92 (1981): 20–54.

Patrides, C. A. "Renaissance and Modern Thought on the Last Things: A Study in Changing Conceptions." *Harvard Theological Review* 51, no. 3 (1958): 169–85.

Pavic, Milorad. *Last Love in Constantinople: A Tarot Novel for Divination*. Translated by Christina Pribichevich-Zoric. London: Peter Owen, 1998.

Pellegrin, Elisabeth. *La Bibliothèque Des Visconti Et Des Sforza Ducs De Milan, Au XV Siecle, Publications De L'institut De Recherche Et D'histoire Des Textes.* Paris: Service des Publications du C. N. R. S., 1955.

Pert, Alan. *Red Cactus: The Life of Anna Kingsford,* Watson's Bay: Books & Writers, 2006.

Peterson, Joseph H. *Twilit Grotto: Archives of Western Esoterica* [website]. Peterson, Joseph H., 2 September 2005 [cited 12 September 2005]. Available from http://www.esotericarchives.com.

Petrarch, Francesco. *The Triumphs of Petrarch.* Translated by Ernest Hatch Wilkins. Chicago: The University of Chicago Press, 1962.

Philipp, Thomas, and Ulrich Haarmann, eds. *The Mamluks in Egyptian Politics and Society.* Edited by David Morgan, *The Cambridge Studies in Islamic Civilization.* Cambridge: Cambridge University Press, 1998.

Phillips, Mark. "A Newly Discovered Chronicle by Marco Parenti." *Renaissance Quarterly* 31, no. 2 (1978): 153-60.

Pitois, Jean-Baptiste. *The History and Practice of Magic.* Translated by James Kirkup and Julian Shaw. II vols. London: Forge Press, 1952.

Place, Robert M. *The Tarot: History, Symbolism, and Divination.* New York: Jeremy P. Tarcher/Penguin, 2005.

Plato. *The Republic.* Translated by Desmond Lee. Edited by Betty Radice. Second ed, *Penguin Classics.* London: London, 2003.

Pollack, Rachel. *The New Tarot.* Wellingborough: The Aquarian Press, 1989.

——. "An Overview of the Variety of New Tarot Decks: Emphasis on European Decks." In *New Thoughts on Tarot: Transcripts from the First International Tarot Symposium,* edited by Mary K. Greer and Rachel Pollack, 123-39. North Hollywood: Newcastle Publishing, 1989.

Powell, Ivor. "Introduction." In *The Tarot,* edited by Joseph Maxwell. Saffron Walden: C. W. Daniel Company Limited, 1975.

Pratesi, Franco. "Italian Cards - New Discoveries: 9. Tarot in Bologna: Documents from the University Library." *The Playing Card* XXVII (1989): 136-46.

——. "Italian Cards - New Discoveries: 10. The Earliest Tarot Pack Known." *The Playing Card* XVIII, no. 2 (1989): 33-38.

Preston, Percy. *A Dictionary of Pictorial Subjects from Classical Literature: A Guide to Their Identification in Works of Art.* New York: Charles Scribner's Sons, 1983.

Pullan, Brian. *A History of Early Renaissance Italy from the Mid-Thirteenth to the Mid-Fifteenth Century.* London: Allen Lane, 1973.

Raine, Kathleen. *Yeats, the Tarot and the Golden Dawn.* Edited by Liam Miller, *New Yeats Papers II.* Dublin: Dolmen Press, 1972.

Ranking, Bayard. "The History of Probability and the Changing Concept of the Individual." *Journal of the History of Ideas* 27, no. 4 (1966): 483-504.

Ranking, D. F. de 'Hoste. "The Tarot." *Journal of the Gypsy Lore Society* New Series II (1908): 14-37.

Rasmussen, Mary. "Kulturgeschichte Des Horns (a Pictorial History of the Horn)." *Notes* 35, no. 2 (1978): 320-22.

Read, Piers Paul. *The Templars: The Dramatic History of the Knights Templar, the Most Powerful Military Order of the Crusades.* London: Phoenix Press, 1999.

Regardie, Israel. *The Golden Dawn: A Complete Course in Practical Ceremonial Magic: The Original Account of the Teachings, Rites, and Ceremonies of the Hermetic Order of the Golden Dawn (Stella Matutina) as Revealed by Israel Regardie.* Sixth, revised and enlarged ed, *Llewellyn's Golden Dawn Series.* St Paul: Llewellyn Publications, 1989. Reprint, Tenth.

———. *My Rosicrucian Adventure: A Contribution to a Recent Phase of the History of Magic, and a Study in the Technique of Theurgy.* Chicago: The Aries Press, 1936.

Riches, D. (2003). "Counter-Cultural Egalitarianism: A Comparative Analysis of New Age and Other 'Alternative Communities'." Culture and Religion 4(1): 119–139.

Rickards, Maurice. *The Encyclopedia of Ephemera: A Guide to the Fragmentary Documents of Everyday Life for the Collector, Curator, and Historian.* London: British Library, 2000.

Riordan, Suzanne. "Chaneling: A New Revelation?" In *Perspectives on the New Age,* edited by James R. Lewis and J. Gordon Melton, 105–26. Albany: State University of New York Press, 1992.

Robbins, Rossell Hope. *The Encyclopedia of Witchcraft and Demonology.* London: Peter Nevill Limited, 1959.

Roberts, Marie Mulvey, and Hugh Ormsby-Lennin, eds. *Secret Texts: The Literature of Secret Societies.* Vol. 1, *AMS Studies in Cultural History, No. 1.* New York: AMS Press, 1995.

Roberts, Richard. "Part II: Esoteric Tarot: Symbolism of the Waite/Rider Deck." In *Tarot Revelations,* edited by Richard Roberts, 39–287. San Anselmo: Vernal Equinox Press, 1987.

———, ed. *Tarot Revelations.* Third ed. San Anselmo: Vernal Equinox Press, 1987.

Robertson, D. W., Jr. "The Concept of Courtly Love as an Impediment to the Understanding of Medieval Texts." In *The Meaning of Courtly Love: Papers of the First Annual Conference of the Center for Medieval and Renaissance Studies State University of New York at Binghamton March 17-18, 1967,* edited by F. X. Newman, 1–18. Albany: State University of New York Press, 1968.

Robinson, David M. "The Wheel of Fortune." *Classical Philology* 41, no. 4 (1946): 207–16.

Rosenberg, Charles M. "Piety and Patronage in Renaissance Venice: Bellini, Titian, and the Franciscans." *Italica* 65, no. 3 (1988): 270–74.

Rüdiger, Johann Christian Christoph. *On the Indic Language and the Origin of the Gipsies* [website]. School of Languages, Linguistics and Culture, University of Manchester, 1782 [cited 17 October 2005]. Available from http://ling.uni-graz.at/~romman/downloads/1/ruediger_translation.pdf.

Runciman, Steven. *The Medieval Manichee: A Study of the Christian Dualist Heresy.* Cambridge: Cambridge University Press, 1960.

Runyon, Carroll 'Poke'. "An Analysis of the Cypher Manuscript." In *Secrets of the Golden Dawn Cypher Manuscript*, edited by Carroll 'Poke' Runyon. Silverado: C. H. S., Inc., 2000. Reprint, Second.

———. "The History of the Cypher Manuscript." In *Secrets of the Golden Dawn Cypher Manuscript*, edited by Carroll 'Poke' Runyon. Silverado: C. H. S., Inc., 2000. Reprint, Second.

———. *Secrets of the Golden Dawn Cypher Manuscript.* Silverado: C. H. S., Inc, 2000. Reprint, Second.

Russell, Jeffrey Burton. *Witchcraft in the Middle Ages.* Ithaca: Cornell University Press, 1972.

Sadhu, Mouni. *The Tarot: A Contemporary Course of the Quintessence of Hermetic Occultism.* Hollywood: Melvin Powers Wilshire Book Company, 1962. Reprint, Second.

Salaman, Clement, Dorine van Oyen, and William D. Wharton. *The Way of Hermes: The Corpus Hermeticum.* London: Duckworth, 1999.

Sargent, Carl. *Personality, Divination and the Tarot.* London: Rider, 1988.

Saurat, Denis. *Literature and Occult Tradition: Studies in Philosophical Poetry.* Translated by Dorothy Bolton. Port Washington: Kennikat Press, Inc., 1966.

Scholem, Gershom. *Origins of the Kabbalah.* Translated by Allan Arkush. Philadelphia: Jewish Publication Society, 1987.

Scoville, Thomas, and Hughes Hall. *The Metrosexual Tarot* [website]. Thomas Scoville, 2004 [cited 30 September 2005]. Available from http://www.thomasscoville.com/metrosexual/.

Seabury, William Marston. *The Tarot Cards and Dante's Divine Comedy.* New York: Privately printed, 1951.

Seguin, Jean-Pierre. *Le Jeu De Carte.* Paris: Hermann, 1968.

Senior, John. *The Way Down and Out: The Occult in Symbolist Literature.* New York: Greenwood Press, 1968.

Seznec, Jean. *The Survival of the Pagan Gods: The Mythological Tradition and Its Place in Renaissance Humanism and Art.* Translated by Barbara F. Sessions. Edited by Bollingen Foundation, *Bollingen Series.* Princeton: Princeton University Press, 1972.

Shah, Sayed Idries. *The Sufis.* New York: Anchor Books, 1971.

Shell, Janice. *Zavattari* [Online reference source]. Grove Art Online, Oxford University Press, 2006 [cited 16 February 2006]. Available from http://www.groveart.com/.

Shumaker, Wayne. *The Occult Sciences in the Renaissance: A Study in Intellectual Patterns.* Berkeley: University of California Press, 1972.

Sidgwick, Henry. "Address by the President at the First General Meeting." In *The Fin De Siècle: A Reader in Cultural History, C. 1880–1900*, edited by Sally Ledger and Roger Luckhurst, 272-75. Oxford: Oxford University Press, 2000.

Sill, Gertrude Grace. *A Handbook of Symbols in Christian Art.* New York: Touchstone, 1996.

Singer, Samuel Weller. *Researches into the History of Playing Cards; with Illustrations of the Origin of Printing and Engraving on Wood.* London: R. Triphook, 1816.

Singleton, Charles S. "On Meaning in the Decameron." *Italica* 21, no. 3 (1944): 117–24.

Smalley, Beryl. *English Friars and Antiquity in the Early Fourteenth Century.* Oxford: Basil Blackwell, 1960.

Smith, F. Harold. *Outline of Hinduism.* Edited by Eric S. Waterhouse, *Great Religions of the East.* London: The Epworth Press, 1934.

Smith, Pamela Colman, and Arthur Edward Waite. "Rider Tarot." Neuhausen: AGMüller, 1971.

Sobel, Robert. *The French Revolution: A Concise History and Interpretation.* Gloucester: Peter Smith, 1967.

Society for Psychical Research. "Objects of the Society." In *The Fin De Siècle: A Reader in Cultural History, C. 1880-1900,* edited by Sally Ledger and Roger Luckhurst, 271–72. Oxford: Oxford University Press, 2000.

Stark, Rodney, and William Sims Bainbridge. *The Future of Religion: Secularization, Revival and Cult Formation.* Berkeley: University of California Press, 1985.

Starkie, Walter. "Carmen and the Tarots." *American Record Guide* 31, no. 1 (1964): 4–9.

Steele, Robert. "A Notice of the *Ludus Triumphorum* and Some Early Italian Card Games; with Some Remarks on the Origin of the Game of Cards." *Archaeologia, or, Miscellaneous Tracts Relating to Antiquity* 57 (1900): 185–200.

Steffler, Alva William. *Symbols of the Christian Faith.* Grand Rapids: William B. Eerdmans Publishing Company, 2002.

Steinitz, Kate T. "The Tarot Cards Painted by Bonifacio Bembo: An Iconographic and Historical Study [Review]." *Art Bulletin* 51, no. 2 (1969): 188–89.

Stephens, John. *The Italian Renaissance: The Origins of Intellectual and Artistic Change before the Reformation.* London: Longman, 1990.

Stevenson, David. *The Origins of Freemasonry: Scotland's Century, 1590-1710.* Cambridge: Cambridge University Press, 1988.

Strathern, Paul. *The Medici: Godfathers of the Renaissance.* London: Random House, 2003.

Summers, Catherine, and Julian Vayne. *Personal Development with the Tarot.* London: Quantum, 2002.

Surette, Leon. *The Birth of Modernism: Ezra Pound, T.S. Eliot, W.B. Yeats and the Occult.* Montreal: McGill-Queen's University Press, 1994.

Symonds, John. *The Great Beast: The Life of Aleister Crowley.* London: Rider and Company, 1951. Reprint, Fifth.

———. "Introduction." In *The Confessions of Aleister Crowley: An Autohagiography,* edited by John Symonds and Kenneth Grant, 13–25. London: Arkana, 1979.

Tacey, David. *Jung and the New Age.* Hove: Brunner-Routledge, 2001.

Taylor, Ed S. *The History of Playing Cards, with Anecdotes of Their Use in Conjuring, Fortune-Telling, and Card Sharping.* London: John Camden Hotten, 1865.

Thomas, Keith. *Religion and the Decline of Magic: Studies in Popular Beliefs in Sixteenth and Seventeenth Century England.* London: Wiedenfeld and Nicolson, 1971. Reprint, Second.

Thompson, C. J. S. *The Mystery and Lore of Monsters with Accounts of Some Giants, Dwarfs and Prodigies.* New York: University Books, 1968.

Thomson, Sandra A. *Pictures from the Heart: A Tarot Dictionary.* New York: St Martin's Griffin, 2003.

Thorndike, Lynn. *The History of Medieval Europe.* Third ed. Cambridge: Houghton Mifflin Company, 1945.

——. "Robertus Anglicus and the Introduction of Demons and Magic into Commentaries Upon the Sphere of Sacrobosco." *Speculum* 21, no. 2 (1946): 241–43.

——. "Some Medieval Conceptions of Magic." *The Monist* XXV (1966): 107–39.

Tilley, Roger. *A History of Playing Cards.* London: Studio Vista, 1973.

Toesca, Pietro. *La Pittura E La Miniatura Nella Lombardia Dai Più Antichi Monumenti Alla Metà Del Quattrocento.* Milano: Istituto editoriale Cisalpino-La Goliardica, 1982.

Trimingham, J. Spencer. *The Sufi Orders in Islam.* London: Oxford University Press, 1971.

Turner, Frank Miller. *Between Science and Religion: The Reaction to Scientific Naturalism in Late Victorian England.* New Haven: Yale University Press, 1974.

Tuve, Rosemund. "Notes on the Virtues and Vices: Part II." *Journal of the Warburg and Courtauld Institutes* 27 (1964): 42–72.

U.S. Games Systems, Inc. *Tarot Catalog #61.* Stamford: U. S. Games Systems, Inc., 2004.

Unger, Tchalaï. *Preface to the Tzigane Tarot (Tarot of the Roms).* Translated by Josee Noel. Paris: Ets J. M. Simon, 1984.

Ussher, Arland. *The XXII Keys of the Tarot.* New ed. Dublin: The Dolmen Press, 1969.

van den Broek, Roelef, and Wouter J. Hanegraaff, eds. *Gnosis and Hermeticism from Antiquity to Modern Times.* Edited by David Appelbaum, *SUNY Series in Western Esoteric Traditions.* New York: State University of New York Press, 1998.

van Egmond, Daniel. "Western Esoteric Schools in the Late Nineteenth and Early Twentieth Centuries." In *Gnosis and Hermeticism from Antiquity to Modern Times,* edited by Roelof and Hanegraaff van den Broek, Wouter J. New York: State University of New York Press, 1998.

van Marle, Raimond. *The Development of the Italian Schools of Painting.* XIX vols. Vol. VII. New York: Hacker Art Books, 1970.

——. *Iconographie De L'art Profane Au Moyen-Age Et À La Renaissance Et La Décoration Des Demeures.* II vols. Vol. I. New York: Hacker Art Books, 1971.

——. *Iconographie De L'art Profane Au Moyen-Age Et À La Renaissance Et La Décoration Des Demeures.* II vols. Vol. II. New York: Hacker Art Books, 1971.

van Rensselaer, Mrs John King. *Prophetical, Educational and Playing Cards.* London: Hurst and Blackett, Ltd, 1912.

Vernon, K. D. "Ueber Die Anfänge Der Signorie in Oberitalien: Ein Beitrag Zur Italienischen Verfassungsgeschichte [Review]." *English Historical Review* 16, no. 61 (1901): 134–36.

Versluis, Arthur. *The Esoteric Origins of the American Renaissance.* Oxford: Oxford University Press, 2001.

Vickers, Brian. "Frances Yates and the Writing of History." *The Journal of Modern History* 51, no. 2 (1979): 287–316.

——, ed. *Occult and Scientific Mentalities in the Renaissance.* Cambridge: Cambridge University Press, 1984.

Vince, Ronald W. "Virtues and Vices." In *A Companion to the Medieval Theatre*, edited by Ronald W. Vince, 373. New York: Greenwood Press, 1989.

——, ed. *A Companion to the Medieval Theatre.* New York: Greenwood Press, 1989.

Vincent, Bill. "Quantum Thoughts on Tarot." *The Bleeping Herald*, no. 15 (2006).

Viscardi, Antonio. "Arthurian Influences on Italian Literature from 1200 to 1500." In *Arthurian Literature in the Middle Ages: A Collaboartive History*, edited by Roger Sherman Loomis, 419–29. Oxford: Clarendon Press, 1959.

Vitali, Andrea. "Arcani Svelati." In *I Tarocchi: Le Carte Di Corte : Bioco E Magia Alla Corte Degli Estensi*, edited by Giordano Berti and Andrea Vitali, 145–57. Bologna: Nuova Alfa, 1987.

Vitti, Paolo, Teresa Rago, Fabrizio Aghini-Lombardi, and Aldo Pinchera. "Iodine Deficiency Disorders in Europe." *Public Health Nutrition* 4, no. 2b (2001): 529–35.

Vogt, Carl. "On Microcephali; or, Human-Ape Organisms." *Anthropological Review* 7, no. 25 (1869): 128–36.

von Franz, Marie-Louise. *On Divination and Synchronicity: The Psychology of Meaningful Chance.* Edited by Daryl Sharp, *Studies in Jungian Psychology by Jungian Analysts.* Toronto: Inner City Books, 1980.

von Stuckrad, Kocku. *Western Esotericism: A Brief History of Secret Knowledge.* Translated by Nicholas Goodrick-Clarke. London: Equinox Publishing Ltd, 2005.

——. "Western Esotericism: Towards an Integrative Model of Interpretation." *Religion* 35, no. 2 (2005): 78–97.

Waite, Arthur Edward. *The Brotherhood of the Rosy Cross: Being Records of the House of the Holy Spirit in Its Inward and Outward History.* New York: University Books, 1961.

——. "The Great Symbols of the Tarot." *Occult Review* 43 (1926): 11–19.

——. *The Hidden Church of the Holy Graal: Its Legends and Symbolism Considered in Their Affinity with Certain Mysteries of Initiation and Other Traces of a Secret Tradition in Christian Times.* London: Rebman Limited, 1909.

——. *The Holy Grail: The Galahad Quest in the Arthurian Literature.* New York: University Books, 1961.

——. *The Holy Kabbalah: A Study of the Secret Tradition in Israel as Unfolded by Sons of the Doctrine for the Benefit and Consolation of the Elect Dispersed through the Lands and Ages of the Greater Exile.* New Hyde Park: University Books, 1970. Reprint, Sixth.

——. *The Pictorial Key to the Tarot: Being Fragments of a Secret Tradition under the Veil of Divination.* Second ed. London: Rider & Company, 1971. Reprint, Fifth.

——. "Preface to the English Translation." In *The Tarot of the Bohemians: Absolute Key to Occult Science; the Most Ancient Book in the World for the Use of Initiates,* by Gerard Encausse, v-xxviii. Hollywood: Wilshire Book Company, 1971.

——. *Shadows of Life and Thought: A Retrospective Review in the Form of Memoirs.* London: Selwyn and Blount, 1938.

——. "The Tarot: A Wheel of Fortune." *The Occult Review* X, no. 12 (1909): 307-17.

Wakefield, Walter L. *Heresy, Crusade and Inquisition in Southern France: 1100-1250.* London: George Allen & Unwin Ltd, 1974.

Waldoff, Jessica. "The Music of Recognition: Operatic Enlightenment in 'the Magic Flute'." *Music & Letters* 75, no. 2 (1994): 214-35.

Walker, D. P. *Spiritual and Demonic Magic from Ficino to Campanella.* Edited by G. Bing, *Studies of the Warburg Institute.* London: Warburg Institute, 1958.

Wang, Robert. *Golden Dawn Tarot Deck.* Stamford: U.S. Games Systems, 1991.

——. *An Introduction to the Golden Dawn Tarot Including the Original Documents on Tarot from the Order of the Golden Dawn with Explanatory Notes.* York Beach: Samuel Weiser, Inc., 1978.

Washington, Peter. *Madame Blavatsky's Baboon: A History of the Mystics, Mediums, and Misfits Who Brought Spiritualism to America.* New York: Schocken Books, 1995.

Wasserman, James. *Instructions for Aleister Crowley's Thoth Tarot Deck.* Stamford: U. S. Games Systems, Inc., 1978.

Watkins, Renee Neu. "Petrarch and the Black Death: From Fear to Monuments." *Studies in the Renaissance* 19 (1972): 196-223.

Webb, James. *The Occult Establishment.* La Salle: Open Court Publishing Company, 1976.

——. *The Occult Underground.* La Salle: Open Court Publishing Company, 1974.

Webber, F. R. *Church Symbolism: An Explanation of the More Important Symbols of the Old and New Testament, the Primitive, the Mediaeval and the Modern Church.* Second, revised ed. Detroit: Gale Research Company, 1971.

Weisbach, Werner. *Trionfi.* Berlin: G. Grote, 1919.

Weiss, Roberto. "Italian Humanism in Western Europe." In *Italian Renaissance Studies,* edited by E. F. Jacob, 69-93. London: Faber and Faber, 1960.

Welch, Evelyn. *Art and Society in Italy 1350-1500, Oxford History of Art.* Oxford: Oxford University Press, 1997.

Wessley, Stephen. "The Thirteenth-Century Gugliemites: Salvation through Women." In *Medieval Women Dedicated and Presented to Professor Rosalind M. T. Hill on the Occasion of Her Seventieth Birthday*, edited by Derek Baker, 289–303. Oxford: Basil Blackwell, 1978.

Westcott, William Wynn. "The Historical Lecture." In *The Golden Dawn Source Book*, edited by Darcy Küntz, 46–51. Edmonds: Holmes Publishing Group, 1996.

——. "Letter to F. L. Gardner." In *The Golden Dawn Companion: A Guide to the History, Structure, and Workings of the Hermetic Order of the Golden Dawn*, edited by Robert A. Gilbert. Wellingborough: Aquarian Press, 1986.

Weston, Jessie L. *From Ritual to Romance*. Garden City: Doubleday Anchor Books, 1957.

Whitaker, Muriel. *The Legends of King Arthur in Art*. Vol. XXII, *Arthurian Studies*. Cambridge: D. S. Brewer, 1990.

White, Karin. "Metal-Workers, Agriculturists, Acrobats, Military-People and Fortune-Tellers: Roma (Gypsies) in and around the Byzantine Empire." *Gouden Hoorn: Tijdschrift over Byzantium* 7, no. 2 (1999).

Wickham, Glynne. *The Medieval Theatre*. Third ed. Cambridge: Cambridge University Press, 1987.

Wilkins, Ernest Hatch. "Preface." In *The Triumphs of Petrarch*. Chicago: The University of Chicago Press, 1962.

Willard, Thomas. "Acts of the Companions: A.E. Waite's Fellowship and the Novels of Charles Williams." In *Secret Texts: The Literature of Secret Societies*, edited by Marie Mulvey and Ormsby-Lennin Roberts, Hugh. New York: AMS Press, 1995.

Williams, Charles. *The Greater Trumps*. Grand Rapids: William B. Eerdmans Publishing Company, 1976.

Williams, Thomas A. *Eliphas Lévi: Master of Occultism*. Birmingham: University of Alabama Press, 1975.

Wills, Garry. *Saint Augustine*. London: Phœnix, 1999.

Wilson, Robert H. "Malory's 'French Book' Again." *Comparative Literature* 2, no. 2 (1950): 172–81.

Wind, Edgar. "Charity: The Case History of a Pattern." *Journal of the Warburg Institute* 1, no. 4 (1938): 322–30.

——. *Pagan Mysteries in the Renaissance*. Revised ed. Harmondsworth: Penguin Books, 1967.

Wintle, Simon. *A 'Moorish' Sheet of Playing Cards* [website]. World of Playing Cards, 1987 [cited 22 August 2006]. Available from http://www.wopc.co.uk /spain/moorish2.jpg.

Wirth, Oswald. *Le Tarot Des Imagiers Du Moyen Âge*. Paris: E. Nourry, 1927.

Wittgenstein, Ludwig. *Philosophical Investigations*. Translated by G. E. M. Anscombe. Second ed. Oxford: Basil Blackwell, 1968.

Wollen, Keith A., and Matthew G. Margres. "Bizarreness and the Imagery Multiprocess Model." In *Imagery and Related Mnemonic Processes: Theories, Individual Differences, and Applications*, edited by Mark A. McDaniel and Michael Pressley. New York: Springer-Verlag, 1987.

Wolpert, Stanley. *A New History of India.* Sixth ed. New York: Oxford University Press, 2000.

Wood, Juliette. "The Celtic Tarot and the Secret Traditions: A Study in Modern Legend Making." *Folklore* 109 (1998): 15-25.

———. *Secret Traditions in the Modern Tarot: Folklore and the Occult Revival* [website]. 2001 [cited 7 September 2003]. Available from http://www.juliette.wood.btinternet.co.uk/tarot.htm.

Woodford, Archer. "Mediaeval Iconography of the Virtues; a Poetic Portraiture." *Speculum* 28, no. 3 (1953): 521-24.

Woods-Marsden, Joanna. "Images of Castles in the Renaissance: Symbols of 'Signoria'/Symbols of Tyranny." *Art Journal* 48, no. 2 (1989): 130-37.

Wortham, John David. *British Egyptology: 1549-1906.* Newton Abbot: David & Charles, 1971.

Yates, Frances Amelia. *The Art of Memory.* Harmondsworth: Penguin Books Ltd, 1966.

———. *Giordano Bruno and the Hermetic Tradition, Routledge Classics.* London: Routledge, 1964.

———. *The Occult Philosophy in the Elizabethan Age.* London: Ark Paperbacks, 1983.

———. *The Rosicrucian Enlightenment.* London: Routledge and Kegan Paul, 1972.

Zaehner, Robert Charles. *Hinduism.* Edited by Christopher Butler, Robert Evans and John Skorupski. Second ed, *Opus.* Oxford: Oxford University Press, 1966.

Zalewski, Pat. *Secret Inner Order Rituals of the Golden Dawn with the Approval of Israel Regardie.* Phoenix: Falcon Press, 1988.

Ziegler, Gerd. *Tarot: Mirror of the Soul: Handbook for the Aleister Crowley Tarot.* York Beach: Samuel Weiser, Inc., 1986.

Zolrak, and Dürkön. *The Tarot of the Orishàs.* Second ed. St Paul: Llewellyn Publications, 2000. Reprint, Fifth.

Zuffi, Stefano. *The Renaissance.* London: Collins, 2002.

Index

Bold figures refer to pages with illustrations.

Printed in the USA
CPSIA information can be obtained
at www.ICGtesting.com
LVHW011224270124
769852LV00008BA/219